WORDS ᴀɴᴅ SILENCES

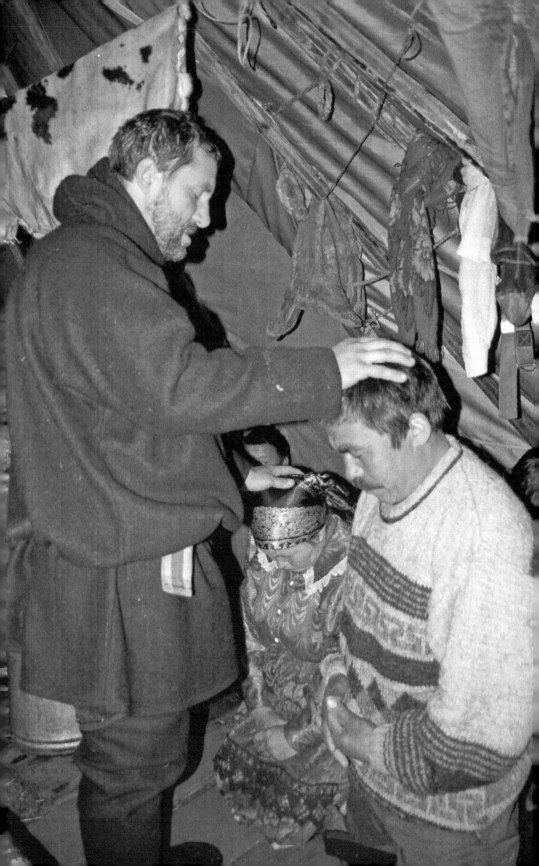

WORDS AND SILENCES

Nenets Reindeer Herders and Russian Evangelical Missionaries in the Post-Soviet Arctic

Laur Vallikivi

INDIANA UNIVERSITY PRESS

This book is a publication of

Indiana University Press
Office of Scholarly Publishing
Herman B Wells Library 350
1320 East 10th Street
Bloomington, Indiana 47405 USA

iupress.org

Manufactured in the United States of America

First printing 2024

Library of Congress Cataloging-in-Publication Data

Names: Vallikivi, Laur, author.
Title: Words and silences : Nenets reindeer herders and Russian evangelical
missionaries in the post-Soviet arctic / Laur Vallikivi.
Other titles: Nenets reindeer herders and Russian evangelical missionaries
in the post-Soviet arctic
Identifiers: LCCN 2023054884 (print) | LCCN 2023054885 (ebook) | ISBN
9780253068750 (hardback) | ISBN 9780253068767 (paperback) | ISBN
9780253068774 (ebook)
Subjects: LCSH: Nentsy—Russia, Northern—Social life and customs. |
Nentsy—Missions—Russia, Northern. | Nentsy—Russia,
Northern—Religion. | Reindeer herders—Russia, Northern. | Russia,
Northern—Social life and customs. | BISAC: SOCIAL SCIENCE /
Anthropology / Cultural & Social | PHILOSOPHY / Language
Classification: LCC DK34.N4 V36 2024 (print) | LCC DK34.N4 (ebook) | DDC
305.894/40471—dc23/eng/20240116
LC record available at https://lccn.loc.gov/2023054884
LC ebook record available at https://lccn.loc.gov/2023054885

To Juta, Johannes, Leen, and Oskar

CONTENTS

List of Maps and Figures   ix

Preface and Acknowledgments   xiii

*Notes on Transliteration, Translation,
and Bible Citations*   xvii

PART I. REINDEER NOMADS AND REFORMERS

Introduction   *2*

1   Dynamics of Avoidance and Engagement   *39*

PART II. CONVERSION OF PEOPLE,
DISENFRANCHISEMENT OF SPIRITS

2   Trajectories of Conversion   *77*

3   Baptist Missionaries on the Edge   *104*

4   Destructive Persuasion   *131*

PART III. SPEAKING AND SILENCE

5   Silence and Binding Words   *171*

6   Speaking Saves, Silence Damns   *197*

7 Pure Subjects *220*

Conclusion *242*

Main Characters *253*

Glossary of Selected Nenets and Russian Words *255*

Notes *257*

References *283*

Index *319*

MAPS AND FIGURES

All maps and photographs are by the author, except where indicated otherwise.

Maps

1   Tundra Nenets areas in Arctic Russia.   *20*

2   Yamb-To Nenets and Ural Nenets areas.   *27*

3   Land-use rights of reindeer-herding enterprises.   *57*

Figures

0.1   Before the water baptism of Yegor and Lida, August 2002.   *2*

0.2   Nenets converts reading the Bible, August 2002.   *15*

0.3   A reindeer-herding camp in Polar Urals, March 2007.   *18*

0.4   A reindeer herd of a thousand animals enables a decent life in the tundra, July 2007.   *21*

0.5   Driving a reindeer caravan on the last patches of the snow at the end of spring migration, June 2007.   *25*

0.6   White reindeer are particularly valued, August 2006.   *28*

0.7   Feeding a pet reindeer called *navka*, February 2007.   *29*

0.8 A Nenets family corralling reindeer near
the Polar Urals, 9 p.m., June 2007. *30*

0.9 Non-Christian Nenets eat a freshly killed
reindeer, March 2007. *35*

1.1 Nenets shift workers, August 1999. *42*

1.2 An icon of St. Nicholas the Miracle-Maker
and coins used as offerings at sacred places,
September 2006. *46*

1.3 Yegor and his family with Russian acquaintances
in Amderma at the end of the 1980s. *59*

1.4 Entering Amderma, July 2002. *64*

1.5 Having a rest after selling and buying,
Amderma, August 2006. *65*

1.6 Passports are issued to Independents,
July 2002. *66*

1.7 Nenets boarding school in Vorgashor,
September 2017. *70*

1.8 Ural Nenets paying a visit to the Sovetskiy
village, May 2012. *71*

2.1 Snowmobiles increasingly replace reindeer
for long-distance winter travel, March 2004. *87*

2.2 A moment of prayer in front of the box for food
and teacups after having lunch on the way,
August 2002. *94*

2.3 Literate youth reading the Baptist journal
Herald of Truth, February 2007. *101*

3.1 Baptist missionaries visiting Yegor's nomadic
camp, March 2004. *106*

3.2 Vorkuta Baptist congregants celebrating
     the sixtieth anniversary of their church,
     February 2007.   *111*

3.3 The sign of the second coming of Christ,
     December 2006.   *120*

3.4 Missionaries driving their all-terrain vehicle on
     the coast of the Arctic Ocean, August 2002.   *122*

3.5 Pavel gives a sermon in a Nenets *mya*, July 2002.   *128*

4.1 Interior of a tent in the Polar Urals, March 2007.   *136*

4.2 Pukhutsya and Iriko, May 2007.   *140*

4.3 Before a baptism in the pool of the Pentecostal
     prayer house, April 2007.   *144*

4.4 Baptism of Iriko, June 2007.   *145*

4.5 Pentecostal missionary Vladislav performing
     Hamlet's monologue with a reindeer head in
     the presence of Baptist converts, April 2007.   *147*

4.6 Vladislav gives a sermon, April 2007.   *152*

4.7 Iriko's *khekheq* and Orthodox icons known
     as *lutsa khekheq*, April 2007.   *155*

4.8 Vladislav saving the Orthodox icons from
     the fire, April 2007.   *158*

4.9 Iriko watching his *khekheq* burning, April 2007.   *159*

5.1 Ural Nenets searching for wood material in
     the forest tundra, April 2007.   *173*

5.2 Alcohol helps to appease spirits,
     September 2006.   *176*

6.1 Pavel baptizing Yegor by immersing him in
     the cold tundra lake, August 2002.   *206*

6.2 Pavel baptizing Lida, August 2002. *207*

6.3 Baptist missionaries and Nenets converts singing hymns, August 2002. *211*

6.4 Pavel performing the laying on of hands for Lida and Yegor, August 2002. *212*

7.1 Mastering lasso is one of the most important skills for men, November 2006. *228*

8.1 A boy and a *myenarui*, reindeer bull dedicated to spirits, July 2002. *248*

PREFACE AND ACKNOWLEDGMENTS

THIS BOOK IS THE RESULT OF MANY HAPPY coincidences and long friendships. In 1999, as an undergraduate ethnology student at Tartu University, I traveled to the Nenets Autonomous Region on the invitation of Nenets poet and artist Prokopi Yavtysyi (1932–2005), whom I had met on his visit to Estonia. This cheerful, talented man, who tirelessly worked to make the suppressed Nenets language and culture more visible, took me to a collective farm reindeer-herding unit in his childhood lands of the Malozemelskaya tundra. This Vyucheiskiy kolkhoz brigade consisted of five men and one woman who were working as paid shift workers away from their families. Prokopi left me there and flew himself with some regional officials for a Reindeer Day to the Yamb-To Nenets, five hundred kilometers further east in the Bolshezemelskaya tundra. When we met again in Naryan-Mar, Prokopi told me of dignified Nenets families who had never been collectivized and who lived in the tundra with their children and private reindeer. As I soon learned, these nomads were unique in the entire Russian Arctic because, unlike the others, they had not been registered with the state institutions and were not school educated during the Soviet period. Prokopi's vivid description of these proud *yedinolichniki* or Independents, as if "from the old times," made me wish to find out more.

A year later, I met Lyudmila Taleyeva in Tartu, a Nenets graduate student of linguistics, who in summertime worked as a teacher in the Yamb-To nomadic school. She gave me information about the migration routes of the Independents and told in more detail about the ongoing proselytization by Russian and Ukrainian missionaries—something Prokopi had mentioned with noticeable regret in his voice. It turned out that many of those never Sovietized Nenets were undergoing a rapid cultural change, as if trying to catch up with the collective farmers in their own way. In December 2000, I took a train to the dark Vorkuta, once the notorious Stalinist labor camp area, and contacted the Baptist pastor Pavel and his family; he welcomed me in his home and prayer house. Pavel introduced me to Ivan, the unofficial leader of the Yamb-To community and the first Nenets convert, who had been a member of the church for five years then. Ivan became a friend who introduced me to his kin in the tundra, among whom some had and many were about to become members of the Baptist church.

Over the years, I made eight field trips (last time in 2017) and spent altogether a year and a half in the area. Most of the time, I lived in the Yamb-To community with newly converted Baptist families. In 2007, I also spent four months with a family that was undergoing conversion to Pentecostalism in the neighboring Ural community of Independents. Furthermore, I also stayed for shorter periods with religiously divided families or with those who resisted the missionaries' attempts and were called *yazychniki*, "pagans." From time to time, I spent an occasional week in Vorkuta or some other settlement, often with Nenets herders looking for necessary provisions as well as attending Baptist and Pentecostal church services.

I am very grateful to the many people in the tundra who shared their tents, reindeer, food, and world with me. It is impossible to mention them all. I owe an enormous debt to the Nenets reindeer herders I lived with—especially to the Veli and Laptander families—who generously accommodated me in their camps, provided me with their insights, and gave gifts ranging from a reindeer coat to harness reindeer. *Ngarka vada!* I am also indebted to the friends in Naryan-Mar, Vorkuta, and Vorgashor, who invited me to stay in their homes and provided practical assistance, especially the Stetsyuk family, Lyudmila Taleyeva, and the late Prokopi Yavtysyi.

I thank the Baptist and Pentecostal pastors and congregants in Vorkuta, who—despite their frustration with me not converting and my regret of seeing them destroying animist cultural heritage—let me observe their church life and have conversations with them over the years. Being a constant object of evangelization gave me a good understanding of what it means to be targeted in a mission encounter. In Naryan-Mar, I want to thank officials from the Nenets regional administration and Vladislav Peskov for making my entry into the closed border zone on the coast of the Arctic Ocean possible.

I owe a deep debt of gratitude to Piers Vitebsky for his remarkable guidance and limitless support over the years. I benefited greatly from discussions of my work in progress in his Magic Circle seminar at the University of Cambridge. I want to express my thanks to the seminar participants, among others to Barbara Bodenhorn, Ludek Broz, Paul Connerton, Prudence Jones, Janne Flora, Elena Khlinovskaya Rockhill, Tania Kossberg, Terto Kreutzmann, Evelyn Landerer, Eleanor Peers, Madeleine Reeves, Hugo Reinert, Vera Skvirskaja, and Olga Ulturgasheva. The Scott Polar

Research Institute in the University of Cambridge, with its wonderful library and bibliographer Isabella Warren, was the perfect setting in which to base my research. I also thank King's College for providing a home to me and my family. For funding my research, I am grateful to the Gates Cambridge Trust, the Archimedes Foundation in Estonia, the Cultural Endowment of Estonia, the Estonian Science Foundation, and the Centre of Excellence in Cultural Theory at Tartu University. The writing up has been enabled by the Estonian Research Council grant PRG1584.

I am particularly grateful to Fenella Cannell, Tim Jenkins, Alex King, Karina Lukin, Joel Robbins, Nikolai Ssorin-Chaikov, and Florian Stammler for their valuable comments on reading earlier drafts of the book. I also want to thank Matthew Engelke, Roza Laptander, Mathijs Pelkmans, Sergei Sokolovskiy, Katherine Swancutt, and Konstantinos Zorbas, who all read parts of my research at various stages and made perceptive comments. Any shortcomings that remain are entirely my responsibility. I have also received useful suggestions and help from Tatiana Bulgakova, Stephan Dudeck, Jenanne Ferguson, Patty Gray, Toomas Gross, Otto Habeck, Caroline Humphrey, Kirill Istomin, Jeanne Kormina, Igor Krupnik, Yelena Liarskaya, Igor Mikeshin, Aleksandr Panchenko, Patrick Plattet, Tapani Salminen, Elo-Hanna Seljamaa, Sergei Shtyrkov, Anna-Leena Siikala, Tatiana Vagramenko, Nikolai Vakhtin, Virginie Vaté, Aimar Ventsel, Vladislava Vladimirova, Maria Vyatchina, and Rane Willerslev.

In Estonia, I am especially grateful to Eva Toulouze, Liivo Niglas, Art Leete, Ülo Valk, Piret Koosa, and Taavi Tatsi, who for more than twenty years have not only offered support and constructive criticism but also their friendship. For various kinds of help, I should also like to extend my thanks to my colleagues in the Arctic Studies Centre, the Department of Ethnology, and the Department of Estonian and Comparative Folklore at Tartu University.

For editing my English, I need to thank Daniel Edward Allen. At Indiana University Press, thanks are due to my editors, Sophia Hebert, Bethany Mowry, and Nancy Lightfoot and others in this highly professional editorial team.

I am grateful to my extended family, including my brother Hannes and sister Mari, and their partners and children, who all play a huge role in my life. My mother and father, Ene and Arvo Vallikivi, have offered their unconditional love, encouragement, and inspiration. As part of a "class enemy" family my father was deported in 1949 to Siberia with his mother and brother. He spent his teenage years in the Novosibirsk area and then moved to Kolyma in 1954, where my grandfather had survived seven and a half years in the infamous gold mining camps. The family was not allowed to return to Estonia for another five years (until 1958). However, my father, who finished secondary school in Susuman and got a "clean passport" by mistake, managed to return after half a year. Back in Estonia, he soon became a writer who gradually developed interest in Finno-Ugric and other ethnic minorities in the Soviet empire. The stories he shared as well as our childhood family trips in Estonia and beyond instilled in me a deep curiosity about Indigenous cultural worlds. I am also grateful to my late maternal grandparents, Leida and Johann Kitse, with whom I grew up in Viljandi and whose many words and silences I carry with me to this day.

Last, but by no means least, my deepest thanks go to my wife, Juta, and to our three children, Johannes, Leen, and Oskar, who have supported my work throughout its long course with their actions, thoughts, and love, and to whom I dedicate this book.

NOTES ON TRANSLITERATION, TRANSLATION, AND BIBLE CITATIONS

THE TRANSLITERATION OF RUSSIAN AND NENETS WORDS FOLLOWS the United States Board on Geographic Names. Throughout the text, I have used established or simplified orthography for geographical names (e.g., "Bolshezemelskaya" rather than "Bol'shezemel'skaya"—from Большеземельская) and personal names encountered in the field ("Gennadi" rather than "Gennadiy"—from Геннадий, except for the names in the bibliography).

I have transliterated Tundra Nenets from the standard Cyrillic orthography (as in Tereshchenko 2003) with slight simplifying adjustments. *q* stands for a glottal stop (at the end of a word it sometimes marks the plural, e.g., *lutsa* "Russian," *lutsaq* "Russians"); "ng" (in Cyrillic ӈ) marks a velar nasal; "yo" (in Cyrillic ё) marks a palatal glide. One apostrophe stands for palatalization (e.g., *mal'tsya*—from мальця).

Unless otherwise stated, I have quoted the Bible in English from the King James Version (1611). The Baptists and Pentecostals in Russia use the Russian Synodal Version (1876), which, like the King James Version, has an archaic tone.

All translations of quotes (except for scriptures) are mine.

Different levels of administrative units in the Russian Federation are translated as follows: *respublika*—republic, *kray*—territory, *oblast'*—province, *okrug*—region, *rayon*—district.

In this work, the English "Nenets" marks both singular and plural forms (and not "Nenetses," "Nentsy," or "Nentsi"), the adjective, and the name of the language.

WORDS and SILENCES

PART I
REINDEER NOMADS AND REFORMERS

Figure 0.1. Before the water baptism of Yegor and Lida, August 2002.

INTRODUCTION

A NENETS REINDEER HERDERS' SUMMER CAMP NEAR THE coast of the Arctic Ocean. Two conical tents are erected next to each other on a sandy rise with a few dozen sledges standing in lines. Between the tents is a big white all-terrain vehicle. Aided by GPS and backed up by a satellite phone in case of emergency, three white middle-aged Baptist missionaries have arrived at this herders' camp after making a three-hundred-kilometer journey across the roadless Great Land (Bolshezemelskaya) tundra from the former Gulag city of Vorkuta, which is their home base. Scattered around the white vehicle are the sledges of Nenets guests who have come from nearby camps. About thirty Nenets, adults and children, have gathered. Many of them burned their spirit figures and were baptized a few years earlier. They have come to witness the water baptism of Yegor and Lida, a middle-aged Nenets couple. This is to take place in a nearby lake through full immersion in bone-chilling water.

Words abound at this meeting, as the rite is accompanied by long prayers, readings, sermons, and hymn singing. Not knowing any Nenets, the proselytizers are speaking Russian with the tundra dwellers, relying on Ivan, the first Nenets convert, to interpret their words. Although most Nenets men and a few women understand some Russian, biblical language remains largely impenetrable. After prayers have been said on the shore, missionary Pavel goes into the water up to his chest and Yegor soon follows him. In response to the missionary's question whether he believes that Jesus is the Son of God, Yegor says, "I believe" (*ya veryu*). Then the missionary immerses him backward into the water. Next it is Lida's turn. During the following service in the tent, the missionary stresses that a few sincere words can save a person. He reminds those present that praying, reading the Bible, listening to sermons live or from audiocassettes, and discussing passages are the best sacrifice to God. The Nenets listen to Pavel in silence (see chap. 6 for more detail).

This scene gives a glimpse of a mission encounter in the Nenets tundra that can be characterized as a negotiation with and over words. Reindeer herders' responses to these outsiders' visits vary, from becoming Christian speakers to repeating imitatively to remaining silent in refusal. Some become engaged in pious self-transformation by carefully choosing their words and gestures, as well as shaping their habits of body and voice through kneeling, reading, singing, and other practices that come from a foreign world. In the long run, missionaries' words inform ways of marriage, raising children, burying the dead, and engaging—or not engaging—in gift exchange. However, many converts struggle to learn the new belief language with its specific qualities of emotionality and movement. This may be due to their poor knowledge of Russian, insufficient motivation, or embodied habits from the past. Furthermore, there are stubborn "old-timers" for whom the missionaries' words seem to be intrusive and intense, their demands insensitive and damaging, as these transform beyond recognition older patterns of sociality with kin, animals, and spirits. They gauge missionaries' words against their earlier experiences with Russians (*lutsaq*), whose dangerous words they and their ancestors have been able to dodge more or less efficiently over the last centuries. They know that the outsiders' words can be binding and make them vulnerable to undesired consequences.

In this book, there are Nenets animists on one side and Slavic conservative Baptists and Pentecostals on the other.[1] Both sides have had a long history of tension with the Soviet state, which desires to control every citizen's mind and property, and both have managed to avoid that control for the most part. This is then, among other things, a story of a striking failure of one of the most invasive and controlling states in the world. Under socialism, two small groups of Nenets in focus here managed to live outside Soviet society, as they were not registered by the state institutions. They avoided engagement with the collective farms, the boarding schools, and the army that so thoroughly shaped the fate of virtually everyone else in the Soviet North. Among those few outsiders who knew of their existence, they were called Independents (*yedinolichniki*), a term for not-(yet)-collectivized peasants from the Stalinist period. Since the mid-1990s, however, they have been gradually integrated into the life of the post-Soviet Russian state. Today these two reindeer-herding communities are known as the Yamb-To Nenets and the Ural Nenets.[2]

Many Soviet Protestants also tried to avoid state intrusion into their lives, although in a different manner. The branch of Baptists whose representatives baptized Yegor and Lida has never been registered with the authorities; as an illegal organization it has carefully concealed its religious activities from the authorities throughout the Soviet period. Others, including their fellow Baptists who abided by state law, called these underground believers "Unregistered Baptists" (*nezaregistrirovannye baptisty*). Even if most of them fulfilled their civic duties as Soviet citizens, members of these congregations were targets of various repressions. Today these Unregistered Baptists still manage to avoid the authorities, who are once again stepping up persecution of minority Christians in Russia.

Even with these similarities between the Independent nomads and the underground Protestants, it is hard to imagine two more dissimilar social groups in Russia. Their differences in their ways of living, thinking, and believing are vast. And yet despite this cultural gap, since the mid-1990s, more than half of Nenets Independents have converted to either Baptist or Pentecostal Christianity. While these two Protestant denominations are bitter competitors for souls in the region today, the more conservative Baptists have been far more successful in their evangelization campaign, having won over a couple of hundred converts compared to a few dozen by the Pentecostals. Furthermore, these conversions within the poorly integrated part of the Indigenous population are especially surprising when compared to earlier, not very fruitful attempts at conversion by Russian Orthodox priests and Communist Party activists.

Ethics and Language in Conversion

The encounter between missionaries and Nenets at the baptism of Yegor and Lida is not an isolated case. Similar scenes of baptism have become increasingly common in remote places across post-Soviet Arctic Russia. After the collapse of the Soviet state and the disappearance of active anti-religious policies, these isolated communities, like many in other former Soviet areas, have seen a significant growth of new forms of Protestant Christianity, both home based and foreign (Pelkmans 2009a). Although Protestant missionaries are only recent newcomers to this part of the world, they have transformed the life of many Indigenous communities on an unprecedented scale.[3]

There is no single answer to the question of why Nenets convert to evangelical Christianity, only multiple interpretations, as this is a story of particular people in specific places that furthermore takes place at a certain juncture of history. Any such interpretation depends on whether one starts the analysis from historical structures, cosmologies, social relations, or individual lives (Hefner 1993a; Robbins 2011). For instance, why have less austere Pentecostals been less successful proselytizers in Nenets nomadic camps than the stricter Baptists? Is the reason in the content of the teachings, the difference of communicative style, the frequency of visits, favorable cultural patterns, or something else? As I shall demonstrate, specific techniques of proselytization and modes of interaction matter more than initially meets the eye. Furthermore, these encounters are shaped by personalities, as well as by vastly different cosmologies, ontologies, and moralities.

In one or another way, I suggest, conversion is related to an ethical question of *how* I, or we, should live. What kind of person should I become? Or what kind of community should we be? What are the decisions taken and choices made on this path? When should I speak or stay silent? And so on. These questions implicitly address degrees of freedom and constraint. Michael Lambek (2015a, 6) has written that "people, both collectively and individually, often freely and deliberately submit to specific kinds of discipline in order to cultivate an ethical disposition in themselves or their children, as though the ordinary social rules or conventional cultural ends were not enough, but equally as though sheer freedom was at least as dangerous an alternative." As he notes, rules and freedom should not be treated as a simple opposition though, as life is replete with situations where people must decide "among several competing or incommensurable conventional commitments or obligations" (ibid.), requiring constant practical judgment. It seems reasonable to accept the idea that some freedom, which is realized while reflectively "standing back," is also part and parcel of ethical life, as James Laidlaw (2018, 188) proposes (see also 2014). We shall see that the Nenets converts' everyday ways, with their tacit assumptions and habits, many of these coming from the past, exist side by side with the newly introduced Christian ways that require constant self-reflection. These two ways of being sometimes operate separately, with limited interaction; at other times, they are sources of unbearable tensions.

What the current ethnography hopes to demonstrate is that ethical decision-making and self-reflection are of a highly varied nature, historically situated and socially entangled. For instance, promise-making and promise-keeping in the mission encounter can bind a person in ways that are unexpected and in hindsight undesired, and yet the person might find him or herself taking the course of action as promised. I suggest that commitments emerge through participation in shared language (e.g., prayers), texts (e.g., the Bible), rituals (e.g., baptism), bodily techniques (e.g., kneeling), institutions (e.g., church), rules (e.g., decalogue), and acts (e.g., helping a brother or sister in faith) that are explicit and can be judged by others. Although various clearly expressed ethical principles have been part of Nenets' lives before, what is truly new with the coming of Christianity is the encounter with its highly systematized and orchestrated nature and its ambition to be a total morality system.

As Christianity comes to challenge that which was earlier, it raises many questions: How do the new ideas, emotions, and practices on offer relate to existing ontological realities and cultural values? What about earlier relationships—bearing in mind that conversion not only creates new relations between human and divine entities but also cuts the old ones (Chua 2012; Holbraad and Pedersen 2017, 254–56; Robbins 2015; Vitebsky 2017a)? What are the benefits of Christianity for now and for the future, considering the promise of paradise or the threat of hell, or the promise of modernity versus the sense of being marginal? What is to be gained and what is to be lost are not only matters of rational calculation; they also require an imagining of what kind of person one wants to be in one's own and others' eyes. On the one hand, ethical judgments and choices are related to one's past experiences, current contingencies, and future aspirations. On the other hand, ethical questions are not only individual but also deeply socially embedded as they emerge in interaction with others.

When discussing religious conversion, it is often assumed that minds are changed from the outside and against the person's will. Jean and John Comaroff (1991) have argued in their account of the conversion of Tswana in South Africa that in the mission encounter "the colonization of consciousness" takes place. The Comaroffs draw on the Gramscian model of hegemony in which dominant ideology comes "to be taken-for-granted" and is, in the end, "habit forming" (23). They think through Pierre Bourdieu's uses of the tacit and explicit and suggest that Tswana had to accept "unspoken conventions" (26) without fully understanding their effects. However, the concept of colonization of consciousness has its analytical limits: it tends to portray converts as passive victims of power and thus eclipses the particular logic of ethical subject formation in Christianity (Cannell 2006; Robbins 2007a; Roberts 2012). As Joel Robbins (2007a, 6) notes, the Comaroffs "manage to a great extent to write Christianity as a culture out of their discussion." Instead, he calls for the logic of Christianity and peoples' freedom to act within it to be taken seriously.

Suppose for a moment we entertain the concept of a colonization of consciousness, mind, knowledge, or imagination—it is "never total, never as expected" (Engelke 2013, 233). In both Christian and Communist rhetoric, "converts" are argued to have gone through a total transformation. However, even the most pious or politically committed person's lived life is far more complex, contradictory, and situated compared to what the governing moral rules would prescribe. Talking of social imaginary in Mongolia, David Sneath (2009) has argued that the colonization of imagination rarely succeeds, as imagining is always open to creative possibilities. He discusses Soviet-style modernism in Mongolia, in which the project of electrification coexisted with divinatory practices such as scapulimancy (foretelling future by reading marks on a burnt shoulder blade of a sheep), "practices that would appear senseless or meaningless if Soviet-style modernism had successfully colonized the imaginations of state subjects" (74; cf. Arzyutov 2019). While electric light and similar technical solutions were "meant to be read as metonymic emblems of a single grand narrative—modernity" (Sneath 2009, 87), local people kept their ancient divinatory practices and generated "an infinite number of narratives in answer to particular questions" (ibid.). Sneath, like many others before him, rightly points out that divination, like shamanic practices, represent not a rigid ideology or belief system but "a set of magical techniques requiring no personal commitment to any single religious cosmology or political ideology" (2009, 87; see also Balzer 2011; Humphrey 1998, 409–17; 2018; Pedersen 2011; Ssorin-Chaikov 2001; Vitebsky 1992, 239; Willerslev 2007). As we shall see, people in these remote settings have been involved in institutionalized projects of self-fashioning in rather limited capacities, if at all.

Similar discrepancies are visible all over Russia where the people have adopted certain Soviet values and rhetoric yet continue to engage with "backward" (*otstalye*) ideologies and activities full of "remnants" (*perezhitki*, "survivals") from the past. These are typical situations when the exclusionary logic of "either/or" is unable to fully eliminate the pluralist logic of "both/and" (Lambek 2015b, 2021).[4] For instance, I was told that among collective farm Nenets, at one moment, a Soviet-period Nenets brigadier (the head of a reindeer-herding unit in a state farm) could preach the Communist values of the planned economy, and the next moment he could carry out a reindeer sacrifice (*khan*) to protect his herd and family. Arguably, there was no tension around these practices, even if an outsider could have taken this as a scandalous contradiction.

As we shall see below, the church and the state both offer rule-based morality systems and ethical procedures. How these are taken up varies considerably, as each system has its own particular history. Compared to evangelical missionaries, authoritarian states like the Soviet Union could use far more coercive disciplinary power in their attempts to transform their citizens. Across the Russian North before the 1990s, Indigenous peoples were involved in the Soviet ideological system and workings of power through various explicit policies (Grant 1995; Gray 2005; Slezkine 1994; Ssorin-Chaikov 2003; Vitebsky 2005). At that time, both individual and collective consciousness (constructs such as "class consciousness," *klassovoe soznanie*) were key categories in the Marxist ideology that the Soviets used widely (Kharkhordin 1999; Vladimirova 2006, 114–26). Obviously, they did not talk about colonizing the consciousness but rather "working on" or "raising" it. Or as the ethnographer Yevgenia Alekseyenko (1981, 91) writes in her paper on shamanism among the Kets, "The main means of fighting the remnants in the consciousness [*perezhitki v soznanii*] was via the gradual introduction of culture, knowledge, and medical care into the life of the Indigenous population." Soviet Marxists argued that, the right ideas could not be introduced without changing the material base, which required a radical transformation of local economies and social organization. Indeed, with sedentarization and other social reforms, the Soviets managed to reorder many of the existing social and cultural patterns in the North.

However, despite the pervasiveness of atheism in Soviet society (Luehrmann 2012; Smolkin 2018), people were able to find ways to transmit their religion to the next generation through everyday actions that remained largely invisible to outsiders. In the case of persecuted Christian groups, this required spatial or temporal separation of religion from state institutions. For instance, Douglas Rogers (2009) shows in his account on Priestless Old Believers in the Perm Territory (a thousand kilometers south from the Nenets areas) how these Christians, historically persecuted by both the Russian Orthodox Church and by the state, became religiously active only when they retired from their occupational activity in the collective farm. Working-age adults kept their religiosity latent while carrying on certain Old Believer values and sensibilities in everyday practices that outsiders did not easily notice. The Russian Unregistered Baptists under focus in this book chose a different strategy, as they hid their activities by carrying out religious services in home churches where the youth were present and active (Panych 2012a). This was a protest culture that was pushed underground; when discovered, they risked their children and houses being taken away.

Obviously, nomadic Nenets were better placed to hide their rituals compared to Old Believers or Unregistered Baptists. However, what makes them different from these Christian communities is that Nenets lacked a comparable kind of moral activism, strict dogmas, formal religious institutions and projects of self-cultivation. Instead, animist reindeer herders interacted with the sentient environment through disparate knowledge originating from personal experiences combined with others' stories of more or less distant origins. One of the central tasks of this book is to tackle this kind of moral and ethical complexity of the mission encounter in which an explicit and systematic set of norms meets more fluid and tacit assumptions.

Although morality and ethics overlap and interact with each other, Laidlaw (2014, 111) insists, following Michel Foucault, that it is useful to keep them separate in an inquiry: "Moral codes and ethics must be distinguished analytically, because they may change independently" (see also Mattingly and Throop 2018). "Morality systems" are recognizable by their explicit rules, texts, disciplines, rituals, and institutions.[5] The way they are taken up varies considerably in different places and at different times. This is related to ethics—the way one acts on oneself, with the aim of becoming a particular kind of person. Without taking the philosophical distinctions to the letter (see Faubion 2011), I follow this rough division of morality and ethics, as it helps to interpret ethnographically some of the most puzzling moments relating to the question of why and how people take on a radical self-transformation such as conversion from an animist world of relatively tacit workings (most principles cannot be easily expressed in words and yet they work) to an evangelical religion of a rather explicit character (each act can and should be interpreted, for instance, through reference to some passage in the Bible). My question is then—to borrow from Laidlaw (2018, 186)—"What happens to ethical life when it is subjected to self-conscious and institutionalized reflexive [reflective] systematization"?

The book shows that with conversion to Protestantism, for the first time in their history, Independents participate in a systematic objectifying discourse on themselves and their community. Instead of using the metaphor of colonization of consciousness, one could then ask what new notions, words, and gestures are offered to people for looking at themselves, others, and the world around them after they have become members of a Christian congregation. Most of those who have agreed to take on the identity of believers enter a regime in which people are supposed to participate in "purposeful efforts at ethical transformation" (Keane 2016, 178). Webb Keane argues that "scriptural monotheisms tend to objectify ethics, exerting pressure on them to become more consistent and cognitively explicit. But objectification also tends to separate ethics from everyday habits and foster the taking up of a third-person perspective on ethical life" (208). In his view, Christian ethical practices rely on seeing oneself from "the third person perspective," which takes the form of "the God's-eye view" (205). Living from God's perspective is also how Nenets converts themselves characterize their strivings for a pious life (see chap. 7).

It is not only a private relationship with God; accepting a new religion changes one's status publicly, as living up to one's promise to God is expected to become a visible commitment. In conversion to evangelical Christianity, a person makes a ritual promise (by a prayer of repentance, baptism, or some other ritual action) and thus marks a new performative relationship with the morality system that is to be followed. This is a strong oath to a particular kind of way of life, principles, and one's community that from now on evaluates the oath taker's behavior in the light of relevant criteria. Catherine Wanner (2007) emphasizes in her analysis on Ukrainian evangelicals—some of them belonging to the church unions that are active in Arctic Russia—that at "the core of morality is *commitment* to particular practices and beliefs" (10, her italics); furthermore morality "also embodies commitment to a group that helps uphold them through shared discourses and disciplining practices, which, in turn, reflect certain understandings of good and evil, of virtue and vice" (11). Wanner's Durkheimian analysis shows how a religious community is primarily a moral community that follows a transcendent moral code and surveils its members' acts and words. Any such community, on Sundays and beyond, also activates itself as a temporal speech community (Gumperz 1968) with specific ways of speaking (Hymes 1974) that rely on newly learned words and notions. As "older" words, topics, and rhetorical styles are shunned, it also produces new ways of being silent, as we shall see below.

A public commitment to a morality system creates a situation in which ethical consistency in one's life must be demonstrated now and again. Even if the lived life (or the "everyday," see Das 2015) is chaotic, ambiguous, and multifaceted and no morality system can guarantee that it is followed in its entirety, striving for coherence as a self-conscious aspirational project is common to piety movements (Keane 2016, 200; see also Laidlaw 2018; Lambek 2015a, 3; Strhan 2015). On the one hand, there are many narratives that suggest coherence can be achieved, and these motivate converts to purposefully transform themselves. For instance, there are exemplary stories of particularly pious persons one can hear during sermons or read about in church journals. On the other hand, even the diagnoses of failure that are signs of incoherence can be used for the same purpose, as when a pastor reiterates that God saves those who are aware of their sins and who are willing to ask for forgiveness.

We should not forget that converts live in larger communities that have intricate webs of existing relationships already in place. Occasionally, one can hear among unconverted Nenets that Christians do not live up to the moral rules they preach—for instance, when believers' (*punryodaq*) reindeer trample non-Christians' pastures. When these accusations reach converts, it can lead to counteraccusations instead of rectifying behavior and searching for forgiveness. What has not changed with the introduction of evangelical Christianity in tundra society is that one's words are measured against one's deeds; only the ways of justification have changed.

This mission encounter in the tundra is significantly about the ethical nature of interaction and of language more specifically. Veena Das (2012, 133) finds that humans are "embodied creatures and beings who have a life in language," as this enables evaluation of oneself and others in their everyday vulnerability. Or as Lambek (2010b, 49) notes, "Language is central to the ethical and the ethical to language." Both Das and Lambek develop their arguments from ordinary language philosophers such as Ludwig Wittgenstein, J. L. Austin, and Stanley Cavell, who offer a fruitful path for thinking about how language shapes human sociality and ethical becoming through evaluative practices. Indeed, among evangelical converts, a great deal of the work on selves and others takes place more in language than anywhere else. My focus on language—and I include here silences—is the way into the main problematics, as speaking, and refraining from it, is one of the most contested sites in the mission encounter.

Of course, one should be careful when presenting Christianity in its various forms as an overwhelmingly linguistic project. While this is especially true with Catholic and Orthodox denominations, which do not regard language to be necessarily central in religious experience (see, e.g., Hann 2007; Hann and Goltz 2010; Norget et al. 2017), Protestants have been consciously and explicitly focused on language in their doings. The world the converts enter is a highly verbalized one, revolving around the quest for meaning and learning right intention (imagined as individual and internal) through the right form of self-expression (Bialecki 2011; Handman

2018; Tomlinson 2009a; Tomlinson and Engelke 2006). For instance, Simon Coleman (2000, 117) describes how Swedish charismatics, Word of Life members, are "akin to a verbal factory, responsible for the production of many millions of words a year in the form of taped sermons, books and magazines." Robbins's (2001a, 904–5) interlocutors in Papua New Guinea, playing with mixed messages regarding values, argue that "God is nothing but talk." Susan Harding (2000, 33–34), in her study on evangelicals in the United States, demonstrates that conversion takes place through "a process of acquiring a specific religious language," which starts from having been "inhabited by the fundamental Baptist tongue" and moves to the next stage when "the listener becomes a speaker." At the end of this process, the person learns to take responsibility for the words uttered and assumes the identity of believer.

In this book, the concept of language surpasses its purely representational (i.e., propositional, referential, denotational, constative, etc.) dimension and concentrates on its link to personhood, body, and emotion in ethical practices. Obviously, there are several ways in which language and body interact (see, e.g., Butler 1997a). For instance, Tanya Luhrmann (2004) argues that more and more people in the United States are leaving mainstream churches seeking "intense spiritual experience," and an intimate God, as "it is *not* words *alone* that convert" (518, her italics; see also 2012, 2020; Jenkins 2018; Webster 2013, 107). Luhrmann charts the religious transformation through which a person acquires a certain emotionality and specific skills and aptitudes in apprenticeship, calling this process "metakinesis," a term borrowed from dance theory (2004, 519). Luhrmann is correct that learning is a multifaceted process that is not only about getting concepts and words right but is also about acquiring and cultivating certain sensibilities. Indeed, speaking is not just a matter of sounds and meanings; it is also a deeply embodied practice, often specific to a social group in which one learns to speak with authority supported by "a certain posture, poise, tone of voice and manner" (Jenkins 2013, 72). And yet as Luhrmann (2004, 522) herself demonstrates, among evangelicals, "learning to have these experiences" requires lots of words.[6]

As I shall argue, in evangelical Christianity, words not only are effective means for self-transformation but also constitute a core ethical value, as one's salvation is imagined to be in one's words, and as such they prevail over all other aspects of life. This is not only an abstract ideal but also a value in practice or, as Lambek (2017, 146) would argue after Aristotle, an issue of practical judgment when "distinct intentions or commitments are specified and clarified" (see also 2010b; 2015a, 34). Furthermore— unlike gestures and other nonverbal communicative means—words have the capacity to make things explicit and thus readily available for reflection.

The Unregistered Baptists I am mainly concerned with in this book impute a huge role to words they imagine to be the source of divine wisdom as well as a path to salvation. As they say, they use the "plain" and "nourishing" word as the main way of being truly religious, and distrust other forms as "mere" emotional behavior. The crux of the whole change is in believing: this needs to be demonstrated to others (and oneself). To put it another way, one's faith (*vera*) cannot be mute; it must be represented loud and clear, in words of repentance, prayer, or discussion of the scriptures. I once heard a Baptist minister preaching that church members should not rely too much on emotions. He went on to say that emotional forms of worship like singing, reading poems, and declamations should give more space to direct communication with the divine, but also to reading, discussing, and hearing the actual Word of God (*Slovo Bozh'e*). As he phrased it, "Songs and poems are just sweets or condensed milk that are additional but not directly necessary."

Nenets converts perceive Russian Baptists' emotionality—even if claimed to be relatively restrained—to be challenging to deal with. Sometimes missionaries reprimand those who pray barely audibly, saying they are not articulate enough. As several Nenets admitted to me and as I could observe myself, this was a highly demanding task, especially for those who have grown up without an extensive practice of explaining oneself to others and—not less significantly—to oneself as well. For a formally uneducated Nenets, becoming a believer requires swearing an oath, learning both oral and written Russian (the language of both missionaries and the Bible, as there is no Nenets translation of the full Bible yet), acquiring propositional knowledge in the form of teachings, and getting "spontaneous" prayer right (in either Nenets or—even better—in Russian) and complete with humble tones and deep sighs (see chap. 6).[7]

There is a specific ideology of personhood and agency embedded in this. In evangelical Christianity, spoken words are taken to reflect the "inner state" of a person as an expression of sincerity, transparency, and truthfulness, which is a crucial precondition for giving the spoken words efficacy in communication with God. The notion of sincerity as a match between inner thoughts and feelings and outer expressions in words and acts does

Figure 0.2. Nenets converts reading the Bible, August 2002.

not exist as a cultural concept among Nenets, as is also the case in many other non-Christian societies (Jenkins 2013; Keane 2007; Robbins 2007b; Robbins et al. 2014, 585; Schieffelin 2007; Vitebsky 2017a). Missionaries have thus been introducing a new understanding of personhood through the pairing of interiority and exteriority.

In evangelical logic, human spoken words can have impact only as far as they are sincerely willed by a speaker whose decision and desire is to submit to God. In these situations, evangelicals assume that sincerity is not only *expressed* but also *produced*, as the ethical world of the self is shaped by the divine. Compelling words of repentance (a "yes" from a "pagan"[8]

Nenets) are seen as a victory, proof of a seed engendered by the Holy Spirit. As we shall see, in some instances of formalized speech, the demand for sincerity tends to wear off and all attention is on the act of speaking in a right way and taking public responsibility for the words articulated. For instance, this can be noticed when a Baptist preacher interrogates a candidate for baptism in the water (as with Yegor and Lida at the beginning of this chapter) or cajoles a reluctant old man to utter a few "saving words" (see chap. 5).

Conversion thus changes language ideology—that is, the way people think of how language and communication work (Kroskrity 2004), and even more broadly how various signs work in the world. When discussing the conversion of Sumbanese to Reformed Christianity through the concept of "semiotic ideology" (a particular set of assumptions about the relationship between words, things, and persons), Keane (2007, 18) writes that "it is a matter of semiotic ideology whether speakers even consider words to be radically distinct from things in the first place" (see also Engelke 2007; Keane 1997; Robbins 2007b). As I shall demonstrate, Christian missionaries in the tundra would regard putting words, things, and persons in the same category as scandalous (see chap. 4). And yet, for Nenets, the idea of language as solely representational is thoroughly alien because words in many cases (e.g., curses, names, and songs) are thought to act as things or (part-)persons able to produce profound social and ontological effects—it is not thoughts and feelings that are externalized but rather certain connections that are created and embodied effects that are transmitted to others (see chap. 5).

The evangelicals' highly verbal culture relies on an understanding that representation stays in the center, as it is tied to a particular concept of agency. In their view, human words can do nothing more than represent and mediate the power of more powerful agents. The only morally approved source of agency, and thus of meaningful change, is the Christian God. However, as a saved person becomes suffused with the divine, his or her words come to be—to use Austin's (1962) speech act theory loosely—performatives that change oneself (e.g., through prayers) and others (e.g., through witnessing and preaching) and commit oneself to a specific identity as a believer that initiates one way of living among other alternatives.

I do not regard speech act theory as a universal theory here (cf. Fleming and Lempert 2014), even if I agree that some performativity is inherent in all speech acts, as Austin (1962, 138, 146) claims. Performativity is an especially useful concept when thinking through particular cultural contexts and language ideologies. Words are deeds in their relations to local concepts of language, personhood, and agency. Starting from ethnographic observations, I look at the local understandings of language and sociality by thinking with speech act theory and seeing how various local theories of words, intentions, and relations might illuminate ethical (un)becoming in this ethnographic scene. My main concern here is with what Austin (1962, 101) calls "perlocutionary"—"saying something will often, or even normally, produce certain consequential effects upon the feelings, thoughts, or actions of the audience, or of the speaker, or of other persons"—and how this aspect is shaped by local epistemological assumptions and ontological sensibilities.

Also, the kind of wordscape to which the evangelical language is introduced matters significantly, as the efficiency of evangelical language depends on how much the cultural worlds that meet each other overlap in the mission encounter. When starting one's journey from a noisy Russian settlement nearby, what one notices straight away is that the Nenets pattern of communication in the tundra is far less verbose. If one stays longer, one realizes that this is a matter not only of style, which differs considerably between Nenets and Russians, but also underlying assumptions of what words do and how one can manage them. For instance, acquiring practical knowledge (e.g., how to tame a lead reindeer at the harness; how to castrate a bull reindeer using one's teeth) goes with little verbal explanation but rather by example, observation, and repeated engagement (see also Ingold 2000; Kwon 1993; Willerslev 2007). Even if practical knowledge remains all-important among Nenets converts, there is a tendency to ethicize words in the light of the new Christian morality system, as learning to become a Baptist or Pentecostal is significantly more dependent on propositional statements and explicit moral rules than any form of practical learning in the tundra.

Both missionaries and Nenets treat various kinds of words as powerful, although their understandings about the origins and economies of word force differ considerably from each other. While Nenets often see humans' words as extensions of personhood or semi-independent agents that transform relations in the world, missionaries believe that only the divine word is a true deed, as it takes place in the Creation. However, they are convinced that they mediate these powerful words of the Christian God and so assume some of his power. Now, those Nenets who meet the missionaries might choose silence—or "silence acts" as I call them—for their response, as this cuts intrusive engagement and makes the missionaries' attempts at change more difficult, if not impossible (see chap. 5). I hope that my concept

Figure 0.3. A reindeer-herding camp in Polar Urals, March 2007.

of a silence act, and its close ethnographic documentation of how to do things with silences, offers a corrective to some of the key assumptions in speech act theory with its logocentric approach to communication and portrayal of silence as being primarily an absence.

The Nenets, Their Reindeer, and Their Others

In many ways, this mission encounter is shaped by the geography and history of the area, which I shall discuss in this section. Nenets live in the vast treeless plains and mountains north of the Arctic Circle. On the west-east axis, their area covers two thousand kilometers from the Kanin Peninsula to the Yenisei River and is divided by the Ural Mountains—the range that splits Eurasia into Europe and Asia. In addition to conspicuous natural borders, there are inner administrative divisions inside the Russian Federation that have considerable influence on these nomads' lives. Most Nenets live in the Yamalo-Nenets Autonomous Region (hereafter "Yamalo-Nenets Region"), the Nenets Autonomous Region (hereafter "Nenets Region"), and in parts of the Komi Republic and the Krasnoyarsk Territory (see map 1). Throughout their history, despite centralized state policies, the nomadic pastoralists in each region have experienced a slightly different fate due to different physical geographies, ethnic compositions, and styles of administration (see chap. 1). With a population of around fifty thousand, Nenets are the biggest of the forty-odd "small-numbered Indigenous peoples," an official category providing certain privileges in the Russian legal system (Donahoe et al. 2008).[9] However, inside these officially designated ethnic groups, those living by traditional livelihoods, such as nomadic reindeer herding and hunting, now constitute a minority. This includes Nenets, among whom nomads are not more than a third (Klokov and Khrushchev 2006, 26; Ravna 2021, 2; Tishkov 2016, 85; Volzhanina 2010, 89–90). Those who live in the tundra (*vy*) consider reindeer herding to be one of the main markers of being Nenets (*nyenetsyaq*, "people"), which is probably more important for Nenets self-identification than, for example, speaking the Nenets language.[10]

The Yamb-To and Ural reindeer nomads stand in contrast to other Nenets due to their poor knowledge of the Russian world and language.[11] The main reason for this is that they successfully avoided collectivization. In the brutal Stalinist period, virtually all northern nomads were forced into collective farms (Forsyth 1992; Slezkine 1994). Being a member of a kolkhoz or sovkhoz defined most relations with the state—as the farms functioned as "total social institutions" (Humphrey 1998).[12] Despite widespread resistance to the collectivization and flight across the North in the 1930s and 1940s, only a few reindeer-herding families managed to evade state pressure for more than a decade or two. Practically all Nenets pastoralists became herders of reindeer they no longer owned (except for a number of personal reindeer mixed into the cooperative herd) and lived on land managed by the collective farm administrations that followed the regulations of the central authorities (Golovnev and Osherenko 1999; Stammler 2005; Tuisku 1999).

The Soviet state presented collectivization as essential to an unavoidable fight of the poor against wealthy reindeer pastoralists known as kulaks (*kulaki*)—that is, better-off herders regarded as exploiters. The reality

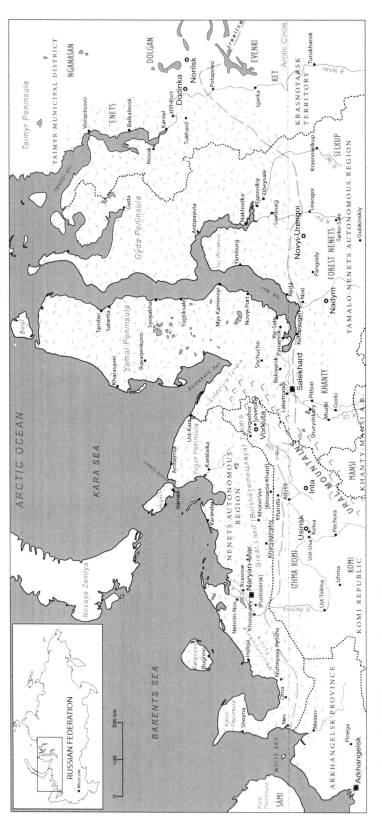

Map 1. Tundra Nenets areas in Arctic Russia.

Figure 0.4. A reindeer herd of a thousand animals enables a decent life in the tundra, July 2007.
The Ural Mountains are in the background.

was that the owners of smaller herds—like many among the ancestors of Independents—were as likely to flee the state's pressure as the owners of larger herds. Those who resisted Sovietization were repressed: their animals were confiscated, and when they did not comply with the new laws and refused to work in cooperative farms, they were ostracized and eventually imprisoned. Not only kulaks but also a number of others found themselves in the category of "class enemy," such as shamans[13] and elders, who were typically blamed for working against collectivization.[14] The vast majority of the tundra population was against the violent Soviet reforms, and this led to various acts of resistance, such as the *mandalada* uprising in the Polar Urals in 1943, which was severely suppressed, and, as a result, dozens of Nenets men were taken away never to return. This was the atmosphere that pushed many pastoralists to hide from the gaze of the state. By and large, throughout the Soviet period, the families in these informal communities of the Bolshezemelskaya (Ngarka Ya, "Great Land") tundra and Polar Urals (Ngarka Pe, "Great Rock") continued to live an independent life in the way their ancestors had before collectivization (see chap. 1).

If we look at the last few centuries, the Nenets Independents' evasion of the authorities in the Soviet period is just the latest phase in a long history of the tundra dwellers' cautious relations with outsiders. Depending on the area, the intensity of contact varied significantly. Even if some large rivers (such as Pechora) and islands (such as Vaigach) were first visited more than five hundred years ago by Russian Pomors and, from the mid-sixteenth century, by Dutch, English, and Norwegian travelers, vast areas of the interior were first "discovered" by outsiders only in the early twentieth century (Zhitkov 1913). The beginning of Russian colonization of the region came with the establishment of the first Russian Arctic town, called Pustozersk, which was founded in 1499 on the Pechora River.[15] This and other settlements, including what was called Obdorsk (today Salekhard) on the lower Ob River, were established to procure highly valued furs from the Indigenous population and to sell them to royal courts in western Europe for a lucrative profit.

Until the mid-eighteenth century, collecting fur tax (*yasak*) often took place by seizing hostages. Samoyeds[16] attacked the forts to free their imprisoned relatives and chase the foreigners away. The Russian military men retaliated with punitive expeditions, hanging hundreds of Nenets on larch trees near Pustozersk (Okladnikov 1999, 23–27; see also Golovnev and Osherenko 1999, 49; Vershinin and Vizgalov 2004). By the late eighteenth century, more peaceful relations had emerged between outsiders and tundra dwellers. Nenets benefited from trading with fur-hungry Russians to obtain axes, guns, flour, salt, tea, tobacco, and other goods. In the long run, this kind of trade created considerable dependence among Nenets on Russians both in terms of debts and for the growing necessity of these distant goods (Kolycheva 1956). One must add to that another dependence, which was addiction to alcohol used by Russians as "means of getting them [Natives] drunk and fleecing them" (Forsyth 1992, 106).

Unlike in many other parts of the world where colonizers and Christian missionaries arrived together, Russian Orthodox clergymen began proselytizing in the Nenets tundra rather late. Although there were already some cases of baptism in the sixteenth and seventeenth centuries when, for instance, Samoyed children were baptized after Russians and Komi had taken them into their households as child labor (Yasinski and Ovsyannikov 2003, 314), the first large-scale attempt to Christianize Nenets took place in the early eighteenth century in the lower Ob area. This attempt failed because of fierce resistance from the nomads (Golovnev and Osherenko 1999, 53–56). A hundred years later, archimandrite Veniamin was given the task of converting Nenets in the European tundra, which proved successful, at least in numbers.[17] After the mission campaign, three churches were built, including one dedicated to St. Nicholas on the Kolva River where the forefathers of Independents had kept their winter pastures. In the long run, this campaign replaced Nenets personal names with Russian ones and added new rituals, such as the baptism of children, burial in the ground (instead of erecting aboveground box graves), and blood sacrifices to icons.[18] Despite the open hostility of missionaries toward "pagan" religion, shamanic practices persisted in the area until the mid-twentieth century, and various animist rituals are still practiced today.

Following the tax collectors, traders, and Orthodox missionaries, Soviet reformers arrived in the early 1920s. The Bolshevik regime marked the first time that every Indigenous family across Arctic Russia had to adapt to unprecedentedly intrusive campaigns of transformation. Compared to those of later decades, however, the 1920s policies were relatively benign. To quote James Forsyth (1992, 284), "This was in fact a kind of reforming missionarism without the Christian religion, but with an equally strong conviction of absolute enlightenment" (cf. Toulouze 2011b). Alongside the formation of national administrative regions, the development of literacy, medical care, and schooling were the main heralded objectives. Special culture bases (*kul'tbazy*) were built, such as Khoseda-Khard in the southern part of the Great Land tundra (Arzyutov 2016, 341–43; Habeck 2005, 208–11; Josephson 2014, 221–33; Toulouze et al. 2017). These were to become sites for economic transactions and teaching literacy, Marxism-Leninism, hygiene, and new gender relations. For instance, Indigenous women were taught that they had to be freed from what were considered to be abusive practices, such as following gender-based purity rules; arranged marriages; and the practice of bridewealth, polygamy, and other "remnants of clan life." Several of these kinship institutions were criminalized in 1928 (Slezkine 1994, 226).

When Stalin launched his industrialization campaign in the late 1920s, hundreds of prospectors came to the North to search for natural resources under the reindeer pastures. In 1930, the young Russian geologist Georgi Chernov discovered high-quality coal on the banks of the Vorkuta River and returned the following year with thirty-nine Gulag prisoners to build the mining settlement that would later become the city of Vorkuta (Barenberg 2014, 15–16). At that time, local Nenets and Izhma Komi, who had been threatened with reindeer confiscation as part of the ongoing collectivization campaign, had to leave and yield their pastures to the rapidly growing territories of the Vorkuta prison camps. Within the space of just a few years, the camp system, known as Vorkutlag, accommodated tens of thousands of prisoners. Smaller prison camps were built on the coast of the Arctic Ocean in places like Amderma and Khabarovo. Each such area occupied by southerners meant fewer reindeer pastures, hunting grounds, and fishing sites for nomads.

A new phase of encroachment into the reindeer herders' territories began in the 1960s when some of the world's largest natural gas and oil deposits were discovered in western Arctic Russia (Dallmann et al. 2010; Golovnev et al. 2014; Rouillard 2013; Stammler 2011). Pastoralists had to withdraw from vast territories as gas wells, oil rigs, and other infrastructure were constructed. Also as a result of rapid industrialization, large areas have been contaminated with chemicals and metal rubbish. Another collateral effect is that Nenets today share their lands with newcomers, mainly urban labor migrants from the south who outnumber the Indigenous population many times over. While nearly all these Russians (here a loose term signifying the Russian-speaking white population of various ethnic backgrounds) live in towns and villages, a growing number of oil and gas shift workers occupy new reindeer pastures each year. Although the Independents roaming in the eastern part of the Great Land tundra are less affected by recent extractive industry developments compared to many other Nenets communities, they have been forced to give up some of their lands to the gas pipelines and service roads that traverse their pastures. Furthermore, some areas north of Vorkuta are used for military training, causing anxiety among herders who are not warned of upcoming missile tests.

Nevertheless, the nomadic lifestyle gives some room for maneuvering in the context of the various pressures coming from the sedentary world. The "art of not being governed" (Scott 2009) among the Arctic nomads is based on a flexibility made possible not only by high mobility but also their specific human-animal relations and technological adaptations. The Yamb-To and Ural Nenets live in tepee-shaped tents (*myaq* in Nenets, *chumy* in Russian) covered with reindeer skins in winter and tarpaulin in summer. A campsite consisting of one or several *myaq* is situated five to fifteen

Figure 0.5. Driving a reindeer caravan on the last patches of the snow at the end of spring migration, June 2007.

kilometers from the closest neighbors depending on the season and size of herd. Families change campsites dozens of times a year over the course of their nomadic cycles on the land, which is covered with snow for about eight months of the year. The two communities under focus here have slightly different migration routes. In summer the Yamb-To Nenets move with their reindeer to the cool and windy coastal pastures of the Arctic Ocean to escape the biting insects that can cause considerable damage to their herds. When winter approaches and green plants die, they migrate back southward to and beyond the Korotaikha River basin in search of lichen-rich pastures. Unlike most collective farm herders, they stay in the open tundra throughout the year. The Ural Nenets take a different route: they move to higher and windier places in summer in or near the northern slopes of the

Ural mountain range, while in winter they migrate south of the Moscow-Labytnangi railway line where there are small patches of forest providing materials for woodworking. Many spend their winters on the eastern side of the Urals in the Yamalo-Nenets Region (see map 2).

The importance of reindeer in the lives of the Nenets herders is difficult to overestimate.[19] Reindeer feed people, pull sledges, provide clothing and tent covers, help to form relations with kin and affines through exchange, relate humans to spirits and predatory animals, and carry the dead to the afterworld. While humans submit reindeer to their will in many ways, it is, in a sense, a mutual relationship, or "symbiotic domesticity" (Stammler 2010), in which reindeer participate in the decision-making process through their particular behaviors (Anderson et al. 2017; Beach and Stammler 2006; Stépanoff et al. 2017). The herders view their environment through reindeer's eyes, using what Andrei Golovnev (2017, 44) calls "reindeer thinking," which is "herders' coawareness and coconcern of their reindeer needs" (cf. Istomin and Dwyer 2021, 180; Ingold 2013). This is a practical perspective-taking which is needed for successful life on the land. Furthermore, living with reindeer entangles Nenets personhood intimately with the sentient tundra landscape, which is suffused with numerous forces and nonhuman beings capable of communicating with one another. The sentience of landscape is related to the idea that there are various masters of places and other agents, endowed with their own agendas, with whom one must learn to live (D. Anderson 2000; Ingold 2000, 24–26). This is a world where humans, spirits, and animals are persons who consume one another as well as make gifts to one another.[20]

Furthermore, there is an aesthetic and affective dimension to the human-reindeer relationship. Godfrey Lienhardt (1961, 16) describes how, among the Dinka in Sudan, cattle give "imaginative satisfactions" to the pastoralists. Like Dinka men, Nenets herders spend most of their waking hours observing, herding, lassoing, or corralling their animals. They cherish the thought of having more reindeer; they take pride in their powerful white castrated bulls (*khabtq*) with big antlers, or hand-fed orphan reindeer (*navka*) who enter the tent whenever they like.

For many Nenets today, such an intimate relationship with reindeer has disappeared because they no longer live in the tundra. Throughout the 1960s, 1970s, and 1980s, Nenets women, children, and elderly people working in collective farms in the Nenets Region were forced to live in settlements. Eventually, Nenets youth became alienated from the tundra way of

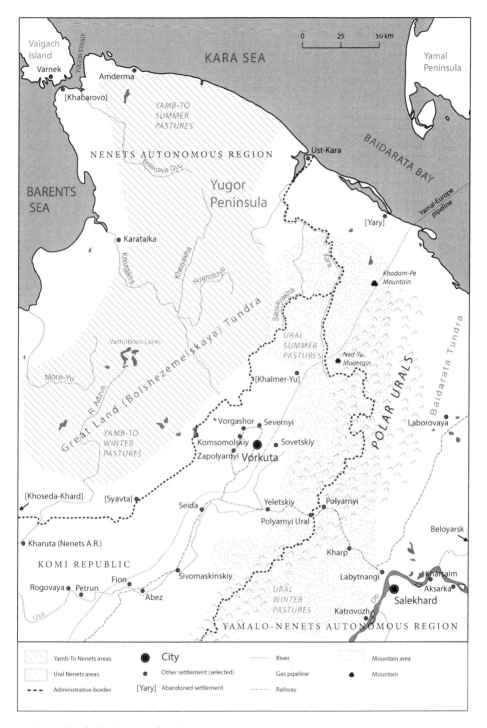

Map 2. Yamb-To Nenets and Ural Nenets areas.

Figure 0.6. White reindeer are particularly valued, August 2006.

life, most of them having never visited a single reindeer-herding camp in their lives (Lukin 2011; Ravna 2021; Tuisku 2001). Nomadic Nenets call their way of living with reindeer *nyeney yil*, meaning "real life" (Kharyuchi 2001, 12; Stammler 2005, 22). From the perspective of most of the tundra dwellers I know, sedentary life is perceived as an undesirable separation from *nyeney yil* (cf. Yoshida 1997, 209). However, there have always been people who lose their reindeer in epizootics, due to unfavorable natural conditions, or during drinking parties, and who, as a result, "sit" (*ngamdyo*) in one place without reindeer.[21]

Losing reindeer and settling down is not merely an economic matter but also, in some sense, an ontological one. As *nyeney* also refers to humanity, settling down and starting to live without reindeer as a Russian, *lutsa*, is perceived as potentially losing one's full humanity (see chap. 1). Becoming sedentary and becoming Russian—living *lutsa yil*, "Russian life"—are thus seen as parallel forms of transformation.[22] However, among the younger generation of Independents, this perception is losing its potency

Figure 0.7. Feeding a pet reindeer called *navka*, February 2007.

as more of them are attracted by city life, even if this usually remains a fleeting wish or unrealizable plan once they understand the various hardships related to it.

For the Independents, calling themselves "the ones who live on their own" (*khariq yilyenaq*), a subsistence way of life with the private ownership of reindeer—even if there are not too many—has long been the only imaginable way of living. A Nenets family can live on two hundred to three hundred animals, although the ideal is to have a thousand or more. Nenets say only a few who have luck (*yab*) or good relations with the spirits—or now, for converts, with the Christian deity—reach this number. During the Soviet period, few Independents were able to live up to this central cultural value of having many reindeer, because they did not want to draw attention to themselves for fear of being labeled kulaks. Those whose herds grew big

Figure 0.8. A Nenets family corralling reindeer near the Polar Urals, 9 p.m., June 2007.

were occasionally targeted by the authorities that tried to confiscate their animals (see chap. 1).

Among the Independents, personal and family autonomy is highly valued in many aspects of life. A social ideal is that a person or a family should not depend too much on others' resources or skills. From their early teens, women work in the camp taking care of small children, cooking, making clothing, and sewing tent covers, while men work outside herding, hunting, fishing, and crafting sledges. There are also women who know how to herd reindeer and check deadfall traps for foxes or fishing nets on the lake and rivers, while most men can cook, and some know how to work with reindeer skins. As in other Siberian Indigenous societies, children are expected to acquire vital skills with relatively little interference from parents, as one's ingenuity and mastery are thought to mature primarily through autonomous acts (Kwon 1993, 155–56; Ravna 2019, 2021; Stammler 2005, 84; Ulturgasheva 2012; Willerslev 2007, 54; see also chap. 7).[23]

In the early 1990s, when the first newspaper article was published on the Yamb-To Independents (Tolkachev 1990), they became a symbol of the last true nomads of the Nenets Region for the local cultural elite in Naryan-Mar. (The Ural Independents in the Komi Republic have never been given such positive public attention.) As Nenets poet Prokopi Yavtysyi told me after he had visited the Yamb-To, "Unlike others [collective farm herders], these people are full of dignity. You can see this right away, as the men stand with their chests pushed forward." For him, the Independents represented witnesses from "a lost past" and thus "authentic" Nenetsness.[24] At the same time, he was expressing his unease that many had converted to evangelical Christianity at the cost of rejecting traditional beliefs and customs. He shared the view, espoused by several others, that for the Independents the state would be a more benign agent than Christian missionaries.

However, Independents see this rather differently. A history of repression has made them wary of outsiders, especially state agents. For instance, years after the collapse of the Soviet state, some Yamb-To and Ural Nenets still fear confiscation of their reindeer by the state. They have also been reluctant to have their rights and obligations written down in official documents. As one herder told me, they are not interested in "setting up another kolkhoz" with its collectivist and hierarchical pitfalls.[25] Yet this does not mean that they desire isolation. In the Soviet period they regularly visited settlements, traded with state fur collectors, and bartered with army personnel or itinerant geologists. In case of emergency, some also sought medical help from hospitals, which was provided to people in reindeer parkas without too many questions asked. One family even sent two boys to boarding school in Ust-Kara in the 1970s; they became the first to convert to Baptism in the 1990s. Today these men, Ivan and Andrei, are the religious leaders in Yamb-To. The younger brother, Ivan, was the initiator of the change: he dreamed of becoming a shaman (*tadyebya*) but instead became a fervent denouncer of shamanism. However, he had never seen a single practicing shaman himself, as they had disappeared in the area by the late Soviet period after decades of repressions (see chap. 2).

Shamans and Missionaries

Once an elaborate and enduring set of rituals and cosmology, shamanism has persisted among Nenets in less visible forms as a set of underlying epistemological assumptions and ontological sensibilities about how seen and unseen forces act on people and how they can be acted upon.[26] I met a few Nenets who said that although they were not practicing shamans, they had related knowledge, skills, and sensibilities. For example, a young Nenets woman, Tikynye, now Pentecostal, told me that she was born with a caul on her head that marked her shamanic abilities (cf. Lehtisalo 1924, 146). A few days after her birth, a wolf made a kill in her family herd. As the family was supposed to carry out the so-called navel sacrifice (*syunggan*) for the newborn, the parents considered the wolf's kill as a substitute to it and they did not undertake *syunggan* themselves (see also Vallikivi 2017). This event, as Tikynye explained, created a strong relationship between herself and wolves. She characterized this with the kin term *syuny*, which refers to the children of two sisters: "The wolf gave me meat. Through this, I became a relative of the wolf. We are now *syunyq*." Since this event, whenever a wolf comes, Tikynye says she feels it as she starts to breathe rapidly. She then convinces the wolf not to kill reindeer by saying quietly "I know that it is you."

This is an example of a common animist ontological stance concerning human-animal relations, although it should be stressed that this stance is not a "dispassionate metaphysical speculation" but an ethical lead for how one should interact with animals, and thus has practical ends (Keane 2016, 15; see also 2013, 189–90).[27] These ethical leads are derived from an understanding of the equality of human and nonhuman agents that stands in striking contrast to the hierarchical Christian model. With the arrival of evangelical metaphysics, things are expected to be reinterpreted, as all direct acts of reciprocity with nonhuman agents (except for the Christian God) must be avoided. Christian missionaries would classify Tikynye's interpretation of her gifts as either a lie or demonic possession—thus themselves sharing animist ontological assumptions about others as potent agents (see chap. 4). Instead, their doctrine would prescribe that the all-seeing Christian God be petitioned to protect reindeer from predation, as God reigns over everyone while his believers share some of his power. Even if Tikynye knew, as a Pentecostal Christian, that she should cut all reciprocal relations with nonhuman others and deal with the predation of wolves through prayers to God, she seemed to treat her relationship as a given and efficacious. She preferred not to talk about this relationship with wolves to her Pentecostal pastor who would have admonished her for engaging with demons.

Many tundra dwellers have had similar experiences to those of Tikynye with various animals, spirits of the landscape, and spirits of the ancestors. Probably everyone over thirty has participated in sacrificial slaughtering of reindeer to local land, water, and mountain spirits, although this and all other "pagan" rituals have stopped in families who have recently converted. Evangelical missionaries teach that God forbids the strangling of reindeer for the spirits. So life has changed for everyone in the tundra, even for those who resist conversion, as many unconverted have abandoned sacrificial killings, or if they still sacrifice, hide their actions carefully from others. This wave of Christianization has an impact on nearly everyone, in a somewhat similar way to the past when the Soviets came and people concealed their animist or Orthodoxy-inspired ritual activities.

It must be stressed that different denominations of Christianity show a great variety of techniques when proselytizing. In Arctic Russia, one can find some accommodating missions, such as charismatic neo-Pentecostals among the Koryaks in the Russian Far East who, among other things, allow shamanic drums to be used during their services (Plattet 2013). However, most evangelical missionaries have chosen an approach that is well rehearsed throughout the history of Christianity, which is to demand a total rejection of everything that they define as "pagan." Like Communist Party activists, Christian evangelists are often driven by a desire to condemn. They have not only urged people to burn their sacred objects (*khekheq*) and banned sacrificial slaughter, they have also discouraged everyday practices such as drinking reindeer blood or marriage between maternal cousins. To overcome the threat of syncretism, contamination, or superficiality, as true

Figure 0.9. Non-Christian Nenets eat a freshly killed reindeer, March 2007. *Christians must substitute vitamin-rich raw meat and blood with vegetables.*

purifiers, the missionaries are busy defining various illicit amalgams of the "pagan" and Christian forms (Latour 1993, 2010).

Missionaries travel to remote corners of the Arctic (where other non-reindeer-herding people almost never go) to conquer the periphery.[28] Their rhetoric of margins conflates the physical and moral outer border in their attempt to accelerate the second coming of Christ (see chap. 3). Although this Christian idea is global, it has a local logic in the former Soviet Union.[29] In the early 1960s, at the height of Khrushchev's anti-religious campaign, many Baptist believers (*veruyushchie*) refused to register their congregations and, as a result, hundreds of active preachers were imprisoned or lived in hiding (Bourdeaux 1968; Sawatsky 1981).[30] Unlike many others who followed the restrictive rules of the government, the Unregistered Baptists tried hard to enact the principle of total separation of church from state. Despite a greater religious freedom in post-socialist Russia, they still have not registered their congregations with the authorities and source their identity largely from their Soviet-era martyrdom experiences and ascetic style of religiosity. Pentecostals in the Soviet Union went through a similar split to that of the Baptists.

Although Baptists and Pentecostals are no longer that "new," they are certainly imagined as not being "traditional" by the wider public in Russia. Today evangelicals are still—in recent years even more forcefully so—branded in the media and beyond as intrinsically "foreign," essentially "non-Russian" (Agadjanian 2014; Fagan 2013; Glanzer 2002; Kazmina 2008; Koosa 2017; Richters 2013). Russianness for most is felt to be tightly tied to Russian Orthodoxy, whose representatives are wary or openly inimical toward evangelicals, sharing this antipathy with the state. Evangelicals again see Orthodoxy as a mistaken form of Christianity, if not outright devil worship. Somewhat paradoxically, the Nenets' historic experience of Orthodoxy has rather encouraged their conversion to evangelical Christianity. Although there is only sporadic Orthodox evangelization in the tundra today (see, e.g., Borisova 2022; Konstantin 2014), the leading Christian church of Russia continues to have a relatively positive reputation among the Independents, especially when they compare Orthodox believers to nonbelievers.

Indeed, many features from Orthodoxy have entered the ritual life of herders. One can see icons in the ritually pure part of the tent, in front of which candles are burned on certain holidays. These rituals are inherited from their ancestors who were baptized by Orthodox priests in the tsarist period and who also witnessed Orthodoxy among the neighboring Izhma Komi reindeer herders (Habeck 2011). Some Nenets go to Orthodox churches to buy icons and candles. For example, among the Yamb-To Nenets, Mikul, the first Baptist convert Ivan's grandfather, was known as "the old priest" (*pop vesako*) because he spoke highly of a Christian sacred book and carried out quasi-Orthodox baptisms of infants (see Leete and Vallikivi 2011, 94–95 for more detail). People who have not joined Baptists or Pentecostals still baptize (*kresti*) their children: this act is expected not only to safeguard a child but also to create relations through gifts received from the godparents. Despite carrying out Christian rituals, nomads have little understanding of the doctrinal teachings. For instance, before the evangelicals came, most people had never heard the name Jesus Christ. So for Protestant missionaries, despite the Nenets' claims of being Orthodox, they are still "pagans" who do not know even the name of God's son. However, as elsewhere in the mission fields, this diagnosis of ignorance serves as the primary initiative for proselytization.[31]

Overview of the Book

My main ethnographic focus is on Baptists, except for chapter 4 which is primarily on Pentecostals, while animists are touched upon throughout the book. Chapter 1 is dedicated to the history of the noncollectivized reindeer herders and their difference from the collectivized Nenets in the Great Land tundra and Polar Urals. The latter part of the chapter gives a short overview of post-Soviet developments, including the Independents' engagement with the state and the appeal of the modern market. It sets a context for understanding the Independents' new wish to engage with outsiders— that is, Russians (*lutsaq*), who are perceived as both threatening and useful at the same time.

Part II charts the process of conversion from both Nenets' and Baptist missionaries' perspectives. Chapter 2 looks at the conversion of the first Nenets convert, Ivan, which grew out of a long-term quest but is yet representable as sudden and radical. I go on to discuss one larger set of motivations in conversion, which is the rejection of alcohol. At that point, I also describe the growing tensions between the imagined futures of older and younger generations of converts. Chapter 3 gives an overview of the agenda of the Unregistered Baptist missionaries, who in their salvation work are driven by their particular views of past and future. Having restored God's true church on earth, they aim to fulfill their role as messengers at the end of time and space. Meanwhile, chapter 4 explores the destruction of Nenets sacred images through an encounter between Vladislav, a Pentecostal missionary, and Iriko, the head of a Ural Nenets family. I shall discuss this not only as an event of material destruction but also as a crucial (de-)socializing and performative speech event.

Part III, which is about speaking and silence, contains three chapters that all treat various aspects of language use and personhood in the setting of the mission encounter. I focus on the limits of verbalizability, the role of the nonreferential power of words, and the aspects of intentionality and agency in the context of emergent and ongoing social relations. I demonstrate that, like words, silences can also have profound ethical consequences on social lives. Chapter 5 investigates the Nenets understanding of words, especially in their capacity to bind and create dangerous relations. In this context, the missionaries' words enter the Nenets wordscape as potentially powerful agents. Chapter 6 portrays the changing understanding of words among Baptist converts who struggle with their constative ("state something") and performative ("do something") aspects. Linguistic practices are tightly situated in the power relations that are shaped by missionaries. The final chapter focuses on changes of personhood and the ethical self-formation of converts who strive for coherence in their lives; it discusses more specifically how new kinds of disposition and sensitivity emerge as patterns of self-reflective ethical habits.

1

DYNAMICS OF AVOIDANCE AND
ENGAGEMENT

Russians: The Dangerous *Lutsaq*

This chapter is on Sovietization and its absence as well as subsequent developments over the course of the early post-Soviet years. During the decades of Soviet modernization, the Independent reindeer herders came to be *different* from their neighbors (nomadic collective farm workers or newly sedentarized villagers), as they created their own Arctic "nonstate space" (Scott 2009, 13). I shall give an overview of the history of the Nenets reindeer herders who chose concealment from the Soviets and who, for reasons to be explained, were successful in this. These Independents lived distinct lives in many respects.

By the late Soviet period, most Nenets working in collective farm brigades (*brigady*) or living in villages had become subjects molded by state policies and Communist values and micromanaged through everyday institutional practices. The generations whose parents had suffered from Stalinist repressions had grown up in a new state and social system they had come to see as "a fact of life" (Gray 2005, 96). However, the elusive Independents had by and large sustained a precollectivization way of life, with the family-based herding of private reindeer. They maintained a typical pattern of migration of the small-scale herders whose animals numbered rather in tens than hundreds; this amount enabled only limited mobility and required extensive fishing and hunting (Babushkin 1930; Kertselli 1911; see also Klokov and Zayker 2010; Krupnik 1976, 1993). By the late Soviet period, many, especially the younger generation of Independents, came to perceive themselves as left behind in the rapidly changing world around them. I would suggest this is why they have tried to break out of their isolated way of life and set up relations with outsiders.

The wider argument I shall make is that religious conversions are linked—at least for the younger generations—to a sense of marginality in the community of Independents.[1] However, reasons for conversion are never singular, nor do they stay the same over time. As Robbins (2004, 86) argues, "The motives that initiate the process of conversion are often transformed as it progresses" (cf. Hefner 1993b, 18). His dynamic model of conversion ties together two dominant analytical approaches, which he calls "utilitarian" and "intellectualist."[2] While the first offers political and economic advantages, the second stresses how a changing world is made meaningful through adopted exogenous categories. These approaches can be successfully juxtaposed, as Robbins (2004, 87) notes, "Good at explaining the initial impetus toward conversion, the utilitarian approach gives way to the intellectualist one when it comes time to explain why in some cases people stay with the new religion and come to engage it deeply." Even if we may doubt whether things necessarily stand that neatly, especially when thinking of the intricately woven new ideas, fears, hopes, (in)conveniences, and constraints that conversion is known to entail, I find this model a useful heuristic for sorting wider social contexts and particular religious developments. In this chapter, I shall look at the initial phase, or impetus for conversion, by examining the experience of the Nenets reindeer herders in the Soviet period. In the next chapter, my focus shall be on the post-Soviet context and deeper engagement with the new religion, or the second stage.[3]

I would argue that to break through their perceived isolation, the Independents have been searching for empowerment from the outside world while trying not to be submerged by its influence. My focus in this chapter is on two brothers from the Veli family—Ivan, the first convert, and his elder brother Andrei, the second convert and later presbyter of "the Nenets church." Ivan has come to be engaged in business projects and set up relations with administrators hoping for some kind of improvement in his and his kin's lives. In this setting, Christian missionaries Ivan met on the path proved well adapted to offer a sense of empowerment and likely more trustworthy than state agents, who carry with them a history of interference and violence from the past. I shall suggest that conversion offers to the Independents a sense of dignity, a rough equivalent to what among collective farmers is glossed with the Soviet term "cultured" (*kul'turnyy*) or "civilized" (*tsivilizovannyy*). There has been a constant struggle to find a balance between leading the old way of life in the tundra (living with reindeer; the men, women, and children gathering around the hearth; etc.) and becoming different kinds of person as a result of the changes that Christianity and modernity offer.

Although much of the Soviet empire was governed by a central ideology and set of rules, there were remarkable differences in the ways in which regions were managed, especially in the post-Stalinist Soviet period (see, e.g., D. Anderson 2000; Balzer 1999; Grant 1995; Gray 2005; King 2011; Vitebsky 2005; Wiget and Balalaeva 2011). This was the case with the neighboring Nenets "national" regions, that is the Nenets Region and Yamalo-Nenets Region, where directives from Moscow were differently implemented due to an interplay of various factors (ethnic composition, regional leadership, economic structure, vast distances, etc.). West of the Urals in the Nenets Region, the full-scale sedentarization campaign—from the late 1950s until the 1980s—turned men into shift workers, who spent a month or two in the tundra and as much time in the village, often drinking heavily. Their wives, parents, and children were moved from nomadic tents into Russian-style log cabins, where they were alienated from tundra life, herding, and reindeer. This policy was carried out to increase control over the local economy and Indigenous population under the labels of "rationalization of production" and "raising the cultural level of the Indigenous population" (Khomich 1966, 261; Lashov 1964). As a result, the family-based nomadic way of life remained in only a few pockets of the region. East of the Urals, in the Yamalo-Nenets Region, mobile pastoralism was (and still is) considerably more viable (Stammler 2005; Golovnev et al. 2018).

In the following, I shall map out the Nenets' relationships with outsiders—especially Russians (*lutsaq*). In the perception of Nenets nomads, there are largely two kinds of human others who have enabled them to craft their local sense of themselves. These are other reindeer-herding peoples, who have specific names, and nonreindeer-herding peoples, who are all labeled *lutsaq*—the word marking a fundamental kind of alterity in a world split into nomadic and settled ways of life. This division is manifest not only in lifeways, but also in language, race, colonial experience, and ideas about origins.

Ivan and Andrei's brother Yegor explained to me that all people who do not live with reindeer are *lutsaq*. Other reindeer-herding neighbors like the Izhma Komi (*ngysma*) and the Khanty (*khabi*) have their own distinctive names, while the nonnomads bear one generalized name (cf. Pushkareva

Figure 1.1. Nenets shift workers, August 1999.
Their children are visiting the herders' camp only in the summer holiday.

2000, 95). *Lutsaq* makes up a category that has evolved to be multilayered and highly relational over the course of time and which can be grasped only in the context of situated naming practices. It is not so much a fixed name for a bounded group but rather a default term that describes different ways of living, subsistence practices, communicative behaviors, and skills.

Those who live with reindeer refer to themselves as *nyeneyq nyenetsyaq*, translated as "real people" or "genuine humans." The word *nyeney* is used to emphasize one's humanity, as in the phrase *nyeney mirkani ngani khamyvq*, "to take on again a human form" (Pushkareva 2007, 79, 201; 2019, 118). However, being Nenets is not only about the human form or having reindeer but also about having certain skills. It is possible to become enskilled (*tyene-vana*) only through an intimate contact with the living environment. When somebody is unskillful in the tundra, the person is called *lutsa* (for men) or *khabyenye* (for women). As such, reindeer herders also use the term as a pedagogical tool. When his children did something wrong, Yegor would call them *lutsaq*, either teasing with a smile or scoffing seriously. Yegor explained his word use like this: "Whenever somebody in the tundra called another *lutsa* or said that he did something like a Russian [*lutsarakha*], this was taken as a serious offense. For example, people called [my father] Sem Vesako *lutsa*. Yet my grandfather Mikul did not tolerate it when somebody did something like a Russian."

Although Mikul did not like it, his son Sem joked by calling himself "Russian" when he was drunk, claiming that his mother's father was Russian. One of the proofs was him being taller than most others. He imitated Russians by being very noisy and talkative. Sem used to say, "I am a half Russian," (*lutsa takharuv*) and "I am talking like a Russian." Sem was simultaneously mocking Russians and his alcohol-induced talkativeness, being self-reflectively ironic. This was not a positive identification but rather took the role of "the other" in a similar entertaining way as the Western Apache mock the white man's intolerable verbosity and noisy bravado (Basso 1979). When Yegor talked about the *lutsaq*, he often referred to his own grandfather. As a fresh Baptist convert, he could not, however, subscribe to his "pagan" (even if "a bit Orthodox") grandfather's views in a straightforward manner. To prove his current position, he would say from time to time that "people did not understand then," a standard phrase from a convert's mouth. Despite this, Yegor was eager to talk about his grandfather's views on the Russians.

The idea that Russians are evil and dangerous has roots in the spiritual realm, as occurs in many other societies that have faced the aggression of colonialists. Yegor once said, with a smile, "My granddad Mikul did not want to send his children to school because, as he said, all Russians are the sons of the younger wife of the underworld's master [*Nga taty nyuq*]. They are monkeys [*ngayatarq*] and evil spirits [*ngylyekaq*]. But [Grandfather used to say] Nenets are from God." Calling Russians "evil spirits" was not an idiosyncratic habit of Mikul. In Nenets oral tradition, too, Russians have their origin from the underworld, and they are described as chthonic spirits, sons of the underworld's master, Nga, who has also fathered all other evil spirits with his junior wife (Chernetsov 1987, 88, 119–20; Golovnev and Osherenko 1999, 1). Amused by what he was going to reveal, Yegor said that when Communists appeared in the tundra for the first time, they themselves declared that their origin was not from God but from monkeys. Because monkeys were portrayed as evil spirits in epic songs, a Darwinian narrative quickly became merged with a Nenets one. Thus for Mikul, the godless Russians were the worst, briefly called "Communists" or "monkeys," who were to be avoided for better or worse.

For Yegor's grandfather Mikul, the most fearsome *lutsaq* were the godless Soviets, collectivizers, repressors, soldiers, officials, and prisoners he had seen in the Gulag camps on the coast of the Kara Sea. Herders used to say when speaking of the outsiders that "the Russians do not joke" (*lutsaq niq yonyenaq*) or "the Russians can kill" (*lutsaq khadangguq*) whenever a situation was tense. "We were afraid of the Russians," Yegor told me many times. However, as with predators, one had to adapt to the situation and find the best kind of relationship with them. Russians, wolves, and spirits of the underworld could not be shunned entirely; instead, they called for sacrifices through exchange circuits, as I was told. Some herders used to say that Soviet fishing inspectors or greedy state fur buyers had to be fed in the same way as wolves (cf. Vitebsky 2005, 273). In this way, Nenets tried to protect themselves from what could be called the witchcraft of the Russians. (I shall return to this topic in chap. 5.)

Today's concerns of the Independents come from a logic of avoidance and engagement that has evolved over several generations. I shall give a brief overview of what constitutes the historical experience of Yamb-To and Ural Nenets with Russians. The families of Independents all have slightly different stories about how they remained outside the collective farms. Yet common to such narratives are motives of fear and escape, especially in the early period of Sovietization when members of the same family would often become engaged in different ways with the power of the Russian "civilizing mission."

The Veli Family in the Stalinist Period

To explain what stands behind this perception of Russians as dangerous agents, I shall give a short overview of the Veli family, who figure as key characters in the changes that the Yamb-To Independents have gone through. During the Stalin era, Yegor's grandfather Mikul and his three brothers were going very different ways: Mikhail joined with most of the family's two thousand reindeer into a collective farm; Ngel disappeared to the front during the Second World War (in 1942); and Vas perished in the Gulag after being arrested in the aftermath of the *mandalada* uprising in 1943. Only Mikul managed to stay behind and live the cautious life of an Independent herder. I shall describe this family's history in detail not only because I have spent most of my time in the field with Mikul's descendants but also because of the diversity it illustrates of the fortunes of most Nenets of the area.

In the nineteenth century, Mikul's great-grandfather Yarki Veli lived in the forest. His children would migrate across the open tundra in the eastern part of the Great Land tundra.[4] Yarki's grandson Taras (Mikul's father) had a big reindeer herd. His grandson Vata, then an old man himself, told me that Taras's herd was "ten thousand strong," a poetic formula meaning "very many." He lost the greater part of his herd in one of the several waves of reindeer epidemics of the early twentieth century (cf. Kertselli 1911). He and his wife died in epidemics of smallpox when whole nomadic camps perished, leaving Mikul and his brothers orphans, all of them very young. Mikul survived smallpox, yet he lost the sight in his left eye. This would later save him from being conscripted in the Second World War.

Like most others to the west of the Urals, the Velis were baptized by Orthodox missionaries, who were active in the area from 1825 until the end of the 1910s.[5] The missionaries used to come to the summer settlement of Khabarovo in the Yugor Strait area on the Kara coast, where as a young man Mikul spent most of his time in the 1920s and 1930s. During the short summers, this area became unusually densely populated, as it offered various options for fishing, hunting, and trade with Russians and Izhma Komi for Nenets (Arzyutov 2016; Krupnik 1993, 209; Kvashnin 2009b). It was a ritually loaded area as well, where a Russian church and a major Nenets sacred site lay close to each other. The first was situated on the mainland coast of the Yugor Strait in Khabarovo and the second on the island of Vaigach across the strait, known among Nenets as Khekhe Ngo ("island of spirits") or Khebyidya Ngo ("sacred island"). Orthodox priests systematically destroyed wooden and stone images of spirits (*syadeiq*) at these sites (see chap. 4). Yet the Nenets still visited them and other sacred locations, where they created new *syadeiq* to whom they made sacrifices and offerings. However, they also visited the Orthodox church in Khabarovo and took their offerings to St. Nicholas, known as the "Russian spirit" (*lutsa khekhe*) Mikola. The Orthodox religiosity of the Nenets was thoroughly integrated into the existing ritual complex. However, as many reports suggest, the Nenets knew almost nothing about Christian doctrines, including the economy of salvation (Igumnov 1912; Jackson 1895, 84–89; Kozmin 1903; Mikhaylov 1898; see also Vallikivi 2023).

Figure 1.2. An icon of St. Nicholas the Miracle-Maker and coins used as offerings at sacred places, September 2006.
Note the Lenin heads.

In the 1920s, the Bolsheviks shut down all the Orthodox churches in the region and repressed the priests. When Stalinist industrialization and collectivization was taken to the North in 1930, Fyodor Eikhmans, the head of the Gulag secret police (OGPU), built the first forced-labor camp in the area, under the label of the so-called Vaigach Expedition. According to the historian Orlando Figes (2008, 210), Eikhmans was looking for gold there after he had heard "ancient legends about the 'golden woman,' a totem doll of solid gold" from some Nenets. However, he found only zinc and lead, which the convicts, most of them geologists and other specialists, extracted in deadly conditions. Like many others both before and after, Eikhmans was fascinated by the idea of transforming scarcely populated frontiers with abundant treasures into industrial hubs. As Kate Brown (2007, 84–88) writes, Eikhmans's idea of the development was reminiscent of the "frontier thesis" forged by the historian Frederick Jackson Turner, who believed in the crucial role of frontiers for American nationhood. We shall see later how the idea of conquest of the world's end is crucial in the thinking of the evangelical missionaries as well. So far it is enough to point out that, although the goals of the two have a great many differences, they both are motivated by the desire to conquer untapped areas and transform local people into believers of the project they carry out (see chap. 3).

Nenets were both attracted to and repelled by the Gulag camps. Male herders were hired to transport geologists in search of metallic ores (Gurskiy 1999; Vittenburg 2003). Like many others in the 1930s living near the newly established Gulag camps, Mikul was hired as a sledge driver (*yamshchik*). His duty was to transport various goods, mail, and people along the coast of the Arctic Ocean between the Gulag camps of Khabarovo and Amderma (the first convicts were taken to Amderma in summer 1933 to excavate fluorite [see Josephson 2014, 272–80]). As Vata told me, his father witnessed there how Communists were particularly dangerous sorts of Russians, who killed their own people, that is other *lutsaq* from the Gulag camps, by throwing them under the ice "like frozen fish."

In parallel with industrialization through the Gulag system, agricultural collectivization became a full-fledged project in which the whole rural population, including the Indigenous minorities, was forced to take part. As described in the introduction, this caused fierce resistance in many parts of the North. Soviet ethnographer Georgiy Prokof'ev writes in his private diary, "Nenets call this nothing other than that 'they were robbed'" (quoted in Arzyutov 2016, 344; cf. Laptander 2017). In summer 1934, the authorities in Naryan-Mar requested the leaders of the Bolshezemelskaya District to intensify the collectivization of Nenets in the Kara tundra, who, unlike in western areas, were lagging behind the official schedule (Yevsyugin 1993; cf. Tolkachev 2000b, 271–72). By that time, very few collective farms had been established in the region, and most Nenets were still classified as Independents (*yedinolichniki*), individual freeholders outside the collective farms or state farms. This category was planned to be eradicated in a few years' time.[6]

The main tools with which to compel reindeer herders into collective and state farms were persuasion, intimidation, and various repressive measures ranging from expropriation to incarceration and deportation. The most respected community members, better-off reindeer owners, and shamans were often victims of dekulakization: their property was heavily taxed and reindeer confiscated; some of them were imprisoned or killed as "anti-Soviet elements." As a result, entire communities reacted either by fleeing or with armed resistance.

A half-Nenets and half-Russian, Arkadi Yevsyugin, the first secretary of the Bolshezemelskaya District, was responsible for collectivization in the region.[7] With a few other members of local Native councils (*tuzsovety*), he began to visit reindeer camps in the area. As Yevsyugin (1993, 24) recalls in his memoirs, "We started to go to tents and joint camps [*po chumam i parmam*] and carry out individual and group political work among the rural proletarians and middle-class reindeer herders [*olenevodov-batrakov i serednyakov*]. We explained what Soviet power was and what it aimed at. We talked a lot of the future tasks in the tundra; we conversed about the Communist Party and Lenin." Yevsyugin refused to be accompanied by the police, as he believed in the power of persuasion, or as he put it, "We shall rely only on the true word of the Party [*pravdivoe partiynoe slovo*]" (ibid.).[8] This echoes Christian missionaries' conviction of the persuasive power of the word, as we shall see below.

A pragmatist by nature, Yevsyugin made a curious move to attract the Nenets to join the collective farm. The reindeer herders had complained to the Soviet officials that they could not use the Khabarovo church on St. Elijah's Day. In summer 1934, Yevsyugin asked Aleksandr Ditskaln, the next head of the Vaigach Gulag camp after notorious Eikhmans had left, "to fix, paint, and limewash the chapel and put the religious items back in their places" (26). The Soviets had been using it as a dormitory. On August 2 (St. Elijah's Day by the new calendar), Nenets arrived and "stopped at the church and were satisfied with the church looking better than before" (ibid.). This took place despite this time being the height of the state's violent antireligious policy. A big tent was erected nearby for the meeting, and herders were given free tea and vodka. Ivan Prourzin, the first secretary of the Nenets regional party organization, and some other high-ranking officials arrived from Naryan-Mar; in addition, representatives of the Gulag were present.[9] The meeting lasted for two days and was said to be a success, as over the following years, a few new collective farms emerged. Yevsyugin was probably hoping to gain symbolic capital from overlapping the Soviet time and place with the Orthodox time and place: following the Soviet practice of replacing saints days with the days of new heroes, events, and professions (Lane 1981; Peris 1998; Tumarkin 1983), in 1932 party officials had declared St. Elijah's Day to be a "mass agricultural-political holiday—Reindeer Day instead of the clerical holiday" (quoted in Tolkachev 1999, 112).

Many Nenets still resisted. Out of four Veli brothers, only Mikhail joined the collective farm, doing so in 1935. He went with most of the family's reindeer and became chairman of the collective farm, which was called

"Yadey Segery."[10] Despite Yevsyugin's efforts, Mikul's family, along with many others, did not join the collective farm. Vata told me that working for the Gulag protected his father: "The chief of Amderma [Gulag] did not let him go to the collective farm, as he worked well for him." In the early days of the Gulag, this was possible because of the different management style when camps bought the service of the Independents: the herders could also rely on individual relations and the supply system outside the collective farm for the time being. Yet soon pressure from the collectivizers grew, and the herders searched for safer places. During the Second World War, Mikul's family escaped to the other side of the Urals after hearing that the "red soldiers" were coming to take their reindeer. On the Ob River, Mikul was caught and forced to work as a log transporter on a Gulag construction site in Aksarka.[11] This time it was not a voluntary or paid job. After working there for a year, struggling with cold and hunger, one night, with the help of local Nenets, he managed to gather some reindeer and flee back across the Urals (cf. Bjørklund 1995; Khanzerova 2003, 2007).

With the beginning of the Second World War, a new threat emerged for the herders. A 1939 law had abolished the military service exemption for the Indigenous minorities of the North. One of Mikul's brothers, Ngel, was conscripted into the army and sent to the front. He never returned.[12] A significant proportion of Nenets adult men (six hundred men with six thousand reindeer) from the Nenets Region were sent to fight against Finland on the Karelian front and elsewhere, not having "the slightest idea about what in fact a war was," not speaking Russian, and considering it a trick to send them "to their deaths" (Gorter-Gronvik and Suprun 2000, 130–32, 141n6; see also Dudeck 2018). Ngel's fate was shared by hundreds of other Nenets men who never returned from the war. While the men were on the front, families in the tundra had to meet extra high quotas, make "voluntary" payments to the defense fund, and tolerate confiscations of private animals. In addition to all female chores, women, often with small children, had to herd reindeer and trap foxes and fish by themselves to survive (see Khomich 1966, 244–45 for a heroic account; Mamoylova 1997, 67).

The excessive work norms and taxes (live reindeer, meat, fish, and furs), recruitment of men for the war, and lack of supplies led to extensive unrest among the Nenets on both sides of the Urals. While in Aksarka in 1943, Mikul met his brother Vas's son and learned that Vas had been arrested in an uprising. This event came to define the relationships between Nenets and the Russians and their collective farms for years to come, forcing many to avoid the *lutsaq* and state institutions at any cost. Most Independent herders today are either direct descendants—including orphans—or close kin of participants in the uprising.

Nenets call this uprising *mandalada*. Families around the Urals had not managed to meet the production quotas set by the state through the collective farms because of the bad hunting season. As a result, the collective farm did not give supplies to the herders. Desperate and infuriated, Nenets families left the prescribed collective farm pastures in Baidarata (east of the Urals), took their reindeer with them, and retreated to the northern slopes of the Polar Urals, away from the trajectories where Russians moved. A few *yedinolichniki* also joined. Yegor's mother-in-law, Tetteya, who was born the same year as the *mandalada*, explained to me that her family, like others, had gathered to discuss how to chase the Russians out of the tundra. Andrei added that from the Nenets' point of view, "there was no difference between dying in the army or here in the *mandalada*." During the spring months of reindeer calving, maybe two hundred to four hundred people were camping around the mountains called Nganorakha. Some participants traveled across the tundra, inviting people to join the *mandaladaq* ("gathered ones"), threatening to kill all the Russians and any Nenets who collaborated with them. *Mandalada* people once attacked a supply caravan and took flour and salt; another time ninety-five reindeer paid earlier as war tax were taken back (Vallikivi 2005; see also Golovnev and Osherenko 1999, 81–93; Laptander 2014; Leete 2005a; Tolkachev 2000b).

On June 24, 1943, a group of Soviet military men armed with machine guns arrived at Ned-Yu Mountain (see map 2). A daylong battle followed. The Nenets killed one Russian officer; the Russians killed six Nenets. "You can still see a skull there," said Andrei's wife, who, when staying in the camp nearby, once went there as a child to search for hidden items left by the *mandalada* participants. After the Russians had taken some Nenets women hostage, the Nenets men surrendered. Over fifty men were arrested (many of them days later), among whom some had no connection whatsoever with the incident, including Mikul's brother Vas.[13] He was taken to Arkhangelsk and perished somewhere in the Gulag. Almost no one returned from the prison camps. Tetteya's father was among the few lucky ones to come back to the tundra. Tetteya was fourteen when, in 1957, she first saw her father. She vividly described to me how wary she was of a stranger arriving and kissing her on the cheek.

For Nenets, *mandalada* was also an event that involved spirits. Tetteya told me of two shamans who performed a ritual seance in the *mandalada*.

They foretold success in the fight against the Russians. Tetteya, like many others I talked to, noted that these shamans had erred in their prophecy. This failure probably contributed to the deteriorating image of shamans, who had become a rare species after a prolonged persecution they could not withstand. As Ivan told me (from whose Baptist viewpoint, this was a chance to condemn "shamanism," or "Satanism" as he also called it), "What is interesting here is that, if the shaman had known, he would have understood what was going to happen—for example, that the authorities would come and that Communism would start and that we were about to be killed. But this was not open to them." When I met Ngelku (a Ural Independent), the grandson of one of the shamans called Sevdya Mishka, he did not wish to talk about his grandfather's role. Some said that he was ashamed of his grandfather; others believed he feared arrest himself for his grandfather's deeds over sixty years earlier (cf. Bjørklund 1995, 78; see also Golovnev 1995, 194; Laptander 2014, 2017; Lar 2001, 217). As I learned from some others, this kind of fear had not vanished completely, even in the post-Soviet era.

The parents and grandparents of several families of Independents managed to escape arrest after the uprising and to remain outside collective farms. For instance, at the beginning of 1943, Yegor Vylka left the Kara collective farm to join the *mandalada*. He avoided being arrested and started living with a few reindeer near Amderma with three other Independent families, forming the origin of today's Yamb-To community. His name appears in two documents: in the first, he is listed with the other "deserters" of the Kara collective farm (Tolkachev 2000b, 302) and in the second with those who had "gathered" but had succeeded in escaping on hearing of the Russians' arrival; he had been declared wanted by the authorities (305). In the following years, many Independents married those who had been widowed during the *mandalada*. For instance, Mikul's third marriage was to a woman with a small child who had lost her husband in the *mandalada* and lived in a trading post in extreme poverty. At that time, there were some thirty to forty Independents living in the area, while probably well over a hundred found refuge in the Urals.

Dodging the Officials after Stalin

In the 1930s, thousands fled inside Russia. While in the Russian agrarian South only a few land-bound Independent peasants could move away from the pressure (Alexopoulos 2003, 7, 9; Fitzpatrick 1994, 154), in the subarctic

North, collectivization triggered large-scale movements of the (semi-)nomadic population (D. Anderson 2000, 47; Brandišauskas 2017, 44; Donahoe 2003, 124; 2012, 107; Lavrillier 2005, 124; Perevalova 2019, 208–9). Nenets, like many other nomads, were used to the tactics of retreat in the seventeenth and eighteenth centuries, when they felt growing colonial pressure, including attempts of Christianization (Golovnev and Kan 1997, 153; Shemanovskiy 2011, tome I, 187). However, unlike that period, in the era of Stalin the pressure had become unavoidable everywhere, and evading the state by flight was now virtually impossible. Most of those who had succeeded in remaining separate were herded into collective farms by the late 1940s, such as hundreds of Nenets who had fled to the northernmost part of the Yamal Peninsula (Lezova 2001).

Across Siberia, there were families or small groups who remained outside the collective farms after that period. Some of them were collectivized in the 1960s—for example, small groups of Evenki (Fondahl 1998, 60–61; Lavrillier 2005, 123; Tugolukov 2005, 230; Vasilevich 2005, 9–11, 21), Eveny (Gurvich 2005, 102–7; Khakhovskaya 2008, 108–9; Popova 1981), and Koryak (Khakhovskaya 2018, 33–34). However, a few families among the Potapovo Evenki and Nenets (D. Anderson 2000, 25, 48), Tozhu in Tyva (Donahoe 2003, 124; 2012, 107) and Ust-Nyukzha Evenki (Lavrillier 2005, 123) appear to have remained in the taiga hidden from the gaze of "Soviet organs" until the end of the 1980s or beyond.[14] Nevertheless, by the late Soviet period, none of these state-evading groups seem to have been of a comparable size to the Nenets Independent groups in the Polar Urals and Great Land tundra.

In the post-Stalinist period, the Independents presented a disturbing problem for the local authorities, although there was no need to deal with this problem intensively because *officially* there were almost no *yedinolichniki* left. According to official rhetoric, in the Nenets Region, collectivization had been completed by 1940 (Abul'khanov and Kovyazin 1977, 66). Furthermore, even if the authorities knew, nobody had an exact idea about the scale of the "problem," even though a growing number of aircrafts flew above the heads of Independents, offering a view of their campsites from the sky. Yet there were those who had met the Independents and described them as surviving "elements" who unforgivably lived outside the gaze of the state, without documents, not fulfilling their "obligations." This was a moral problem. Some Soviet activists tried to solve it, while most others ignored it.

Journalist Viktor Tolkachev, arriving in the Nenets Region from Donbas, Ukraine, in search of "romanticism of the North" is a telling example. In the mid-1960s, he took a job as a culture worker (*kul'trabotnik*) in the "agitation group" (*agitgruppa*) of the Ust-Kara "Red October" collective farm. Its brigades migrated in the easternmost area of the Nenets Region where Independent families were numerous. By traveling from one reindeer-herding brigade to another, his job was to screen films, organize games, and give talks on Soviet life and politics. When staying in a brigade in October 1965, he met a family of Independents. This was Mikul's son Sem (father of the then five-year-old Yegor) with his wife and eldest daughter. Tolkachev admits that Sem, with "the narrow and darkened face of an Indian, with high-pitched guttural voice and pure Nenets speech," caused contradictory feelings in his "Soviet consciousness." He writes:

> A family came to visit the Laptander family—secretive and strange *lichniki* [*yedinolichniki*]. They do not join the collective farm; they do not send their children to school or lads to the army. They do not have passports, and nobody knows how many they are and who they are. And yet they have their OWN reindeer, and they are their own MASTERS. Every family has its OWN chum. Nobody takes cinema to them. Maybe they do not have this kind of need. . . . I look at these unusual and rare guests, experiencing a difficult feeling of curiosity, respect, and hostility. Say what you like, in front of me—to say the least—are passive enemies of Soviet power. (1999, 206–7, capital letters in original)

Back from the tundra in 1967, Tolkachev went to a meeting for culture workers in Naryan-Mar where he spoke of "the problem of *yedinolichniki*." Officials there were dismissive and refuted Tolkachev's claims by saying that in the Nenets Region there were not "these" (*takikh*) and the ones he met must have come from Yamal. But in Salekhard, the center of the Yamalo-Nenets Region, Tolkachev believed, they were said to come from the Nenets Region. The "problem" was just written off from both sides (Tolkachev 1999; 2004, 504). Apparently, the Independents themselves occasionally used the same tactics. Ivan said to me, "When in Komi, we said that we were from the Nenets Region; when in the Nenets Region, we said we came from Komi."

The existence of the Independents was known among the farm chairmen, chairmen of village councils and party workers of the area who reported on them to the regional centers from time to time. The complaints that reached Naryan-Mar contained accusations from unlawful use of collective farm pasture to parasitism and to parents not giving their children to school or lads to the army. The collective farm chairmen were above all concerned about the use of the pastures. They argued that as the Independents were tramping the transit corridors of the collective farm pastures, they should be "called to account" (Tolkachev 2004, 499).

While most of the time the regional leaders ignored these reports, a few concerted efforts were made to "liquidate the problem." For instance, in 1958, the chief prosecutor, the police chief, and a specialist from the agricultural department from Naryan-Mar went to the coal-mining settlement of Khalmer-Yu to prosecute the Independents for social parasitism (*tuneyadstvo*) (Tolkachev 2004, 505).[15] According to the law, any adults who refused to engage in socially useful work were considered "parasites" and could be jailed (Alexopoulos 2003, 10; see also Konstantinov 2015, 324; Vladimirova 2006, 108–11).[16] The officials went on a hunt for these "parasites" by all-terrain vehicle (*vezdekhod*), following the sled trails from the village and hoping to catch up with Independents who had just left Khalmer-Yu. Having found only a few children and women in camps, they returned empty-handed. Geologists working in the tundra confirmed that *lichniki* were "not hospitable, trying to be silent, and when Russians come to a chum, the men go to the tundra" (Tolkachev 2004, 507).

Another attempt was made by Yevsyugin who was imprisoned in 1937 and released from the Gulag after Stalin's death. He became a leader of the Bolshezemelskaya District once again, this time as the chair of the executive committee (*okrispolkom*). During his short tenure (1958–59), he felt responsible for tackling the issue. He approached Independents on a small market in Khalmer-Yu. There they sold fish and with the cash earned bought necessary provisions from the shop. While most ignored his repeated addresses in Russian (Yevsyugin had forgotten his childhood language), he managed to talk to an Independent herder called Dmitri Fedotovich Taibarey, who knew some Russian. Yevsyugin recognized him as a "collective farm activist" from the Yusharskiy Tundra Council from the early 1930s. Dmitri's brother Ivan had even become the chair of the executive committee of the Nenets Region in 1936, one of the highest officials in the region. Like Yevsyugin himself, only two years later he was sent to the Gulag during the Great Terror (Tolkachev 2000a, 43–44). Dmitri learned from Yevsyugin that his brother had died in the prison camp. Struck and angered by the news, after a long pause Dmitri asked in Nenets whether Yevsyugin himself was not "with stars," in other words, a masked agent of the NKVD, the secret police. Dmitri left the village, never to appear again (Tolkachev 2004,

504–11). Yevsyugin's naive hopes to build a "trusting relationship" with the Independents were destined to fail because they considered any approach by officials dangerous.[17]

Having relatively small herds—which protected them from excessive interest from the local authorities—the Independents needed cash. They relied on selling valuable furs that could give a substantial income. Yet according to the law, furs could be sold only to the special collection points, which belonged to the state-monopolized auction organization called Soyuzpushnina. Although herders sold pelts on the black market (from hand to hand) as well—for instance, to the military officers in Amderma or geologists working in the tundra—most of the steady income came from fulfilling contracts with Soyuzpushnina (see Yevsyugin 1979, 79). Andrei explained to me how it worked:

> Now we get cash from fish but then we had foxes. We gave these to the collection point by agreement [*po dogovoru*]. The head of the Khalmer-Yu collection point even gave us award letters [*gramoty*]. It would have been better if he had given us money instead. He cheated us. He wrote down a good sort of the fur for his friends; others were credited with a lower sort. Some other people made a statement [*zayavlenie*] against him, as he put pelts aside and paid less money than prescribed. He was imprisoned for a couple of years. But afterward he worked there again and continued to cheat. Once, he even stole pelts from a sledge.

In essence, the Independents carried on with the old-style fur trade their ancestors were practicing before the Bolshevik revolution.[18] Even the claims of cheating had not changed (see Yevladov 1992, 70). Despite his criticism against the head of the Khalmer-Yu fur collection point, Andrei admitted that thanks to the written agreement, he could obtain the documents necessary to protect himself from the pressure that came from state officials. In this way, in the 1970s, several Independents of working age got residence permits (*propiski*) through the Khalmer-Yu fur collection point, where they were registered as hunters (*okhotniki*) (cf. Alekseyenko and Its 2005a, 116–17; 2005b, 238–39).[19]

While in the available publications the past tense was used when talking of the Independents (Yevsyugin 1979), they were still mentioned as "contemporary" in the classified reports written by Soviet ethnographers from the 1960s to the 1980s for the regional and central authorities (Khomich 2006, 149; Vasil'ev 2006a, 2006b). Vladimir Vasil'ev stated that the biggest concentration of Independents was in the southwestern part of the Yamal

Peninsula and the Polar Urals. Writing from the perspective of the Yamalo-Nenets Region, he was implying that the source of the problem was the Nenets Region, reflecting the way the officials in the Yamalo-Nenets Region were accusing the Nenets Region (as discussed above). Vasil'ev describes, "From behind the Urals every summer, reindeer herds of Independents from the Karskiy and the Yusharskiy Village Councils of the Nenets Autonomous Region, Arkhangelsk Province, arrive here. Moreover, these Nenets families, to whom these reindeer belong, are not registered in any of the village councils of either autonomous region. Apparently, the time has arrived to join the efforts of the executive committees of the Yamalo-Nenets and Nenets Region for family and numerical registration of the Independents as well as the reindeer herds in their possession" (2006b, 195).

The efforts were never joined though. The Independents were profiting from living at various kinds of borders. The division was even more complex as collective and state farm lands stretched across administrative borders (see map 3). The farms did not use the pastures further away that were allocated to them (Tolkachev 2004, 499–512; cf. Stammler 2005, 136). For instance, the Ust-Kara collective farm "Red October," which was surrounded by Independents was officially based in the Nenets Region but also had pastures across the border in Komi and the Yamalo-Nenets Region. Yet in practice they rarely used their winter pastures in the Polar Urals because of the rough terrain, deadly avalanches, exhausting herding on foot, and abundance of wolves, which had found refuge in the mountains from the mass culls carried out from airplanes. Instead, dozens of Independent families were using these unwanted pastures.

In addition to this, the Yamb-To Nenets, who were living on the plains, took advantage of the favorable division of lands on the Yugor Peninsula, as their animals predominantly grazed on the pastures of the Komi state farms, the offices of which where hundreds of kilometers further south. Izhma Komi reindeer herders rarely came to the coast of the Arctic Ocean (cf. Habeck 2005, 31–32), where the Independents spent their summers. During winters the Yamb-To people stayed in the middle Korotaikha River in the Nenets Region, which was allocated to the Komi Usinsk state farm as a spring and autumn transitional passage (this was still the case in 2007). Nevertheless, the Komi herders were tolerant toward the Independents, who were scattered with their small herds, a few hundred strong, over a large area. The Komi herders I met spoke of a good bartering relationship, which had lasted over generations with the Independents.[20]

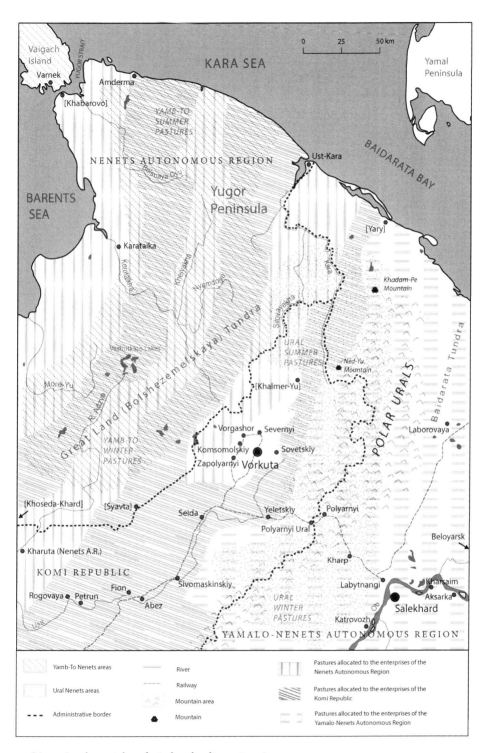

Map 3. Land-use rights of reindeer-herding enterprises.
The map shows the usage rights of kolkhozes and sovkhozes at the end of the Soviet period.
Yamb-To Nenets and Ural Nenets areas are as of 2007.

However, Independents were reminded of their "illegality" from time to time. According to Yegor, when he was a child, Karataika collective farm "Friendship of Peoples" wrote a letter to Moscow, claiming that there were "bandits" in the tundra. A "land committee" and police officers arrived in Karataika. Independents were chased to the village and a meeting was carried out there that lasted for three days. Their names and migration routes were written down. When they were told to join the collective farm, Yegor explained, "Kulei Van [a Yamb-To Independent] even gave a speech and said that he had been in the collective farm, but there was nothing good in it." They all gave promises that they would join a collective farm, not in Karataika but further away in Salekhard or Ust-Kara, which they never did (except for Yegor and Tyepan in the 1980s, see below).

The threat of collectivization had not yet disappeared. Andrei's wife, Lyuba, grew up in a Ural Independent family that had a herd three thousand strong, the size of an average farm brigade. One day in 1976 people from the Baidarata state farm administration (Yamalo-Nenets Region) flew to Lyuba's family camp in the mountains. On board the helicopter were state farm representatives and an armed police officer. They ordered the family to give up most of the herd and told them to join the Baidarata state farm. Taking advantage of rugged terrain and poor weather, Lyuba's father and uncles managed to hide parts of their herd and gave away only around eight hundred (cf. Golovnev and Osherenko 1999, 98). Lyuba told me that while her father and uncles were taking the to-be-collectivized reindeer to Laborovaya, they stopped every now and again, killed a reindeer, ate the best parts of it, and left the rest behind, saying that "these are not our reindeer anymore." This was what many rich reindeer herders did in the 1930s and 1940s when reindeer threatened with collectivization were slaughtered or "lost" (Donahoe 2012, 107; Golovnev and Osherenko 1999; Grant 1995, 91; Leete 2005a, 2005b; Prokof'eva 2018, 137; Stammler 2005, 137). After this confiscation, Lyuba's family escaped to the west and joined the Yamb-To Nenets. Lyuba's father was sought by "people from Salekhard," although without success. An Independent herder who was thought to be Lyuba's father was arrested in Khalmer-Yu, although he was released after the mistake was discovered.

Probably only in the late Soviet period did the problem of Independents reach the highest authorities, when, in 1983, a typhus outbreak erupted in Yamb-To (Zuyeva 2017). Eight Nenets were hospitalized, and all the tents of the Independents were sanitized. Lyuba's first husband died during this outbreak. Others survived. After the epidemic was brought under control,

Figure 1.3. Yegor and his family with Russian acquaintances in Amderma at the end of the 1980s. Private collection.
Soviet militaries and civilians were interested in buying valuable furs from reindeer herders.

the local authorities tried to deal with the "problem" of *yedinolichniki* more thoroughly than ever, relating the typhus to absence of hygiene, lack of education, and general "savagery" (cf. Shearer 2009, 250–51). The regional administration issued a decree (*reshenie*), "to register all members of the Independent families and issue them passports,[21] to register their firearms, to carry out medical checks, to count reindeer and determine migration corridors, to make contracts on procurement of reindeer meat, to assist with acquisitions of foodstuffs and manufactured goods, to teach children in boarding schools, and to give accommodation to families who become sedentary" (Tolkachev 2000a, 491). The deadline was set for 1985, but the regional leaders preferred to leave things as they were (Golovnev 2000a, 139).

Almost nothing from this plan was carried out, except for Vata's family, whose two children were forcibly taken to boarding school (*internat*). People recalled that whenever they heard helicopters flying, children were told to hide behind reindeer skins and bedding rolled at the low edge of the tent. However, when, on an early September day in 1983, a helicopter came to take children to school in the camp of Vata, there were no parents, as they had gone to the settlement to renew their supplies. Like birds of prey, the officials took two school-age children away from an unguarded nest. Yegor witnessed the event from the neighboring tent but dared not do anything. Vata's daughter Tyepas and son Yegor stayed in Naryan-Mar for eight years without seeing their parents or receiving news from them.[22]

By that time, only two children had attended school in Ust-Kara for a short time in the late 1970s. These were Ivan and Andrei. Andrei explained that free school meals probably motivated his father to send them to school: "We were poor and probably this is why father sent us to school." Their father, Sem, had decided to follow the example of the collective farmers. It is likely that he hoped to later benefit from his sons' experience with the sedentary world. Yet he took them away after two years (as Ivan said, "We ran away"). This was enough time to learn some Russian and Komi (the main spoken language in Ust-Kara among the Komi and the Komified Nenets called Kolva Yaran). In many ways, these were vital experiences for them as they later paved the way to deeper engagement with the sedentary Russian world, and, as I shall suggest in chapter 2, made conversion to Christianity more imaginable.

By the late Soviet period, a considerable cultural gap had evolved between the Independents and the collective farm workers. Alongside the collective farm, media, and army, the school probably had the greatest impact on the formation of a new kind of person in the Indigenous Arctic (Liarskaya 2003, 2013; Ravna 2019; Yadne 1995, 2006; cf. Bloch 2004). Many from the younger generation of collective farmers that passed through boarding school, pioneer camps, the Communist Youth League, and the army considered themselves an enlightened new kind of people (Thibaudat and Desplanques 2005, 236–37) and were as knowledgeable about society and history as most others in the Soviet state (Stammler 2005, 96; Vitebsky 2012, 189). They became fluent in formulaic Soviet language, even if their thoughts and words were in an ambiguous relationship. Alexei Yurchak (2006) has described how, for most people by the late Soviet period, the constative dimension of language, with its "literal" meaning, had lost its importance. Following speech act theory, he shows that it was not the "truth" of the text that mattered but the reproduction of the text for the sake of participation in "normal" social life.

Yet language and other state rituals paved the way for the "Soviet consciousness" emerging here and there. In a published interview, Khabecha Yaungad, a Nenets journalist, recollects his realization of how different he had become in comparison to his father, who lived in the tundra. Speaking of the time around 1973 from a post-Soviet perspective, he recalls:

> I had served in the army. There I joined the Party. I sincerely believed that there was no place on earth for any ideology other than Communism. Twenty-three years old, I came home as an ideological person [*ideynym chelovekom*]. I tried out, "Father, do you know what times these are now?" He says: "Daytime." I tried from another angle: "Do you know about socialism?" Father became interested: "Did he serve with you in the army?" I started to reeducate him. But my agitation did not succeed. My father preferred to remain a thick coastal hunter and did not wish to take an interest in the trends of the time. (quoted in Shestakova 2002)

The older generation, who had limited contact with Soviet institutions, did not "speak Soviet."[23] They had not even learned the Soviet "evocative transcript"—that is, the use of previous texts, which are reproduced even while "there is a shared sense that the official truth is not true" (Humphrey 1994, 40). People like Yaungad were living proof of the existence of committed speakers of Soviet, as were many other "sincere young communists" (Yurchak 2006, 104, 209). They had acclaimed the truth of the Soviet cause (Humphrey 2008; see chap. 2).[24]

The Independents were in a different position, as there were certain things that they never heard because they did not "speak Soviet." I realized this when living in the camp of Poru, a middle-aged Nenets man. He was different from other Yamb-To men because he had spent his teenage years in Khalmer-Yu and Vorkuta. His father, after marrying a daughter of an Independent herder from the Urals, left the collective farm—having been an illiterate party worker in his youth—but soon lost all his reindeer because of excessive drinking. As a result, his family moved to an abandoned shed in Khalmer-Yu that they refurbished with reindeer skins imitating the interior of a nomadic tent. From there Poru was taken to a school in Vorkuta where he spent four years. In the mid-1970s, he met a Yamb-To man who invited him to the tundra. He agreed.

In the beginning, Independents called Poru Russian, *lutsa*, because he had forgotten Nenets and when he got drunk he sang Russian songs. Now with thirteen children and over three hundred reindeer, he has stubbornly resisted the pressure of the Baptists. On the day we met, he told me, "In

Vorkuta, I became an atheist, a Communist. Uncle Brezhnev taught us that way." This was language that reflected Soviet-style ideological indoctrination and which could never be heard among Independents. He had appropriated this language and related values through his formal education and reading habits. When reflecting on why there were so many conversions among the Independents and not among the collective farmers, he said to me that the illiterate nomads never resisted verbally but instead they "listen to the missionaries silently and are easily made to agree" (see chap. 5). Although he portrayed his neighbors as naive (as did usually ordinary Russians in the city), he also argued that once the missionaries had left the converts kept gossiping, deceiving, and stealing from one another. He explained that they "pray, then they are forgiven and are free to sin again. They deceive thus both themselves and God."

The school's influence on Ivan and Andrei was different in comparison to Poru because they attended for only a short period, being younger than ten years old. Now a few decades later, both men recall this period as particularly difficult because only Komi and Russian were spoken in Ust-Kara, and they were bullied. Fed by their contradictory experiences of hardships and attraction to the village, the brothers remained fascinated with life in the settlement. Once back in the tundra, they felt that their families were too different from the others, who were better integrated into the Russian world. As Ivan said to me, many collective farmers laughed at Independent herders because they did not understand how things worked in the city (*markana*). In a way, they were discovering their "backwardness" even compared with other reindeer herders whom wider Soviet society considered "backward" (Slezkine 1994).

Ivan and Andrei also learned some Russian at school, which later gave them an advantage when making relationships with city dwellers. For instance, Andrei's father-in-law gave him a reindeer every time he engaged in some kind of business with Russians on his behalf. The other two brothers, Yegor and Tyepan, were the first to become even more closely engaged with the outside world. They joined the collective and state farm respectively a few years before perestroika started. In the early 1980s, after marrying a kolkhoz girl called Lida who had been to school for ten years, Yegor formally joined the Kara collective farm as a hunter. This category was the group least managed by the collective farm administration (see Vasil'ev 2006b, 195).[25] But the change was not significant for him. Yegor was obliged to fulfill the hunting plan and to take his fox furs to Ust-Kara instead of

Khalmer-Yu. As he recalled that time, Yegor was amused by the fact that the collective farm even paid for firewood that he cut for his own tenthold.

Shortly after, Yegor's younger brother Tyepan, who was a bachelor, went to work as a herdsman (*pastukh*) at the Vorkuta state farm. He did so "in the search of discipline," as his Soviet-style explanation was years later. In addition to this, his decision to leave the life of an Independent also stemmed from his lack of any prospect of having his own viable share of his father's small herd, as well as the relatively good salary the state farm paid. Already during the period of perestroika, he settled in Vorkuta as a reindeer skin boot maker selling to city dwellers. At that time, his brother Ivan organized a reindeer-herding cooperative with a couple of Russians, which soon went bust, as one Russian shareholder left for the south with all the money.

Despite the discourse of unease toward the *lutsaq* among the Independents, all four brothers felt an urge to become "modern" and earn money, which came to denote the realization of modernity in many ways. This was accompanied by an urge to overcome the embarrassment of neither knowing the Russian language well enough nor having a basic understanding of the mechanisms and technologies of the Russian world.

Becoming Citizens in Post-Soviet Russia

In 1990, the local newspaper in Naryan-Mar published an article on the discovery of the last true Nenets of the region, titled "The Recluse of the Tundra, or the People Who Do Not Exist" (Tolkachev 1990). Since then, the regional administration has paid institutionalized attention to the Independent herders. Largely emulating the decree of 1983, the administration proposed that it would count reindeer, register herders, and send children to boarding school. Unlike the Ural Nenets, who remained outside the "titular" Nenets areas and thus did not gain much attention, the Yamb-To Nenets became for many a romantic image of a lost tribe. The Yamb-To herders themselves were also looking for contact in the quickly deteriorating economic situation that hit the collapsing Soviet Union. Because at that time much of the food was sold using a system of coupons (*talonnaya sistema*), the documentless Independents were no longer able to buy salt, sugar, vodka, tea, and other necessities from the village shop because they were not on the list based on residence permits. They addressed the Amderma Village Council to obtain coupons. This could not yet be done without procedures of identification and documentation.

Figure 1.4. Entering Amderma, July 2002.
Amderma was a closed military settlement until the early 1990s, after which it was quickly depopulated and left in ruins.

With the collapse of the Soviet Union in 1991, the existence of Independents was no longer illegal. With the new laws on privatization, the Independents gained the *right* to own private reindeer herds, falling into the same category as hundreds of ex-collective farmers (Osherenko 1995, 1091). For many, privatization was seen as a "progressive" way ahead. Yet in the eyes of the regional administration, the main problem was that the Independents—like reindeer herders who had recently left collective farms—had not been allocated usage rights to pasturelands (the land belongs to the state), which were distributed by the land resource committees of the region. In 1992, Naryan-Mar officials proposed the establishment of a reindeer-herding community with the invented name "Yamb-To" for the Independents. Ivan became an elected representative of this community-to-be and a middleman for the new world of bureaucracy and paperwork.[26] He was now coordinating relations with the regional administration (whom the Independents call "Naryan-Mar" for short). Among other things, this was

Figure 1.5. Having a rest after selling and buying, Amderma, August 2006.

the opportunity for an ambitious young man to raise his status through his skill in dealing with the *lutsaq* better than others.

As in the 1930s, Reindeer Day became the time when Naryan-Mar officials visited the tundra to manage relations with the Independents. Every year in early August, representatives from the department of ethnic issues, and a few journalists, doctors, photographers, and entertainers, arrive by helicopter with appreciated gifts like tarpaulin for tent covers, binoculars, some foodstuff, and vodka. As in the Soviet period, urban singers in Nenets folk costumes with added glitter give performances, reindeer races are held, prizes are awarded, and officials make speeches. In 1995, when the registration of the families started, Reindeer Day offered an opportunity for administrators to carry out medical checks, take photos, and collect other information required to start the process of issuing birth certificates and passports (see fig. 1.6).

At the beginning, as many admitted, they were not very comfortable with the registration procedures, especially the taking of images and calling out names, which are both perceived as intimate extensions of one's

Figure 1.6. Passports are issued to Independents, July 2002.

personhood (see chap. 5). For instance, mothers refused to say the Nenets names of their young children in fear of the loss of the child's life force. Irina Khanzerova (2003), who participated in the process of registration, writes what one woman told her, "Write down [a name] you want; in our lives, we do not need them anyway" (see also 2017). As a result, the officials gave children Russian names to their own liking. From the state's perspective, these new Russian citizens became properly represented in their rightful place within the bureaucratic system.[27]

However, the Independents were quick to learn that they needed the documents with names on them in bureaucratic dealings with the authorities, especially to receive various allowances. The Yamb-To Nenets were given the right of residence in the village of Amderma, which was rapidly depopulating in the 1990s (like many other Arctic settlements, see, e.g.,

Thompson 2008). Once registered, pensions and child benefits were allocated through the Amderma village administration. However, confusion with names was frequent. For instance, one child was given the wrong surname because of a misunderstanding and the officials' ignorance of the Nenets language. When an official asked "father's name," the child's mother said not the surname of the child's father's but her father's surname, which was again different from the child's mother's "official" surname. As a result, the child had a different surname from his mother and father. When the discrepancy was discovered by the officials, the case had to be taken to court to legalize the relationship between the child and his parents.

Formal education has been another big change for Independents. In 1991, a couple of children were given to boarding schools in Karataika and Ust-Kara for the first time (except for Ivan and Andrei); many more started in the late 1990s. Although enrollment in elementary school was still compulsory after the collapse of the Soviet Union, the schooling of children was no longer a matter to which the authorities paid close attention (Liarskaya 2003, 68; 2013; Yadne 1995, 27–28). Yet an increasing number of parents—although not all—have been willing to send their children to school. In 2006, I witnessed how thirty-four Yamb-To children were flown from Amderma to Karataika school in a helicopter. Most of them declared loudly that they did not want to go to school. These children usually spend from September to May away from their family camps, during which time they become fluent in Russian, reading and writing. They also experience new disciplinary practices, mandatory visits to the village sauna (*banya*), and the occasional fight with village children—the source of traumatic memories for many. Some parents take their children out early after realizing that the tenthold did not have enough workforce, even if some children, and especially girls, themselves would have liked to continue with school (see chap. 2). Those tundra children who develop a deep antipathy toward the school quit after their first year. Boys are often less keen to study, partly because there are rumors that studying for a longer period might make them eligible for army conscription.

Andrei once said to me, "Army, prison, and school are all the same. They can all corrupt people." What he argued was that these institutions had the power to transform Nenets, including his own children, into the *lutsaq.* Another time his brother Yegor explained why too much education was not good: "You see, all these Kara collective farmers in the second and seventh brigades. They have lots of children but none of their sons live in the tundra. One of them tried living in the tundra but did not like it. He went on learning. Education and army turn them into half Russians." Yet Yegor and Andrei both admitted that some education, especially the ability to read, was indispensable, as it helped not only to orientate people in the Russian world but also to bring them closer to their salvation.

Illiterate parents had some initiation into reading and writing through a special program that emulated the liquidation of illiteracy campaign (*likbez*) of the early Soviet period (Khanzerova 2004). Every summer for a month or two from 1997 until 2007, four Nenets teachers from Naryan-Mar taught adults and children in the tundra. This so-called Summer Nomadic School (*letnyaya kochevaya shkola*) was initiated by Norwegian anthropologist Ivar Bjørklund, the first foreigner to pay visits to the Independents (Bjørklund 1995, 2000; Zhuravleva 2000). Financed by the Norwegian state and organized by the regional administration, representatives of the Nenets intelligentsia saw their role as teachers of the outside world to the Yamb-To Independents. Tellingly, one of the subjects was the "surrounding world," which taught the technological advances of the modern world and the basic mechanisms of the market economy. Those who were thinking about becoming Baptists made a particular effort to learn literacy. Some others who were less motivated avoided it, claiming to have no time for "non-serious" things.

Baptist missionary Pavel contended that the state education program for the Nenets was part of the divine plan. He said, "I think the presence of these teachers comes from God's thought . . . to enable these people . . . our people to believe in God's Word and read." Yet he was disturbed by the teachers' "propaganda" against the faith (see chap. 3). To balance the harmful impact of the state school and the hostile Nenets teachers of the summer school, in 2001, Pavel organized a private boarding school in Vorkuta, located near the prayer house, for the children of converts. Running costs came from Nenets families selling reindeer meat in the market. In the first year, twelve children attended the school; the second year the number increased to twenty. Yet this project was abandoned after two years because of too much hassle with "material" and bureaucratic problems. Rather, sisters in faith from Ukraine, Belarus, Saint Petersburg, and elsewhere began to visit converts in the tundra to teach reading, singing, and the gospel. As with the state teachers, church teachers moved from one family to another, staying with each for a couple of weeks. Unlike with the Nenets summer school teachers, the curriculum was in Russian and Bible based.

Compared to the Yamb-To people, the Independents from the Polar Urals had a rather different experience with the authorities, who mainly saw in them trouble. The Ural Independents have always visited Vorkuta and adjacent settlements in the Komi Republic. Unlike among the Yamb-To, a significant proportion of the Ural families had very few reindeer, or none at all, and thus lived in destitute conditions.[28] Partly because of that, they started to send their children to school to get them properly fed. A makeshift boarding school in a kindergarten in Sovetskiy village (near Vorkuta) was open in 1996, where children from the age of three to fourteen were admitted.[29] This was a profoundly traumatic experience for the children as they were unable to communicate with Russian teachers who were totally unprepared for the task (Drama 2000; Murashko 2013). As one visiting pedagogue described it, children in the classroom "were just sitting on their chairs and were silent. . . . On their faces, there were no emotions. Total closure [*polnaya zakrytost'*]" (Aromshtam 2002). Echoing similar descriptions from the 1930s, the teachers tried hard to teach children to wear manufactured clothes, sit at the table while eating, sleep in bed, and use towels and toilet paper. Uninterested in colorful cubes or toy cars, children discovered plasticine from which they masterfully crafted detailed reindeer for hours on end. Seeing the high quality of the craftsmanship, Russian teachers were surprised that "nobody had taught it to them" (Aromshtam 2002; cf. Ravna 2021). Children's "education of attention" (Ingold 2000) was exceptional while they struggled with formalized teaching, the Russian language, and the abstract world of plastic toys.

The village of Sovetskiy was a new place for the Ural Independents. Until the early 1990s, the Ural Nenets had visited Khalmer-Yu (*khal'myer*, "dead" in Nenets, *yu*, "valley" in Komi) village, which served as their main base for trading (as for the Yamb-To) in the winter period. In 1995, it was closed down as unprofitable (*neperspektivnyy*, "lacking in prospects"). The three hundred or so Nenets who relied on the place for trade started to frequent Sovetskiy. Reluctantly, the officials in Sovetskiy began to deal with the visiting herders, only then realizing that there were dozens of families that had no documents, were unable to speak Russian, and were totally "uncivilized." The village administration started their documentation. The new status gave the Independents access to the pensions and benefits for families with many children, who profited considerably from welfare payments.

When I visited the Sovetskiy Village Council in 2007 with local reindeer herders, a Russian woman, a middle-aged social worker responsible for

Figure 1.7. Nenets boarding school in Vorgashor, September 2017.

"the problem of the unregistered Nenets," argued that these Independents spent all their allowances on vodka and lost their passports, saying, "This is why we keep their passports here." The Nenets sitting next to me were not protesting against the arrangement, as long as they were given their allowances. Furthermore, the official was troubled by a few people who were unwilling to address the local council and register themselves. She also told of an unregistered Nenets who by rumor lived somewhere in the mountains and who had never visited the village. It was as if a sense of incompleteness disturbed her.[30]

Many scholars have rightly argued that from the viewpoint of administrators and missionaries, nomadic reindeer herders in the Russian Arctic have been the most difficult to subdue (Krupnik 1993, 86; Znamenski 1999). Yet their relationship with the state has always been more complex than just confrontation or submission. On the one hand, the Independents have feared becoming *lutsa*, losing the specific kind of humanity they gain from living with reindeer. On the other hand, they have always tried to benefit from engaging with the Russian world. This has been largely driven by the potential material gain and a sense of overcoming their marginality.

Figure 1.8. Ural Nenets paying a visit to the Sovetskiy village, May 2012.
Parents have come to collect their children from school and buy necessities.

Perceived marginalization is a common cause for conversion. Some have argued that the Roman conquest instilled a sense of marginality among the population of the eastern Mediterranean, which became a catalyst for the emergence of Christianity (Hefner 1993b, 31; Kee 1980). Probably the best ethnographic example of this phenomenon today has been given by Robbins, who describes conversion of the Urapmin in Papua New Guinea (2004). Having had less contact with Westerners than some other neighboring groups and having lost their earlier high status in the local ritual hierarchy, the Urapmin came to sense themselves as lagging. As a result, they eagerly embraced Christianity (of a Pentecostal kind), which took place in a sudden "revival" in 1977. This happened after a few individuals had received Baptist Christian educations elsewhere and brought new teachings and skills into the community. The community itself had never been targeted by any outside missions. Drawing on Marshall Sahlins (1992, 24), Robbins (2004, 9) argues that Christianity became the "means of cultural debasement" (Sahlins's phrase), as it convinces "people in meaningful terms to regard their own traditions as unacceptable" (cf. Tuzin 1997). Robbins (2004, 85) goes further, saying that the Urapmin had a fertile cultural ground to understand themselves as "humiliated" and "sinful" because of their heightened sense of marginalization. He claims that neither missionary pressure nor socioeconomic change triggered the embracing of Christianity but that Urapmin culture did from its "internal" sources, "motivated by their own culturally given goals" (ibid.).

Among the Nenets, conversion to Christianity had certainly offered a sense of cultural debasement, as they—especially the youth—started to see their own way of life, at least partly, as unacceptable. However, unlike with the Urapmin, for the Nenets the long, complicated history of avoidance and engagement with the *lutsaq* and the dynamics of the missionary encounter with its inherent relations of power have defined the outcome somewhat differently. One can say that the encounter with missionaries is just the latest among many similar earlier encounters with outsiders that have significant similarities with one another. Perhaps for their earlier experience the older generation is not willing to give up too much, while the younger generation would be ready to leave tundra life altogether. However, the image of the dangerous *lutsaq* still haunts many, and this is what I shall look at in the next chapter.

PART II

CONVERSION OF PEOPLE, DISENFRANCHISEMENT OF SPIRITS

2

TRAJECTORIES OF CONVERSION

Prologue: A Service in a Nenets *Mya*

On a cold Sunday toward the end of 2006, in the dull half-light of a late morning during the months of polar night, a few families arrived on their reindeer sledges to attend a service in the camp of Andrei, the Nenets presbyter of the Baptist church. Among those who arrived from nearby camps—at a distance of a few dozen kilometers—was Andrei's brother Yegor, with whom I had recently completed the autumn migration. By December, all the Yamb-To Nenets had made their way from the coast of the Kara Sea to the winter pastures after two months of isolated travel southward, being once again capable of trips to one another's *myaq* and to the city to sell and buy. This was also the time when the missionaries paid occasional visits to the camps. Most of the church life still took place in the tundra, as people found their way to the city prayer house not more than a couple of times a year. Missionaries did not like this infrequency. I heard Pavel, the presbyter of the Baptist church in the city, reproaching herders now and again, saying that "the brethren from the tundra" came to Vorkuta without attending services in his prayer house. As usual, the Nenets were silent when admonished. However, since Andrei had been ordained a presbyter, some said that they no longer needed to visit the city church that often. Although they did not cast doubt on the need for utmost commitment to the teachings introduced by Pavel and other missionaries, this was one of the signs that the Nenets converts were trying to carve out their own cultural space and style of being *punryodaq*, "believers."

In most ways, in the morning before the Sunday service, except for a prayer before and after eating, nothing would betray that these herders were different from non-Christian herders. Neither their outfits nor the way they spoke marked the distinctiveness of the day of repose or the Christianity of their "inner lives." Indeed, until recently, Sunday (*khekhe yalya*, "sacred day") visits were accompanied by vodka, tobacco, and cards, these now being taboo. In addition, Nenets songs, wrestling, reindeer races, and drinking of raw blood after butchering a reindeer for guests were no longer part of social life. While some of these activities, such as wrestling, were claimed to be just vanity and a potential source of unhealthy rivalry, drinking blood was said to conflict with God's Word, which banned it outright. Singing personal or epic songs had been outlawed because of the perceived danger that this would pull a person back into the old way of being, and so was somewhere between vanity and "paganism" (*yazychestvo*) (see chap. 5).

After eating, some casual chat, and occasional laughter, Andrei declared that it was time to start with the service. Sitting on reindeer hides, congregants became somewhat more serious, and everybody's gaze turned to the pastor who was about to lead the service from where he was, sitting near the pure part of the *mya* under the kerosene lamp (*si*, i.e., the part where foodstuff is stored, and, before conversion, sacred items). Rather than the spatial structure of the confrontational pulpit and pews—segregated by gender—in the prayer house, people stayed where they usually were (by a loose principle, the most honorable male guests are closer to the *si*). Andrei gave an introductory prayer, with a deep and measured voice, in which he called for the Holy Spirit to come among them. Then, he took out his Russian Bible from the leather case and read slowly but firmly a preselected passage from Matthew, translating it sentence by sentence into Nenets and further explaining the message with his own words in the vernacular. After finishing the passage, he continued with a short sermon using examples from everyday life and thus shifting listeners' imagination between the doings of Jesus and of the "we" here and now. The written word unfolded into a spoken word of instruction, transferring some of the authority hidden in the text to the one who voiced it. People were listening, fiddling, and looking at one another. From time to time, the hostess of the *mya*, Lyuba, added long willow branches to the metal stove. The fire was crackling, and a stew was boiling.

Just as the spatiotemporal configurations were not fixed, so the language of Andrei oscillated between the two idioms. Although he mainly spoke Nenets, some Russian words had found their way into Nenets, like "be alert" (*bodrstvuyte*). Some Nenets words were also struggling to free themselves from their history—for instance, the word for "Satan," *ngylyeka*, "an underworld spirit" that carried a whole gamut of experiences from the "pagan" past, especially for the older generation who had engaged with local and ancestral spirits during their lifetime. As always, Andrei harangued—although considerably more mildly than the Russian missionaries—the congregants about the need to try harder to study the Bible, follow what it prescribed, and pray to God more often. As he said, without these actions, there was no hope of God's protection here on earth or thereafter. His language was based on "a grammar of desire and fear" (Kulick and Schieffelin 2004, 363; cf. Luhrmann 2018, 314–15), reminding listeners how their fates were tightly related to rewards and punishment.

In his sermon, Andrei also quoted Bible passages by heart, a skill that only a few Nenets commanded. His greater ability subtly hinted at his greater holiness and authority at that moment in an otherwise egalitarian community of brethren and sisters. As Yegor's wife, Lida, told me after, "We all pray for him, and so God must have given him more than others." Lida referred to a fundamental point that has its source in Christian understanding that ordained presbyters like Andrei acted as a composite agent entailing both human and divine components. Whereas "ordinary" believers were also composites, the overall sense was that the Holy Spirit was acting more powerfully in Andrei, Pavel, and other pastors whose greater skills were a sign of God's greater investment in them.

Closing the Bible, Andrei called for prayers in Russian: "Let us pray" (*davayte pomolimsya*). This had become an evocative phrase that the missionaries repeated again and again. After a short silence, Andrei's sister's husband, Yevgeni, was the first to start. Fluent in Nenets, Komi, and Russian, as are many youngsters, he began the first sentence of his prayer in Russian but finished it in Nenets: "Great God, glory and gratitude is yours!" (*Velikiy Bog, slava i blagodarnost' pydar nyand!*). Others kneeling nearby were attentively listening; a few were moving their lips in silence accompanying Yevgeni's prayer, which was interspersed with his sighs suggesting that the words were coming from the heart and were deeply felt. Then Yevgeni's wife, Ksenya, performed her prayer, which was barely audible, like the ones from other female converts. The prayers contained, as usual, a thanksgiving for how things are, no matter whether good or bad, followed by an admission of one's sinfulness, a request for forgiveness and purification, petitions of a general or particular order (the well-being of one's family and reindeer, a safe journey, etc.), all these elements bracketed with phrases praising God and with repeating of "Not my will but thine be done." The short prayer session, in which nearly all present made their petitions in Nenets, was finalized by Andrei, who prayed louder and more fluently than the others who were unable to speak with similar authority.

Without leaving too long a pause, Andrei said the number "seventy-four," which marked a song called "Oh, I Am a Poor Sinner! Truly I Am One" (*O! Ya Greshnik Bednyy! Pravda, Ya Takov*) from the Baptist hymnal in Russian (*Pesn'* 2004). This melancholy hymn speaking of Christ's gift to sinful humans had become one of the favorites among the church members (alongside a hymn on Vorkuta; see chap. 3). All who were able to read, even if not that well, opened the hymnal. Others who were illiterate sang along with the parts they had memorized. Now and again, the tune slowed, as if on an old record player. Following the principle of the priesthood of all believers—or more precisely, "the priesthood of all male believers," as women were not allowed to sermonize—in the next round, Yevgeni did the reading. The cycle of reading and singing intermingled with prayers was repeated twice more.

As in the city church, individual believers were encouraged to sing or read a poem they knew by heart in front of the congregation. Yegor, who struggled with reading and whose ability to sing Russian songs (*yanggerts'*) was modest (in contrast with his masterful performances of epic songs, see chap. 5), moved with his literate daughter Alla to the door area, which offered a square meter for a stage. Alla started singing, her father following her with evident lack of self-confidence, yet performing until the end. As Andrei commented afterward, God must have been very pleased to see Yegor taking the stage despite his inability to stay in tune. His comment characterizes the overall expectation and pressure among the Baptists: one must do more than one thinks is possible as the Holy Spirit helps out. The service ended with men and women shaking hands and with brotherly or sisterly kisses on the lips among people of the same gender. The Baptists stressed that kissing reinforces brotherhood and peace, taking a lead from Romans 16:16 ("Salute one another with an holy kiss. The churches of Christ salute you"). After the service, Lyuba served tea, meat, and fish. Then, in the complete darkness of afternoon polar night, the guests left toward their camps.

Modernity and the Urge for Change

Non-Christian Nenets say that the Baptist services with prayers, singing in Russian, and kisses look strange. Yet converts argue that the new behavior, with this kind of touch, is vital to enjoy God's protection and future salvation. In this chapter, I shall ask how the scene described above has come to be an intrinsic part of many families' lives across the camps of the Nenets tundra. In other words, what has motivated more than half of the Independents to become converts and to change radically their personal and social lives? What kind of self-transformation has become imaginable for the reindeer herders, and how is it related to becoming "modern"? My ethnographic focus will stay with the Veli family.

In the last chapter, we saw how contact with the Russian world—education, state offices, the market economy—have led to substantial changes in the lives of the Independents. The state started to model the *yedinolichniki* through the process of passportization (i.e., granting citizenship), clan-community forming, and schooling. The missionaries joined the scene a few years later (in 1994, see Bjørklund 1995) than the state officials, yet they were to have a considerably more profound impact. Even if they strove from different rhetoric and ideologies, the two conversions—conversion to modernity and conversion to Christianity—gradually converged.

I would argue that the appeal of modernity and the message of Christianity have become inseparable in the conversion of Independents. What many ethnographic accounts reveal is that what is called "modernity" (often pluralized as "modernities") is rather diffuse, variable, and does not presume the same forces or outcomes everywhere (Asad 2003, 12–16; see also van der Veer 1996). Modernity is a confusing concept being a source of numerous heated debates, including on the danger of smuggling a metanarrative of modernity into anthropological analyses (Englund and Leach 2000). While modernity remains hard to pin down, it is undeniable that in colonial contexts, some versions of modernity and Christianity have often arrived together.

Following Talal Asad (1996) and Keane (2007), I would suggest that modernity becomes a site of imagination, and this becoming is by itself part of a significant transformation. Keane has described modernity as a metanarrative of a moral character that has developed hand in hand with Protestant ideas and Enlightenment, "a story of human liberation from a host of false beliefs and fetishisms that undermine freedom" (5). Emancipation and self-mastery lie at the heart of this narrative, which usually includes "rupture from a traditional past, and progress into a better future" (48). Becoming preoccupied with oneself as my "self" that needs remolding shifts perspective to a more global plane in which conceiving of an identity of a new kind is a common way of thinking (Cannell 2006). But as Keane (2007, 42) stresses, "it is not merely a matter of imagination" but also a matter of material medium as new kinds of idea, value, skill, disposition, and relationship emerge through engagement with mass media, formal education, literacy, medicine, global market, various technologies, and means of transport.

But how then can modernity and religion—usually depicted as direct opposites to each other—be seen interacting in conversion? Asad (1996) argues that there is a certain convergence between becoming modern and becoming a religious convert, as they are both shaped by a new defining logic: "Religious conversion is usually thought of as 'irrational,' because it happens to people rather than being something that they choose to become after careful thought. And yet most individuals enter modernity rather as converts enter a new religion—as a consequence of forces beyond their control. Modernity, like the convert's religion, *defines* new choices; it is rarely the result of an entirely 'free choice.' And like the convert's religion, it annihilates old possibilities and puts others in their place" (263, his italics).

The Christians I know would agree with Asad in this respect that this is not purely one's "free choice": it is God who defines one's choices. Yet they would also say that one needs to wish to be chosen as a child of God in the first place (even if this wish is put in the heart by God, see chap. 7). So, the determinism of modernity like religion is a matter of definition as there is always a component of self-reflection involved (Laidlaw 2014); these can be described rather as "affordances" that can be picked up but do not necessarily determine the outcome (Keane 2016). Obviously, there are many ways in which a new religion is entered, and in some cases, it may take place without the defining power of the teachings of the new religion. What is important to stress, however, is that when one engages with it more deeply, it starts to define one's choices more forcefully. This is why we should not assess the initial decisions to be the *same* as the ethical deliberations taking place in renewed circumstances of further learning. Old possibilities are annihilated, as Asad says.

Evangelical logic requires a rupture (in practices, ideals, and rhetoric) from the old life and the fraudulent traditions now doomed to belong to "the past" (Robbins 2007a, 2020; cf. Freeman 2017; Holbraad et al. 2019). As this move takes away one kind of possibility from people, it offers them other kinds for constituting themselves as new persons or groups through connection and disconnection, both imaginary and real. Fundamentally, this is a shift in ethics, as one must ask what it means to be a good person or a good community (Laidlaw 2014; Lambek 2015a; Zigon 2010). Furthermore, this introduces new understandings of society and temporality, as hopeful new Christians understand that they become connected to wider worlds and a better future (Englund 2003; Robbins 2004; 2009, 234; Wanner 2007, 207, 253). It happens as if people had suddenly become claustrophobic in their own world, although this sense is not the same for everyone. I suggest that differences in the case of Nenets converts are generational, as is often the case in revolutionary projects in which youth find themselves more at stake personally than older people. While parents are worried, their children feel liberated as they give up old ways (cf. Vitebsky 2012, 186; 2017a).

For many converts, there is certain ambivalence in their attitudes toward modernity. On the one hand, as with the Ewe Christians in Ghana who demonize modernity and yet are attracted to it (Meyer 1999), Nenets are trying to find their way through both the maze of Christian prescriptions and the appeal of secular modernity that has a shadow of dangerous Russian, *lutsa*, in it. On the other hand, they have joined a church that regards itself as thoroughly "antimodern," an aspect they must adapt to in their modernist desires (see chap. 3).[1] Being antimodern is especially relevant when it comes to distancing oneself not only from "modern people" (*sovremennye lyudi*) or "people from this world" (*lyudi etogo mira*) but also from mainstream Protestant churches (which is less a concern for Nenets).

To return to Asad (1996, 265) once again, one could argue with him that "the changed epistemic structure" brought about by conversion has given Nenets "new possibilities for constituting themselves," or in other words, self-formation becomes available through the "politics of consciousness." Without doubt, for Independents this is a radically new experience in which new ideas play a significant role. Nenets converts claim they have the truth, which they did not have before, and which the nonconverts still do not have. Andrei once explained to me that he truly comprehended what it meant to be a Christian only when he understood what happened to Jesus, that he gave his own blood for the sake of saving sinful humanity. He presented this as an event in which he realized that he and Jesus were intimately linked through the most important event in human history, the resurrection of Christ.

Conversion is thus aligning personal and cosmic events. Here, I would like to briefly touch upon Caroline Humphrey's (2008) discussion—inspired from Alain Badiou—on subject and event (see also Bialecki 2009; Engelke 2010; Laidlaw et al. 2018; Robbins 2010). Humphrey suggests that the subject potentially emerges in this situation when enmeshed in the new logic through a disruptive event. According to Badiou (2001), the event is an extraordinary happening that changes the whole sense of oneself by abolishing previous knowledge and by offering a radically new truth. He presents a discussion of how subjects emerge in an event and the truth of the event by examining Saul's (Paul's) conversion on the road to Damascus (Badiou 2003). There are two aspects in this Badouian formal scheme I wish to stress, as I see these as having some benefit in thinking about religious conversion. First, the event is not an event for everyone but only for those who decide to declare it, pledge themselves to the event, and thus emerge as subjects(-in-becoming) in their fidelity to the declared event. Second, the event—despite being subjectively acclaimed—is universally addressed to everybody, as in Paul's call to repentance for Jews and non-Jews alike.

I would describe the conversion of Nenets (at least some of them) as what Humphrey (2008, 364) calls a "decision-event" in which "a new truth" is acclaimed or "a new position by leaping across what is not known" is chosen or discovered in a new setting. Humphrey rejects Badiou's theory of ordinary people as incapable of understanding the situation they live in (in Badiou's version they resemble animals) and argues that many are capable of acclaiming the event. She writes that we "need some further ideas to explain how people ordinarily attain individuality, how they track through, gather together, or sort out the multiplicities of their being, and how indeed someone is (or becomes) the kind of person capable of acclaiming the event when others around them do not. It is necessary, therefore, to have a theory of actors who are not subjects in Badiou's sense, but have the potential to become so" (363).

I would suggest that some Baptist converts among the Nenets had this kind of potential of becoming a subject, seeing themselves in a new light and declaring their fidelity to the event in the new language. According to Badiou, as an archetypal convert, Paul was unprecedented in history, since his claims were universalizing by their nature. The resurrection of Christ was the most important truth-event ("the Christ-event," Badiou 2003, 73) in Paul's eyes. Remaining faithful to this truth-event was at the center. Furthermore, the event must be declared, narrativized, and explained to oneself as to others. So, the emergence of the subject is inseparable from becoming a new kind of linguistic agent who has made a long journey from a different language world (see chaps. 6 and 7).

In the following section, I shall describe Ivan's conversion, which entails elements from both a Pauline and a shamanic self-transformation. My sense is that Ivan's shamanic quest partly paved the way to him becoming a Christian, as both can be seen as particular—although qualitatively rather different—kinds of self-fashioning. I shall then move on to the main "utilitarian" motivation, shared by nearly all converts in the tundra, which is the frequently expressed wish to abandon drinking alcohol and improve one's (family's) economic situation. I would propose that abstaining creates a path for an enhanced self-control, an exercise that modernity and Christianity both exploit to a significant extent (Weber 2001). In the second part of the chapter, I shall move to the unintended consequences of conversion, as families are threatened with a split along generational lines (something that many went through elsewhere during the Soviet period, as discussed in chap. 1). On the one hand, non-Christian parents have been distanced from their Christian children, while on the other hand middle-aged converts face their children's desire to leave the tundra, causing their parents great anxiety.

Ivan: From Prospective Shaman to Evangelical Entrepreneur

Sociologically speaking, I agree with Mathijs Pelkmans (2009a, 2) when he argued that "dislocations wrought by postsocialist change and the advance of free-market capitalism" have set the scene for conversions in Russia, through "the messages of hope and the sense of community offered by new religious movements." However, in the case of Nenets Independents, postsocialist dislocations alone can hardly explain the recent wave of conversion. The Independents did not enjoy services from the state and did not see in church-based infrastructure and humanitarian aid a substitute for state sources (even if some aid was received). There are other dynamics at play that are not only sociological but also ideational, affective, and rhetorical.

Christian conversions in small-scale communities often take place through one or two key local persons who trigger conversions of larger communities (Engelke 2007; Vitebsky 2017a). Without doubt, in the case of Nenets Independents, Ivan has become a nodal point in a network of new emergent connections, not only with state officials and business people but also with missionaries. As with many kinds of cultural change, this was one that was elicited from outside and inside simultaneously through a person being on the border of the two worlds. Acting as both an assistant for the missionaries and an independent lay preacher (later ordained as an evangelist, *blagovestnik*) himself, Ivan inspired a series of conversions. Without his assistance with navigation, translation, and social relations, the Russian missionaries would have found it much harder if not impossible to convert a substantial part of the Yamb-To and the Ural Nenets to Christianity.

Importantly, Ivan's quest to become different, and the missionaries' quest to make others different, converged. Ivan became especially suitable for an evangelistic project (see chap. 3). When he went to the Baptist prayer house, presbyter Pavel saw in him a God-given challenge that could not be ignored. He was not, however, the first Nenets to step over the threshold of the Vorkuta prayer house in the quarter of old wooden houses on the outskirts of the city. For instance, his brother Tyepan, who had settled in Vorkuta, had visited it a couple of times, but he did not like it there. Yet Ivan was different from his brother and the other Nenets who had come to the prayer house a few times, sitting there silently and never reappearing again. He was more curious and less taciturn than others, being skillful in talk, including the everyday Russian that he acquired at school and while doing business. Most importantly, he was willing to take missionaries to the tundra when Pavel declared that God wanted him to do that. This let him act as a mediator between the herders and *lutsaq*, something at which he felt himself to be expert. He introduced untypically "friendly" Russians (such non-Nenets acquaintances are called *yuryo*) to Nenets in the tundra and offered knowledge about reindeer herders' families and their movement patterns on the land to the missionaries.

When I met Ivan for the first time in late 2000, he surprised me with his ambition, assertiveness, and eagerness for reform. As we saw in the last chapter, this was reflected in his entrepreneurial endeavors. He hoped to harness external knowledge and power to become a part of the "modern" world. He ceaselessly dreamed of engineering nearly every aspect of tundra life. In our conversations, Ivan often spoke of his latest ideas of technological innovations, such as bringing a washing machine to the tundra tentholds or developing floating sledges to cross dangerous rivers during spring and autumn migrations, though none of his plans was realized over the years. Rather, he spent much of his energy and reindeer buying the consumer goods that the recently emerged market economy had to offer. Most significantly, he became the first Independent herder to own a snowmobile and an electric generator in the mid-1990s introducing fast travel and cold urban light into the tundra. Snowmobiles particularly gathered enormous popularity among herders. Russian missionaries readily gave advice on which snowmobiles to buy and how to repair them when they failed, as

Figure 2.1. Snowmobiles increasingly replace reindeer for long-distance winter travel, March 2004.

they often did.[2] Yet Pavel repeatedly warned them not to make idols for themselves out of these things (see chap. 4).

Like many other youngsters in the community, Ivan sensed that his parents' life in the tundra was far too different from the Russian world. More exciting things and ideas seemed to go past, leaving out the reindeer herders. Ivan often complained that his parents were illiterate and had a poor understanding of the "Russians and their things." However, the sense of embarrassment was turned into empowerment. He once told me of an incident around the table when his grandfather Mikul told a Russian man that one had to behave *kruto* ("cool"). Ivan explained that he meant *kul'turno* ("in a civilized manner"), adding that meanings of both words remained vague for his grandfather. When he told this story, other converts laughed at the matter. This laughter echoed both embarrassment for the grandfather and pride in being *different*. Unlike their parents, the younger generation sensed they had become knowledgeable in the new vocabulary and had acquired new skills in their suddenly enlarged world.

Ivan had become a kind of a supernomad moving beyond the Nenets areas, once even flying to the United States with Pavel to visit Russian diaspora congregations. He made occasional trips to Naryan-Mar to discuss matters of clan-community-in-formation with regional officials, who urged him to travel from one camp to another and explain the benefits of setting up a clan-community of reindeer herders. These events became ideal opportunities for Christian proselytization. During these meetings, he made introductions and conclusions with references to the Bible and evidence of God's will. In a scene in a TV documentary Ivan gives a speech at such a meeting: "Today God has gathered us here so we can live. So I think. This gathering takes place for us to go forward and not to look back. Also, we need not to quarrel with each other. It is written in the Holy Book: 'I sent God's son.' We have to live according to this book. So we can go forward. Then God will give us goods. And these children will start to live. We need to look at our own lives. When there is an old dispute, then forget it" (Barayev 1997).

"Living" has not only a spiritual but also a material and social aspect to it, as in a cargo cult. Acquiring goods was important for Ivan and many others. Ivan earned his living as a middleman. He bought products like reindeer meat, antlers, or fish and sold goods like spare parts for snowmobiles. Although many were happy with his role, others were increasingly uncomfortable that Ivan made a profit out of his brothers in faith.

However, Ivan's desire was to be a mediator in a positive way. He presented himself as a seeker, stretching his aspirations back into his early childhood when he wanted to become a shaman. He once told me, "Since my childhood I have wished to learn, to achieve something and to become a spiritual person, a healer or a shaman." To put this into a correct perspective, he promptly added that his shamanic endeavor was just something that was never to be realized because God had already fixed his eye on him. Thus, the rupture had a prelude, as it is often the case with a conversion. He continued, "In my childhood—after the age of six—I was afraid of something, and I started to pray inwardly. Nobody taught me, but I already had the fear of God. . . . I thought about going to town to get the Bible, the book I had heard about from my grandfather."

Nevertheless, this did not happen. Instead of becoming a shaman or a healer, he became an active Christian when he was twenty-six years old.

It was evident that he was one of those who had his own aspirations long before missionaries came. Based on that, I would suggest that the image of shamanic transformation had a significant role to play in his conversion, maybe more than meets the eye at first. The discursive space he used to live in before conversion acknowledged the potential for a radical transformation of a person. But an *event* was to be awaited to turn him into a committed believer, the event that realizes itself through a narrative and a gaze from elsewhere (divine, missionary) and from elsewhen (in retrospect and through imagining a better future).

Ivan's conversion narrative is dramatic. Starting with his drunken arrival in a bus station in Vorkuta, he is literally stripped down to awaken to a new reality (like in a shamanic initiation, see below), as he tells it in the same documentary that was shot a couple of years after the experience: "I felt a great fear. I had never experienced such a fear. In a bus station I saw a woman whose face appeared to me like that of the devil. I called out to God and said, 'Lord, you see me; save me!' After that I took off my clothes and started to freeze. The temperature was minus thirty degrees. I undressed completely. The police and an ambulance were called. I was taken by them. I found myself in the psychiatric hospital. Then, I thought, I must follow the way of the truth" (Barayev 1997).

The situation required an interpretation in order to become a decision-event (Humphrey 2008). This took place when he went ("God sent me") to the prayer house, met Baptist presbyter Pavel, and repented. Only then he could understand the agencies at play: how he was acting and how he was acted upon at the same time, caught between divine and demonic forces.

For Pavel, meeting Ivan was also a life-changing moment. Years later, on visits to other churches, he told Ivan's conversion story from his own perspective. As he put it, before meeting Ivan, he sometimes found himself thinking that God had forgotten the reindeer herders who lay drunk in the snow on the streets of Vorkuta. Ivan's arrival at the prayer house changed the way he saw the reindeer herders. Pavel once narrated this at a gathering:

> One day a man in a dark blue jean outfit arrived at the prayer house; he had his hair below his shoulders and his face was darkened from the wind. This was a Nenets called Ivan. He came to sit in the back row once. Then he came for a second time. And the third time he prayed and repented. I got acquainted with him. He came to the prayer house because he had gone through a deep trauma. A few weeks before, he had come to the city on his reindeer for a reindeer race. These were his best reindeer. . . . Soon after he arrived, all his reindeer were stolen; only the harnessing belts and his sledge remained. He got drunk

and fell into a state of delirium tremens [*belaya goryachka*]; in other words, he started to hallucinate. He was taken to the psychiatric hospital. When he became sober again, he ran away from there. Somebody showed a way to our prayer house.

Pavel argued that the hallucinations were the work of the devil. Ivan agreed. He learned that God loved him and wanted him to reject his past life. Only when the new language became available was he made aware through this language that he was going through a crisis of a specific kind (cf. Harding 2000, 38). Now Ivan had a truth. From his newly gained perspective and language, this frightening monster could qualify only as Satan and not a shaman's spirit helper (*tadyebtso*).[3] As he explained, the enemy lured him to drink to the point of delirium and then appeared to him. He was convinced that he had to suffer the attack by the devil to become aware of his sinfulness and of the need to ask Jesus's forgiveness. In his words, this dramatic moment in his life was not a coincidence but God's plan to save him from his "past life," as he called it, which consisted of drinking, playing cards, cheating, and stealing others' reindeer. Speaking of his sinful life and the radical change were constitutive for sustaining a sense of being a true Christian who had left the past behind.

In another version of Ivan's conversion story written by Pavel (in 2002, for circulation in the church), he paints a detailed picture of Ivan's hallucination at the bus stop—a more detailed account than I ever heard from Ivan himself: "Suddenly this woman began to turn into a monster, ready to devour the young reindeer herder. Around him dark beings with horns and tails appeared, and all this filth [*nechist'*] took him hostage [*brala ego v kol'tso*]." Pavel then quotes Ivan's thought during his nightmare in the hospital: "Satan wanted to destroy me. He was about to do it."

After meeting Ivan, the first task for Pavel was to cleanse the lost person. Not only his soul but also his body needed purification from "the filth." Pavel continued his talk in the same gathering: "Ivan was invited into a Christian family, where he later acquired kin, friends, and blood [*obrel i rodnykh, i druzey, i krov'*]. His clothes with worn appearance were washed; his long hair cut; his head, covered with lice, was carefully worked on with a special shampoo and combed. A person from the tundra learned to believe in the Bible and learned urban life—how to use the toilet, bath, and other things." This "Christian family" in the quote was Pavel's own family. (The anonymity marks his instrumentality as a tool of God.) Initially the pastor's wife forbade him to take Ivan into their home because he was full of lice, but then she relented, as Ivan agreed to have his long hair washed and cut. Pavel taught Ivan that apostle Paul instructed the Corinthians that it was shameful for men to have long hair.[4] He argued that this was obeying God's will: it was the Law that had to be followed on the outside to enable a person to become different in his interiority.

Significantly, Pavel described Ivan not only as an uncivilized person but also as somebody who lacked family, saying that the church was to become his true family. Like Soviet and post-Soviet officials, Pavel was putting a stress both on cleanliness and on the new "family" replacing actual kin ties. In the 1930s and later, Nenets children were washed and their hair cut against their will when they were taken to school (Kharyuchi 2001, 151; King 2011; Leete 2014, 212–15; Liarskaya 2003; Yadne 1995, 23). In the 1990s, the state was doing that again with the children of the Ural Independents at the Sovetskiy boarding school, quarantining all the tundra children for a couple of months before any teaching started. This was like a new kind of initiation rite. In addition, in the state ideology, boarding schools (like reindeer brigades or other similar collectives, *kollektivy*) were thought to be a worthy substitute for one's family (Khlinovskaya Rockhill 2010; Rethmann 2001, 30). Now the church was doing something similar. Independents were supposed to become a family, cleansed and civilized, in a way that many collective farmers had experienced before, but that was rather different from Independents' earlier experience (cf. Vagramenko 2014, 2017a).

Ivan's long hair had been part of his spiritual aspirations. For Nenets, human hair contains a person's shadow soul (*sidyangg*), and a shaman's long hair is a site of extra power (Kharyuchi 2001, 151; Lapsui et al. 2023, 29; Lar et al. 2003, 83; Yadne 2006, 168). I witnessed how people used to take great care not to leave their cut hair behind in a campsite when moving to the next. The fear was that malevolent spirits in the form of small birds (*venzyoy leqmorq*) would take this hair and make the owner fall ill. As one non-Christian herder explained to me, you would "lose your shadow soul" (*sidyangg syalmde*) and then with that you would lose the ability to do any work. He told me of a man to whom this had happened recently. To avoid misfortune, some even gathered their hair and nails throughout their lives. For instance, before his death in 1999, Ivan's "pagan" father asked his children to place his nails and hair in his coffin to retain his soul force in one place. However, this never happened because he was buried by his children who had already distanced themselves from what they called, in Russian, "ritual" (*ritual*) and "superstition" (*suyeverie*). In a way, cutting off his hair was no less a profound change for Ivan than learning to use the bath and the Bible. Instead of becoming a composite of shamanic spirits gained from outside, he was equipped with a different kind of power—the unambiguously good Holy Spirit.

Even if this was ideologically downplayed by missionaries, this transformation was thus not only spiritual but also bodily (cf. Vilaça 2016). In Ivan's change, aspects like bodily suffering, social role, and source of agency paralleled the ideas that can be loosely related to a shamanic experience. In both shamanic and evangelical initiations, there is a complex interplay of submission in which an exterior agent plays a significant role. Both Saul/ Paul and Ivan are deeply frightened during their conversion experience. Saul encountered the resurrected Christ, was blinded by him, and heard his voice asking why he was persecuting the Lord. Once he gets his sight, Saul discovers that he is Christian and that his name is Paul. His identity and volition were changed from outside.

Anxiety and fear are a common state when becoming a shaman. Ivan's own experience at the bus stop would have qualified for an encounter with spirit helpers, although now they were just *ngylyekaq*, a general name for evil spirits. Ivan explained to me that spirit helpers were frightening by telling me a story of one of his ancestors who desired to become a shaman. He went to Yamal, where an initiated shaman blindfolded him and told him to run around the tent. Suddenly, spirits appeared to him and he was frightened half to death. "Playing with spirits" was utterly dangerous, in Ivan's words, something that he knew firsthand. Remarkably, in the literature, one can find similar initiation stories ending with a frightened person becoming a Christian instead. In the early 1840s, the Finnish linguist Matthias Castrén traveled among Nenets who were recently missionized by the Orthodox Church. An ex-apprentice of a shaman told him how he had started learning the art when he was fifteen years old. Two teaching shamans blindfolded the initiate and told him to beat a drum. The shamans hit the novice on his head and back. Suddenly the boy saw a crowd of spirit helpers (*tadyebtsoq*) dancing on his hands and feet. Being very frightened, he fled to the local Orthodox priest and had himself baptized. After that he stopped seeing *tadyebtsoq* (Castrén 1853, 191–92).[5]

Instead of becoming a shaman, Ivan became an evangelical preacher under the influence of an external agent, taking on the role of leader in the community, which historically in Nenets society was thought to require shamanic abilities (Golovnev and Osherenko 1999, 58). Although there were no shamans left by the end of the Soviet period who would carry out once-elaborate ritual seances with a drum, pendants, or other instruments, the idea of the possibility of going through a personal transformation remained. The emergence of Christian priests in the post-Soviet period seemed to offer a less demanding path to dealing with spirits.

Others' conversion narratives I heard were not as dramatic as Ivan's. After Ivan's conversion and baptism in early 1995, there was for a couple of years a gap before others followed his example. Ivan's brother Andrei and his wife, Lyuba, were the next in the tundra to be baptized. On their second meeting, Andrei made an impression on Pavel by having thoroughly read parts of the Bible and having begun to act like "a true Christian" by giving away clothes or other personal belongings to others. Enthralled by "the work of God's Word," Pavel performed the rite of baptism in a tundra lake in 1997. Lyuba was the first Nenets woman to be baptized by Pavel. Because of the lack of common language and the gender barrier, she was baptized rather as an extension of her husband and not as an individual who had her relationship with God properly validated as viable. As I shall discuss later, this happened not only among Baptists but also similarly among the few Pentecostals alike (see chap. 4).

Andrei was convinced that God decided who was saved and who was not. Although God performed his "saving work" person by person, Andrei believed there was a collective dimension to it as well (see Vallikivi 2009, 69–73). Comparing the Yamb-To and the Ural Independents, he summarized the process like this:

> People in the Urals understood only now that one could not live any longer in this kind of darkness. In our area there was not so much paganism and evilness. People here made sacrifices but did not understand to the full extent what they were doing. But in the east, people were following in detail the norms [*normy*]. They knew exactly who they were sacrificing to. They said these were gods. But God had mercy upon us [the Yamb-To Baptists] and sent his Word to us. We quickly accepted it. When we heard about salvation, we wanted to learn more about it. And God liked that. He sent the Holy Spirit. . . . I think this all happens through the Holy Spirit, as when it is coming down. It is in God's hands. And he sends it only when people are seeking. Conversion then takes place like a flare of fire.

Andrei's unusually deep faith expressed in the new language appealed to Pavel. As a result, he proposed to the Nenets converts that they elect Andrei as their presbyter. In 2004, when Andrei was ordained in the Vorkuta prayer house, "the Nenets church" was founded with thirty-four members

Figure 2.2. A moment of prayer in front of the box for food and teacups after having lunch on the way, August 2002.

(unbaptized believers not included).[6] This was a year of abundant harvest for Pavel, as a revival took place among the Ural Nenets as well. That year adult members of the Vorkuta church from among Independents reached well over a hundred, outnumbering the Russian membership twice over.

Alcoholic Hiccup Worms

For the new believers, *punryodaq*, this was not only a break with sacrifices, offerings, sacred items, old-style singing, and the consumption of raw blood but also—perhaps most importantly—a break with vodka (*syarka*). Alcohol played a significant role in Ivan's conversion. For him, it was a radical movement away from alcohol, and this has been the case with nearly all herders, whatever the variations in their personal stories. Making a complete break with alcohol played a pivotal role as both a practice and a narrative for the

Independents. An acute perception of the destructiveness of alcohol consumption has made people susceptible to the new promising temperance program that Christianity has turned out to be.[7]

Discussing conversion in different parts of the post-Soviet space, scholars have pointed out that the anti-alcohol stance of evangelical churches has been very attractive.[8] Undoubtedly, becoming an evangelical Christian offers a chance to quit the habit of excessive drinking. Furthermore, I would like to suggest that rigorous abstaining practices are the first steps toward introducing the new ethics of self-control. Among the tundra dwellers, drinking sessions take place only occasionally, as vodka or its surrogates are not available all the time (Lukin 2011, 122–26; Yoshida 1997, 123–25). Among non-Christians, social drinking is common during visits to other tentholds, especially on Orthodox Church calendar holidays, if there is any vodka available. When herders go and barter with their trading partners (usually every head of a family has one) in settlements, they expect to be served tea, something to eat, and a shot or two as a sign of hospitality. After having a taste of vodka in the mouth, a day or two of binge drinking might follow in the village. Unlike many Russians who drink in the privacy of four walls, Nenets often drink in public places, which has turned them into an easy target for contemptuous remarks by Russians.

Alcohol has the capacity to unleash rage among herders who otherwise value restraint. Examples of the destructiveness of alcohol need not to be sought from afar. When tracing genealogies, I learned that in the post-Soviet period alone more than a dozen Independents were killed during drinking sessions or were frozen to death in the snow when drunk. In one case, all four participants of a drunken binge died, as they consumed suspicious ethanol sold to them by local Russian traders (*kommersanty*). This problem was not specific to the Independents but also to the villagers and collective farmers who drank a lot, especially from the late Soviet period. For instance, the neighboring Ust-Kara collective farm was said to have collapsed in the 1990s from the curse of drink, as herders exchanged most of the communal reindeer for vodka.

For the Independents, there are no communal reindeer to barter for vodka; instead, one's family herd (or racing reindeer, as with Ivan) may disappear. In the late 1990s, a young Yamb-To family lost its entire herd, three hundred strong, as the reindeer ran astray during a month-long drinking party near Vorkuta. Since then, the family has been "sitting" on a lakeshore living from fishing. Alcohol has meant occasional hunger for many. A few herders described how from time to time in their childhood they suffered empty stomachs because their parents spent all their cash on vodka. However, often children were given vodka by their parents. Yegor recalled how when he was a child, grandfather Mikul used to give him a shot. "When I was eleven, I did not want to drink anymore," he once proudly said. Yet later he returned to the habit.

Missionaries have banned drinking for good among converts, and the ban has been strictly followed. From the perspective of Nenets, becoming teetotal probably marks the biggest challenge in their lives. The first time I met Yegor I asked him how many years he had been Christian. He replied, "I have not been drinking for two years now." Significantly, he took the true change from the day he abandoned drink. Before that Yegor had another two-year period when he slid back into drinking from time to time, even if he was willing to become a Christian in his own words. Among converts, such abstinence is the clearest statement of genuine transformation one could ever give to oneself and others.[9]

When asking about his way of finding God, another young reindeer herder called Khriska told me a story about how God stopped him drinking. He had bought vodka in the village of Amderma as usual. When he came out onto the street, the plastic bag gave way under the weight and all the bottles fell on the concrete pavement (*betonka*) and smashed to pieces. As he said, this was God's hand protecting him from the actions that were about to destroy his life, both here and in the hereafter. I heard numerous times from many converts that if they had not converted and given up drink, they would have been dead by the time we met. Even if the new discourse gave the option to somewhat overplay it, many, including non-Christians, saw in drinking a risk to their lives and well-being.

Pavel often blamed drinking as the reason why there were no more conversions among the Yamb-To Nenets. He said that Satan kept people back through alcohol, and as such whole families were in danger of being deprived of salvation. He argued that nobody other than Jesus was able to free the Nenets from their addiction. For example, Pavel talked of Poru (the same man who told me he was an "atheist" taught by "Uncle Brezhnev," see chap. 1), "Poru has heard the Word many times. Today he listened to it like for the first time and remained very pensive. Sandra [Poru's wife] was inclined toward God for some time. But without their husbands, women don't do anything. A woman waits for the husband's decision. But Poru loves to drink. Yet our Jesus is able to make his heart receptive."

Pavel's remark about gender relations mirrors above all his own inability to communicate directly with the women. Despite some public male dominance, Nenets women in many families have significant authority. I happened to witness how husbands and wives made important decisions together concerning migration, trade, and schooling their children (cf. Niglas 1997b). It is true that some women are more interested in conversion and in influencing their men to become sober by getting their husbands to accept conversion. Other anthropologists make similar observations elsewhere: for instance, Colombian women who, as Elizabeth Brusco (1995, 5) argues, "domesticate" their husbands through conversion to evangelical Christianity. As she describes, the 20 to 40 percent of the family's budget was spent on alcohol by the husband, which was saved after conversion.[10]

Vodka has an important place in rituals. Older people who have not converted and have not demonized the Nenets spirits say that alcohol (and tobacco) help to hold back and appease certain spirits. Non-Christian Nenets keep some reserves of vodka to feed spirits by pouring "spirit water" (*khekhe yi*) into an upper recess of spirit figures, onto stones and trees, or into the rivers and lakes in which spirits are known to live. For the missionaries, this is living proof of Satan's workings. However, there is also a category of agent that lives inside a person and demands vodka. *Ikota khalyq*, or "hiccup worms" (known in the wider area as well, see Il'ina 2008, 74–78; Khristoforova 2016; Napolskikh et al. 2003, 300–302), are said to demand alcohol through their host's voice by hiccupping and shrieking. Once Yegor explained that when drinking together with his "pagan" uncle Vata on a Sunday, he nearly caught *ikota khalyq* from him. Yegor described how a few times an unwanted hiccup came out of his mouth asking for drink. When he was relating this story, I could see from his face how horrified he was merely by the thought of being possessed by *ikota khalyq*.

While I was staying with Vata in September 2006, he often complained to me that *ikota khalyq* were giving him hard times when he had no vodka at hand. Indeed, most of the time the old man was just lying on reindeer hides and suffering in pain. As he said, the hiccup worms were moving in his body and making his arms and legs painful (cf. Khomich 1976, 25; Kvashnin 2018, 27; Lepekhin 1805, 266; Schrenk 1848, 549–50; Yevladov 2010, 164). Yegor had stopped visiting his "pagan" uncle, like most *punryodaq* who—if they had not completely severed the bonds of kinship with non-Christians—avoided kin who were drinkers. Once he went to see Vata to tell him that *ikota* was Satan, who was making him drink, and that only

Jesus could heal him from his possession. Despite a promise that Jesus would heal him, Vata avoided missionaries. Like some other older people, he preferred to give vodka to his hiccup worms, as he could be certain that in these moments his limbs stopped aching (see chap. 5 for more detail).

Another person who was said to have an *ikota* was Yegor's mother Granny Marina. As she lived with her daughter Ksenya and son-in-law Yevgeni, both Baptists, she heard Bible readings and prayers every day. Like most people, she did not object to the need to pray to God. Now and then, when there was a communal prayer, she went onto her knees; at other times she just sat and sometimes fell asleep during the service. To my question at the beginning of my fieldwork, whether Granny Marina was a believer, Yevgeni said that she was possessed by an *ikota* demon and because of that "her head is not well, and she does not understand what has been said." I lived in the same camp for many weeks over the years and my impression was that she was just silently ignoring what her children were doing, disguising it with madness. She had old ideas about how to relate to the spirit realm. Sometimes she said that this or that thing should not be done because it was taboo. When I once mentioned the word "cholera" (*kholera*, referring to spirits that cause anthrax or other epidemics) during a conversation when sitting around the table, she abruptly told me not to say the word again, as it would attract the spirit of the illness. Baptist children somewhat nervously laughed at her and told me not to pay attention to what she had said.

Becoming Russian: Tensions between Old and Young

For the non-Christian older generation, the young people had gone too far in their dealings with *lutsaq*. Paradoxically, the oldest among the converts, like Yegor or Andrei, found themselves with the same problem, which they did not expect when they initially became members of the church. The single biggest problem was that their children wanted to leave the tundra. This new economy of desire had reached the Independents with a significant delay compared to many collective farmers whose children had for years preferred to abandon the nomadic lifestyle (see Rozanova 2019).

This was a source of anxiety for Christian parents, who thought one should remain in the tundra and live with the reindeer, whether one is Christian or not. The young generation of Independents, born after the 1980s, was generally willing to convert, having witnessed little of the old Nenets religion. There were a few exceptions though, as with a young herder who told me that he "was not going to believe" because he wanted to have a big herd. He had heard that Christians should give away their reindeer and live a life of poverty in order to be saved. Some others had not converted because they wanted to avoid conflict with their nonbelieving kin. But in general, one could sense among the youngsters a fervor to become Christian that was related to the imagined future trajectories of adult life.

I realized this most clearly when talking to Andrei's daughter Vera. Eighteen years old (in 2007), disciplined, and hardworking, Vera confessed to me, "There is only one thing that makes me sad. I do not like living in the tundra anymore." She added, "Almost every young person wants to leave the tundra." City life appeals to Vera for various reasons. Life is hard and dull in the tundra, she argued. The coal-mining city Vorkuta, which was the image everybody bore in mind, was what was seen as full of life and intensity, compared to the repetitious life in the tundra where there were never enough socially entertaining events. Vera attended school for seven years, longer than most others in the community, and she wished to go to Naryan-Mar to obtain secondary education in order to get out of the tundra (cf. Vladimirova 2018, 11).[11] Moreover, for Vera there was a question of whom to marry in the new era when alongside "arranged marriages" the first "love marriages" took place. She declared that she did not wish to marry anybody from the tundra. "My parents should not choose a husband for me," she said. Vera then recalled with excitement her first trip to Saint Petersburg to a church youth gathering where she met a nice Russian lad who expressed his interest in her. When I asked Andrei what he made of his daughter's wish, he sighed and said with resignation that God would take care of it (*Bog usmotrit*). He could not say much against it, especially when Vera argued that living in the city would allow her to be in tighter communion with her sisters and brothers in faith.

Pavel supported her wish to leave the tundra, as Vera said. Although missionaries do not make overly forceful attempts to make reindeer herders sedentary, they implicitly share the view of wider Russian society that a nomadic lifestyle is unnatural in the current period. Unknowingly, they had adopted a view according to which nomadism is "a sociological cul-de-sac," something that Soviet evolutionist ideologues believed in as well (Gellner 1988, 106; cf. Sneath 2007, 121–56; Stammler 2005, 21). Even though Pavel admitted that there was a greater concentration of devilish dangers in the settled world, he told me another time matter-of-factly that "sooner or later, they [the Nenets] are going to be tired of this way of life in the tundra and move to the settlements" (cf. Vagramenko 2018, 73). Some converts like Ivan had already proved the case, as he had finally moved to Vorkuta in 2005. He was a pathbreaker for the youngsters. However, when visiting Andrei's family in 2012, Vera had been married to a Ural Nenets and become a mother. Her worst fear of moving to an unknown family had not realized, as her groom moved to Vera's parents' tent. This was an exceptional arrangement in a patrilocal society (Vera's father had followed the same rare pattern). Vera was not the only one who stayed, as most other young adults who had enthusiastically told me about their wish to leave still lived in the tundra.

For Yegor, too, becoming *lutsa* was an issue that touched his family acutely. Although he said that he belonged to God's people (*nuv khibyariq* in Nenets, *narod bozhiy* in Russian) in which different ethnic groups were involved and would be united as one in heaven, he did not like the prospect of his children moving into a settlement and becoming Russian. Yegor's children, who were the first converts in the family, convinced him to become a *punryoda*. Now, most of the children dreamed of moving to the city like the pastor's daughter Vera once had.

From Yegor's perspective, his brother Ivan, who had moved to the city recently but still owned reindeer and often visited his brothers in the tundra, was in an ambiguous position. "My brother Ivan is *lutsa*," Yegor once declared. Then he paused for a second and continued, "All right, maybe he is still a Nenets [*nyenets'*], but his daughter will be a Russian woman [*khabyenye*] for sure." The fact that Ivan's family was Nenets-speaking did not make them Nenets, *nyeneyq nyenetsyaq* ("real people"). Those who live or do things like Russians and who do not have reindeer are *lutsaq*, was Yegor's diagnosis. The fact that Ivan did business like a Russian businessman (*kommersant*) only confirmed that he should be called *lutsa*. Many did not regard Ivan as a true believer anymore because, as mentioned above, he was now acting more as a middleman for his own greed and not for God.[12] Tellingly, another nickname he had was Monkey (*ngayatarq*), which referred to his Russianness (see chap. 1), although nobody told him this directly (cf. Ssorin-Chaikov 2003, 160). Again, Ivan wore a Russian suit with a homemade reindeer skin tie with antler-motifs on it, showing that he still valued his "Nenetsness," while his Russian suit made it possible literally to blend into the Russian Baptist world.

For Yegor, this boundary between the nomadic and settled way was neither impermeable nor final. He argued that if Ivan returned to the tundra, he would be a *nyeney nyenets'* again. However, what he feared more was that the metamorphosis of his children could become irreversible. Thus,

Figure 2.3. Literate youth reading the Baptist journal *Herald of Truth*, February 2007.

his practice of naming (e.g., *lutsa*) was not so much classifying for the sake of classification but a production of performatives that were about trying to maintain a certain togetherness of his family. In other words, labeling somebody *lutsa* served as a ridiculing discourse that fought against the epidemic wish of the youngsters to leave the tundra—a move that would cause them to lose their skills and bonds. Despite competing Christian concepts, these abilities and connections were still considered essential for being human (*nyeney*). Youngsters moving out of the tundra and living without reindeer would thus mean, in the eyes of their parents, losing the part of their personhood that was tightly entangled with reindeer and the land. And yet, Yegor's and Andrei's attempts to fight against their children's wish to—as they saw it—become *lutsa* would go against the Christian logic of the insignificance of one's "ethnicity" or "culture" in one's life. They said that faith was not a matter of Russianness or Nenetsness—what mattered was serving God. Therefore, Yegor and Andrei were caught by the evangelical ideology crafted by Russian Baptists they loyally followed.

In this chapter, I pointed to a link between Ivan's conversion and the Nenets shamanic cosmology where there is a place for a radical self-transformation.

This is not to argue that a shamanic self-transformation was replaced by a Christian one, and as such, would just be the continuation of the old mode of existence under the guise of Christianity (like the Nenets "Christian shaman" that one encounters in a report from early Orthodox missionization, see Znamenski 2003, 47–50). Ivan went through a rupture in a very different sense than would have been the case if he had become a shaman. He becomes thinkable for himself in a radically new manner, as a subject in a Badiouan sense, helped by the newly acquired Baptist language. As I shall discuss in chapter 7, this involves an ideal of fixation of God's gaze on oneself accompanied by an inevitable threat of sliding back to one's former sinful self.

New relations with Russians, becoming sober, and acquiring modern technologies were all part of Ivan's journey to Christianity. However, his path to Christianity is not to be understood *only* by the drive to become modern. As Cannell, Harding, Robbins, and others have pointed out, Christianity has its own compelling logic that makes people become Christian. On the one hand, it seems that in the case of Ivan, Christian logic arrived late—as it often does—and that the initial impetus lay somewhere else. On the other hand, it was not only *his* desire and decision to become a mediator, a businessman, or a shaman but also new relations and events that made him into a Christian subject.

My wider point is that evangelical Christianity offers tools for transforming one's ideas about available and expected transformations over the course of an extended future. In this respect, it must be stressed that Christian logic with its message starts to work on its own; as it sinks in, other trajectories emerge through daily engagements with disciplinary practices of a linguistic, emotional, and cognitive nature. Missionaries taught the converts to reject their desires for "mundane" or "material" and instead to focus on their new "spiritual," a church-based interiorist identity with a Russian tint to it. This is directly related to the endless work that missionaries do all over the world by separating "religion" and "culture," being an example of a constant "work of purification," as Bruno Latour (1993) would characterize it (cf. Keane 2007). The result is that the relationship with God and his community makes any other senses of belonging irrelevant because relevance lies only with the divine and persons filled by the Holy Spirit and living as the Body of Christ.

Unexpectedly, the new "life-giving God" makes youngsters wish to leave the tundra and live a life that old people compare to a kind of death.

As one herder told me, there was not much difference when somebody stayed to live in the city or died. Remarkably, the Baptist parents have been actively repudiating their past ritual engagements, while their children have not had much to repudiate in these terms. Yet as if they felt a need to repudiate something, they are ready to cast off their tundra life altogether. Being pulled by various forces of modernity, Nenets converts have joined a movement that sees itself as thoroughly "antimodern," which is what I shall look at next.

3

BAPTIST MISSIONARIES ON THE EDGE

Insiders and Outsiders

The Baptist brotherhood has been missionizing in the Nenets areas since the mid-1990s. Known as the International Union of Churches of Evangelical Christians-Baptists (hereafter International Union) or Unregistered Baptists (in the literature also Reform Baptists or Initsiativniki), this was the biggest illegal religious union during the Soviet period. Today it remains one of the most conservative and antiworldly Protestant movements in post-atheist Russia (Bourdeaux and Filatov 2003, 185–94).[1] In recent decades, the brotherhood has been the most active mission among northern Indigenous peoples, having converted, among others, many Nenets Independents. As already mentioned, Pentecostal denominations also proselytize in the area (see chap. 4), although none of them has been as successful as the Unregistered Baptists (cf. Vagramenko 2014; Wiget and Balalaeva 2011, 173).

Throughout their existence in Russia, the Protestant denominations have been shaped by their relations with the state, and they continue to be. This has probably been the single most important factor in interdenominational dynamics as well: during the Soviet period, the state was the direct or indirect cause of all major splits of church unions. Both Baptists and Pentecostals, the two biggest Protestant denominations in Russia, were united during the Soviet era under one union by the state. As a result, they all split into so-called registered and unregistered branches.[2] Although in the post-Soviet period the religious landscape has changed radically, the divisions that emerged in the Soviet era among the evangelicals are still playing a significant role today.

The Unregistered Baptists' separatist history, strict morality, and heightened discipline have all played into their conversionist ideology, missionary techniques, and church-building in the tundra. Members are convinced that they have restored the initial church and that the eschatological end is not far away. They call themselves a spiritually awakened brotherhood (*probuzhdennoe bratstvo*), *the* true church, *the* people of God, and *the* direct followers of the early apostolic church. The long-term charismatic leader Gennadiy Kryuchkov (1926–2007), who authored the official historical narrative of the union, argued that three hundred years after Christ, the true church grew tired of persecution and Christians were entrapped by the new tactics of Satan, who approached them under the guise of powerful rulers like Constantine. By Kryuchkov's words, if the early church had remained firm in its separatism or world-rejecting ideology then "it would have won the whole world and possibly already then evangelized up to the ends of the earth" (*Tserkov'* 2008, 183; see also Kryuchkov 2008, 33). Having survived decades of harassment, the International Union, also known as "the persecuted church" (*gonimaya tserkov'*), is there to complete the process.

I suggest the attention of the International Union in the North is not random but has its cosmological reasons embedded in its specific concepts of space and time. I realized this partly because of my own positionality while doing fieldwork. Anthropologists have always aimed to become insiders to some extent. However, fundamentalist evangelical logic sets certain limits to this—at least this was what I found to be the case. The anthropologist's position is not fully of one's own making, especially in a missionary culture whose sole aim is to change all outsiders, including researchers (Harding 2000; see also S. Coleman 2015; Crane and Weibel 2012). Some church members saw in me a "sympathizer" or potential convert (*priblizhayushchiy*), as I was interested in spiritual topics. I realized that converts saw me above all through the future, through the potential of change, through God's plans. I sensed some of my best Nenets friends' concern as they tried to convince me to become a believer. For instance, Yegor, when trying to persuade me of the need to become a member of the church, insisted that he would like to meet me in heaven. Yet negotiating my position was even more prominent in my relations with Baptist missionary Pavel.

In April 2007, Pavel invited me to his home in Vorkuta to inquire about my scholarly project. We had had numerous conversations during occasional meetings in both the city and the tundra over the course of eight years. Being convinced that God had a purpose in sending me to the tundra,

Figure 3.1. Baptist missionaries visiting Yegor's nomadic camp, March 2004.

he proposed several times that I should quit my academic work and "start to work for God." Despite his overall friendliness, this time I felt that he was trying to vet me more seriously than ever before. We were having a conversation sitting behind the kitchen table in his flat situated in a five-floor concrete building on the edge of the tundra.

To his question of what my interest was in living with herders for so long (far longer than any evangelists had), I explained that I was exploring reindeer herders' "culture" (*kul'tura*). I tried to accommodate my vocabulary to the local setting, or at least what I thought it to be. Pavel replied that everything about Nenets culture was in a book written by Yevladov. There, one can find descriptions of Nenets clothing, dwellings, and reindeer herding in great detail, he said.[3] When I mentioned that I was not only exploring material aspects of reindeer herders' culture (that had not changed much over this period) but also their worldview (*mirovozzrenie*), Pavel became noticeably tenser. With an authoritative tone, he said that worldview was not culture and that I was going beyond the boundaries of ethnography (*etnografiya*). "Culture is their clothes and tents," he insisted. This statement was in line with the wider Soviet-period understanding of material culture being the true object of ethnography. Although one could find chapters on ethnogenesis, social structure, and religious conceptions (*religioznye pred-stavleniya*) in the works of the Soviet ethnographers (see, e.g., Khomich 1966, 1995), the lay understanding of ethnography was above all related to material objects displayed in museums (Vakhtin 2006; cf. Pelkmans 2007; Vaté 2009).[4]

As I understood it, Pavel's remark was not so much concern about my academic work for the sake of its quality but concern about unwanted attention by an outsider into spiritual matters of the born-again Christian Nenets for whom he felt responsible (cf. Crapanzano 2000, 91). Every time I returned to Vorkuta and met Baptists in their prayer meetings, I sensed that the overall atmosphere was changing slightly. As some openly said, they felt a growing pressure from outsiders (*vneshnie*). Hints about that had become more common over the years in both sermons and my conversations with Baptists. Congregants tried to protect church life from the external gaze more keenly as the ideal of secrecy (*konspiratsiya*) and alertness or vigilance (*bodrstvovanie*) were in high gear once again.[5]

Unregistered Baptists feared that the current period of relative freedom has weakened their ability to oppose the world, the state, and Satan, which are all intricately linked. Their ethos depends on opposition, similarly to the early Christians. Furthermore, this understanding matches the Unregistered Baptist myth of origin—being spiritually the direct descendants of early Christianity and the only true continuation of it. While others change around because of the world's (or the devil's) pressure, they claim to have not changed. This is why in the post-Soviet period, their central mission has been keeping up secrecy and alertness, which backs up their identity as the holy people.

In the eyes of Pavel, I belonged to the category of outsiders, even if he referred to me as *drug*, "friend" (but not *brat*, "brother") and prayed for my soul by saying my name out loud in my presence. I guess he had become slightly impatient at not seeing my heart change despite my interest in faith matters over the years. He still welcomed me with a smile on his face, but growing concern on the matter of outsiders made him apprehensive.

Most Nenets Baptist friends were less obsessed with me being an outsider, probably because of the closer relationship we had developed over an extended period. When I was staying with Nenets presbyter Andrei in 2007, he once openly admitted, "I was warned about you." As a sign of trust, he then quickly assured me that he did not regard me as a threat: "If you had evil purposes, God would have revealed it to me in my dreams. I said it to them as well." Although he did not say it directly, "them" must have been Pavel and other Russian missionaries. I had lived with Andrei's family several times over eight years, and he encouraged me to take an interest in the Nenets way of life. However, even with Andrei I did not discuss faith as a matter of knowledge. For him, believing was to be enacted in a very specific way. It could be spoken only in performative contexts through the Holy Spirit and not just discussed for the sake of "exchanging information" (Crapanzano 2000, 88; see also Tuzin 1997, 26; chap. 6).

Toward the end of the conversation with Pavel at his kitchen table, I explained that my aim was to gain a better understanding of various points of views that reindeer herders possessed, including those of the believers. My statement must have sounded hopelessly wrong. Pavel was silent for a moment and then asked, "Do you know what tolerance is?" He went on, explaining, "Tolerance is everything other than being on the narrow path after Jesus." For him, I was another typical secular person who did not understand that various viewpoints could not exist that were right at the same time. For instance, his assessment was that other Protestants—not speaking of the Orthodox, who were simply "mistaken idolaters"—were known to be treading a wide path that did not lead to paradise but to hell.

Pavel was there to guard proselytes. Nenets converts belonging to those few who were saved had to be protected with extra care. Childlike in their innocence, according to Pavel's words, they were not used to outside pressure from the world and could fall into its traps more easily. Their souls belonged to God, who had sent him to save them. The "infantilism" of the reindeer herders—a motif repeated in descriptions by Christian ministers on Nenets (see, e.g., Makariy 1878; Shemanovskiy 2011; cf. Balzer 2011, 222)—had yet helped to open their hearts to God more easily, the evangelist assumed.

Pavel tried to open my eyes to what the world's actual intentions toward the Nenets converts were. There were many signs, he said. His intention, I guess, was to warn me not to become complicit, explaining that "in these days, many have become interested in the Nenets as God's people. This is not without reason. We are currently heading toward the times we have had earlier—persecutions [*goneniya*]. The interest is abnormally big. Last year there were attempts to write down all the Nenets. All believers. Have you heard of that? This was done because they wanted to control God's new people. Where were they before [conversion]? Earlier, nobody was interested in them. They lived without passports, without being registered. But now they are being registered."

Registration was a stimulus to extra alertness by Russian Baptists and Nenets herders alike, although not always for the same reasons. Both had avoided one or another form of registration that they felt threatened their way of life (even if they knew that being unregistered was against the law). Although the census he referred to was an economic survey, according to Pavel, this was a mere smokescreen, as every kind of registration was just another cunning way of the world (and Satan) to attempt to control God's children.[6]

I asked Andrei what he made of that census. Andrei seemed to be more concerned about his herd, the size of which was asked by enumerators. Converts, like nonconverts, feared that the state was trying to take control of their reindeer because—as older people used to say—after the census takers had left the tundra, new restrictions, additional taxes, or confiscations of animals followed. The Nenets shared wariness toward the state with the Unregistered Baptists, although they were only learning that the Russian Baptists' reasons were bound to their historical experience, of a very different kind though, as I shall explain below.

The Birth of the Vorkuta Church in the Gulag

To understand the self-perception of the Russian Baptists in Vorkuta, one must look at the wider history of the evangelical movement in Russia and its ecclesiology (see H. Coleman 2005). Baptists have been known for their schismatic tendencies (Troeltsch 1960, 694ff.; Weber 2001, 92–101). As mentioned above, in the Soviet Union, the schismatic groups declared their total independence from the state and state-managed church unions. Paradoxically, in the long run, this drove them to depend on opposition to the state. In their publications as well as in their church services, Unregistered Baptist ministers boasted that they had always kept the church separated from the world (which evidently comprised the state). They did not engage in political activities or even in any kind of social work among the unsaved.[7]

The only thing the church of the Unregistered Baptists was obliged to offer to outsiders was God's Word. For Baptists, this was an issue of relationship with God, who did not give power to "the ones who loved the world." As older ministers of the International Union proudly said, they had never committed "the sin of cooperation with the world" (*grekh sotrudnichestva s mirom*).

Vorkuta, with its Gulag history, has a special place in the imagination of the Unregistered Baptists. Many consider it "a symbol of the suffering of God's people," as Pavel said (see also Belyakova and Dobson 2015; French 2018; Panych 2012b). One of the songs I heard frequently sung by both Russian and Nenets congregants was a hymn called "Infertile Land, Uninhabited Expanses" composed around the motif of prisoners of faith in Vorkuta. Nenets converts seemed enchanted by its march rhythm, even if the lyrics portrayed the area rather counterintuitively (e.g., "uninhabited") to the Indigenous sensibilities: "Harsh region you, the North. . . . Your harsh polar elements, and the dead tundra, wild taiga. Let the whole country, vast Russia, hear the news from Christ's witnesses" (*Pesn'* 2004). In this song, Vorkuta is the place where "holy seeds" start growing and where "the soldiers of Christ" become free and "take the banner of the truth to the nations." The union journal refers to the prophetic hymn: "Today with joy we can witness these words come true. The Indigenous inhabitants of the Far North turn to God" (Dolzhno mne 1995, 30).[8] Nenets converts were expressing themselves in a language that had a transcendental (and southern) origin. They were about to accommodate the gaze of "the other," which was one of a Soviet schismatic church.

Pavel had been a member of the Vorkuta Baptist church from the early 1980s and had been a presbyter since 1990.[9] Although he had not suffered repressions himself, he proudly promoted the history of "the persecuted church." In 2007, sixty years of the Vorkuta church was celebrated with photos on the walls of the prayer hall and past events recalled from the pulpit. The Vorkuta church, like the city itself, had its roots in the penal labor camp that was set up there to excavate coal. Throughout their existence, Vorkuta labor camps, like others of their kind, had—in addition to political prisoners, kulaks, and criminals—people convicted for their religious views or activities from virtually all Christian denominations represented in Russia. Despite the efforts of the camp guards, there was a lot of religious activity. Bibles were smuggled into the zone, and services were held secretly

Figure 3.2. Vorkuta Baptist congregants celebrating the sixtieth anniversary of their church, February 2007.
Most of the Nenets congregants were absent at the time.

(Noble 1970). As a result of illegal missionization in the camps, many prisoners converted to Christianity.

Vorkuta had been a temporary home for hundreds of Baptists, including later Baptist schismatic leaders such as Nikolay Baturin (*Podrazhayte* 2001) and Nikolay Boyko (2006; see also Kovalenko 2006). Those who were released but did not have the right to leave Vorkuta organized church life on the other side of the barbed wire in "the work zone." One of those was Grigoriy Kovtun, who in 1947 founded the Baptist church of Vorkuta and became its first presbyter. Like many other isolated congregations elsewhere, the church did not attempt to register its congregation with the authorities

(*Podrazhayte* 2001, 72). By the mid-1950s, the congregation had around sixty members (many of them Germans from the Volga area of Mennonite background) but did not have a prayer house; instead, they gathered in private homes of the members (Boyko 2006).

In 1944, the authorities decided to allow Baptists, Evangelical Christians, and Pentecostals to legalize their activities—on the condition that they were all governed by one centralized organization called the "All-Union Council of Evangelical Christians-Baptists" (hereafter "All-Union Council"). However, not all joined the union. Many remained autonomous, like the church of Vorkuta. Others soon splintered off from the artificial conglomerate and became illegal again. Pentecostals, who are not allowed to speak in tongues, perform faith healing, or wash feet during their services, lost half of their churches through secession from the union after 1946 (Mitrokhin 1997, 405–10).

As the only officially accepted central body of evangelical Protestant churches in the Soviet Union (except for a small union of Seventh-day Adventists), the All-Union Council was closely monitored and managed by the state. Everything had to go through a system of registrations with state organs; it was not possible to open new churches at will or appoint presbyters without the approval of local Communist Party officials. Furthermore, union leaders and senior presbyters (some of them registered as agents of the secret police) were on a short leash, giving regular reports to the special councils for religious affairs and making pro-Soviet statements at home and abroad. Despite the obedience of the leaders to the state, church members were harassed in oft-repeated campaigns against believers not only during services but also at work, school, or in the army (Marsh 2011, 90–98; Nikol'skaya 2009; Sawatsky 1981).

De-Stalinization after 1953 and the gradual release of Gulag prisoners mobilized a cohort of young, uncompromising evangelicals who were dissatisfied with the state-managed official union. After an upsurge in the activity of committed Christians at the end of the 1950s, the first secretary of the Communist Party and Stalin's successor, Nikita Khrushchev, launched a new campaign aimed at the eradication of religion (J. Anderson 1994). He revived the use of groups of atheist agitators and the methods of the notorious League of Militant Atheists in the 1920s (Peris 1998; see also Suslov 1931 on the League's fight with "shamanists"). This campaign reached the remotest areas, including Vorkuta. Soviet historian Yuriy Gagarin (1978, 292) reported that at the end of the 1950s, Komsomol (Communist Youth League) members from the Vorkuta coal mines were carrying out "individual work"—taking into account one's denominational affiliation, age, sex, social background and so on—with sectarians (*sektanty*) under the guidance of "experienced atheists" (cf. Barenberg 2014, 211–12). Next to the individual work, the government launched an atheist propaganda campaign through newspapers, radio, and television, which was not always well received by Christians or a wider audience (Smolkin 2018; Wanner 2007, 2012). In 1961, by command of the city party organization, a Club of Atheists was founded. They claimed their words to be "weapons" that find "a road to the hearts" of the people and save them from "a fog" (Zhilin 1963, 10, 15, 27). The underlying idea was to offer their own positive program and rituals in place of religion. However, Soviet commentators argued that success was poor because "mistakes" were made during campaigns (Gagarin 1978, 304).

From the perspective of the regime that was in rush, educational measures alone were not enough. Councils for religious affairs and the KGB launched so-called administrative measures to eradicate religion and accelerate the arrival of Communism. As they had done several times earlier, the state used the requirement of registration as its main tool to control and suppress Christian congregations. Between 1959 and 1964, hundreds of prayer houses were shut down. As many congregations were not allowed or not willing to register, the state forced a substantial number of churches underground. Many other congregations registered (Prokhorov 2013, 345; Smolkin 2018, 80; Walters 1993).

The All-Union Council leaders decided to comply with the new antireligious policies that aimed to cut off the transmission of religious knowledge to youth while hoping that "the old people, illiterate fanatics" would take their religious zeal with them when they died (Kryuchkov 2008, 498). In 1960, the All-Union Council changed the church statutes and composed a secret "Letter of Instruction," which they sent out to all senior presbyters controlling local congregations in regions. This notorious letter ordered ministers to preach less, keep children away from services, minimize the number of baptisms among under thirty-year-olds, and stop "unhealthy missionary tendencies" in general (Bourdeaux 1968, 20–21; Koroleva et al. 2013; Mitrokhin 1997, 414; Sawatsky 1981, 139, 177).

Many Baptists had been dissatisfied with the All-Union Council leaders' overt obedience to the authorities. But the new rules triggered more widespread discontent, especially among young Baptist men. Gennadiy Kryuchkov, Aleksey Prokof'ev, Georgiy Vins, Mikhail Khorev, and some other hardliners formed an Initiative Group to fight submissive union leaders. Nicknamed "Initsiativniki" by seculars, they called for a general congress to be convened and urged leaders of the official union to stop collaborating with the state, to repent, and to become sanctified again. As expected, the government did not give a permit to convene, and the leaders of the All-Union Council gave a hostile reaction to the call as well. The Initiative Group saw in the leaders of the All-Union Council apostates through whom Satan worked, and as such they declared the excommunication of those alongside with most senior presbyters (Bourdeaux 1968, 44–45). This was an attempt to take over the union. Yet it was only partially successful. After having won around half of the All-Union Council congregations and many unregistered churches, in 1965 they resorted to establishing a new central church body, called the Council of Churches of Evangelical Christians-Baptists (hereafter "Council of Churches") (Sawatsky 1981, 146, 179). The leaders of the new council claimed that, being full of the Holy Spirit, only they were the true children of God and the true church on earth. Another schism was complete.[10]

Staying outside the World and Welcoming Persecution

Although the state repressed all Christians in the early 1960s, the Unregistered Baptists (including members of autonomous congregations, such as the Vorkuta church) were arrested more often than others because of their stubborn refusal to register or to give up instructing their own children and evangelizing among Soviet citizens. In the 1960s alone, more than five hundred activist Unregistered Baptists were imprisoned for three to five years on average (Khorev 1988). Until the end of the 1980s, nearly all the leaders of Council of Churches were either underground or imprisoned. Despite this, they managed to run the union through a dispersed network of activists and to print in underground offset printing houses journals (*samizdat*), church literature, and appeals addressed to the authorities in the USSR and in the West.

The relationship with the state remained highly controversial. This was the area where Baptists' literalist reading of the Bible was tested to the fullest in the maze of contradicting messages about the state in scriptures (cf. Kee 1980, 119–25). All Baptists agreed that the worldly authorities required respect because God had instituted the rulers. What the respect required from a believer was, however, interpreted radically differently among the

Registered and Unregistered Baptists. One of the most debated passages in these disputes were Christ's words, "Render therefore unto Caesar the things which are Caesar's; and unto God the things that are God's" (Matthew 22:21). While the Registered Baptists stressed Paul's urge to obey the state and law, the Unregistered stressed Acts 5, where Peter and John expressed the idea that "we ought to obey God rather than men" (cf. Sawatsky 1981, 189–90). While the All-Union Council ideologists quoted passages that recommended quietism and obedience to the state (e.g., Romans 13:1–4; Titus 3:1), the Council of Churches argued that when the matters *inside* the church (i.e., "spiritual matters") were at stake, they did not need to be obedient to the state because in their words, the church stayed *outside* the world.

Outworldliness or out-stateness was not a result of free theological debates but of tension with the Soviet state, which made the Unregistered Baptists resort to a rigid concept of it. Against the Baptists' own understanding, both the Soviet and Western authorities saw them as political dissidents. Reformers stressed that they were dealing with purely spiritual matters and that they were not anti-Soviet, as God did not allow dealing with politics. They fought for their biblical and constitutional right (which recognized the separation of the state and church) to be left in peace in matters of religion. Despite what was said, the state was always an implicit addressee of the Baptists' texts.

The principle of noninvolvement was frequently repeated. Referring to Paul (1 Corinthians 5:12–13),[11] Unregistered Baptists argued that they were not called to criticize or comment on the authorities in any way because only God could judge outsiders. They declared that "making tsars is God's work and not for humans. He puts them in place, overthrows and humiliates them (Job 12:19; Ezekiel 17:24; Daniel 4:32; Romans 13:1)" (*Tserkov'* 2008). Kryuchkov preached forcefully the ideology of noninvolvement until the end of his life. In his ideological testament, he wrote:

> And the authorities are not the Antichrist for us, nor is the Kremlin an enemy for us, as some well-known authors would suggest [to be our position]. Yes, we must tread on all the power of the enemy (Luke 10:19) and we are obliged to resist the devil (James 4:7), but only in the Church and not beyond its limits. If he penetrates inside and defiles the sanctuary, if he acts through apostate ministers, then we shall be commanded to lead with him an uncompromising war. But to fight outside the Church on his own territory (or equally to cooperate with the world) is a sinful, anti-evangelical, unsuccessful, and fatal act. Thanks to God, our brotherhood never went that way. We fought against sin

in the Church, we did not let the world govern inside it, we kept watching at the altars of the Lord, but we never (!) touched Caesar's government beyond the borders of the Church! God was with us on this holy road. (*Tserkov'* 2008, 11; see also Kryuchkov 2008, 32)

Border maintenance had become the ultimate issue for Unregistered Baptists; what they called the external world, meaning nonspiritual, worldly, contrasted to the internal, which was spiritual. They boasted that they had remained unpolluted while the All-Union Council had let outsiders govern the church from inside. In the true church, there could be no place for outsiders because the church and the world could not be merged without damage. This ecclesiology has ultimate importance for understanding what was at stake. The church, both universal and local, is a collective of individual believers who constitute Christ's body, "a holy place" (Kryuchkov 2008, 33). This body is regarded as a collective of interiorities that is in tight relationship with God. Like individual believers, so the church needs to have a pure "heart," or as Kryuchkov put it, "Only by finding freedom inside the church and liberating it from all the sinful, do we free its heart so that God could act in it powerfully, soundly, and strongly" (*Tserkov'* 2008, 201). This shows how the imagined interiority shifts between individual and collective dimensions. (I shall return to the importance of the notion of heart, and "internal" and "external" in the concept of personhood of Baptists, in chap. 7.)

To reconcile two seemingly contradictory commands of behavior, one of the law-abiding person and another of the obedient God's child, Kryuchkov and some other church leaders worked out a conceptual division between an individual-as-church-member and an individual-as-citizen. All the matters recognized as the sphere of the state's interests, like education and military service, were considered to remain out of the reach of the church. These were institutions that believers had to work out their relationship with and participate in only as citizens. The church as a collective body had arguably no right to intervene. An explicit command to the presbyters was phrased categorically: "Do not take any church resolutions in our congresses or membership meetings about military issues, state politics, the electoral system, social issues, education, or health care. Every Christian can only form independently his own position in these questions as a citizen" (*Tserkov'* 2008, 202). The Unregistered Baptists did not intend to change the social order but only to take as many people as possible outside the world, by following the principle of "spreading the news out to the world, holiness of the brotherhood inside the church" (*blagovestie spas-eniya—vovne, svyatost' bratstva—vnutri*) (*Tserkov'* 2008, 201).

As Louis Dumont (1986) has argued, renouncing the world is always a relative position as it entails an inherent tension between living in the world and trying to be already otherworldly. Relying on the work of the well-known Protestant theologian Ernst Troeltsch, he offers an apt characterization of this kind of tension among Christians:

> It follows from Christ's and then Paul's teaching that the Christian is an "individual-in-relation-to-God." There is, Troeltsch says, "absolute individualism and absolute universalism" in relation to God. The individual soul receives eternal value from its filial relationship to God, in which relationship is also grounded human fellowship: Christians meet in Christ, whose members they are. This tremendous affirmation takes place on a level that transcends the world of man and of social institutions, although these are also from God. The infinite worth of the individual is at the same time the disparagement, the negation in terms of value, of the world as it is: a dualism is posited, a tension is established that is constitutive of Christianity and will endure throughout history. (30)

The same tension is constitutive in the identity of the Unregistered Baptists who struggle with the classical theological question of how to be *in* the world without being *of* the world. The answer is "the brotherhood of love in and through Christ, and the consequent equality of all," (31) which enables "the emancipation of the individual through a personal transcendence, and the union of outworldly individuals in a community that treads on earth but has its heart in heaven" (ibid.). Notably, the practice of constantly defining what is inside the church and what remains outside has offered the Unregistered Baptists the possibility to uphold their separatist identity and a necessary distance from the state.

In the tundra, I heard Nenets reindeer herders dutifully mentioning rulers in their prayers every fourth Friday of the month. They followed what their printed prayer plan prescribed. Most had only a very vague idea about state politics. The only one among the Independents who was interested in politics was Andrei. Yet this was more a curiosity about the Russians' world "over there" that had only a limited impact on the life in the tundra.

Among urban church members in Vorkuta, persecution was a topic that came up again and again. Believers shared stories of martyrdom (*muchenichestvo*) and persecution they had experienced, heard of, or read about (cf. Prokhorov 2013, 107–8, 252–55, 333–35). The usual motifs were how police and vigilantes disrupted services and arrested congregants, how homes were confiscated, how children were taken away to state orphanages, and how brothers and sisters in faith suffered in prison. I heard a few testimonies from older Vorkuta congregation members recalling how they gathered in private homes or how they carried out baptisms in the tundra away from external gaze. Many accounts were also printed in Baptists' journals, which were the main reading material, after the Bible, for all age groups. All these stories stressed that repressions did not end the activity of local churches due to the high morale of their members who, in the case of raids and arrests, found other places for services and had new ministers ordained (cf. Wanner 2007). For Nenets converts, these stories illustrated the evil of the state and bravery of the church.

With the arrival of greater religious freedom after the collapse of the Soviet Union, reformers paradoxically faced significant difficulties in maintaining their identity of that of the persecuted. To maintain the earlier zeal, they increasingly glorified their past and cherished the memory of the martyrs.[12] After twenty-odd years hiding, in the late 1980s, Kryuchkov came out and began to rally churches with this purpose in mind. His main message was that the new freedom was only a temporary break and that new persecutions were coming soon. For example, this idea was reflected in the union journal *Herald of Truth* from 1994: "We shall be beaten and persecuted. Let our children see it. That will be their best Sunday school. . . . Let our children become new people. . . . Let them see that we are cocrucified with Christ and that every day we are given over to death for the sake of holiness and piety" (quoted in *Tserkov'* 2008, 201). In 2004, I met the Russian missionary Viktor in Ivan's tundra camp. With obvious regret in his voice, Viktor said that in recent years, the younger generation, who had not experienced persecution, lacked the zeal of the older believers. In his assessment, new persecutions were unavoidable—and even necessary—because the world hated the true church.

Attacks against evangelicals (what the Russian media called "totalitarian sects") intensified in the late 1990s and have increased since. The signs of hatred of the "outsiders" became ever more frequent after the passing of restrictive laws on religion in 1997 and 2016, which made registration requirements once again more stringent (Witte 1999; Zagrebina 2017).[13] Behind the menaces and attacks were both state agents and vigilantes. In the Nenets areas or nearby, there had been many incidents. In Syoyakha, a Nenets village in Yamal, a senior official of the administration threatened to burn down the prayer house of the local Baptists in 1999 (Neverov 1999).

In 2003, some "ill-wishers," as Baptists called them, did burn down a prayer house in Arkhangelsk (Severo-Zapadnoe 2004, 11; cf. Bur'yanov 2007, 80). In 2009, the local authorities in Naryan-Mar tried to force a Baptist congregation to register its prayer hall that was accommodated in a private house. Although the Vorkuta church had not seen direct assaults, parallels between the Soviet and current period were increasingly a topic for discussions there, which echoed a mixture of fear and expectation. Some older Russian members, probably hoping for the zeal of the old times to be restored, seemed to be ever more thrilled about new tensions.

Pavel's Mission at the End of Space-Time

In the imagination of the Unregistered Baptists, the world is like a huge litmus paper. It suffices to look around and see that the world has reached a level of moral degradation characteristic of the end times. The Baptists know the future from the Book of Revelations, which, as Ivan repeatedly said to me, is very difficult reading. Those who were more knowledgeable, like Kryuchkov, presented the present time as "the period of the Laodicean church," being the last among seven periods depicted in the Book of Revelations and known for its wealth and corruption (Bourdeaux 1968, 34; *Bratskiy listok* 2001, 556; Prokhorov 2013, 126–27; *Tserkov'* 2008, 57, 166). Like other "everyday millenarians," as Robbins characterizes this kind of Christian, the signs of the end can be seen everywhere, even if people have different ideas about the imminence of the arrival of Christ (2001b; 2020, 105–27). For those who evangelize and keep looking for signs in the North, the area is a source of great excitement, as it shows that the time is drawing near.

During fieldwork, I was referred to various signs of the end. Some of them were visible and recognizable for the chosen but not for outsiders. I shall give one example. While staying in Yegor's camp one afternoon in December (*ngarka pevdya*, "the great darkness"), I admired a vista of the sky with an intense patch of light above the cloudy horizon and took a photo of it (see fig. 3.3). The next day, Pavel and a young Russian preacher, Zhenya, from Karelia, arrived in the church vehicle. They had seen the same vista while on their way to the camp, but their interpretation was eschatological, not aesthetic, like mine. Immediately after arriving, Zhenya asked Yegor whether he had seen the unusual light in the sky the day before. Yegor, who must have been used to similar vistas, confirmed—although not too eagerly—that he had seen "something unusual." Zhenya explained that this

Figure 3.3. The sign of the second coming of Christ, December 2006.

was a sign of the approaching Second Coming. He argued that the North was an especially good place to witness it, referring to Job (37:22): "Fair weather cometh out of the north: with God is terrible majesty." Effortlessly, Zhenya moved to a related topic, speaking of other signs such as Satan marking people through various forms of registration, using his number 666,[14] and gathering them through the Internet: "As it is written, before the end, Satan gathers people together. This has happened via the Internet." Yegor and other Nenets were listening to him, nodding from time to time, not probably having much of a clue how the Internet enabled the evil work. However, they did not question what Zhenya was saying. It just *had to* make sense.

The world was trying to do everything possible to hinder those who were fulfilling Jesus's command for mission. During the conversation at his kitchen table, Pavel had given me another example of how evil forces tried to hold the true church back from doing its "saving work." He said that recently the authorities had restricted missionaries' access to the border zone by enlarging it from five to twenty kilometers in the Nenets Region. "This was done with the purpose of stopping us," he claimed. It was difficult to get permission to enter the restricted area with the motive of evangelism. It turned out to be not only a bureaucratic matter but also a part of the decisive cosmological fight, as the devil was making obstacles for the preachers to reach the literal end of the earth.

Although freedom is a source of worries for the church, it is also praised. Freedom offers a unique chance to enact the command of Jesus and take God's Word to the ends of earth, including to "the lost tribes" (Kirsch 1997). Missionary work is imagined to be sowing of the Word in a straightforward manner through a public performance of one's faith or witnessing (*svidetel'stvo*), conversations, singing, and handing out literature. In remote Arctic areas, several options for mission trips are used to alleviate the "friction of terrain" (Scott 2009, 43) hindering or slowing movement on the swampy, rocky, or snowy landscape. Missionaries cruise along rivers on boats or over vast plains on all-terrain vehicles or snowmobiles. As described in the opening scene of the introduction, Pavel used to move across the tundra on a big-wheeled Trekol, which gave him access to the remotest reindeer-herding camps that outsiders rarely visited. Another option was to dispatch families from the south to live with the reindeer herders for short periods, motivated by a conviction that they were making history on the edge of space and time with and for God.

Pavel had described how on one of his first mission journeys to the tundra in 1997, he was standing on the shore of the Arctic Ocean and predicted, "The gospel will be preached to the ends of the earth [*do kraya zemli*], and then comes the end." God's promise was unfolding in front of his eyes, or as he explained, "These were historical days when the all-powerful God fulfilled his Word. The ends of the earth were only ten meters from us." By the conquest of this ultimate periphery, the missionary, empowered by the situation, was participating in the completion of God's plan, being full of his Spirit. Pavel showed his true source of inspiration, the Acts of the Apostles, quoting, "But you will receive power when the Holy Spirit comes on you; and you will be my witnesses in Jerusalem, and in all Judea and Samaria, and to the ends of the earth" (1:8).

He followed a geography of apocalypses that entailed not only space but also time: only after the Gospel reaches the margins of the world will

Figure 3.4. Missionaries driving their all-terrain vehicle on the coast of the Arctic Ocean, August 2002.
A herder shows the safe passage across the river to the next campsite.

the second coming of Christ be possible. The space and time become interchangeable. Although nobody can know exactly where the time edge lay, his use of "meters" sounded more like "days" or "years."

In many ways, Baptists' focus at the ends of the earth is not random. Instead of preaching in Vorkuta or other densely inhabited areas, Pavel and other missionaries from Nadym, Syoyakha, and Novyi Port tried to reach as remote areas as possible (like Soviet workers in search of "the romance of the frontier," Ssorin-Chaikov 2003, 20). Their trajectories of movement themselves followed the logic of the conquest of the ends. Pavel made trips to the shore of the Arctic Ocean, Vaigach Island, and even as far as the northern parts of the Gyda and Yamal Peninsula. The latter was a rhetorical favorite: nearly every report from there that I heard or read about referred to the etymology of "Yamal" (*ya mal*), meaning "land's end" in Nenets. It was as if God had already made his imprint into non-Christians' language to prepare them for his eschatological plans (see Vallikivi 2014b for more details; cf. White 2020, 111–14).

In the perceptions of the Baptists, the margins were described as the most difficult areas to conquer because they were full of evil forces and devil worshippers. Among Russian Baptists and Nenets, there was a certain convergence (or rather, an inversion) between the ideas about the edges. In Nenets cosmology, gods live on the farthest edges of the known world (Golovnev 2000b, 232). The most powerful sacred areas are the northernmost part of the Yamal Peninsula (Yamal Khekhe Salya, "cape of the spirit of the land's end"), Belyi Island (Ser Ngo, "white island"), the end of the Ural Mountains (Khadam Pe, "Grandmother's mountain"), and Vaigach Island. Ivan told me that to evangelize in these places, a particularly powerful minister full of the Holy Spirit is needed. Pavel was convinced that he was qualified for the job. In 2003, he made two trips to Varnek on the isle of Vaigach, a village where almost a hundred Nenets lived by fishing and hunting for the Karataika enterprise "Friendship of Peoples."

To demonstrate the idea about the dangers on the edge and the perception of the missionary role in conquering it, I present here a longer extract from Pavel's mission notes circulated in the church:

> We stopped at the first houses. From the darkness, somber human figures began to appear. How will we be met? I told brother Pyotr: "Go out and get acquainted." He replied, "I am scared." There is a lot to be afraid of. The land here has been drenched with human blood to satiety. They drink, shoot, and cut. . . . Some are drunk. Another asks for a bottle. We try to extinguish any flare of aggression with kind words and courteous addresses. It is time to reveal to the people who we are and why we are here. Someone immediately goes away. The village headman asks to give him at least a hundred gram [of vodka]. He was driven by this thirst to the extent that he pestered us even during nighttime. We went to his home. It was filthy inside, with worn oilcloth on the table and unwashed dishes. In another room, the TV was playing at full volume and screening horrors. Here they do not have Russian TV but have only video players with which people feed their souls greedily. The aged parents of the headman took pleasure in this "cultural" program. We asked to lower the volume of the idol.
>
> They put on the table locally caught herring that were tiny and very salty. Tea was poured out into dirty mugs. Praying ourselves, we ate and drank. From another room an old, disheveled woman with the appearance of a fairy-tale monster came out to us. My [Russian] brethren, Pyotr and Oleg, sat under great strain. The son of the headman told us about his wife and the power she had. She could walk on the water, go into the sea up to her neck and after

coming out [of the water], remain absolutely dry, and so on. We had an internal prayer accompanying us, and God was all the time with us. Glory to Him!

We were invited to the clubhouse. . . . They were united by the hopelessness of life on the island. We said that the Gospel will be preached to the ends of the earth—also to them. Somebody asked, "What do you think of our sanctuaries?" We answered with Paul's words to the Ephesians [which ones was not explained].

The next day brought a powerful snowstorm and hurricane winds. This though did not prevent us from going from one house to another and from working for the Lord. Some said, "Our gods raised the snowstorm against you." We said, "No, instead the almighty God sent the blizzard to make all of you stay at home and not let you go out for a hunt and thus to let everybody hear God's Word. When we are done, the snowstorm will stop and we shall leave." We evangelized for two days. Most islanders heeded God's Word with interest. Some wanted to ask forgiveness from God, and we helped them to pray. Opponents were few. It was evident that spiritual wickedness in high places was tied by God's power through the prayers of all the saints [*po molitvam vsekh svyatykh*].

Referring immodestly to his fearlessness in his conquest of faraway places full of evil forces and possessed people, Pavel implicitly framed himself as an apostle working at the end of time. When listening to him or reading his text, my impression was that he saw himself as a tool who enjoyed his own instrumentality. It is evident in the language he uses. As one can see, he writes *in* biblical language. The random character of using quotations like "the abomination of desolation" (Matthew 24:15) or "spiritual wickedness in high places," referring to "pagan" sanctuaries (Ephesians 6:12) illustrates how his language was to be taken as a reenactment of divine words and early apostolic travels, only to be enhanced by elements of prophecy ("the snowstorm will stop") and confirmations of God's supremacy over Satan.

There are many parallels between Christian and Communist ideologies. As briefly discussed above, one of them is the idea of mastery (*osvoyenie*) of the remotest areas and an implicit attempt at the mastery of time in its linear logic (see chap. 1). When analyzing the socialist temporality of the Stalinist period, Nikolai Ssorin-Chaikov (2006, 359), referring to Boris Groys and some others, has argued that socialist acceleration of time and frantic rushing on the surface actually froze time. A similar tension, although somewhat inverted, can be found in the Baptist ideas of temporality. They preach a complete change to outsiders while claiming that true Christians are not entangled with the changing world. Pavel claimed that the true church would always remain the *same*, "early apostolic" by its nature (despite all the material innovations they used eagerly). None of the other self-proclaimed Christian churches, including the ones of the registered union, could remain the same because they were hopelessly enmeshed in the changing world.

As the early apostolic church had stopped short before the work was finished, the task of finishing the job fell on the shoulders of a small community of the saved people in the land where the Antichrist had recently hit the hardest. As a visiting missionary from Petrozavodsk once said in a sermon, "Lord gave the honor to reach the last edge to our brotherhood," making clear that they were unique in their endeavor to conquer the land's edge. Pavel, with his fellow ministers, was there in a frenzied haste to save others. They shared with Communists a sense of being the chosen ones as well as a model of abrupt rupture on the axis of the past and future; they read the present through the lens of a utopian future and operated on an assumption of speeding up the fulfilment of cosmic promises and being involved in conquering space to its ends (cf. Etkind 2005; Halfin 2002; Ssorin-Chaikov 2006).

Pavel seemed to be always in a rush, usually not staying longer than half a day at one place when on a mission trip in the tundra—to talk and not so much to listen. His, like others' accounts of mission trips, reveal the quality of hurrying across the tundra, overcoming constant obstacles on the way. Often, they entail fewer descriptions of witnessing and conversion (which tend to be short and standardized), and instead entail long descriptions of all kinds of perilous situations on the road, including mechanical problems with their all-terrain vehicle, satellite navigation, and threats from administrators.

Missionaries needed to hurry up, because there were many who had not heard of Jesus yet, as they said. Pavel had become one among many enthusiastic collectors of unevangelized Indigenous peoples. In his statements, he was talking of saving *the* Nenets people or *the* Komi people. Converting a few members from one ethnic group seemed to fulfill Jesus's "missionary command." It was important that *all* nations be proselytized (Matthew 24:14; see also Kryuchkov 2000, 4). Evangelizing all ethnic groups living in the ex–Soviet Union alone appeared to shift the balance and remove the last obstacles for the big final events. (As in Roman times, all nations seemed to live in "the known world.") From the pulpit, senior Baptists expressed their joy that in their brotherhood there were over fifty nationalities (unquestioned objective entities) from all over the ex–Soviet Union, including twenty-odd "small peoples" (i.e., northern minorities), which allowed them to call their union proudly "a multinational family" or "multinational brotherhood."

Every year plans were made for a year ahead at the highest administrative level in the International Union. As in Soviet state practices, the element of fulfilling a plan and reporting even bigger numbers was a ritual part of annual conferences. Some report makers remark apologetically that numbers were not important; however, they then go on to provide a detailed account of how many trips, how many kilometers, and how many converts they have achieved during the last year. A conversion of somebody from a "new" ethnic group causes particular excitement, as it enables one more "nation" to be added on the list (see, e.g., *Bratskiy listok* 2001, 501–2, 513, 532; Ural'skoe 1999, 34; Yamalo-Nenetskiy 1998). The Unregistered Baptists were full of confidence that they were moving toward a completion encompassing all peoples and areas.

However, the variety of ethnic groups speaking in different languages complicate everyday practical arrangements for the missionaries, especially in terms of effective communication. Notably, learning local languages and translating scriptures have no significance whatsoever in the agenda of the Unregistered Baptists. Pavel was neither learning Nenets nor organizing translations of scriptures into it. Rather, he relied on the Russian version of the Bible, local interpreters, and especially schooling of the young Nenets generation in Russian.[15] In everyday workings, Russian was seen to have an instrumental value for communicative purposes. And yet, as they said, this was already planned by God, as there was nothing left to chance—a concept that does not exist among evangelicals—on the path of historical progression. To confirm this, Pavel told me that the creation of the Soviet Union was in God's plan exactly for the purpose of bringing more believers together who could communicate with one another in the same language, implicitly working in the paradigm of the Russian (Slavic) messianic mission. Like other Ukrainians, Pavel knew that Russian had advantages in "godly matters" over Ukrainian or Nenets (cf. Wanner 2007, 26).[16]

Unwittingly, Unregistered Baptists had been forming a new myth of Holy Russia in which events of cosmic importance were unfolding. According to Kryuchkov, it was not a coincidence that the true and incorruptible church emerged in the Soviet Union. Satan had chosen "one-sixth of the earth" for its battlefield by establishing the first atheist state in the world there. God responded by carrying out a great spiritual awakening of the true church in 1961 (Kryuchkov 2008, 210). Kryuchkov argued that members started building the church from scratch, as they had nobody to take a tradition over, or as he put it, "The style of the brotherhood's spiritual life we took from the texts of early apostles, gospel, and the Holy Spirit" (*Tserkov'* 2008, 201). Like so many other accounts of seceded Christian groups, they seemed to need both an element of continuity for the sake of universal claims and an element of a fresh beginning for the sake of emotional intensity and purity. They thus acted as restorers of the divine will and revolutionaries at the same time (cf. Humphrey 2014).

Paradoxically, despite or because of their outworldliness, Baptists believed that they were making world history. Even if everything happened because God had planned it, in one or another way, the deeds of "his people" were silently assumed to make a difference because God was dwelling in them. For example, one did not need to propose any sociological explanations for the collapse of the Soviet Union. Pavel and others argued that on Christmas Day 1991, the day Mikhail Gorbachev resigned, "atheism capitulated" because loving Christ came to annihilate the devil's work after the blood of the saints had been spilled and a multitude of prayers were said for thirty years (see also *Tserkov'* 2008, 24, 196–97).

In their sermons, the Unregistered Baptist pastors called upon church members to stay "strangers" to the world. As noted above, although Soviet Baptists were a product of the political predicament in which they lived, most of them, and especially the Unregistered Baptists, never discussed politics publicly, as they were not supposed to delve (*vnikat'*) into it. The only exceptions to this political disengagement occurred when policy infringed on religious freedom, a constitutional right that existed only on paper in Soviet times. As a rule, the Unregistered Baptist pastors preached against participating in contemporary "sodomite culture" (*sodomskaya kul'tura*) in which the main channels for Satan's work were television, theater, cinema, concerts, sport events, and, eventually, the Internet. Russian Registered Baptists were known to increasingly participate in these sins.

Unregistered Baptists claimed that they were just different from the others. This distinction was partly visible, or as visiting missionary Viktor told me, "Outer appearances mirrored what was inside the person." Inner purity had to be achieved through disciplined behavior—in everyday life, Christians were expected to follow certain standards of conduct, outlook, and cleanliness. Some rules could be traced directly back to certain scriptural passages; others were said to correspond to the spirit (*po dukhu*). Unlike Registered Baptists, Unregistered Baptists avoided wearing mainstream

Figure 3.5. Pavel gives a sermon in a Nenets *mya*, July 2002.

or "fashionable" clothes. This concerned women more than men. Nenets women fitted easily with these demands, as they never wore trousers or used makeup anyway. Their colorful dresses were accepted as part of their "culture." Men were far less restricted in their outlook. While some younger Nenets men wore fake designer jeans and jackets bought at the Vorkuta market, others wore secondhand suits, often too big for men of such small stature. Most other aspects of "sodomite culture," like secular forms of entertainment and mass media, were largely out of reach for tundra dwellers.

Even more serious accusations toward the Registered Baptists were that they practiced marriage with unbelievers (i.e., non-Baptists), divorce, and birth control. Supposedly, this never happened in the unregistered brotherhood that functioned as an endogamous unit. If one did not follow the rules, other church members were quick to point to one's misconduct, which sometimes led to excommunication or to not being accepted as a church member in the first place. For instance, birth control was not used among the Independents until very recently. Yet I heard of a Nenets woman who had a contraceptive device and because of that she was not baptized before she had it removed (cf. Prokhorov 2013, 350–51). This was revealed only at the last moment in a closed session before baptism in which missionaries systematically inquired about the candidate's readiness for the act. Although this was a doctor's prescription that she dutifully fulfilled, in the imagination of the Baptists, this was yet another example of Satan's cunning and evil work.

At first glance, there are some striking parallels between the Unregistered Baptists and the Independent Nenets, especially in the way they have delineated the borders of their communities and managed to avoid the state interfering in their lives. The issue of registration is especially relevant in this context. Yet, in detail, these two societies can hardly be more dissimilar. The main difference lies in the way ideological borders are drawn and managed. While the Independent Nenets were literally living outside state institutions to pursue the lifestyle of their ancestors and engaged with Russians cautiously, Baptists were defined by their militant opposition to the state. Most of them were employed and schooled by the state. Practically, Unregistered Baptists were living as separated from the world as possible. Wanner (2007, 77) has stressed the importance of homes for unregistered believers, "The home not only became a sacred place, but it also functioned as something of a total institution, the hub of social, leisure, often professional, and, of course, spiritual needs." They actively sought to stay outside the state as an enclave by claiming to have become a transcendent collective body, believing that their souls were outside the world and their bodies were in the world, which was declared to be close to its end. The antagonism of great forces defined the scene. In everyday life, the state and corrupt "moderns," including the state-sanctioned Registered Baptists, enabled the Unregistered Baptists to sustain their identity.

Unlike the Unregistered Baptists of the Soviet era, the Independent Nenets did not develop an elaborate ideology of withdrawing from the state. They did not have disciplined practices for group formation, nor did they entertain the discourse of strict exclusion and inclusion (cf. Humphrey 2001). Independent families, autonomous in their decisions (on the scale of Independents versus others), were living as they found best. Indeed, they regarded outsiders as a danger and the Russian (*lutsa*) world as highly pol-luted but in a very different and negotiable way. The borders were perme-able (as I have discussed in the introduction and chapter 1). Nenets argued that there were risks and these were a part of their life. With the coming of Christianity in the late 1990s and the early 2000s, there were new rules that introduced unnegotiable convictions and fixed forms of belonging. One re-sult of this was the segregation of the community into different groups in entirely new ways.

4

DESTRUCTIVE PERSUASION

Materiality, Mediation, and Language
in the Mission Encounter

In this chapter, which forms a bridge between the first and second part of the book, I shall move to the issues of materiality, mediation, and language, by discussing cases of burning Nenets' sacred objects and the discourse that surrounds these actions. The acts of destruction are key events in the mission encounter, as they radically change relations among those involved, cutting earlier relations and forming new ones. The destruction of sacred objects—which Nenets call *khekheq* and Russians call *idoly*—as well as what precedes and follows constitutes a complex event. It is defined by dynamic and tense social relations between people, their words, and things and by different ontological assumptions. Do these things entail any power? If yes, are they dangerous? Which agents are linked to them? What are the consequences of destroying or leaving them behind? Who is responsible for these consequences? The questions and the answers to these questions are not the same for Christians, non-Christians, and those in-between, as they see *things* differently.

As Raymond Corbey (2003) admits, analyzing the destruction of images on the colonial Christian frontier is difficult because of the nature of the sources we have. By studying examples from diverse missionary contexts from various parts of the world, he tries to make sense of whose actions these actually were, and he insists that these were not only the missionaries' but also, often mainly, Natives' initiatives. Corbey (10) writes that "these various forms of agency were so entangled that it is difficult to sort them out, all the more so because of the scarcity, brevity and biased nature of source material, which usually has to be culled, with much effort, from missionary archives and periodicals" (cf. Rutherford 2006). Obviously, the past is a distant land, and it remains a challenge to make sense of the ontological and moral ambivalences inherent in these events, especially when mediated by written sources.

While agreeing with Corbey that these are instances of "entangled agency," I suggest that we need a more nuanced understanding of these destructive events where words, feelings, and actions form multifaceted and dynamic relations with one another. Part of the complexity lies with different ideas about what things and signs do in the world. Discussing the case of the Dutch Calvinist missionization among the Sumbanese of Indonesia, Keane (1998, 2007, 2008b) shows that missionaries accuse the "fetishists" of being captives of the material objects to which they falsely attribute agency. This claim has its roots in the history of Christianity. Keane argues that agency and materiality have been central issues in the Euro-American semiotic ideologies since at least the Reformation. As a result, in Western modernity, people are pulled "between the desire for transcendence and abstraction on the one hand, and the persistence of material embodiment and social embeddedness on the other. Transcendence . . . haunts modernity in three unrealizable desires: for a self freed of its body, for meanings freed of semiotic mediation, and for agency freed of the press of other people" (Keane 2006, 309–10). Indeed, these desires are never fully realized, as I shall demonstrate below, despite the press of missionaries to free Nenets' consciousness from the press of the material, the demonic, and the neighboring "pagans." Although the Baptists and Pentecostals in Arctic Russia would agree with Calvinists in Indonesia that the source of idolatry is found in one's heart, they yet argue that if a person *owns* an idol, the devil may act merely through the relationship of belonging, without the person knowing about it. In a way, Russian Protestants seem to share some ontological presuppositions with Nenets: for both, the *khekheq* and their "masters" have real power and a quality of distributedness over persons and things. Unlike the Dutch Calvinists, the Baptist and Pentecostal missionaries in the Russian North thus rely simultaneously on the modern ideology of representationalism and the nonmodern ideology of entangled persons and things.

How do Russian missionaries see things and words and their relationship to one another? While touring around in the Nenets tundra, the Baptist missionaries, in their first encounters, focus their attention equally on telling the "good news" and denouncing idols. They present a short account from Adam's and Eve's fall to the last judgment. After this "act of witnessing," Nenets are asked two questions. The first is whether the person believes in God, and the second is whether the person possesses any idols. Receiving usually positive answers to both questions, the evangelists claim that there is an incompatibility between the two and declare that God wants them to destroy the idols, usually referring to 1 Corinthians 5:11.[1] In the tundra, missionaries find "true" idols, which they imagine to be especially dangerous because people are said to regard these as their gods in a literal sense. Therefore, idol destruction is central to the systematic cutting of earlier relationships with spirits but also with kin, friends, and one's own past. As we shall see, the question remains whether such cutting is final.

The Baptists are not the only ones who argue along these lines. In this chapter, I shall also focus on the second most influential mission in the region, which is the Pentecostals. Although in many respects they are not as strict as the Unregistered Baptists, they are "literalists" who take seriously the biblical claims on the dangerousness of idols. Both Baptists and Pentecostals maintain that the hearts and minds of Nenets are transformed after they burn their idols, having thus been freed from the shackles of the devil. In an important sense, a person's consciousness is seen to be bound or located "physically" in the idols (cf. Vagramenko 2017a, 157; 2018, 79). As a result, in accusations of idolatry, an ideology of automatic efficacy dominates, which goes against the idea of conscious choices based on the right Christian values.[2] If a person possesses idols and is thus possessed by these, the person cannot exercise free will as a Christian.

Before discussing the current situation, let me outline the historical background. Since the nineteenth century, in some areas even earlier, Nenets began to integrate Orthodox icons known as *lutsa khekheq* ("Russian spirits") into their rituals, in which they are treated similarly to their other *khekheq*. Nowadays, Protestant missionaries hostile to any such images must decide what to do with these items, as these are part of ancient disputes over correct understandings on God and materiality. This is a continuation of an old fight over the issue of how the divine can be made present and how the demonic can be made absent, and what kind of objects (if any) can mediate sensuous engagement with the divine (e.g., in sacraments). Protestants have extensively accused one another of idolatry from the very beginning. For instance, Martin Luther cast out the image-smashers from Wittenberg, accusing them of attributing too much power to the images and warning them not to become idolatrous about the absence of material items (Eire 1986, 2; Michalski 1993; van Asselt 2007, 300).

Developing further the Byzantine iconodulic theology, Russia became a place where sacred images (and relics, holy water, incense, neck crosses, etc.) famously came to occupy the heart of not only religious but also various everyday practices (Hanganu 2010; Paxson 2005; Shevzov 2004; Tarasov 2002). Partly as a reaction to Eastern Christian image worship, Russian (many of them ethnic Ukrainian) Protestants grew into a significant religious movement in the nineteenth century. They argued that only the Word of God (accessible above all in the form of scriptures) is a true medium that acts directly on the heart and consciousness of a human being. From this stance, they addressed their accusations toward the Orthodox who venerated icons, wore crosses, and otherwise "wrongly" invested materiality with spiritual efficacy. Yet, for the Orthodox, Protestants seemed preposterous in their claims of being able to communicate directly with God, denying the possibility of representation of God who became incarnated (H. Coleman 2005; Michalski 1993; cf. Keane 2014).

As in the days of the Reformation, different strands of Russian Protestants today fiercely accuse one another of idolatry, even if they have very few ritual objects except for the printed or written letter. This accusation of idolatry comes from Paul's claims of investing too much power in certain objects that should be invested into serving God instead (and recall Luther's stance mentioned above). Furthermore, this is exacerbated by modernity. The Unregistered Baptists believe that other self-claimed Christians are engaged in idolatry, as they visit sports events, concerts, and the cinema, where worldly people do not hide the fact that they go to admire "their idols." No member of the Unregistered Baptist church can have a TV set at home without being accused of idolatry. It is not only screened violence and obscenities that prove their case but also more fundamental "misrecognitions" in the matter of the right kind of mediation of the divine and the proper use of human senses (as exemplified in chap. 3).

As the Bible is silent on the new technologies, Russian Baptists resort to Paul's teachings on the value of hearing and seeing. Like many times earlier in the history of Christianity, the concepts of visual and aural are perceived to be key issues here (Michalski 1993, 185). They emphasize that faith comes by hearing, referring to Romans 10:17.[3] This takes place at the expense of the visual or tactile, which is distrusted. An Unregistered Baptist writes in *Herald of Truth* that even screening the film *Jesus* is not acceptable, as that "would close access to the true, saving blessed Word" (Chukhontsev 2000, 14). In the Baptists' view, God rendered himself into flesh and after leaving his flesh; his work was made available through the readable text (i.e., the Bible, which is the source of valued orality, be it live or cassette sermons, hymn singing, poem reading, or artistic declamations in front of the congregation). "The repudiation of the material is a selective process," as Matthew Engelke (2007, 224) has aptly commented. His own study shows how the members of the Friday Masowe Church in Zimbabwe reject the reading of the Bible to avoid any material mediation with God and let instead the Word of God to be experienced "live and direct" through the Holy Spirit.

The Russian missionaries in the tundra, however, admit that the Word of God requires some kind of visual media. Using elected humans, God had his word written down, which is replicated, usually on paper, in endless forms. Pavel encouraged Nenets converts to draw colorful banners with quotes from the Bible and decorate their tents with these (cf. Prokhorov 2013, 177). This was to imitate otherwise plain prayer houses in the city where behind the pulpit one could read a quotation, "God is love," on a bare wall. In many Nenets families, I saw these banners hanging inside the tent (see fig. 4.1), in the pure part where earlier people used to have a shelf with Orthodox icons hanging above a box with a few Nenets sacred items (or a pike head attached to the central pole protecting against curses, see chap. 5). The "dead matter" was replaced by the "living word," as missionaries put it.

One had to believe that the banner with biblical words was not an idol but the *viva vox* of God. In a sense, the text was supposed to render its material carrier invisible in a way comparable to how early ascetics did not look *at* the icon but looked *past* it (Buchli 2010, 192). However, there is a danger of misjudgment lurking in the background. This is especially the case with illiterate Nenets for whom the letters on the banners remain inscrutable. The same goes for the Bible that one carries along but is unable to read, while possibly assuming that the physical Bible offers divine protection.[4] And even if one can read, it is not self-evident how to ensure the correct interpretation: How does fearing God, which one reads about on the banner, differ from fearing the demons against which missionaries warn in their harangues? As I shall demonstrate below, not only readable words but also spoken words may become vulnerable to misrecognition.

In the evangelicals' view, reading words in the Bible or hearing these retold by someone is the only valid form for recognizing idolatry and dealing with the idolaters. Viktor, a visiting Baptist missionary, characterized idolatry among the Nenets to me like this: "This is exactly as written in

Figure 4.1. Interior of a tent in the Polar Urals, March 2007.
The text on the banner translates to: "And I will give them one heart, and one way, that they may fear me for ever, for the good of them, and of their children after them (Jeremiah 32:39)."

the Bible—they make everyday items from wood, but from the leftover they make their idols. So do the Nenets. From the skins they make clothes and tent covers, and from the rest they make these dolls." Like all authoritative statements, Viktor's claim has its source in the Bible, in this case from Isaiah 44:15–17, which was frequently used in the very first disputes among Reformers (Karlstadt, Hätzer, and other so-called fanatics) but also later in Russia. As the art historian Sergiusz Michalski (1993, 165) writes, "Another Russian sectarian related that after reading Isaiah 44 about the idols made of wood he decided to destroy his idols by burning them to gain some warmth—since this is implied by the Bible passage," and later he adds, "This passage served as an incentive for an iconoclastic act committed by a Russian Biblicist Stundist as late as 1900" (188). Present-day Russian Baptists who are descendants of the Stundists (Shtundists) allow us to move Michalski's observation to the early twenty-first century.

Russian evangelicals are leading a third wave of iconoclasm in the High North today after the Russian Orthodox and the Soviets. From the 1820s onward, Orthodox missionaries destroyed Nenets spirit statues in the landscape and family spirit effigies in the herders' camps for a hundred years. This was initiated by archimandrite Veniamin who led a baptismal campaign by burning and smashing wooden and stone spirit statues (with the help of freshly baptized but hesitant Nenets) at dozens of sacred sites scattered all over the tundra west to the Urals, including the most important one on Vaigach Island, called Vesako ("the old man"). Veniamin (1851, 25, 53; 1855, 117) boasts in the reports that he erected wooden "life-giving crosses of Christ" in these places instead. Other priests followed this example.[5]

In the late 1920s and 1930s, at the height of the anti-religious campaign, Soviet activists confiscated shamanic paraphernalia and other sacred items in reindeer herders' camps (Glavatskaya 2006; Yadne 2006, 388; see also Skachkov 1934; Suslov 1931).[6] From the Nenets' point of view, these incidents, among others, produced stories about deaths of Communists whose attempts to destroy sacred items backfired—sometimes literally. I was told about a Communist who fired at a female spirit effigy, *myad pukhutsya*, but the bullet bounced back into his forehead. In the later Soviet period, the devastation was continued by extractive industry, which destroyed numerous sacred sites (CAFF 2004; Kharyuchi 2013, 98–101; Murashko 2004). In addition, many items ended up in museums, taken there by atheist agitators, ethnographers, archaeologists, and others. As one Nenets explained to me, when a famous seven-headed *syadei* of Vaigach Island was taken to Moscow by an expedition, the people who held it fell severely ill (cf. Kharyuchi 2013, 104; Murashko 2004, 11). Museums containing sacred items became places that were perceived to be loaded with spiritual agency. Against the intentionality of the Soviet regime, local people saw these places as either dangerous or attractive places to visit (Liarskaya 2011).[7]

The early twenty-first century offers a continuation to this account of destruction and displacement. While cultural activists and scholars are seeking to give legal protection to Indigenous sacred sites (Dudeck et al. 2017; Fedorova 2004; Kharyuchi 2001, 2004, 2013, 2018; Kharyuchi and Lipatova 1999; Murashko 2004), Protestant missionaries see the existence of these objects as a direct challenge to God's will.[8] Baptists and Pentecostals claim that among the Indigenous Siberians they have discovered the existence of idolatry in its quintessential or prototypical form as it is described in the Bible. Nenets' household god images correspond to the scriptural "graven images" (see, e.g., Exodus 20:3–6). They argue that, knowingly or unknowingly, the "pagan" Nenets follow Satan, whose ambition is to obtain and destroy as many souls as he can—this link must be severed.

As mentioned, one of the first questions the missionaries ask in their initial visit to a reindeer herders' camp is whether the family has any idols. Consider the following case that Baptist Pavel conveys in a mission report (that was circulated in the congregation) on his first visit to a Yamb-To family in 1997:

> We go to the Laptanders, where the head of the family plays the role of a shaman. . . . There is a teacher-trainee called Rita. She is also a Nenets but she does not want to hear anything about God. All people there regard themselves as believers but in their own way [*no po-svoyemu*]. We explained to them the difference between the living God and the idols. We said that serving idols is serving evil spirits [*sluzhenie idolam est' sluzhenie zlym dukham*]. I asked whether they had any idols. The old ones [*stariki*] exchanged glances, and the hostess pointed her hand toward the pillows in the tent. The Lord enabled us to persuade them [*Gospod' pozvolil ubedit' ikh*] that the idols needed to be burned. The hostess already wanted to throw them in the stove, but then the teacher interfered and started to dissuade and to resist. The old ones began to waver. Another conversation took place, this time with the teacher. We planned to leave but the hostess stopped us, asking that I prayed that she could burn the idols in my presence. Rita yet talked them into [*ugovorila ikh*] saving the clothes of the idols for the museum. The idols went into the fire. Thank God! The hosts asked forgiveness from God.

Missionaries believed that in idols, as in humans, the inner core entails the essence. This explains why Pavel did not object too much to Rita's wish to protect what she regarded to be Nenets cultural heritage (cf. Liarskaya 2011, 19). Pavel let her take the rags from around spirit figures for the museum, as he did not see these being as relevant in Satan's workings. He failed to understand that in the Nenets' perception, the clothes set aside for the museum were powerful and as much a part of the relationality with spirits as the core of wood or stone. The whole "body" of the spirit, with its history, could not be divided into the core and a mere decorative outward addition. Furthermore, some *khekheq* had no "hard" core at all but only cloth or reindeer skin in layers. Together, these constitute both the biography and the essence of the figure (see below).[9]

In general, I was surprised how little open resistance there was to the missionaries who came to destroy Nenets spirit figures. In many cases (like the one of the Laptanders' above) people burned their spirit effigies before they understood even the basics of the new message. They had just accepted that it was better to get rid of these items, but in a seemingly safe way through the missionaries.[10] However, next I describe a case in which there is considerable resistance to burning of *khekheq*, even if it appears to be a voluntary act.

Baptists and Pentecostals Competing for Idolaters' Souls

I did not see the burning of *khekheq* among the Baptists. Yet I saw one such event in the family being converted by Pentecostal missionaries, which I am going to describe and discuss in detail below. Although there are a few differences between the Baptist and Pentecostal take on idolatry, their main thrust and logic of divine and demonic agency *and* the dichotomous understanding of materiality and immateriality are similar. The case below also allows me to discuss the relations between Pentecostals and Baptists in the region as well and the choices of a denomination by potential converts.

In 2007, I lived for four months in a Ural Nenets family that was then being converted to Pentecostalism. Iriko and Pukhutsya, both nearly sixty years old, had four daughters and four sons, between eighteen and thirty-three. They were all living with their parents, except for the eldest daughter, who had married a Khanty reindeer herder. Others had not found partners. Tikynye, the second-oldest daughter, told me that this was because they lived most of the time on their own, and their parents did not visit other camps often enough to be able to arrange marriages. Recently, the prospect of finding a partner had become even slimmer, as they were Pentecostals and most others in the vicinity were Baptists or non-Christians. The borders of potential kin were being redrawn, and each person was compelled to make a careful choice whether to become a Baptist, a Pentecostal, or to remain outside these bounded groups. There were only two other Pentecostal Nenets families, although they were not eligible for marriage, as they belonged to the same patrilineage.[11] For part of the year, three Pentecostal families migrated close to one another. Sometimes they conducted lay services together; at other times, pastors from Vorkuta paid a visit to their small tundra flock.

One day before the end of my year-long fieldwork, my host mother, Pukhutsya, called me aside and gave me two items. She asked me not to tell the other members of her family, except for her daughter Tikynye, who was standing nearby. One gift was an old Orthodox neck cross that belonged

Figure 4.2. Pukhutsya and Iriko, May 2007.

to her husband, Iriko. He had inherited it from his great-grandfather, who probably received it from the Kolva Orthodox church in the nineteenth century. Iriko had not worn this cross around his neck for a couple of years from the time when the Pentecostal and Baptist missionaries had started to visit his family and when his daughters had been baptized in 2005. The other item Pukhutsya gave me was a curious piece of reindeer skin called a *tarq pad*. This is a special piece of fur that can be found, on rare occasions, on the inner side of the skin on the neck of a reindeer. When a reindeer is slaughtered and *tarq pad* is discovered, people say that this family has reindeer luck (*ty yab*) and that this luck will bring an increase in the number of reindeer in the herd. This luck is seen as the favor of spirits and gods (Khomich 1977, 14–15; see also Niglas 1997a).

Iriko and Pukhutsya's family luck was visible. They were called rein-deer-rich (*tesavei, teta*) people and were seen as a success story, especially considering that many in the Urals lived in poverty. Their herd had grown to more than a thousand animals from a few reindeer when Pukhutsya and Iriko married thirty-five years earlier. They had managed to restore the herd to nearly the size of their grandparents' day before the animals were confiscated by the Vorkuta sovkhoz and Gulag administration following the *mandalada* uprising of 1943. After the collapse of the Soviet state, Iriko's family herd began to grow quickly. In his perception, this growth did not come so much from the altered economic situation and changes in legal en-vironment but from care, luck, and a good relationship with the spirits. He told me that "there are many reindeer dedicated to god in my herd. These are reindeer I do not harness. Because of that, god pastures my reindeer well." By "god" he meant Pe Mal Khada, "Grandmother of the Mountains' End," to whom he had dedicated twenty-five of his reindeer. These majes-tic, castrated bulls were called *myenarui*.[12] They were neither harnessed for everyday work nor earmarked, nor were their antlers cut, as they had to be kept in peace, because they were the nodal points between guardian spirits and the rest of the herd (Kostikov 1930a; Niglas 1997a). Until recently, Iriko made sacrifices to Pe Mal Khada by strangling a reindeer and feeding the *khekheq* with sacrificial blood and vodka. He asked Pe Mal Khada for pro-tection from malevolent agents like diseases and Russians.

In summer 2007, when we arrived at the northernmost camp (*mya-dyrma*) of Iriko's family, we could see on the horizon in the northeast three mountains called Ngutos Pe, Khadam Pe and Khabtam Pe. These formed the very end of the Ngarka Pe ("big stones")—that is, the Ural Mountains. Iriko explained that in the middle, the mountain of Khadam Pe, was god-dess Pe Mal Khada's tent, north to this stood her sledge for tent poles (*ngu-tos*), and south to it was a lying bull reindeer (*khabt*). This sacred site is one of the major Nenets sacred sites, next to those in Vaigach and northernmost Yamal.[13] When visiting these or other sacred mountains, men took stones from there for the inner part of the *khekheq*.[14] In return, they sacrificed a reindeer and left some offering like a cloth ribbon or coin alongside the reindeer head and skin. The stones were clothed and they grew more vo-luminous every time when the deity was sewn a new miniature overcoat or a scarf was added as an offering. In Iriko's family, the *khekheq* were Pe Mal Khada and her children. While Iriko had inherited three *khekheq* from his father, he had made himself two for which he collected stones from an-other sacred mountain in the Urals called Yabtam Pe. These, he said, were also daughters of Pe Mal Khada. Until recently, most people had similar anthropomorphic figures on their sacred sledges (*khekhengan*)[15] but most, like Iriko, had gotten rid of theirs. As I was told, Pe Mal Khada helped with giving birth, healed, guarded reindeer, and kept away disease. One could see that among Iriko's *khekheq*, Pe Mal Khada was most powerful, as she had the thickest layer of coats on her. In other words, all the sacred items were charged with power over the life of their existence: they had their bi-ographies, which people considered when solving their problems. In Nenets thinking, a *khekhe* is thus not a mere representation of a deity—it *is* a deity, or rather, it is a relational being tied to the sacred site of its origin, being a *person in person*.

When Pukhutsya handed the cross and the *tarq pad* to me, I hesitated and said that they should stay in the family. Nevertheless, she insisted that I should take them, saying, "One day, these things would be thrown into the fire anyway." She spoke of this as if it was unavoidable. Yet she did not sound too emotional. I suppose that one reason why these things had re-mained untouched so far was that these were not exactly "graven images" and thus not idols proper.

Three months earlier, I had witnessed why some *things* caused an acute problem. Vladislav, a Pentecostal missionary from Vorkuta, made Iriko burn spirit figures that were kept in his sacred sledge. A few years earlier another Pentecostal evangelist convinced Pukhutsya to set on fire her female helper, *myad pukhutsya*. This is the most "public" effigy, as it is kept in the tent sepa-rately from the other *khekheq* of the sacred sledge because of her relationship with the dangerous female power (Golovnev 2000b). Tikynye recalled that a big quarrel took place between her parents after that event. This is why Pukhutsya did not want me to tell Iriko that she had given these things away. It was a sensitive matter. While Tikynye and the other children were eager to burn the "devils" (*yavolq*), the parents were troubled and obstinate, Iriko more so than Pukhutsya. After some resistance, they relented.

Iriko, like some other Nenets, had visited the Vorkuta Baptist church once or twice in the early 1990s but did not stick with it. Toward the end of the 1990s, the family had gained contact with a Russian Pentecostal man who was working in the Sovetskiy Village Council near Vorkuta. He was helping the family and other paperless herders apply for documents and welfare payments. From that time, Iriko's daughters paid occasional visits to a Pentecostal church in Vorkuta. However, it was only after they met Pentecostal pastor Vladislav that the girls became more seriously engaged with Christianity. As a result, in 2005, Vladislav baptized Iriko's daughters Tikynye, Netyu, and Maranga. An energetic man in his early forties, he ran a Pentecostal congregation next to the Vorkuta railway station while also working as a railway inspector. His congregation was one of seven Pentecostal churches of the same union in the Vorkuta area.[16]

I met Vladislav in April 2007 in his home church during a service, in the basement of a block of flats. Iriko's children took me there. During the service, his style of reading scriptures and sermonizing reminded me of what I had seen among the Baptists. Pentecostals and Baptists shared not only the basic evangelical tenets but also many other features (e.g., the same hymnals), which was partly the result of their shared Soviet history (Wanner 2007, 76). But when Vladislav started to sing a song to a pop tune with a guitar in front of a dozen congregants, it hit me that I had arrived in a rather different aesthetic space. The singing was followed by a prayer in which (unlike the Baptists) all the congregants were speaking in Russian simultaneously, and many of them were waving their raised hands. Vladislav led the rhythm of the prayer, gradually speeding up at the beginning and slowing down at the end in order that everybody could start and finish together. Although mostly I could understand Vladislav in a sea of chaotic sounds, as he was louder than the others, at one moment his inspired Russian transformed into glossolalia. Many Russian congregants followed, which reflected that they also had the Holy Spirit acting in them.

Vladislav was welcoming and encouraged me to do research in his church. He invited me to witness the rite of baptism of Iriko's three sons (Pubta, Kolye, and Tyakalyu, who made a slower start compared to their sisters), which was to take place the next day (see fig. 4.3). Unlike Baptists, who baptized only in natural sites, the Pentecostal rite took place in a small pool in the church building. This time, though, in April, the parents were not invited to be baptized because they had not yet burned their idols. A week after the baptism of the three brothers, Vladislav had planned to visit Iriko's family in the tundra to "prepare" others for water baptism as well. Basically, he came to convince Iriko and Pukhutsya to burn the spirit effigies kept in the family. Like Baptists, so the Pentecostals considered idol destruction as an essential step before one could become a member of the

Figure 4.3. Before a baptism in the pool of the Pentecostal prayer house, April 2007.
From the right: Pubta, Kolye, Tyakalyu, and three Russian candidates; the texts on the wall
translate to "He that believeth and is baptized shall be saved. Mark 16:16" and "Except a man
be born of water and of the Spirit, he cannot enter into the kingdom of God. John 3:5."

church. Two months later, in early June 2007, I attended the baptisms of
Iriko and Pukhutsya (see fig. 4.4). With them was their son Ngelya, who
had thought about joining the Baptists but finally decided to become a Pentecostal.

Despite the children's rhetoric of commitment, one could not see
much Christian activities in the tundra camp. There was almost never any
prayer. After Vladislav had visited and convinced them that this was the
most important thing to do, Iriko's children prayed a few times, but after
a couple of days, they stopped. Occasionally, Maranga and Netyu took

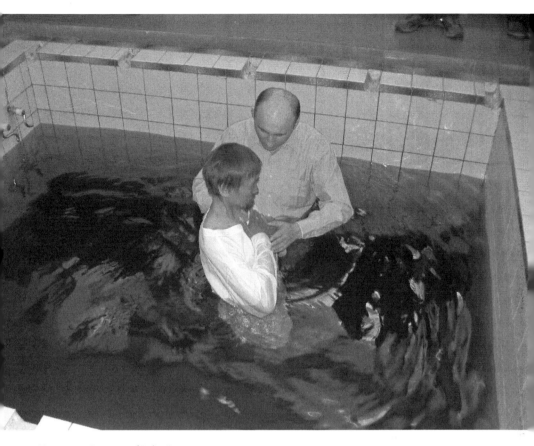

Figure 4.4. Baptism of Iriko, June 2007.

out their Bibles and with great effort read a few words from it. They used to say it was a pity that Baptist Pavel had not sent anybody to their tent to teach them. Not denying the importance of Bible reading, Vladislav argued that illiteracy was not too big an obstacle, as the Holy Spirit gave wisdom and instructions directly. While Pavel would have agreed with Vladislav about God's power in this respect, he regarded reading very important. Furthermore, there was a vital difference between the two in terms of creating dispositions: most Baptists were expected to carry out public acts of praise of God or confession under the pastor's guidance, while the Pentecostals did this all simultaneously, erasing the position of a controller during services. Baptists were expected to scrutinize their inner life, to talk about it: they were more successful in introducing the mechanisms for bringing one's—to use Charles Taylor's (1989, 184) words—"thoughts and feelings into line with the grace-given dispositions of praise and gratitude to God."

Pentecostals and Baptists were competing against each other in the tundra. Baptists had not only preceded everybody else in their white vehicle—*serako masina*, much admired by Nenets and Russians alike; however, missionaries avoided open admiration, as this would have qualified as a fetishistic act—preaching at places that remained inaccessible for the Pentecostals, but they had also dispatched young female teachers to instruct new Nenets believers. On the same day, when Vladislav was about to arrive, a Nenets family from a nearby camp came to visit Iriko. With them on the sledges sat Ira and Sveta, two Baptist female teachers from Ukraine in their early twenties. They were staying in the camp of illiterate Venu, who had been Baptist for nearly three years. They taught Venu and his family the Bible and Russian, reading, singing, and playing the accordion.

The guests entered Iriko's tent. After an hour without much chatting, the Ukrainian girls proposed reading the Gospel. Although, as Baptists and Pentecostals stress, Paul had in his letters explicitly forbidden women from carrying out a service ("Let your women keep silence in the churches . . . ," 1 Corinthians 14:34; see also 1 Timothy 2:12), they could still read and explain scriptures, if they were not doing it in a prayer house or as a formal service. Before taking the floor, they asked Venu, the only Baptist man present, to pray, to invoke the presence of the Holy Spirit. Then Ira started to read aloud a passage from the Bible. Her voice was full of victorious pathos, somewhat reminiscent of the scenes of Soviet pioneers performing inspired declamation (cf. Lane 1981).

Soon Vladislav arrived. Tyakalyu had met him in the railway station on a reindeer sledge. On a three-hour journey, Vladislav was clad in an extra-large thick reindeer fur costume specially sewn for him by Iriko's daughters. He entered the tent and took off his coat, under which he had his dark blue railway inspector's uniform with epaulets, adding an aura of authority to him. While the Baptist girls had a reserved and serious look, Vladislav was relaxed and busy cracking jokes.[17] Behind the table, while eating, he took a boiled reindeer head in his hand and imitated Hamlet's monologue (see fig. 4.5). The Baptist girls smiled with embarrassment. Venu's wife, Lina, giggled. Feeling uncomfortable, the young Baptist instructors proposed to go back to Venu's camp.

Figure 4.5. Pentecostal missionary Vladislav performing Hamlet's monologue with a reindeer head in the presence of Baptist converts, April 2007.

In the competition between Baptists and Pentecostals for the souls, without any doubt, Baptists had been far more successful. Even Iriko's children, especially Maranga and Ngelya, could not decide where to place their loyalty (partly because of not wanting to restrict their options for marriage). From time to time, they visited the Baptist prayer house as well. Surprisingly, Vladislav did not object to this. Instead, he encouraged Iriko's family to carry out services together with Baptist families in the tundra because, as he said, "There is only one God. . . . I do not like when people draw lines between churches. There are Lutherans, Baptists, Pentecostals . . . but I am a Christian." He liked to present himself as "tolerant." As we have seen, Baptist Pavel was different, claiming that the Pentecostals were fake Christians possessed by Satan. So, after Pavel learned that Iriko's daughters had been baptized by the Pentecostals, he stopped visiting Iriko's tent, which disappointed the children. Pavel was convinced that there was no place for "ecumenism," and he preferred to evangelize the remaining non-Christian population instead, who lived out of the Pentecostals' reach.

The Persuasion of Iriko

After the Baptists had left, the floor was fully Vladislav's. He filled the tent with fast speech, inspired prayers, and melodic songs from the hymnal *The Song of Resurrection*, which the female Baptists had used a few hours earlier. Like most Pentecostals, for Vladislav the force of the word lies in abundance and repetition (cf. S. Coleman 2006, 169). Vladislav related how he received his Spirit baptism and how powerful he felt when the power of the word came upon him. (From the Baptists' point of view, not controlling what one was uttering was an unambiguous sign of demonic possession.) He recommended being open and waiting for a similar event in the lives of those who we were listening to him.

Vladislav then started a prayer in which he asked Jesus to increase and strengthen faith in Iriko's family members and to give them Spirit baptism and the ability to speak in tongues. This time the foreign tongues did not engulf Vladislav, as often happened in the city. He finished his freely arranged prayer with a fixed rhythmic Lord's Prayer (*Otche Nash*, "Our Father"). Until then, Iriko and others were muttering in a low voice; they now joined in louder, as they all knew the prayer by heart. In the background, the voices of Nenets echoed the minister's words. As there are rarely individual prayers performed in front of others, Iriko's family was less fluent in this genre than the Baptists, who were supposed to speak to God one by one. Yet I never heard any of the Pentecostal Nenets performing glossolalia either. Tikynye once admitted that a Russian sister taught it to her, but she gave it up, as she was not able "to get it right" (cf. Bialecki 2018, 212).

In the following sections, I analyze extended extracts of the speech event that took place after the service when Vladislav addressed Iriko. I suggest that the "act of persuasion" at the center took place in an inherent gap between different understandings about language, agency, and authority.

> VLADISLAV: [Iriko's Russian-style passport name and patronymic, which is the polite form of address among Russians], I want to say something to you.
>
> IRIKO: Yes?

VLADISLAV: I would like you to take the decision to serve God forever. For that, as I told you already, there is something you should abandon and burn.

IRIKO: Yes.

VLADISLAV: Do you agree with that?

IRIKO: I agree.

VLADISLAV: [Iriko's Russian-style name], perhaps we could do it tomorrow morning in the presence of others? [There were Iriko's family, his brother, his nephew, and me.]

IRIKO: Okay.

VLADISLAV: Burn the idols?

IRIKO: Let's burn them.

VLADISLAV: You agree with that?

IRIKO: I agree.

VLADISLAV: [Iriko's Russian-style name], I just want to say that they give nothing to one's life. To keep them just as a memory from ancestors does not make sense because behind the idols stand the devils. These idols were once dedicated to another spirit. These spirits acted in the lives of those who believed in them. And they still do. I was convinced of that. I was in the Yamal Region among the people who worship [*poklonyayutsya*] devils. And these devils simply keep these people in fear. They appear to them in visible forms [*v vidimykh obrazakh*]. Get rid of . . . burn the idols, and the devils will not have power over you! So we could dedicate our lives to Jesus Christ. God is only one. The devils take the form of God, but they are not God; they are subject [*podvlastnye*] to him. When Jesus came, there were the devils. The devils were trembling and pleaded [Vladislav speaks in a fearful voice]: "Jesus, don't chase us away!" They are subject to God. Jesus said, "Devils, go out!" They went out. We shall have the same power when we burn these idols. God give us good weather! [Vladislav looks upward.] God, I ask you that tomorrow. . . . [He interrupts his prayer and looks again toward Iriko.] Is this the last devil that is kept in this tent? It has to be given a good kick on the bottom [*pinok pod zad*] and then you can serve Christ with the whole family. Do you agree with me from your heart?

IRIKO: [With a dry and subdued voice] Yes, I agree indeed.

VLADISLAV: I want this to be done. Then I shall empty my heart and start to teach you water baptism and tell you. . . . In fact, you should have been baptized first. Not the boys but you first. But now I have to make you into a Christian last. They [sons] have long been free. They do not hold to these [idols]. These are not valuable to them. If they are valuable to you, I want you to change these values. Let Christ be valuable. He gives life, but the devils take life away. I saw how they [in Yamal] worship their idols; some even do not return to the tundra [camp] but die of the vodka right there. I saw them lying like that [Vladislav bending forward and letting his arms hang at his sides] on sledges without consciousness after this idolatry. Because they drank blood at the beginning and vodka after. And that is it. They die at a very early age. Suddenly they start to drown at a very early age. They hang themselves. These are the devils' deeds [Iriko loudly: "The devils' deeds indeed!"]. God gives life, Satan takes it away. This is why today Satan has to be chased out from this family. And these fetishes [*fetishi*], these idols [*idoly*] need to be discarded. It is good that you sincerely [*iskrenno*] said it. [Iriko: "Yes."] And do not change your mind by [tomorrow] morning! [Iriko: "Okay!"] In the morning we shall do it.

Iriko was *apparently* agreeing, although one could sense that he was disturbed by the whole event. Iriko's children confirmed my impression but added that it was good that their father was made to accept the situation and disengage from the devils.[18] After Vladislav had left, Iriko demonstrated his disagreement with much of what Vladislav had said, as I witnessed. Evidently, he was far from becoming a disbeliever in idols. Vladislav could not understand that, for Iriko, this had never been an issue of believing *in* the idols in a sense of loyalty as the concept of belief in that sense was not relevant in Nenets' relations with the spirits (see chap. 6).

Although Vladislav talked of the need for changing values, it was not a matter of mere reevaluation. He placed individual consciousness at the heart of the fight between good and evil, which took place simultaneously on a cosmic and individual scale. Essentially, he argued that these doll-like objects displaced a "pagan's" mind. The herders lying without consciousness after drinking reindeer blood and vodka were deprived of their own agency, hence their wretchedness and the absence of God's protection. Along similar lines, the devils became visible, and people were living with fear because of their displaced minds. All this proved that these "pagans" were not free human subjects but distributed persons, hybrids of human substance and dangerous objects—a possible but illicit combination. The problem was that it was the wrong kind of distributedness. According to Pentecostal logic, one should become a hybrid of human and divine through Spirit baptism. However, this can take place only when the God-given freedom and agency proper to humans has been restored by stopping their enslavement to the devil.

After this near-monologic dialogue, Vladislav and all the others knelt on reindeer skins. Only Iriko remained seated on an empty bottle crate, just moving his lips from time to time, his look wandering back and forth from Vladislav to the floorboards. Others closed their eyes, and Vladislav started an inspired prayer, which was basically a continuation of his sermon, containing now direct addresses to God:

My Lord, I wish that you would keep a final victory over the devils in these places. [With an increasingly more inspired and emotional voice.] Because you are the only God. We started to believe in you [*uverovali*], there is no other God. But Satan, Lord, is a fallen angel. He always wanted to imitate you, he always wanted to be higher than you. But he never succeeded in this because he did not resurrect in Christ and did not show us the eternal life. He only takes from us health and life, and does all kinds of dirty tricks, destroying whole nations [*narody*]. O Lord, suppress their freedom! O Lord, suppress their intellect [*razum*]! Tie them up, my God! Destroy all kinds of occultism [*okkul'tizm*]! Today, we want to finish it in this territory, in this family. O Lord, I ask you, my Lord, give us tomorrow a possibility, any possibility—as you, God are the governor of all nature—give us a chance to make the fire and burn these idols in the fire. If we cannot do this in the fire, we shall do it right in this stove [kneeling just in front of the stove, his eyes closed, Vladislav points his finger toward the stove]. For that there would be a final defeat over the forces of the evil which until now have held back the consciousness [*soznanie*] of the people living here. O Lord, let the final freedom appear! O Lord! And your victory, Lord. Because Jesus was always a winner and is still today, and in eternity and nobody else, except you, defeated death, the power of death. Only you, My Lord! We are very grateful to you for this truth. That you, Lord, you did not hide from us [still eyes closed, he takes up his Bible and waves it in his hand] but revealed to us that we are eternal. But it depends only from our decision, which eternity we go into, the eternity with the devils, with Satan in the fire of hell or the eternity in the kingdom with you.

The next morning before the idol burning was to take place, Vladislav gave a long sermon (see fig. 4.6). Somewhat surprisingly, it was not about idolatry but about love. Eventually, he covered the core narrative of Christianity, from the Creation to the Last Day, in one hour. He spoke quickly. Iriko's family, who (except for Pukhutsya) had a relatively good command of everyday Russian, struggled to understand. Vladislav used unfamiliar words and examples from the unknown world—for instance, he referred to TV programs, the heroism of the "Great Patriotic War" (Second World War), or the projects of industrialization (the kind of worldly references that Baptist missionaries almost never made).

Although much of the content must have slipped away, Iriko repeated Vladislav's words from time to time. Vladislav was obviously taking these as an act of agreeing. What the missionary did not realize was that repeating was a part of Nenets communication pragmatics, something that many did as a sign of respect or participation. I observed several instances when people were *as if* agreeing by repeating missionaries' words. Evangelists took this for propositional and not for performative value, which potentially had a subversive component to it. (I shall return to this point

Figure 4.6. Vladislav gives a sermon, April 2007.
From the left: Iriko, Tyakalyu, Vladislav, Iriko's nephew, Pubta, Maranga.

in chap. 5, where I discuss how silence replaces repetition in the mission encounter.)

Inspired by 1 John 4, Vladislav's sermon was on three kinds of love: *eros*, *philia*, and *agape*. He explained that these were Greek words, and Iriko nodded, although this (including the word *Greek*) was Greek to him. At no moment did Vladislav seem to be troubled by whether the message reached the listeners. For Iriko and others, it was almost as if he was speaking in tongues. Lying on his back on reindeer hides, he was explaining. He said that while *eros* was restricted to marriage and having children, *philia* (in his version, *philio*) is a love between children and parents or between brothers and friends, which often triggers heroic deeds and even deaths. His example was from a Soviet propaganda text: "Especially during the Great Patriotic War, many heroes quickly emerged. People went and covered the embrasures with their bodies for the sake of their comrades." He claimed that while this kind of self-sacrifice was good, this love was not yet perfect. The main problem with it was that it was based on the wrong ideas of exchange. He said that this love "depends on reciprocity—I love him because he loves me. This is so. But when he starts to do evil to me, my *philio* towards him fades away." Vladislav then arrived at the culmination of his sermon by explaining that *agape* was the perfect love that was taught in the Bible. "This is the love," he went on, "that does not depend on whether you do good to me or not." It is a "free gift" that denies one's profane self, the idea that flourishes in "ethicised salvation religion," as Jonathan Parry (1986, 467–68) has characterized it (cf. Laidlaw 2000). Vladislav went on arguing that God loved people because they were his creation:

> Like a potter loves his pots because he has spent his time on these pots. Yes? [Iriko: "Yes."] You love your reindeer because you have spent [*tratili*] half of your life on them. [Iriko: "Yes."] You have spent your best years on the reindeer. [Iriko: "Yes."] God loves us because He has spent time on us. He created man and he loves him. This is not a love of that kind. But you know, I say, if your reindeer constantly attacked and wounded you, you would probably slaughter these reindeer, you would not be bothered to herd them anymore. You would slaughter rebellious reindeer. [Iriko listens more attentively and stops his absent-minded affirmatives; Pubta says that "there are indeed this kind of reindeer . . ." but Vladislav does not let Pubta finish his sentence.] If pots rebelled against a potter—forgive me for this kind of comparison—a potter would destroy these. True? This is with everything like that. If God had had not love, *agape*, but some other [kind of love], he would have judged [*sudit'*] us long time ago. [Iriko: "Yes."] Look, every person violates the divine order [*ustanovlenie Bozhie*]. God in this world [Iriko: "In this world . . ."] has created his system, how it all has to go. Humans are constantly interfering in his system and keep corrupting everything [Iriko: "Corrupting."]. He [man] tries with his intellect [Iriko: "Intellect"] to prove that he is cleverer than him [God].

Vladislav then continued with a description of a TV documentary on how the Soviets were diverting rivers against their natural flow and thus destroyed nature in Central Asia and elsewhere. He brought an example closer to home, flirting with the concerns of the herders. These words triggered Iriko's attention. Vladislav said:

> In your place, you see what man has done in your own pastures. God has created the beautiful tundra, grass, greenery for reindeer that you could herd them; that the life would flourish here; that the animal kingdom were here. He

[man] started in this tundra to lay out gas pipelines and other things. As if God were not hurt that somebody is defiling [*poganit*] his creation [Iriko loudly: "Yes, defiles!"]. I think God should have long ago put on trial [*posudit'sya*] us. [Iriko: "Yes."] But God possesses a perfect love, *agape*, loving despite the fact that evil things have been done to him. And in the Bible it is written: "For God so loved the world, that He gave his only begotten Son, that whosoever believeth in Him should not perish, but have everlasting life" [John 3:16]. Man was constantly at enmity with God and said: "There is no God" [Vladislav shaking his fist vigorously upward, acting a grotesque militant atheist]. In the Communist times we were made to say that there is no God [Iriko loudly: "Yes, there is no God!"]. And many people lost their faith in God because in his place were set other gods. "Believe in Lenin, believe in Communism [Iriko: "In Communism"], believe in the bright future, there is no God." And only this reason alone, that he was not acknowledged, God should have wiped all humanity from the Earth.

A gas company was currently constructing a pipeline and dirt road right through Iriko's summer pastures (see map 2). He had repeatedly complained to Vladislav that the gas people were destroying his pastures and that he was hopeful Vladislav would do something about it. However, the pastor recommended praying to God whose love and tolerance was almost unlimited. His message was that, in the end, the environmental or economic concerns were futile compared to those of the heart and mind.

Vladislav finished his sermon with a detailed description of what was going to happen at the end of time. "They make the fire under. . . . One cannot escape it. This goes on forever. One wants to drink. It is very hot. One cannot escape it. The major torment is going on in here [he put his finger on his head]. The person realizes, 'I could have avoided it. I was offered salvation.'"

Vladislav had come to replace the fire of hell in the afterlife with the fire of idols here and now. Iriko's reading of the evolving situation was something else, though.

Burning Iriko's Sacred Images

Iriko was affirming, repeating, and quoting lots of what the missionary said. The sequence was only interrupted after the morning service ended, when Vladislav proposed, "Let us go to search for the idols where you have hidden them. Do they fit in the stove?" As usual, Iriko started affirmatively, saying absentmindedly, "They fit in the stove." Then he quickly corrected himself, "No, not in the stove. They need to be . . . in the field." As I understood later from children's comments, Iriko feared that burning them in

Figure 4.7. Iriko's *khekheq* and Orthodox icons known as *lutsa khekheq*, April 2007.

the stove would have caused the rage of the deities to come to his tenthold, his family (cf. Vagramenko 2014, 203–4). The fire spirit (*tu yerv, tu khada*) is known to safeguard the people in the tent. It could be fed with sacrificial meat and vodka but not with *khekheq* (see fig. 4.7).

Everybody moved out of the tent. Vladislav gathered some firewood while Iriko went with Pukhutsya and Netyu to the sacred sledge behind the tent and took out a box with Nenets *khekheq* and another thin box with Orthodox icons (*lutsa khekheq*). Surprisingly, not so much the doll-like Nenets *khekheq* but the icons became a source of tension in subsequent moments.

Vladislav went ahead, carrying willow twigs on a low metal sledge that he pulled after himself with a rope. Every time he stopped and suggested making a fire, Iriko told him resolutely to move further away, until they reached a mountain slope outside the area where reindeer were lassoed. This was apparently to keep the reindeer away from the potential revenge

of the spirits-to-be-rejected. The very same *khekheq* had helped him to increase his herd to such numbers as they were now. There Iriko put the box
with the *khekheq* down. He looked around and asked where the box with
the Orthodox icons was. Vladislav said that he had left them behind, for
these could be given back to the Orthodox Church. Iriko was unyielding
and said, "Of course, they have to be burned!" Pointing at Pukhutsya, he
continued with an irritated voice, "The fool said, 'We need these.' I bought
these in vain. It cost five hundred rubles each." Vladislav was silent.

While Vladislav was not interested in the slightest what the Nenets
spirit effigies were thought to do, because their true nature was explained
in the Bible, the icons seemed to be a different case. Once the box with icons
was brought, he opened it and started to explain:

> Look, this is Jesus, and this is Jesus but their faces are different. There cannot
> be different Jesuses. But these [icons] are in millions and on all of these, Jesus
> is different. That is not right. Who can paint Jesus without having seen him?
> These are contemporary people who painted these. We do not worship icons.
> These are mere pictures [Iriko: "Pictures, of course!"]. This is art. This is why I
> sometimes propose people not to burn these but to give them to the Orthodox
> Church for whom they are valuable. Somebody has worked on all of these. If
> they are valuable for them, let them use these. At the same time, the harm lies
> in the fact that people begin to kiss them.

Vladislav took an icon and kissed it while saying the word "kiss" to
demonstrate how people misplace their devotion on a *mere* material item.
Unlike with the idols, there was nothing "behind" these things. Iriko, who
was bending over the shoulder of squatting Vladislav, took another icon in
his hand, said another affirmative "yes," and kissed the icon as well.

> VLADISLAV: They begin to worship these. [Iriko: "During Easter. . . ."; Vladislav
> does not let him finish.] This is not right. God says not to worship any
> images [*izobrazheniya*]. This is an image. Do not worship it. But when it
> hangs as a picture [*kartina*], then there is no damage. This is why I do not
> teach burning [of icons]. But if you want to get rid of these. . . . They are not
> valuable. Just give these to an Orthodox church. . . they are not valuable.
>
> IRIKO: But we bought these from a shop in the church.
>
> VLADISLAV: Yes, a shop. Furthermore, icons are sold in shops. That is why . . . I
> say that these are not Christian valuables. God is alive. Paint and worship
> are not good for. . . . When one worships pictures and not the living God
> [Iriko: "Yes, the living God!"]. For that reason, do not feel pity for these.
>
> IRIKO: Should they be burned then?
>
> VLADISLAV: As you wish!

After a moment of confusion, Vladislav gave up the idea of returning the icons to their place of origin. He tried to salvage the frames of the icons, inspired probably by Iriko's comment that he had paid money for the pictures in a church shop. Vladislav took it as a matter of rational calculation and an attempt to avoid wasting the investment in the frames as commodities. He proposed to Iriko, "Take out the pictures and put photos of your family in there." Iriko said abruptly that this should not be done. For him, most likely, the magical efficacy of the icons was not only in their image-like representations but also in the objects as wholes (like the *khekheq* with their stones and clothes). Furthermore, placing their own photos in the frames of the Russian *khekheq* would have potentially set their own selves on a dangerous conjuncture of human and spirit worlds. As these *khekheq* are sometimes called *sidyanggq*, meaning "shadows" in Nenets, and as photos are also called *sidyanggq*, this move would have possibly caused a clash of perceptions (more on *sidyanggq* below).[19] Despite Iriko's protests, Vladislav took the icons out of the box, where they were placed above the *khekheq* to be burned all together. Iriko was once more overridden. As soon as the flames covered the box, he left in a hurry (see figs. 4.8 and 4.9).

After Iriko had moved away, Vladislav told me in front of the fire, holding under his arm the salvaged icons, "Thank God! You see how the person had been sinning. Many years he had resisted. His sons were worrying. They were saying that their dad was keeping idols there. Today the person made the last step on his path to God. I am pleased. It is written in the Bible that an idol is nothing in the world. Let this [fire] burn them up! Would it no longer bring misfortune!" Vladislav continued:

> What is remarkable is that it is done on a hill. The Nenets and other northern peoples—not only the northern peoples but [all] oriental peoples—they always worshiped idols on high places. They dedicated them in high places. High places are the best places they could choose for their idols. Today, in these places, these idols are finished. Let us dedicate this hill to our God and to the Lord Jesus Christ. For believing people would visit these places and would praise God, who gives everything so abundantly [he gestured toward the flat snowy tundra below]. That people could enjoy life here. And he gives the eternal life. [He pointed at the icons under his arm.] From these we shall do beautiful frames with photos. These all can be used.

I asked Vladislav whether he still planned to give these pictures to an Orthodox church himself. He replied,

> No, I shall not. I shall simply take out these pictures and put in here [frames] mother's [Pukhutsya] and father's [Iriko] photos. Let them . . . as already they

Figure 4.8. Vladislav saving the Orthodox icons from the fire, April 2007.

have spent money on these frames, let them be used normally [*v normal'nom ispol'zovanie*]. I do not teach burning the icons or smashing them. There is no point in tilting at windmills. You know how it was in Cervantes. One has to fight what is there inside [he pointed his finger at his heart]. But to smash the icons . . . no . . . . In the beginning thinking has to be changed. If you destroy the icons, he would buy the new ones. Thinking has to be changed.

Vladislav did not make the same argument about the Nenets *khekheq*, which the flames had completely engulfed by that time (see fig. 4.9). He did not consider these as replaceable items, nor did he call them "pieces of art" that represented somebody's work. As he had said the previous night, Nenets idols were not good for souvenirs ("a memory from ancestors").

Figure 4.9. Iriko watching his *khekheq* burning, April 2007.

Most importantly, they were not something one could just change an opin-
ion about. They had to be destroyed to effect a physical transformation
in their owners.

From Iriko's perspective, obviously, there were too many asymme-
tries at play (as it must have happened in colonial or mission encounters
so many times before in various parts of the world, see Latour 2010, 2–7;
Masuzawa 2000, 251–52; Pietz 1985). For Iriko, it was difficult to understand
why Vladislav was keen to preserve the icons or dismantle them, because
this would not have changed the fact that these were related to the spirits,
"the Russian spirits." The question was obvious: Why did the Nenets images
have to be destroyed, while the Russian ones did not?

In addition, with the tension over the Orthodox icons, the introduction of the ideology of immateriality threatened to fail. On the one hand, Vladislav seemed to be convinced that there were positive prototypes for the icons (e.g., Jesus, Our Lady) but he insisted that these could not mediate any divine power despite the expectations of those who kiss these (cf. Keane 2014; Luehrmann 2010). On the other hand, because of their link to devils or Satan, he was ready to claim that the idols mediated evil power (cf. Meyer 2010). As the Nenets images could not be reevaluated, they had to be destroyed because they *made* people drink, hang themselves, and drown, independent of people's volition and thoughts. A mere verbal disavowal of the idols and keeping them as souvenirs would not have been enough because they carried in themselves automatic efficacy. Vladislav did not notice Iriko's irritation over why Nenets *khekheq* needed to be burned while Russian *khekheq* did not. Like Baptist missionaries, Vladislav was not interested in how the Nenets economy of the sacred was working.

The whole scene was thus taking place in a gap where the two sides had different understandings, sensibilities, and motives at play. Their intentions never seemed really to match. Vladislav was never quite able—and as we saw, he was not really trying—to control what and with which intentions Iriko was quoting and imitating him. The moment of kissing alongside Iriko's quotations (e.g., "There is no God!") encapsulates the floating quality of the whole dialogic event. Like things, words did not submit themselves to one interpretation. Seemingly overdetermined spoken words like the affirmatives of Iriko were in fact heavily underdetermined, as they eluded control and worked *against* the semantic context that Vladislav was trying to impose. In a way, one can say that Iriko was recycling Vladislav's words while Vladislav was recycling icon frames, both sides departing from their own cosmological and ontological assumptions.

When I later asked Iriko if he was afraid of any consequences, he said, "I do not know what is going to happen." After a pause he said, "Vladislav—not I—wanted to burn them. The spirits will take revenge not on me but on Vladislav. You see, he already got divorced from his wife." Tikynye interrupted, "His wife was a drunkard. That is why he left her." From time to time, the daughters kept on at their father because he had not abandoned his "old ways." After the *khekheq* were burned, a week before Iriko's baptism, I heard him saying to Netyu, "You think that you will go to God after your death. Who will want you over there? This is a deception made up by people. I have not yet seen Jesus. If he sat just next to me here, I would believe then."[20]

For Iriko, this was a matter of visible evidence. I asked him whether he had seen Pe Mal Khada. He replied, "Of course, I have seen her many times in my dreams!" Iriko continued talking about Christians with a burst of irritation, "This is all Communist shit. The Communists will come again. Vladislav is a prick. They all lie. You think that God is here. Where is he?" Tikynye said, "In one's heart." Iriko reacted, "This is all bullshit [*khamban-ziq*]." Netyu interrupted, "I am going to fly to heaven anyway." Iriko replied, "When I see you flying, then I shall really believe in God. But I have not seen it yet." Netyu started to sing an evangelical hymn quietly in Nenets, and at the same time her father continued in an agitated voice, "This is all deceit. The believers are weak. If they were strong, then the pastures would open up more quickly." (It was late spring and because of the deep snow, the reindeer cows with newborn calves were struggling.) After a while, he said (despite having just called Vladislav "Communist"), "I recently dreamed that the Communists would come, and the believers would be imprisoned first. Then my dream stopped." As laid out in chapter 1, the trope of destructive Russians (*lutsaq*) was still very strong.

Another time, Iriko made a remark to his daughters that one did not need the *khekheq* right now, but once one fell ill, then one might need them again. Tikynye, on the other hand, said to me that when they had the idols, they were frequently ailing. She described a case when she had fallen seriously ill. Her father went to Vorkuta and bought a scarf and a bottle of vodka. He poured vodka on the mouth of the effigy of Pe Mal Khada and tied the red scarf around her *khekhe*. I asked whether this helped. Tikynye did not deny that the offering might have helped with her recovery, although she still called it "devil feeding." She also recalled how she and her sisters, in their childhood, secretly took these images (calling these *vandako myu*, "the internals of the cargo sledge") and unwrapped their many layers to see what was inside. They discovered stones in there. At the time of our conversation, these stones were already on the mountain slope blackened in the fire.

Although I never directly asked Iriko about this matter, I think he might have considered it the least disruptive way to disengage from the spirits by leaving the stones in an undisturbed place, "where feet do not tread," as he characterized such areas (cf. Lehtisalo 1924, 116). He seemed to be cautious about the impact of these stones that came from sacred sites and were thus still connected to their spirit masters (like his special reindeer, who belonged to Pe Mal Khada, still sustained a connection with the deity).

Spiritual and Linguistic Dissonance

In general, most Nenets, both Christian and non-Christian, were not ready to engage too much in discussing spirits. This topic did not belong to the realm of verbal discourse (although some people like Iriko or Vata talked about it more freely than others). In the eyes of the devout Yamb-To Baptists, one should not know too much about idolatry; because of that, they told their children virtually nothing about their firsthand experiences with spirits. This kind of talk or knowledge was by its nature an engagement with the spirits. Yegor and others insisted that it was dangerous even to verbalize the names of the spirits, as this was unpleasant to God and attracted Satan's attention (as his "pagan" mother Granny Marina did, see chap. 2). Also, writing about these matters could be damaging, as Yegor once warned me, "Don't you think that those who will read your book may come to believe in these spirits?" By "believing" he did not mean to deny the reality of the spirits or devils but rather to avoid engagement with them, as they were utterly dangerous.

In Yamb-To, the longest conversation on the spirits (or rather "demons") I had was with Ivan, who must have felt that, as an experienced believer, he could give the right biblical explanations on the matter (see chap. 2). Ivan explained to me that, according to the Bible, there were only two options for how the idols could be discarded: by burning or burying them. As digging through the permafrost was too daunting a task, only the first option from this recipe was practiced. Everyone agreed—non-Christians, converts, and missionaries—that the idols could not just be left behind in a campsite. Both Christians and non-Christians argued that they still had power over their owners or that they could cause harm to those who accidentally found them. Yegor's eldest son once explained to me that an idol left behind could be picked up by somebody, and thus that person could become a victim of the idol and the person who left it behind would be responsible.

Both Baptists and Pentecostals were convinced that destruction of the material form was the key to change, as it freed people from the shackles and kept them from returning to Satanism. Baptist Pavel writes in his mission report:

> Sorrow had befallen our brothers here. Nyeteta, the daughter-in-law of Nisya had a psychic breakdown after her first birth-giving in Naryan-Mar, and she was dispatched with a medical helicopter to Vorkuta for recovery. Teta was

accompanying his wife with the child. "Lord, why?" we asked and looked for an answer. The answer could be in the Ural Mountains. While in June staying in the tent of Nyaku, brother by birth of Nisya, we were speaking of the sin of idolatry. In this reindeer-herding family, they had sacred sledges, where they carefully preserved and carried along wooden idols. There were also idols owned [*sobstvennost'yu*] by Nisya, who in the past gave these to the brother for preservation. We asked the older brother [Nisya], "Is not here hidden the source of the misfortunes that struck the family?" He became anxious, asked forgiveness from God, and promised to go to his brother at the first opportunity and to burn the idols. Fasting and praying, we asked God to be merciful to Nyeteta.

Nyeteta was possessed by Satan through her father-in-law's—that is, her husband's family's—possession of the idols. Nobody questioned the personal, "inner" condition of Nyeteta because the mere existence of an idol in the family—even if absent from its usual location in the camp—served as a source of her problems (cf. Vagramenko 2017, 157). Nobody discussed whether she "believed in" or worshipped Satan. From the Baptist perspective, there was no need for that, as her possession was a symptom of her sinful condition, not being really concerned at that moment about the question of whether the sin comes from inside or outside the person (cf. Robbins 2020, 61).

Pavel explained that for Satan, everything was possible in order to hold people back from burning the idols, and that Satan became especially active when he realized that somebody was about to convert. He told me that some Nenets would not convert because they had heard about people who had lost their reindeer after conversion. A specific example he gave me was about a herder who had converted, but afterward could not find any of his reindeer in the communal herd. Despite the missionaries' promise of powerful protection from the Christian God, many were not convinced. One Yamb-To herder told me that soon after an old woman had burned her female spirit effigy, *myad pukhutsya*, she died. Reindeer herders who decide to eliminate their *khekheq* dare not do it by themselves but wait for the missionaries. The idea is to avoid possible retaliation of the angered spirits, and to transfer it onto missionaries.

Missionaries say that the destruction of idols is solely a decision of the reindeer herders and not in the least theirs. They only assist; they never burn the idols themselves with their own hands. As Pavel put it, "I have never even touched any idol in my life. The only thing we do is to reveal the true nature of these idols; it is up to the herders to decide what to do next."

Missionaries whose hands were "clean" insisted (somewhat inconsistently) that it was entirely an outcome of an individual's changed mind and heart (cf. Jorgensen 2005, 454). Yet at times Protestant individualist rhetoric was blurred, as we saw when Nyeteta's mind and heart could not change because her family had not completely severed the link with their idols.

Before moving to Iriko's camp, I briefly lived with another Independent family in the Urals. Vasnyu's family had been Baptists for three years by then. Vasnyu complained that his reindeer had been dying since baptism. He argued that this was because of the overgrazing of the fragile mountain slopes he was pushed to because of the growing density of people and reindeer. When I moved to Iriko's camp, I heard an alternative explanation. Pubta and Tyakalyu said that when deciding to become a Baptist, Vasnyu had left his sacred sledge in the Khadam Pe sacred place, Pe Mal Khada's home.[21] In the following three years, he lost hundreds of his reindeer: he had had over one thousand reindeer but now only a few hundred were left. Pubta gave his theory of severance by saying:

> Look, Vasnyu's *khekheq* took revenge on him. The shadow soul [*sidyangg*] of the *khekhe* still wanders around and causes harm to people. It is like with a person whose shadow soul moves around for forty days after the death. The shadow soul of the *khekhe* does it as well, the one who is left behind and not fed. But if one burns the *khekhe*, its breath-soul [*yindq*] or spirit breath-soul [*khekhe yindq*] [Pubta paused and smiled, I guess realizing that what he had just said coincidentally also meant the "Holy Spirit" in the Christian register of Nenets] will go to heaven as the human breath-soul does. Once in heaven, it cannot do any harm.

Pubta's brother Tyakalyu, who stood next to us, added to this what was behind the sacrificial logic in this particular case: "Look, the one who took care of the reindeer, he is hungry now and comes and takes revenge by eating the reindeer." Pubta added to this, "You see, the spirits of the dead [*khal'myer ngylyekaq*] cooperate with one another. That is why his reindeer are dying."

According to Iriko's sons, just as with any other human or nonhuman person, a *khekhe* has a shadow soul and a breath-soul, the image that copies a living person who consists of three parts: *sidyangg*, *yindq*, and *ngaya* ("body") (cf. Lar 2003, 64; Lehtisalo 1924, 115). In Pubta's and Tyakalyu's view, idols do the same things as recently deceased humans whose shadows wander around for forty days (the number is borrowed from Orthodox Russians or Komi) before they finally move to the hereafter and cease to be overtly dangerous. It also seems that once the idol's breath-soul has gone to the sky through burning, its *sidyangg* would not be able to take revenge. At another time, Tikynye explained to me that spirit figures cannot be stored on a sledge with other items or left alone and not fed over the winter or summer "because the *sidyangg* would then leave the body of the *khekhe*." Although there are many overlapping and contradicting claims about "part-persons"[22] and the names and shapes they come with, what is significant here is that the biggest changes in the lives of human and nonhuman persons alike take place when one or another part is gained or lost.

Furthermore, what escapes missionaries is the nature of temporality and locality of sacred objects and sacred sites. Among Yamal Nenets, as Vera Skvirskaja (2012, 159n4) comments, *khekheq* belong to a sacred place: "Those things that have, in fact, been taken from sacred places in the tundra tend to be considered 'borrowed' and should, ideally, one day be returned" (see also Lehtisalo 1924, 65, 102, 104). Yevladov, on his expedition to the Yamal Peninsula in 1928–29, asked Pudynasi, a Nenets guardian of the Khaen-Sale sacred place, to give him a wooden spirit statue (*syadei*). Pudynasi gave it to him but warned Yevladov that he should return this statue in three years' time and that if he or his son would not be able to do that, then the idol should be burned, as then "the spirit of this *syadei* [*dukh etogo syadaya*] will come to its own place" (Yevladov 1992, 150).[23]

As we see, the burning of items can be an alternative to returning them, as it frees the soul of the *khekhe* who is able to return to its home place. While Christian missionaries took burning idols as total destructions, Nenets could consider it as a phase in a larger cycle.[24] Even if Iriko burned his *khekheq* and had himself baptized—what he saw as Pentecostal Vladislav's acts—he had not necessarily passed the point of no return. As he was not counting on the protection of Jesus, he could only shift the responsibility to Vladislav to avoid possible dire consequences from the spirits. Having destroyed the *khekheq*, which had so far helped him raise his herd as well as protect against all kinds of malevolent agents, including Russians, Iriko could only hope that the relationship with missionaries would not make things worse. In this ongoing mission encounter, finality was obviously not understood in the same way by all sides.

As I have shown above, a mission encounter can produce moments of collision and collusion where different cosmological assumptions and ontological sensibilities meet. While the evangelists argued that the tundra dwellers were "persuaded," Nenets who lived in settlements (like teacher-trainee Rita) were convinced that the missionized tundra dwellers were "coerced" into burning their sacred images (also they hinted that the missionaries were interested only in the reindeer meat that congregants must give to them as a tithe, cf. Kibenko et al. 2017; Vagramenko 2014); the reindeer herders themselves used neither persuasion nor coercion in their explanations. Analytically speaking, I would align myself with the reindeer herders and suggest that, in some cases, "becoming a Christian" is not necessarily best described as a result of "coercion" or "persuasion" but rather a result of a complex interaction in a gap between different understandings about words and agents. It is thus not solely a matter of the intentionality of individual actors but situational relationships that emerge between people, be they missionaries or missionized, converted or nonconverted family members. Iriko and Pukhutsya (unlike their daughters) were not convinced that their lives should be changed in any radical manner. Neither were they actively seeking to be agentive toward their own thoughts and feelings: they did not become subjects in a comparable sense like many converts around them (see chap. 7). And yet, the hope for protection from the powerful Russians (e.g., the gas people, a state farm boss) and relations with their children and neighbors played a vital part in their public acceptance of Christianity. But, like many other elderly people, their acceptance was less enthusiastic and was set against a general background of dislike toward Russians and their projects.

To sum up, both the wider context and particular communicative acts should be taken into account to better understand why people burned their sacred things.[25] First, stories of failures and successes matter. Herders in the tundra observe and discuss the lives of those who burned their sacred objects first. Since missionaries have arrived, the reindeer herds of most converts have grown steadily, especially in the Yamb-To (but remember the case of Vasnyu's family in the Polar Urals), and the number of violent deaths, virtually all alcohol related, has decreased. Many agreed that there was not much to fear from cutting relations with the local spirits, as "the Christian God was more powerful" (cf. Wiget and Balalaeva 2011, 169). Second, the idea of burning or discarding the *khekheq* is not necessarily incommensurable with local practice and cosmology (as we saw in Yevladov's description). In the end, sacred objects could always be replaced. Third, despite the evangelists' claim that destruction is an individual decision of a convert, people might not see those as their own actions but that of the missionary. These images are thus destroyed in a complex communicative situation with its inherent imbalance of authority, verbal power, and assumptions of responsibility. As we shall see in the next chapter, evangelists' verbal intensity and intrusiveness into personal autonomy make Nenets sense their vulnerability.

PART III

SPEAKING AND SILENCE

5

SILENCE AND BINDING WORDS

Silence Acts

Like many other Indigenous groups in the circumpolar regions, Nenets are described as silent or taciturn compared to the non-Natives in the region.[1] Anthropologists have argued that the relative scarcity of verbal interaction among the Siberian aborigines is not "an absence" or "inadequacy" but rather a specific way of being and a cultural form of communication.[2] When starting my field research among Nenets, I quickly realized that the herders' world was far less verbal than the "Russian" towns and villages where, for instance, in prayer houses people address and explain themselves to one another and to God using, in a couple of hours, more words than one can hear in a Nenets tent during several weeks of a lonely spring or autumn migration. And yet at other moments—for instance, when kin arrive—the tent is gradually filled with vivid talk slowly resuming its habitual state of few words and long silences after they leave, occasionally interrupted by loud shouts of men who lasso reindeer or the fire crackling or a snowstorm howling. These sounds take on meanings for those who can hear them as meaningful in the world full of sentient beings, and thus these sounds become voices.

In this chapter, my focus is on how words and silences are challenged in the mission encounter. Yet silence is a relative category, the usage of which depends on social contexts, one's mood, and many other circumstances (Bakhtin 1986, 134; Basso 1970; Bauman 1983; Braithwaite 1990; Enfield and Sidnell 2022; Jaworski 1993; Tannen and Saville-Troike 1985). This category is shaped by local theories of language and personhood, which includes assumptions of what words and silences can do in the world. Furthermore, it is a matter of ethics—that is, how people evaluate their and others' words and in which circumstances silences can be broken or words imposed. In the tundra, as in many other places, lots of things go without saying. It can be habitus-related silence (taken for granted as "the universe of the undiscussed," Bourdieu 1977, 168) or it can be a lack of need to say out loud or an explicit restraint (e.g., avoidance of uttering names of persons, spirits, diseases, etc.). Indeed, especially for an outsider, it is often hard to determine whether silence means that something is unsayable because this something is not there to be said or is there but is not usually put into words because this something does not belong to the verbal realm, or something is actively avoided. The question is when silence is revelation, concealment, or self-defense or all of them at the same time.[3] And because of the intense ambiguity of silence, people can interpret the same silence differently, especially when it involves people from different cultural worlds.

As we have seen in the previous chapter, there is a clash between Russian and Nenets communication styles—their language ideologies are different and, in some aspects, incompatible, as in the case of addressing, persuading, or repeating. I suggest that in certain contexts, Nenets take words as binding and silence as protecting. They do not see silence necessarily as an absence but a constitutive part of life in the tundra, sometimes an essential means of self-protection against binding words and unwanted relations (as a Western Apache said to Keith Basso [1970, 217], "it is right to give up on words" in ambiguous social situations). This has significant bearing on the outcomes of mission encounters. While some non-Christians avoid talking to missionaries to resist conversion, most Christians avoid speaking of what is unpleasant to God in order not to lose his grace. Importantly, in both wordscapes, speech and silence are seen as shaping relations between humans and spirit agents. Sometimes the rules are rather straightforward. Nenets parents tell their children not to be noisy when it is dark outside (Nenyang 1997, 228; see also Lehtisalo 1924, 117–18; Laptander 2020a, 55–56) and not to shout out in the winter forest to hear whose voice echoes louder, as this is said to attract the attention of malevolent spirits (Golovnev 1995, 320–21).[4] In converted families, keeping silence in similar contexts may be justified with the idea that any playful noise is unpleasant to the Christian deity, who expects from his subjects the obedient following of rules with full seriousness and restraint.

In the eyes of Nenets old-timers, evangelical converts look, or rather sound, noisy, like most *lutsaq* (cf. Fienup-Riordan 1991; Wiget and Balalaeva 2011, 173). Yet this is not a mere noise, as it is potentially dangerous. Words have a power to create undesirable relationships: they affect existing

Figure 5.1. Ural Nenets searching for wood material in the forest tundra, April 2007.

understandings of sociality and personhood but also go against underlying values, such as autonomy, respect, and dignity. In the eyes of the Baptists, the loud moments in the old-timers' life is taken as a noise. Missionaries argue that the babble, laughter, songs, and curses of the so-called pagans lead them to eternal damnation. Although Nenets converts struggle with the new kind of verbality, as I shall show in chapter 6, they see it as a fundamental value and skill. Baptist Yegor agreed by saying that as a "pagan" he had been disorderly and noisy, and that other nonconverts still are. For him, speaking in a right manner had become living his life meaningfully. In his eyes, Christian talk and song is productive and protective. It can also be emotionally rewarding, as what young Vera once characterized as "an exciting life out in the city where people can talk to one another and pray together." To their ears, the verbal world of prayers, sermons, and instructions is not a noise but a purposeful way of being together with the Christian God and fellow believers. Saying the right things is a moral requirement, as this is the only way to prove one's sincerity and loyalty, which guarantees God's protection and ultimate salvation.[5]

I shall argue that speech acts are inseparable from what one might call *silence acts*. Silence as refraining from speech is an ethical choice for both Christians and non-Christians. When silences are used depends on local communicative patterns. Both evangelicals and non-Christians actively avoid speech (any utterances or specific words) in some contexts: speaking is always a choice of what to say and what to repress, be this conscious or otherwise. Michael Billig (1999, 261), a scholar of discursive psychology, has argued that "in conversing, we also create silences." He rethinks the Freudian concept of repression by claiming that it is produced daily through discursive avoidances and commands. When one is taught what can be said, it always implies what cannot be said. Children are exposed to demonstrations or are explicitly taught *what* is unspeakable (and undoable or even unfeelable) and *when* one needs to refrain from speaking (Schieffelin 1990). There is a certain parallel with political and religious regimes that aim to silence their subjects, producing discourses that consist of the said and the unsaid (Foucault 1978, 27–30; see also Carrette 2000; Grice 1975; Humphrey 2005; Jaworski 1993). Or, to take an example from the Soviet context: every day after reading the fresh *Pravda* ("Truth"), a local party activist and patient in Aleksandr Solzhenitsyn's *Cancer Ward* (1991, 210–11) knew, by reading between the lines, not only what he could speak about but also on what matters he had to keep silent.

Baptist missionaries, who aim to control the speech and silence of those they try to convert, must get people talking in the first place. It is not always successful though. While a silence of not responding means failure for evangelists, it may mean maintaining habitual freedom for Nenets. Let me give an example of performative silence acts that work as protection against an unwanted transformation.

Yegor's uncle Vata was one of those reindeer herders in the Yamb-To community who had decided not to convert to Christianity. He saw himself as one of the most defiant opponents of the new faith. Still, the missionaries kept visiting him, with the hope of saving this family. Vata's resistance can be seen in what he did and said, but also in what and when he did not say. When I stayed with Yegor, everybody there was joking about

Vata, ridiculing the way he lived. "His tent barely stands, and his clothes are full of holes," Yegor said, and laughed. This kind of comment worked metonymically: it characterized not only the dwelling but also the spiritual situation in which Vata was living. Before the beginning of the autumn migration, I arrived at Vata's camp, where he stayed with his wife, Tado, and two adult sons. The youngest son had recently moved out to his married sister's tent after a drunken fight between the brothers. Yegor told me, "You need to see the life we all used to live." He spoke as if there were two different speeds of development. In a way, he did not only send me a few dozen miles away but also back to his "pagan" past. A linear temporality had certainly become prominent in his and other Christians' thinking.

When arriving at Vata's camp, I found a small tent ahead with sheets of tarpaulin indeed full of holes. Inside there was a mess compared to the tidy tents of the *punryodaq*. Unpainted floorboards (*lataq*) were a sign of "an untidy household," as I was taught. Vata did not come out to greet me, as his limbs were aching; he explained later, he had hiccup worms (*ikota khalyq*, see chap. 2) in his body, which caused pain and made him to want to drink vodka. Vata's tent and clothes were shabby, but not because he did not have enough reindeer, as one might have expected. He had more than a thousand, but he had just not gone along with the campaign of home embellishment, like Baptists around him.[6] Another reason for the dilapidated state of affairs was that Vata's wife was old and feeble—especially taking into account that her adult sons had no wives—and was not able to keep up with the demand for new garments and tent covers.

After a couple of days, I had developed a very friendly rapport with Vata. In many ways, the atmosphere was much less tense and controlled than at Yegor's where disciplining selves and others was pervasive. At one point, Vata started to sing old songs (*yarabts, syudbabts, yabye syo*). After hours of singing every night Vata was in an unusually good mood. He had not done this for some time, as he said, he was not willing because of illness. The singing practice was vanishing even more importantly because rarely did anybody ever come to listen to his songs, as most people around had become Baptists who denounced Nenets singing.

I heard conflicting versions from both Vata and missionary Pavel about their encounter. Like Iriko, the first time the Baptist missionaries visited him, Vata was approachable and repeated words from sermons and prayers. But as we saw in Iriko's case, repetition can misfire. In this repetition, Pavel saw Vata's sincere attempt to transform himself into a believing person by

Figure 5.2. Alcohol helps to appease spirits, September 2006.

responding to God's call. Vata's repetition was interpretable not only as a sign of apparent eagerness, "thirst for God's Word," but also as a sign of the Holy Spirit working inside him. As I have argued (see chap. 4), from the Nenets vantage point, this was a participatory act or a sign of respect but did not necessarily agree with the meanings of the words said (the separate question is, as with Iriko, to what extent the semantic content of missionaries' talk was understood). I had seen several times how somebody repeated words of a storyteller or in an everyday conversation as a part of Nenets communication pragmatics.[7]

To Pavel's surprise, the next time he visited Vata, the old man maintained a silence throughout his stay. In the meantime, as Vata explained, he had come to a decision not to repeat or talk to the missionaries but to stay silent. He described the last visit by Pavel, who tried to prompt him to talk back. "When last winter Pavel Ivanovich came to my tent, I did not tell him a word. Pavel Ivanovich said, 'At least say one word to me.' No, I did not say anything. [Vata smiles victoriously.] I was silent. I am now always silent when he comes. . . . If I became a Baptist, everybody would become a Baptist. Khriska told me that if I became a Baptist, he would as well. The late Ekhor told me the same."

By stopping his repetitions, Vata tried to avoid a wave of change coming from the *lutsa* world. Having understood that participatory repetitions are misunderstood by evangelists, Vata decided to avoid even a yes, as if realizing that this might be taken as an act of promising and commitment to a dreaded change (cf. Cavell 2010, 320–21). He saw missionaries' words as harmful weapons that had a power to change people. The social ties existing around him were being broken, and new ones, undesirable in his eyes, were being formed. The engagement with Russians seemed to have severe consequences: people were giving up the Nenets ways of sociality like singing epic songs, gift exchange, visits with drinking, card and sport games, and eating meat and blood together around a freshly slaughtered reindeer. His explicit restraint from words was a refusal of this type of engagement, an act of self-defense and a protection of the old kind. It was an act of avoidance of the unwanted force of missionaries' language, as any verbal response would have made Vata vulnerable to the missionary's intrusive and demanding utterances.

This tactic of maintaining silence is not Vata's ad hoc invention. In Nenets language ideology, especially in situations of negotiation, silence is understood as a lack of agreement. An example of this kind of silence act is the case where a father does not want to give his daughter away. When a matchmaker or the father of the potential groom comes to negotiate a future marriage, the father of a potential bride (*piribtya*) may remain silent, which means that there will be no easy deal or no deal at all. (The *piribtya* is usually silent anyway, as she goes out or hides under fur coats.) When the girl's father is not ready to negotiate at all, he remains silent throughout the stay of the matchmaker. He may even extinguish the fire and go to sleep. However, matchmakers who are known as good speakers are sometimes able to break resistance with their tenacity by rekindling the fire and remaining in the tent overnight (Kostikov 1930b, 14–15). The Russian ethnographer Leonid Kostikov, who visited the Gyda Nenets in the 1920s, notes that if the father of a girl remains silent three times when he is asked about his willingness to allow his daughter to marry, then this is taken as a firm refusal.[8] This kind of silent resistance in the marriage arrangements is also a widespread motif in oral poetry: "The stew in the cauldron can be brewed; Lamdo is still silent" (Kupriyanova 1965, 201, see also 35, 206; Lar 2001, 95). In a way, Pavel's pressure and Vata's silence parallels the situation of matchmaking. Vata is resisting Pavel's efforts to make him a member of the church, what Pavel would call the Bride of Christ (cf. Prokhorov 2013, 144). Unlike Iriko, Vata tried to avoid creating a shared field of words with missionaries and thus avoid engagement in a potentially binding exchange.

In Baptist language ideology, as mentioned, a silent response in a mission encounter is a sign of a refusal to accept God's words. The missionaries regarded this as a severe hindrance to salvation and stressed that one needed to accept the Word (*prinyat' Slovo*). As believing starts with speaking to God, the soul can be saved not by silence (as an explicit restraint from responding to the call) but by articulate speech. In contrast to the Nenets model, among evangelicals this is above all a moral issue that is thought to reflect one's inner state.[9] For Pavel, Vata's falling silent and keeping it recalcitrantly was the silence of a sinner. It was not a random silence; rather he was specifically not responding to the Lord's call mediated by God's authoritative workers.

Vata's unresponsive silence act was not idiosyncratic (cf. Khristoforova 2006, 90). Missionary Pavel described how they were welcomed with silence in another Yamb-To family, the one of Ulyana and Vasili. "We evangelized in the name of Jesus Christ, his substitutive death for our sins. The hosts' tense silence descended. Ulyana did not consider herself a sinner. Vasili was silent [*promolchal*] for the whole night. Later we learned that this family was bogged down in the sin of drinking and other sins. It is a pity that our witnessing was only for the sake of witnessing and not for the sake of saving."

While Ulyana somewhat protested, Vasili preferred to remain silent. In trying to break the silence and create a spiritual kin relationship, missionaries use "direct" addresses. Once when Pavel and Vasili met, I heard the missionary asking, "Vasili, when will the day come when I can call you 'my brother'?" Vasili, who was standing next to me, did not say anything and looked elsewhere. Pavel was certainly aware that using personal names ("Vasili") and a kin term ("my brother") had power to bring about relations, although I am not sure that he ever understood how sensitive this was among Nenets compared to Russians or Ukrainians who use personal names extensively in communication. Among Nenets, addressing adults by name is disrespectful and sometimes outright injurious (Baklund 1911, 100–102; Lapsui et al. 2023: 26; cf. Fleming and Slotta 2018; Viveiros de Castro 1998, 476). Juniors are not supposed to pronounce the name of a senior person in the person's presence. As among the Mongols, the ideal among Nenets is not to have their names pronounced in their presence, or as Humphrey

(2006, 173) puts it, "In this way, one can escape from being compelled by one's name" (cf. Stasch 2009, 86; 2011). As I shall argue below, it is not only using personal names but also singing another person's song in the person's presence that is believed to make the owner of the song vulnerable, suffering severe consequences, even death.

Drawing on Louis Althusser (1971) and Judith Butler (1997a, 1997b), one could suggest that naming as a form of address subjectivates and potentially injures. This takes place through hailing or, in Althusser's vocabulary, "interpellation." He invites us to imagine a situation in which the police call to someone "Hey, you there!" on the street and the person turns around and responds to the call. According to Althusser, this is the moment when the person becomes a subject of the dominant ideology (1971, 174).[10] A person is thus interpellated into a subject from outside by a powerful other as by a divine performative when God addresses Moses by his name or Jesus names Simon as Peter (177–79). While following Althusser's sinister version of subjectivation, Butler (1997a) nevertheless proposes that name-calling, despite it being violent, a kind of linguistic injury, can also empower a person and enable a different response. She writes: "By being called a name, one is also, paradoxically, given a certain possibility for social existence, initiated into a temporal life of language that exceeds the prior purposes that animate that call. Thus the injurious address may appear to fix or paralyze the one it hails, but it may also produce an unexpected and enabling response. If to be addressed is to be interpellated, then the offensive call runs the risk of inaugurating a subject in speech who comes to use language to counter the offensive call" (2).

Even if Butler's version presents subjectivation as a primarily violent and largely unreflective process (see Laidlaw 2014, 101), it nevertheless entails some freedom of action. In the scenes described above, subjectivation does not occur, despite missionaries' attempts to mediate God's call (who in Althusser's account is the Subject *par excellence*, see 1971, 179). Some of their addressees may respond at the beginning, even if somewhat formally, but stop talking back at some point. Vasili and Vata use silence for self-protection as well as protecting others around them (recall what Vata said: "If I became a Baptist, everybody would become a Baptist"). Interpellation thus does not automatically predict the result (also considering other aspects such as that missionaries do not operate as state agents who have tools for violence). Furthermore, Nenets' understanding of how words work is different from that of the evangelists—and this is a crucial point. In her critical engagement with Butler's theory of naming, Humphrey (2006) notes that Butler's "work cannot fully answer to an anthropological analysis, because it ignores the presence of different 'linguistic ideologies'" (see also Bodenhorn and vom Bruck 2006, 17). Indeed, we need an interpretation that considers Nenets' and Russian evangelicals' assumptions about language, personhood, and sociality.

In *Excitable Speech*, Butler (1997a) uses a concept of hate speech as an example of injurious address and consequent subjectivation. In both the Baptist and Nenets worlds, I would suggest, it would be more appropriate to talk in similar contexts of "love speech." Evangelicals approach Nenets with "the message of love" ("God loves you"). Yet, as with hate speech, love speech may have undesired consequences in the reindeer herders' eyes. This has roots in the Nenets understanding of binding words that work through quarrel and affection. Sometimes the two are hard to disengage from one another, but as I shall argue below, what really matters is the strength or weakness of a person as well as the intensity of a relationship between the persons involved in relation-making. So it is a question not only of "which words wound, which representations offend" (Butler 1997a, 2) but also of whose words injure in which kind of relations.

As Butler (1997a, 34) claims, in hate speech, as in subjectivating acts of naming, speakers are to some extent responsible for hate speech, but they are not necessarily "the originators of the discourse," in a sense that the words uttered exceed one's self and the moment of utterance. This understanding echoes with the Nenets model of agency and responsibility. As I shall discuss further below, influencing others with words is related to the idea not only of language as representation (as Butler's model has it) but of words as agents that form relations through being extensions of persons— words can thus be seen to function as part-persons (see chap. 4).

Pavel failed to subjectivate Vasili or Vata, at least in the way he would have wished. The missionary attempted to prompt his targets into speaking with the aim of silencing their earlier ways of speaking in the long run. Only then does it become possible to break a person away from his or her "pagan" past. On the one hand, missionaries believed that communication enables persuasion (as we saw with Vladislav in the previous chapter). Even if there were any verbal resistance, it would be still better, as this can be a fruitful way for a discussion in which propositional arguments can lead to "an understanding" (*ponimanie*) and a consequent conversion. Without revealing in speech what is inside of a person, what the person thinks and feels, it is impossible for an evangelist (and the targeted individual) to access, let alone remedy, the self. As in a confession, sinful thoughts must be uttered, made explicit, to suppress them (Foucault 1978; see chap. 7).[11]

On the other hand, speech is necessary, for the divine could start acting in one's life. Once a person utters words of repentance, there is a chance for a heart to be transformed from outside by the divine Other. I was told a story of an old Nenets woman who was about to say a prayer of repentance, but somehow the words "forgive me" did not come to her lips. A Baptist preacher told her word by word how to repent, so she could repeat it. She still failed. The missionary later realized that the reason behind this was that her mouth was full of chewing tobacco, which did not let her speak. For the insiders, it was apparent that tobacco was a devil's tool because it did not release the soul of the woman from his sphere of influence.

Sometimes missionaries read the silence of reindeer herders as an act of attentive listening and reflection. In contrast to Nenets, who tend not to speculate openly about what others are thinking or feeling (as in so many other places in the world, see Danziger and Rumsey 2013), missionaries believe that others' minds are accessible (even if they say that only God sees in the heart of another person), as they do not hold back from discussing what others think. Pavel described how on an evangelistic trip, Sem (Vata's older brother) traveled with missionaries who gave him a lift to Amderma to check on his weakening health: "He listened to all our conversations silently. Although he likes to drink, now he was ruminating and pensive." Pavel's act of mind reading in taking Sem's silence as positive pensiveness was, however, premature, as it turned out that the next time they met him was on his deathbed in the hospital. Sem, who was in the final stages of cancer, did not show much interest in the missionary's attempts to save his soul. According to his Baptist son Andrei, his father became very bitter at the end of his life: "When he was in hospital in Amderma, the preachers paid him a visit and asked whether he knew what was going to happen with him after his death. Sem replied that he was not going to die yet."

The more the Nenets were silent, the more power had to be invested in the message of love, even if it took the form of a threat. I once overheard a conversation between Pavel and Andrei; they talked about old Mitro (Andrei's neighbor in the winter pasture), who had recently died without showing any interest in the Christian faith. Pavel reprimanded Andrei that he had not made enough visits to the old man though it was evident that he was going to die: "You could have saved him. You should have told him directly what was going to happen to him—that he was going to hell." Andrei agreed. He looked like a scolded schoolboy for a moment, maybe thinking about his father, whom he could not save either. As others in the tundra, he had grown up with a disposition or sensitivity that challenging one's parent, and elderly people in general, was unthinkable.

Personal Songs and Epic Songs

The contrast between Christian and Nenets singing is vast. Not only are Christian hymns sung in Russian (except for a few translated hymns) with the specific quality of Russian singing tradition (*yanggerts'*), but there is a different kind of ideology behind them as well. Christian songs are essentially praise to the divine: they must be sung to keep up one's relationship with God. In the eyes of Nenets converts, singing Nenets songs in the old way (*khynots'*) is "bad" (*veva*). I was given various reasons for calling Nenets songs sinful. For instance, Ivan, who believed only in the fixed texts (i.e., scriptures), once told me that when people sing songs they have heard from somebody, they add new bits and some other bits are left out: "These songs are not correct anymore." However, a more pervasive understanding among converts was that these songs invoked sins, and this was a far more serious issue. Ivan told me that it is not good to sing old songs, as "these are all related to shamanism and Satanism." Furthermore, they were often sung during drinking parties, thereby adding one sin to another. In short, people singing Nenets songs are imagined to lose control and give themselves over to dark forces.

Indeed, drinking and singing often go together, especially when singing personal songs called *yabye syo*.[12] The word *yabye* means "drunk," although its root is related to "luck" and "happiness" (*yab*, *yabda*). The genre of personal songs is intimate, as it is the main way for expressing one's emotions, including love and pain, in the otherwise restrained emotionality of everyday life. These songs may depict an important scene of one's life or they can be a condensed version of one's life story (Laptander 2020a, 49–52). The usual motifs are finding a partner, raising many children, becoming an owner of a big herd, or similar. "It is a song of one's fate," as a Nenets woman, Anastasia Lapsui, characterized it to the ethnomusicologist Jarkko Niemi (Niemi and Lapsui 2004, 79).

On the one hand, this is the only format in which expressing what we might call "feelings" becomes possible and morally acceptable. Lapsui explained, "For example, if a man says that he loves some woman, it is not decent and not according to the etiquette, but if he sings it (in his *yabye syo*), then the people may learn about it. . . . Actually, it is possible to reconstruct a person's character through his song. . . . Only through one's *yabye syo* can I know everything; it has all the information" (79–80, italics in original). On the other hand, this is also an act of self-exposure that might have dangerous consequences. There are certain rules while performing these songs. A person who has created the *yabye syo* usually does not sing the song in the presence of others, except among a few close people. I never actually heard anybody singing their own personal song. However, I heard numerous *yabye syo* that belonged to somebody who was not present but whose songs were sung by others. Each song had its own specific tune, and songs circulated like quotations. They were discussed a lot, felt empathy for, or laughed at. Nobody sang these songs in the presence of the creator and owner of the song. Even the songs of the recently deceased were not sung.

A *yabye syo* might convey the most intimate feelings (e.g., secret love) of a person, and through that it makes the person vulnerable to gossip. Then again, presenting somebody else's song itself is dangerous for the owner of the song, because the words and tune of the song are part of one's personhood. In some cases, the trajectories of personhood and relationality become even more complicated. Lapsui's mother refused to sing her deceased husband's song to her daughter, saying, "How could I sing his song? He is a part of me! I shall not pronounce his name any more aloud, after he died. It would cause pain to my soul. I remember him only in my thoughts" (Niemi and Lapsui 2004, 83–84).[13] It appears that personal songs, like personal names, make vulnerable not only those who own the songs or bear the names but also those close to them who have survived.

However, it is possible to sing the song of someone who is long dead. Vata's father Mikul had died thirty years before, so there were no threats involved in singing his song. By that time, one's name can be called, while the name of a recently deceased person is forbidden (as in many other places in Siberia and beyond, see, e.g., Vitebsky 2005, 125; cf. Frazer 1911, 349–74). The relationship of the *yabye syo* and the name is more than coincidental, as each song contains the person's name. And the *yabye syo* itself belongs to the person like a "true name" (*nyeney nyum*), which is known only to the closest of persons (Liarskaya 2002; Pushkareva 2007, 2019).

There is a widely shared taboo against singing a *yabye syo* of a family member who is alive. Not yet knowing about the prohibition, I asked Tikynye to sing her mother's or father's song. She refused by saying that "something bad could happen" if she did this. "Father or mother could fall ill or even die," she said. What I also learned was that if somebody sang another's song in the presence of the person, the potential harm depended on the relation with the person and the singer's power. Tikynye recalled that when her brother Kolye was little, he sang his father's *yabye syo* in his father's presence but surprisingly their father did not interrupt him. She guessed that he was too small to do any harm to their father with singing his song. This shows that the power of one's words is tightly related to the power of one's personhood, as we shall see below.

Singing epic songs is not as intimate an act as singing one's own *yabye syo*. Yet they have a different kind of power to take the person on a journey into a different world (not unlike shamanic singing). Yegor told me that he could not tell me an old story or sing an epic song because there was a danger that it would damage our souls. He said that "before" he did believe in these stories as being actual, but not anymore. Now he knew that these do not belong to the truth and are Satanic deceptions or human inventions. But he could not trust himself entirely because the song and his past self could take him over against his will, as I witnessed (cf. Rosaldo 1980, 57–60; Vitebsky 2008, 2017a).

One night in March 2004, Yegor, then a third-year convert, agreed to sing a *yarabts* and tell a couple of mythic tales (*lakhanako*) for me. He sang a long *yarabts* called "Pilyu Sev Nyu" ("The Son of Gadfly's Eye") for the whole evening. He was unusually merry after that (like Vata when he was singing). Next morning, he woke and said that he dreamed all night about having a drinking party and being in an overwhelmingly cheerful mood. Now overwhelmed by the feeling of guilt, he was upset about his merriness and partially blamed me, as I had asked him to sing. He ardently prayed to God for the sin *we* had committed, which was singing old songs and telling tales. On another occasion, he said that every time he dreamed about drinking, he fell ill.

Significantly, it turned out to be not a mere representation but an actual return despite his earlier statements that he "did not believe in these songs." By singing an old-style song, he seemed to have moved away from his current Christian self: he became the old-time person he used to be before conversion. My fault was that I had asked him to present something as a token of his past life, and I listened to the song with this attitude. However, I failed to predict that for Yegor there could not be representation of his past self, but there was only an actual journey into the song that was also Yegor's past life. This was an unwanted ontological shift for him: it was impossible to take a different perspective without a risk, even if—or especially because—this was a perspective of his own past self that was "pagan." When singing and dreaming, he lost the perspective that he knew to be right in the eyes of God.[14] As we shall see later in chapter 7, as sliding into the perspective of one's past self is the biggest threat of all, believers try to be anchored to the present—that is, bound to the promise of future salvation.

For Nenets, singing is thus just not a mere representation of faraway times but a continuation of past relationships into the present. Furthermore, it is building a relationship with the song and its characters—sometimes in a rather intimate and dangerous way (cf. Niemi 1998).[15] This was so especially "in the time of the shamans" (*tadyebya yol'ts'*) when *tadyebyaq* made their journeys to the realm of spirits through singing and thus invoking their presence. Moreover, not only a *tadyebya* was seen as singing himself, but he could also lend his voice to various otherworldly agents, thus acting as a human animator for words of spirits.[16]

Harmful Words and Vulnerable Affection

In Nenets language ideology, words not only express one's thoughts and feelings but also, in some social contexts, are understood to constitute personhood and so they carry forward a person's qualities. The underlying principle is that once words are spoken out loud, they become partly independent from their originator, as a person who has uttered words is no longer their full master. In certain situations, words are imagined to be containable and can even be turned against the person, as in the case of curses, gossip, or incautious use of words. Therefore, the effects one's words create in the world are not necessarily related to one's intentions (as this is commonly thought to be the case among Russian Christians).

When I lived in Iriko's tent (see chap. 4), there was lots of talk about various words, both benevolent and malevolent. In this unusually verbal family, whose members were being converted to Pentecostalism at the time, I understood better how this relatively silent Nenets environment actually swarmed with various kinds of powerful words, from sacrificial prayers, curses, and spells to words that are harmful because they are extensions of personhood. Earlier, Iriko made short verbal requests during sacrifices or offerings through sacrificial words (*khan vadi*, cf. Lehtisalo 1947, 547–50; Stammler 2005, 173). For instance, when pouring vodka into the water, Iriko said (using a flattering diminutive), "Dear Grandfather-Master of waters, give us fish" [*yid yervkotsya, khalyamda yeremdei*]. Most of the prayers were short, rather colloquial, in otherwise almost wordless sets of actions.

Tikynye recited one prayer—slightly more poetic than the others—for me. As she said, this was a prayer her father most often used when strangling a reindeer to Pe Mal Khada (her *khekhe* was put on the back of the reindeer for the ritual). The same incantation roughly in similar wording was said among the Independent herders in the Urals, as I had been told by some others. Tikynye recited, "Pe Mal Khada, let my reindeer hooves tread the hills by turning them bare. Protect us from the harmful word of the Russians [*lutsa vevako vada*], Pe Mal Khada, you are stronger. Let the words of the Russians fall down on the land [*yan khaqmorngaq*]. Let the Russians become powerless [*nykhysyalma*]."[17]

Iriko and others were convinced that the *lutsaq* were using a curse-like "evil word" (*vevako vada*) to harm their families and reindeer. This was seen as a kind of collective witchcraft performed by those who targeted their reindeer, such as state officials or poachers who once and while shot and stole their animals. This was why one needed to get protection from the Russians' words, because they were always planning something against reindeer herders. The historical experience of the Nenets had proved how the *lutsaq* used words as weapons, either on paper or orally. People say that the Russians have always come and referred to the words of some "masters" (*yerv*) like the tsar, God, or Lenin. For instance, when the Communists came, they showed their papers with words written down, to confiscate reindeer or take their children away to school (cf. Perevalova 2019, 119–20).

The *vevako vada* Iriko referred to in his prayers worked as a projectile. The word *vada* itself is linked to an image of an arrow, as in an expression *ngyn vada yangu*, which means "the bow does not work," while its literal translation would be "the bow does not give a word" (Tereshchenko 2003, 31; cf. Pushkareva 2004, 2007, 2019). The projectile-like qualities of words are revealed best in witchcraft (Siikala 1978, 204), which is an important although largely hidden topic. For example, much dangerous word traffic takes place during or after marriage negotiations. As noted above, when the father of a bride candidate remains silent, this is understood as a refusal to give his daughter away. This silence act contains a great risk for the daughter, as she becomes most likely the target of witchcraft. Among the Ural Nenets, I heard of several cases in which somebody died or fell ill or lost her fortune because of this kind of witchcraft after rejecting a candidate. For instance, Tikynye's mother Pukhutsya admitted that she had not wanted to marry Iriko (who had been her husband for nearly forty years by then), but her grandmother warned that she would die from a curse if she refused.

In the Nenets tundra, shamans were often involved in harmful magic. Nowadays parents of the rejected groom (usually the mother) are still accused of putting spells and cursing the girl. According to Tikynye, one of the spells used in these cases is "Let Nga eat . . . [the name of the intended bride would be said here, as Tikynye explained]. We would feel no pity for her." Nga is the master of the underworld who "eats people" and "pulls the breath-soul out of the body." To my question how dangerous it was if somebody says these words, Tikynye said, "Of course, Nga would eat, if one says [the spell]." I thought this was Tikynye's Pentecostal "self" that featured Nga as an absolute evil having an agenda to destroy people. But Nga seems to have been a powerful agent long before the appearance of the Protestant missionaries. He is a death-maker himself, and mentioning his name was perceived as utterly dangerous (as with the taboo word *kholera* mentioned in chap. 2; see also Fleming and Lempert 2011).[18] This reminded me of Ivan's explanations of the actions of Satan, who would take on the job whenever a person addressed him.

Young women are not defenseless against the charms that are made after a failed matchmaking, as curses can be deflected. Tikynye's mother told her daughter to take precautions after suitors had left (*ngevtana sita portingu*, "the matchmaker may bewitch you").[19] Pukhutsya taught her a technique to catch and redirect the *vevako vada*. After the rejected suitor leaves in the evening with his parents, the girl must wake up before dawn and put a bag of female boots (*syaqmei pad*) across the entrance. This bag is usually kept just next to the door, the farthest end from the pure part of the tent, as it is polluting (*syaqmei*) for men (more on that in chap. 7). She must ensure that nobody notices the procedure. Then she opens the mouth of the bag, catches the *vevako vada*, and closes it by tying up the bag's mouth firmly again. She must be very quiet and careful, as the evil word can easily become frightened (*vada ngapra ni tara*, "don't frighten the word"). Then she puts it back to its place and says with a low voice: "Evil word, go back [*vevako vada punya kheya*] from where you came and catch the ones who sent you. Let you do harm [*khebyakha*][20] to them." The *syaqmei pad* acts as a gateway that serves here as a path to the world of spirits where the evil word finds its way back to the originator (cf. Lepekhin 1805, 117). Such ritual deflections are not public but secret.

Tikynye also used another technique. Once after the family of the groom candidate had left, Pukhutsya told her to throw salt in the direction of the camp of the suitors. Salt helps against the spells of harming (*porti*). While throwing it, she said a formula: "The evil words do not come across the salt" (*vevako vadiq ser tyakha niq tutaq*).[21] When I asked Tikynye whether she was afraid of being cursed, she said no: "Let them curse me, if they like." There was not only resignation but also bitterness in her voice. Tikynye then told me that the mother of the first hopeful groom candidate, Tarko Khada, had said that the girl who would not accept her son would suffer. "One girl died soon after she was not given to Tarko Khada's son," said Tikynye. Tikynye herself had managed to avoid the worst consequences of curses. Yet she had not succeeded in securing a partner.

Evil words thus have some kind of corporeality, as they are containable and deflectable. When somebody releases evil words, they carry harming potential. However, they can be freed from the link with their originator (and thus from the initial intention) and given a new direction by a new verbal command and by manipulation of substances. The words become thus a force independent from their source and recyclable and reversible by others. One can spell out the *vevako vada*, but not claim final power over it.

Various other steps can be taken to intercept evil words. Catching them by putting up a trap of *syaqmei pad* or throwing salt are active measures when one knows to expect a curse. However, there are also means that work like apotropaic "standing" traps. Once, when visiting the tent of Khasavaku (her relatives with the same clan name), Tikynye was surprised to see a dried pike's head (*pyrya ngeva*), mouth full open, tied to the central vertical pole (*symzy*). As she later learned, the pike's head was supposed to catch all the evil words sent by other people and neutralize the curses and gossip that reached the family. Tikynye explained, "Khasavaku's wife is afraid of people; she fears *porti*. In that area, people are talking a lot of one another with the *vevako vada*. Ngelku also dried a pike's head and put it up." The location of the pike's head is not incidental: a pike on the sacred pole that connects the lower and upper worlds has the power to protect, as it is a predator that can catch all kinds of malicious agents from the lower world. Shamans had their spirit helpers in the form of a pike, which is also the master of waters (*yid yerv*). I also once saw pike heads in the boxes of spirit items on a sacred sledge in the camp of a non-Christian Nenets.[22]

The border between curses and gossip is fluid. Tikynye said that she felt it physically when somebody was speaking ill of her. After she had a quarrel with her sister Netyu, she complained of a headache and explained that Netyu was saying bad things about her. Tikynye also noted that "in some camps, when you have hardly left the tent, you can feel that they are talking of you behind your back." People are anxious about gossip for various reasons. Certainly, to avoid gossip, reindeer herders guard their behavior, including words, as these can be used against them and damage their reputation in the form of abusive information. However, as we can deduce from the incident above, there is more at stake than merely "a good name" or following conventions.

To block the *vevako vada*, spirits and wolves planning to attack the herd or the family, it is possible to carry out purification (*nibtyeva*) through fire (see chap. 7). Tikynye explained that when there was a danger lurking around, the fire sometimes spoke: "Earlier, when the fire said 'tuuu,' we used to take a piece of a burning coal [*moryo*] and throw it to the two sides of the *symzy*, one toward the door side [*nyo*], the other toward the back end [*si*], and say, 'Old man, old woman, do not cut across the fire's face' [*yiriko, khadako, tu syadm nyon madaq*]."[23] Tikynye's mother used to "throw fire" (*tu mos'*), but for the last couple of years she had stopped doing it, as her Pentecostal daughters always scolded her and accused her of feeding demons. The last time Pukhutsya threw pieces of burning coal to the *symzy* area, the next day a bear killed a reindeer from their herd. Her daughters then had a good reason to nag their mother that she had invoked a demon to come to the herd instead of warding it off.

During my fieldwork, I witnessed only some rare moments of confrontation in Nenets families that escalated into verbal intensity. Depending on the dynamics of intrafamilial relations, verbal outbursts of irritation took place either between siblings or between parents and children. Like many others, Iriko's tent included unmarried sisters and brothers that had a special relationship of mutual assistance. A sister makes and maintains clothes for one of her brothers while the brother takes care of her draft reindeer and fixes her sledge. Iriko's youngest son, Kolye (then eighteen years old), a tempestuous person, was the loudest and enjoyed verbal assaults on his sister Netyu. He scolded her for not mending his reindeer parka (*mal'tsya*) or for not serving food in time. Netyu did not answer Kolye's attacks loudly but instead went around nagging in a low voice at Kolye and occasionally others. The rest of the family called her "a nagger" (*tedorik*). Usually nobody paid this much attention.

I was told that constant verbal disputes in the family can be dangerous, as this potentially creates bonds that last beyond one's lifetime and can become perilous for the surviving family members. These bonds were not of hatred but of affection, as Tikynye explained. To illustrate the point, she told me how her mother's father, Stepan, and her father's mother, Katya (who were brother and sister), died after each other (in 1983) because of this kind of affectionate relationship. Stepan died drunk at the Serakonabts feast (which marks the first time the sun rises above the horizon in January) on his way back to the tundra from Sovetskiy village. After her brother's death, grandmother Katya put out cards every day to learn her future. "Grandmother sensed that she was going to die. She wanted to see when and where she was going to die, as she did not want to be buried far from her brother and mother," said Tikynye. After four months, in May, Grandmother Katya went to visit her relative Khasavaku. In the middle of a drinking party, she passed away there. I asked why she expected that she was going to die. Tikynye said, "She knew that her brother would pull her to his place sooner or later. They often quarreled [*pyoda*] with each other. They felt pity [*syanz'*] for each other. People say that if somebody quarrels a lot with another, they are going to die together." It is not unusual that such ambivalent relationships cross the border of this and the afterlife, and the emotions of the dead can be threatening for the living (cf. Vitebsky 1993, 2017a).

I also heard of another kind of love speech that can have fatal consequences, as it entails a hazardous combination of vulnerability and force. Tikynye told me of her little brother Yepim, who died when he was five months old. She first said to me that an old woman, Nasta, had killed him through witchcraft. Another time, she said that an old man called Nyaku did it, a wealthy reindeer herder who I understood to be on friendly terms with Tikynye's family. Nyaku also bore the same surname as Tikynye, being thus a distant relative (*yarq nya*) from a parallel lineage. This time she did not mention Nasta at all, and I did not ask either (by the time I knew that she was blamed for some other misfortunes in the family).

I was surprised by the change in Tikynye's explanation of Yepim's death, but I did not want to counter her previous explanation. She said, "Yepim was five months old, in his cradle. My mother swung the cradle on her knees.

Nyaku was there, visiting us. He looked at Yepim, and smiling himself, he said, 'This is my grandchild. How nicely he plays with his little hands.' Yepim got scared and started to cry. He cried and cried and cried. He was just inconsolable. When he stopped, in the end, Nyaku Vesako said something again, and Yepim cried again, loud and long. Right after the old man's visit, he fell ill, and after a couple of weeks, he died."

"Did he want to do anything bad with what he said?" I asked.

"No," said Tikynye. "He has just got a heavy word [*sanggovo vada*]. The heavy word found its way to Yepim. When one has a heavy word, a child falls ill. . . . He did not want to make him ill. . . . Later, my mother met Nyudyaku Nye Khada [an old woman, also a Ural Independent], who said that she should have not shown her child to Nyaku."

Himself a father of thirteen children, Nyaku is known for having killed or afflicted others' children merely by verbally addressing them. Tikynye inferred that he was unaware of the "heaviness" of his own words. She also added that people said that the only one who could calm the child down was the same person who had made the child ill. Tikynye could not, however, explain how undoing the harm worked. Instead, she said that it is like "when a shaman harmed someone and he fell ill, the doctor could not help this person. Only the one who harmed could help. You had to go to the one who had afflicted you." So, in a sense, the person from whom the heavy words emanated remains connected with them.

I later learned that this was not an isolated case: there were some others who had a "heavy word" that children could not bear. Tikynye gave another example—surprisingly—from her own family. Once she said, "I have also told my sister Netyu not to address small children, as they usually start to cry when she is speaking to them." Although I had seen Netyu having arguments not only with Kolye but also with Tikynye—often they fought indirectly by ridiculing and harassing each other's puppy—it was not an attribution of evil intentions or even a moral condemnation of her character but rather an assertion that children are vulnerable to her *sanggovo vada*. As Tikynye said, the words found their way to make harm through certain people. She did not suggest that Nyaku or Netyu *meant* to cause any harm to children (being thus not a question whether they did it on purpose, by accident, by mistake, involuntarily, and so on, see Austin 1961). My explicit question about Nyaku's and Netyu's objectives did not make Tikynye comment on their possible motives: it was not so much their intentions or responsibility that mattered but a causal link that emerged between an adult who has a *sanggovo vada* and a small child who is vulnerable to a forceful adult.[24]

What role has the semantic content of the sentences that Nyaku said ("This is my grandchild. How nicely he plays with his little hands.")? Naming the child as his grandchild could be seen as a kind of intrusion in the mother's eyes, either injurious or establishing a relation, as Butler would argue (similar to Pavel using names in the hope of winning a person over). However, from Nyaku's point of view, he had a reason to call Yepim his "grandchild," as Yepim did indeed belong to the same kin group. When discussing the case, Tikynye did not attach any significance to the semantic side of the utterance. She emphasized instead that the old man's words were too heavy and that they got stuck to Yepim. Yet Nyaku gave his words a direction—there was an act but not malevolent intention.

For Tikynye (and her mother), it was important to be alert to both Nasta and Nyaku, as real effects mattered more than people's hidden thoughts and motives (complicated by the fact that it is often impossible to know who carries malevolent words in themselves).[25] Although Tikynye had been exposed to the strong intentionalistic concept of words through her engagement with Pentecostalism, she still did not present this case as a moral issue in the Christian sense in which a purported inner state of the person would play a role. This is not to argue that she might have not pondered over others' intentions (as this is part of being human everywhere, see Duranti 2015) or not made personal accusations in other cases, but it is not necessarily always part of the local ways of explaining each instance of witchcraft (which, as we see, may take the form of "negative kinship"; see Sahlins 2013, 59). So, this was not so much a matter of ability to read others' intentions or hide her own thoughts about others' intentions than as a choice Tikynye made to explicate in retrospect this particular social situation that had grave consequences.

Although most of the time people are seen as sources of their deeds and words, now and again they as persons may not control what departs from them, as the person is multiple, relational, and extendable rather than a sovereign individual committing only voluntary acts. This does not mean that Nenets would argue that there are no hidden thoughts or feelings involved, or that people would not try to get access to these. But unlike among Christians, thoughts and feelings need not be located inside the person and then imagined to be *expressed*. Hidden feelings can be revealed through personal songs and through the things and animals that circulate between people, in a way that the person may not realize that his or her feelings are disclosed. For example, when somebody receives a reindeer as a gift (this reindeer is called *padarak*, from *podarok* in Russian), kills the animal for meat, and boils the heart, if the heart remains hard to chew, it is said to mirror the giver's greed and negative attitude toward the recipient. Herders say that the donor keeps thinking of this gift-reindeer in terms of pity or regret.[26] As an illness in a child triggered by an adult reflects who has heaviness in his or her words, so the heart of the gift-reindeer reflects hidden feelings or the attitude of the donor. In either case, people saying words or making gifts might not know and might never learn about what they have done, as the effects of their acts and the traits of character are discussed without their presence, often in hindsight, when the following events make others think on these particular instances in the new light.

The cases above reveal that in Nenets ideology of language and personhood, words do not only communicate but also carry force and effects outside the semantic content and ordinary meaningful communication. Words have a capacity to reach targets and produce destructive consequences. Old-timers who are reluctant to convert seem to attribute Russian missionaries' words a similar capacity to harm. Some choose to respond with silence acts. Those who have declared their loyalty to the Christian God and committed themselves to the new teachings, however, believe themselves to be unharmable by evil words.

Embodied and Disembodied Speech

The evangelicals believe in the power of God's Word. This is a creative entity, capable of changing one's fate completely. Yet one needs faith in God for the Word to act in one's life. Although there are moments when Baptists imagine God's Word to create effects in one's life without a person necessarily understanding this, they yet stress that one needs to understand what God wants to say. Unlike divine words (which have the power to create a world), for Baptists, human spoken words cannot have any automatic efficacy (with some exceptions though, see chap. 6).[27] If any such thing appears to take place, the effects of words are said to be mediated by Satan. As we shall see in the next chapter, one must *mean* what one says. In Christian language ideology, there is an assumption that, when speaking, people express intentions that come from their insides, as if one's intentions could always exist *before* an act of expression.

I would suggest that non-Christian Nenets do not always see words as having intentions *behind* them coming from inside a person. It seems that the moments are not rare when intentionality is not lodged in an individual thought but emerges in a constellation of relations and acts in which power and vulnerability have a constitutive role to play (cf. Gell 1998). This can be described as a dispersed or collaborative intentionality, which is played out not in an abstract context but in situated relations. To put it another way, words in various contexts are seen not as signifiers but as part-persons that participate in relational complexities. In this sense, words are not that different from the things, puppies, or reindeer that people have, as, like words, these have the capacity to act as part of distributed persons and constitute embodied relations.

We could argue that all acts of speech have potentially extra effects that are not necessarily meant by the speaker. In the framework of speech act theory, this phenomenon could be classified as words being performatives, with effects coming from convention and context and not from an immediate meaning of the saying as such (Austin 1962).[28] In her Derrida-inspired speech act theory, Butler (1997a) moves toward acknowledging some sort of materiality to the language (cf. Derrida 1982). For her, a speech act is not only a linguistic but also a bodily act. She writes: "In speaking, the act that the body is performing is never fully understood; the body is the blindspot of speech, that which acts in excess of what is said, but which also acts in and through what is said. That the speech act is a bodily act means that the act is redoubled in the moment of speech: there is what is said, and then there is a kind of saying that the bodily 'instrument' of the utterance performs" (11). Butler describes the relationship between language and body as chiasmus. She refers to Shoshana Felman (1983), who argues that speech and body are incongruous but inseparable, which is a "scandal" that "consists in the fact that the act cannot *know what it is doing*" (96, Felman's italics).

How different, then, is Nenets ideology of language and personhood from that of Austin's or Butler's universal theories? Even if Butler, in her too gloomy courtroom-like account, goes as far as to say that calling "an injurious name is embodied" and that "the words enter the limbs, craft the gesture, bend the spine" (1997a, 159), she is yet mainly concerned with "meanings" and "signification."[29] For instance, when Yegor slid back into his past self for a moment, this happened to him possibly because the new ideology of signification had failed to eradicate his old dispositions. His earlier habitus, with a whole set of linguistic and extralinguistic features (e.g., singing, merriness, drinking, and dreaming), worked—perhaps unconsciously or as visceral "moral moods" (Throop 2014)—against the formation of his new self, even if in other moments he consciously tried hard to surpass his past self (see chap. 7). As Nenets language ideology also attributes effects of words outside the sphere of signification and human inner intentionality, words wound not as representations but independently of the ordinary meanings because they are parts of personhood and of relations. Speaking and cursing can thus gain an extralinguistic (extrasemantic) dimension as the words act semi-independently, get stuck to the person as substance, and influence life outside the usual understanding of intentional speech. This creates an entirely different kind of a blind spot.

Part of my argument builds on Tim Ingold's (2000, 103) criticism of the Western understanding of person. He suggests that human speech among non-Westerners is not about representing inner thoughts or expressing mental states outwardly. Following Martin Heidegger and Maurice Merleau-Ponty, Ingold argues that human speech is a way of being alive: "And the dichotomy between interior mental states and their outward physical or behavioural expression that underwrites this conception of the distinctiveness of speech also applies to the way we tend to think about other aspects of personhood—sentience, volition, memory. Thus volition implies the intentionality of action, but Western thought sees intentionality as residing not in the action itself but in a thought or plan that the mind places before the action and which the latter is supposed to execute" (103–4).

Furthermore, non-Western people often do not conceptualize others as intentional individuals who convey in their speech what they mean "from inside" (Duranti 2015; Du Bois 1993; Rosaldo 1982). Alessandro Duranti (1993) shows that the words of Samoan orators who represent politicians as their spokesmen are not taken as personally "intending"; yet they take personal responsibility for the words spoken. In her analysis of Ilongot linguistic practices, Michelle Rosaldo (1982) has argued that reading one another's personal intentions is not primary in communication in this community because subjective meanings do not fully define social relations. She writes, "For Ilongots, I think, it is relations, not intentions, that come first" (210). Words are thus linked to the practices of personhood that are different in different ontological regimes.

This does not mean that, in some settings, various kinds of intention are not imputed to others or to oneself. But in general, as discussed, Nenets usually avoid talking not only about their own but also about others' thoughts, feelings, intentions, and future plans.[30] The consequences of action and known properties of a person constitute the focal concern and not one's intentions per se. Therefore, Tikynye's family members did not stop engaging with more powerful people around them; for example, they did not cut relations with Nyaku. Or take the person who receives a gift that reveals the giver's greed would still need to return a gift-reindeer. Nenets' *economy of words*—understood both as a concise use of words and as the ways words act among and upon speech-enabled agents, such as humans, animals, and spirits—has deep roots in the local concepts of personhood and social relations.

What this chapter has tried to show is that missionaries' attempts to subjectivate old-timers, such as Vata, do not always succeed because words' and silences' performative effects only occur when they are seen as changing the world in the same way by everyone involved. As I shall argue in the next chapter, among Christians the concept of sincere speaking becomes dominant. At least as an ideal. As we have seen, for non-Christian Nenets, the notions of representation and intentions do not operate in the same manner as they do for Baptists or Pentecostals. I shall suggest that there is an important shift toward a model of representationalism and intentionalism, although this shift itself is not as smooth and unproblematic as one might expect.

6

SPEAKING SAVES, SILENCE DAMNS

The Steering Tongue

As shown in the previous chapters, there are conspicuous differences between Nenets and Christian language ideologies. There have always been Christians who value silence highly, like Quakers (Bauman 1983), Benedictine monks (Bruce 2007), or Greek Orthodox (Lind 2021; see also MacCulloch 2013). But this is an institutionalized silence (usually categorized as "a spiritual practice") that needs lots of explanatory words to introduce and not a habitus-like silence that is learned without too much verbal explanation and rather by example. Compared to Nenets' universe that does not require many words, evangelicals live in a highly verbalized environment that leaves little space for the nonverbal. The one who converts to evangelical Christianity is supposed to speak oneself into a new person. However, this new kind of speaking also requires some restraint, as Christian ideology explicitly prescribes avoiding sinful speech and the talk of the world (see, e.g., S. Coleman 2007; Hovi 2016; Koosa 2016; Szuchewycz 1997; Strhan 2015, 69; Tarkka 2013, 127; Tomlinson 2009a). Let me give an ethnographic example.

On a chilly day in September 2006, Yegor's family was making preparations around the tent for the coming busy period of autumn migrations toward winter pasturelands. Sitting on an unfinished transport sledge, Yegor was dissecting the head of a slaughtered reindeer so that Lida could prepare a "head stew." This is one of the tastiest meals of all. After finishing the job, a knife in his right hand, he took the tongue into his left hand and said in Russian with a smile on his face, "There is a good tongue and there is a bad tongue [*yazyk*]. This tongue is good." "But which one is bad?" I asked. "The one that chatters," he replied with laughter. Then his look and tone turned serious, and he continued, "The tongue makes lots of sins and the tongue makes lots of good. That is why the tongue can be good and the tongue can be bad. The tongue blesses and the tongue damns. One needs always to choose a good one [tongue] that does not chatter [*boltaet*] too much. Of course, earlier we chattered more. When a person becomes a believer, then he already understands that this cannot be done anymore. When we did not believe, we spoke a lot, chattered [a lot]." "Is there indeed less chattering now?" I asked. "Of course, there is less now," he quickly replied, then paused for a second and finished less enthusiastically, "A bit. Sometimes we do not yet understand what has been said. We do not understand. We must try to understand."

Yegor went on by telling a story about a slave whose master sent him to buy the best food he could choose. The slave came back with a tongue. Then the master asked him to buy the worst food he knew to exist. The slave came back with a tongue once again.[1] Yegor still had the tongue of the reindeer in his hand, and he finished his exhortation with a biblical figurative example: "Though it is a small part, it steers the person. If the tongue is bad, it would lead the person badly. When the tongue is good, then it steers him well. It is a helm of a person. . . . It is the same on a ship. That is also written in the Bible" (see James 3).

Yegor's description of the "pagans" who chatter excessively contradicts my account of the taciturn becoming talkative through conversion. From the Baptists' normative point of view, my account is an inverse because it reverses the biblical logic that attributes to "pagans'" excessive and idle speaking. Yegor claimed that, among the nonconverts, sinning with the tongue, teasing others, and making rude jokes was widespread (maybe thinking of his own father, Sem Vesako, who jokingly mimicked Russians by being verbose and loud; see chap. 1). He painted a picture of "pagan" herders drinking and speaking all the time. Yegor admitted that he himself still had moments of misuse of his tongue. As we saw in the previous chapter, by singing an old song, his tongue took him back into his old personhood and made his relationship with God insecure for a moment.

To understand why there are contradictions or tensions between different views, I continue with the topic from the previous chapter and describe what it means to speak among the Baptists, whose language ideology is based on the principle of representationalism and intentionalism and not on that of magical words and entanglement with various human and nonhuman others—although with some significant exceptions, as we shall see.

I also ask what speaking does or what words can do using some aspects of speech act theory by exploring how constative and performative dimensions in speech acts fit together and allow language to become the main channel of transformation in conversion.

Austin (1962, 146) argued that all speech acts both potentially convey meanings (are constative) and produce effects (are performative). Or as Butler (1993, 11) has put it, drawing on Austin and Derrida, "In philosophical terms, the constative claim is always to some degree performative" (see also Hollywood 2002).[2] By taking performativity as a matter of degree, I suggest that evangelical language acquires efficacy from its oscillation between a capacity to refer and a capacity to bring into being. Even if Baptists' language ideology is focused on the constative dimension (describing or stating something that can be evaluated as true or false), Baptist speech can be highly performative (doing things in the world), having the potential to change oneself and others. All that is said can and should be evaluated as belonging on the side either of truth or of falsehood: when people speak truth as God's children (*Nuv ngatsekyq*), they become channels for godly truth to produce effects in the world. For this reason, everything that a *punryoda* says must serve a purpose, which is to save one's own and others' souls, or at least not to create obstacles to one's salvation. Thus, from the evangelicals' perspective, any speech act is not only constative but also performative (in Austin's terms, carrying illocutionary force), enabled by the omnipresence of the divine.

In his account of the tongue, Yegor offered a description, which is a constative dimension. He retrieved from scriptures the truth to persuade his listeners. It was a kind of witnessing (cf. Bielo 2009, 113–34), a verbal activity to convey truthful statements about different uses of the tongue. In addition, there is a performative dimension. Yegor's account about the good and bad tongue was not only a predicative description of the world but also a tool that helped transform his listeners and his own self, enabling to fix the self—if only for a moment—into secure fellowship with God. Most importantly, he demonstrated his own obedience to the right discourse, and by this act of obedience, his "inner man" (Ephesians 3:16; see also *Ob osvyaschenii* 2006, 18) was to become firmer in belief. His tongue was what made the difference in his endeavor to anchor his interiority and become saved.

The oscillation of constative and performative dimensions can be seen also in the following statement by missionary Pavel, which he made when he had invited me to his home to ask about my project (see chap. 3). He told me that it would be impossible to describe the believers' spiritual life in a "scientific way" (*nauchno*) because the spiritual cannot be described for the sake of description. One can only be engaged, be immersed in it, to serve God's purpose, or be against it.[3] As Harding (2000) has masterfully demonstrated in her ethnography of American evangelicals, in the universe of believers, there is no place for neutral information. Likewise, new language ideology among Baptist herders implies that all speaking must have a good purpose.[4]

On another occasion, when discussing how people should use their words, Yegor quoted a phrase from Matthew: "For by thy words thou shalt be justified, and by thy words thou shalt be condemned" (12:37). As he confessed, in the scene with a reindeer tongue, it was not that easy always to stay on the right track. By the time of this speech event, he had been a Baptist for four years. It was no longer alcohol that he fought against but his own tongue, excessive laughter, and outbursts of anger that needed correction (see chap. 7). He knew he had to get his tongue right—without it, there was no hope of having a pure heart and a saved soul. As he said, the helm was the means to save the ship and, with it, what was inside.

The reindeer tongue in his hand, Yegor began his explanation about the vices and virtues of a tongue in a joking mode, pretty much in the way non-converts liked to joke. Note the sudden shift to a serious mode, which can be read as a shift in his discursive subject position and ontological perspective (see chap. 7). When explaining what a good and bad tongue was, he—with the help of the Holy Spirit—was performing a right kind of speech act that let God's words out into the world. As on many other occasions, when speaking *of* God, his voice and his posture slightly changed. This was a speech act *from* God as well as a speech act directed *to* God. I see this move as part of the hard work he had been doing over the years as a born-again person, even if he struggled to maintain this for longer than limited periods. And a large part of this hard work had been learning the new language.

To be saved, one is pulled into the world of words, as one is called to listen, speak, and read abundantly. Believers pray, promise, repent, witness, read the Bible aloud and silently, quote or retell passages by heart, teach, and comment on one another and on the unsaved. Among all speech acts, prayers are seen as especially important. Yegor once said, "Times when we do not pray, this is very bad. One has to pray all the time. One who believes and prays a lot will be saved." Justification by faith and its evidencing expression in prayer is a simple recipe that most Baptist Nenets believe to be efficacious for unbroken communion with God and salvation. Furthermore, in this human-cum-divine community, praying for forgiveness allows one to undo or repair consequences of one's unfortunate, unforeseen, or unintended acts, especially when benefiting from hindsight or from others' evaluative comments.

Unlike humans' words, God's utterances are perfect performatives, as he does things with words. Almost every believer in the tundra can say by heart the beginning of the Bible and the beginning of John's gospel where God's cosmic words are said to have created the universe from nothing. This pertains to the past as much as to the future. Believers keep repeating that all that God has said in the Bible is a promise that will be fulfilled, and not a single word of God remains without a corresponding act in the world. God's word, like a judge's verdict, is a deed, a perfect kind of performative that needs no conditions (Austin's "felicitous or not," 1962, 22) to take action on the world. An omnipresent God does not require the right context, because he himself is the context. However, a believer's words can succeed only when conditions are right, which is granted by God's presence inside.

Not all Protestants reason in this way and claim to entertain such an intimate relationship with God. Keane argues that for most Protestants, divine agency has been treated "as an assumed background against which the person acts" (2007, 208–9n6). Likewise, he says in his analysis on Calvinist ideology, "It is not for humans to speculate about the purpose of a transcendent being" (2007, 2n2, 145; see also Miyazaki 2000; Tomlinson 2009b, 184–205). While for Indonesian Calvinists, the divine presence is largely symbolic, for Russian and Nenets Baptists, the purpose of a transcendent being is not to remain a mere "background" but to assume the position of ultimate source of agency. For them, God, with his intentions, is knowable as he is claimed to be present in their lives through the acts of the Holy Spirit, the divine word, and miraculous deeds.[5]

Nenets converts argue that each spoken word in the world is overheard by God (who is a "higher superaddressee" in Mikhail Bakhtin's [1986, 126] theory of the text). There is no place where believers could speak without God hearing what is said, or even thinking without God knowing what is thought. By representing (quoting, retelling) God's words, they render their own words efficacious and their selves renewed. Baptists assert that the Holy Spirit had made them pray and utter the concrete words. Or as some believers said, "God moves lips and puts words in the heart of a believer."

Here is a strong circular logic by which God speaks to himself through believers whose role is to be perfect channels. This circle must be kept uninterrupted. All behavior (including one's speech) is thus about a complete submission to the agency of God, the erasure of all actions derived from human willfulness (except acts of obedience that are not fully of human origin either, as ultimately only God deserves praise for these). Yet converts are taught that they should not attribute to spoken words any power on their own, as Nenets old-timers would.

God's words are known from the Bible. Nenets Baptists who have just become readers have been introduced to a tradition of literalism, according to which a word is imagined to have a true natural meaning and people are supposed to use words at their face value. They are not expected to discuss the contextual pragmatic or rhetoric qualities of words (Crapanzano 2000) or to speak of human words as creative force. In Bakhtinian terms, Baptist ideologists imagine language to be functioning straightforwardly as a "direct, unmediated discourse [*slovo* in Russian] directed exclusively toward its referential object, as an expression of the speaker's ultimate semantic authority" (Bakhtin 1984, 199). This is not to say that parables would be read literally and that sermons would not entail metaphors, but figurative reading is just another kind of literalism. It works on an assumption that there is only *one* interpretation behind parables that reflects the divine intention.[6]

Literalist ideology has a great potential to fix meanings in the world. Everything that is not fixed, in the eyes of the born-again Christians, resembles a lie. This is a lesson that is easy to prove by pointing at the bearers of orality. Recall that Ivan used to make disapproving remarks about old Nenets songs and tales (see chap. 5). He argued, among other things, that these were not "true" because they were constantly changing. He spoke about the "confusion" people had before they knew the Bible: "They knew a bit but they did not understand." By "knowing," Ivan meant that some people, like his grandfather Mikul, were aware that there was the heavenly God (sky deity Num), but he did not know about his son, Jesus, and the resurrection. He also argued that people in the tundra confused St. Nicholas with Christ. "Idolatry and the divine became confused; everything was put into one pot," Ivan said. To my question asking how people knew at all of God before the current revelation, Ivan gave me two explanations. First, ancestors had heard from Orthodox priests and Izhma Komi herders some dos and don'ts. Second, Nenets had some knowledge retained from early times when they "still lived in the Middle East," as all peoples once did: after leaving the area, they had gotten things hopelessly wrong because all the transmission was oral, and mistakes piled up. The true revelation, in Ivan's words, had arrived to the tundra for the first time only today.

The Baptism of Yegor and Lida

Baptists emphasize that human words gain their efficacy from one's sincerity—as if speech externalizes inner thoughts, feelings, and attitudes. If one stops being sincere, this will have severe consequences, as this deficiency is visible to God. Sincerity can take different forms. Anthropologists have shown that ritual is the site where sincerity loses its significance, as its publicly binding nature eradicates the necessity for the match between one's thoughts, words, and acts. Protestants are well aware of the problem, as they consider rituals to be vulnerable to insincerities (Keane 2007, 185). Nevertheless, evangelicals still require formats in which one's public commitment to particular statements and actions could be read by others regardless of one's intimate thoughts or feelings.[7] Roy Rappaport (1999) argues that to undergo a ritual is to commit to the effects of it regardless of one's personal motivations, or as Lambek (2010b, 45) comments, "The participants performing or undergoing a ritual demonstrate to others and to themselves their acceptance of both its message and its form. They do so whether or not they 'believe' in any specific propositions associated with it; hence the outward, public consequences prevail irrespective of the inner states of the participants. This evades the problem of recursiveness inherent to theories of intentionality, as well as the instability of subjectivity" (see also 2015a, 22–23; van der Veer 2006, 11). Lambek (2010b, 45) continues that one's sincerity, or what one "believes," is in some sense irrelevant: "I can pray effectively, for example, without being certain that I believe in God, that I want to do so, or that prayer is the means to address God; I can successfully ask for forgiveness without feeling particularly contrite." What really matters, it seems, is one's commitment to the public criteria of the ritual. Or, to return to Iriko's conversion—even if others may have doubts over Iriko's sincerity, he is identified as a Christian in the eyes of church members around him once he has burned his idols and undergone baptism (however, this may change if others judge Iriko when he does not back up his new status in action, see chap. 4).

And yet, when listening to the evangelical Christians, we learn that one's intentions determine the efficacy of the event that would determine one's fate beyond this life. As all-seeing God oversees the ritual events, this gives it all the necessary felicity conditions, and if one is insincere, uncertain, or doubtful in a ritual, then it is void in God's eyes (cf. Prokhorov 2013, 105). Evangelical logic seems to consider this kind of vulnerability of the human condition, and this is why it stresses that God can change the person from outside and turn him or her into a sincere believer. In this sense, one's sincerity is always a possibility, even if it is missing at the very moment of performing a ritual. Or, to put it in more mundane terms, as Lambek (2015a, 188) writes, "We only 'catch up with ourselves,' come to realize that we do indeed mean what we say (or intend what we do), after the fact, in light of felicitous performances."[8] This kind of learning process is part of Baptist procedures. To discuss how "speaking Baptist" in rituals *produces* sincere believers and how the tension emerges in the ethical language of converts, I shall return to the opening scene of the introduction and give some more details about the baptism of Yegor and Lida.

Initially, three people had come forward for baptism at this time—Yegor and Lida (whose oldest, unmarried son, Ngarka, was already baptized) and an older woman whose husband, who was unwilling to convert, had recently died. The night before the baptism, the church congregants gathered for an examination of the candidates to assess the sincerity of their wish and their readiness to live the life of a born-again. Nonmembers, including me, were not permitted entry. Most people graduate from this test of merit and faith, but not everyone is successful: potential converts may be rejected if, for example, they are ignorant of the main doctrines, incapable of conforming to Baptist values by failing to renounce vodka, or still keep *khekheq*.

Yegor had wanted to be baptized several years earlier, but the members of the congregation had then deemed him unready. This time, however, he had abstained from drinking alcohol, smoking cigarettes, playing cards, and singing old songs for some time. He was now also able to demonstrate sufficient knowledge of the doctrine and perform a prayer of repentance. Lida, his school-educated wife, understood somewhat better the teachings presented in Russian and had less to do with alcohol or idols. Only half a year earlier, Yegor had participated in drinking parties. Under pressure from his Baptist children and missionaries, he decided to make another attempt to get things straight. He finally gave in under the pressure and burned his great-great-great-grandfather Yarki's soul-image (*ngytarma*), passed down to him through his patrilineage from the nineteenth century.

He had now become "free" from the dependence of the statue, or, as he said, "the attachment to Satan through this idol," and was thus considered to have passed his probationary period successfully.

The following day, the church members were told not to eat throughout the day, as collective fasting was planned to make people closer to God and thus the appeal more powerful (cf. Prokhorov 2013, 316–17). Words gain an extra force by such bodily acts, the meanings of which are carefully explained to everyone. The cool and rainy Sunday morning of August 4 started with a service at which Pavel explained the significance of the act of baptism. He stressed that this was an act of promising good conscience to God (*obeshchanie Bogu dobroy sovesti*) and that it was a death of the old self and birth of the new. Yegor and Lida were ready to pledge themselves as loyal children to their new (heavenly) father, Num—as they now called the only God when speaking Nenets.

Wearing their reindeer parkas, the congregants walked together to a nearby lake chosen for water baptism. Pavel explained that true believers are baptized only as adults (a common practice from the age of fourteen years onward) in natural water reservoirs and by full immersion. All other forms like sprinkling or pouring water on the head or even full immersion indoors were said to go against God's will. Pavel and the candidates wore white nurses' gowns they had obtained from a hospital. Rain was drizzling, and the temperature was around five degrees Celsius, a perfect summer day for grazing reindeer but not so much for the shivering participants of the rite.

Yegor walked first to Pavel, who stood in water up to his chest. The presbyter raised his arm above Yegor's head and asked in Russian: "Do you believe that Jesus Christ is the Son of God?" Yegor replied in Russian, "I believe." Pavel continued, "By the command of the Lord and by your faith, I baptize you in the name of the Father, and of the Son, and of the Holy Spirit. Amen."[9] Yegor replied, "Amen." Then Pavel immersed Yegor fully into the water, sliding him backward. Lida followed, frightened stiff by the cold water for a moment, and continued to Pavel. The same words and movements were repeated (see figs. 6.1 and 6.2).

There are several aspects I want to draw attention to in this short, ritualized question-answer format. First, these are relatively rare moments in Baptist speech practices, when words have a fixed character and participants of the dialogue have no freedom to choose their words. Not surprisingly, this kind of fixedness is needed, especially at the most crucial life-changing rituals. These few sentences can be seen as authoritative words *par excellence*, as

Figure 6.1. Pavel baptizing Yegor by immersing him in the cold tundra lake, August 2002.

they cannot be changed; they can only be used (Bakhtin 1981). They enact a kind of "Law of the Father" in Lacanian terms, contradicting the Baptist ideal, which stresses spontaneous speaking that mirrors words of one's own making coming from inside.

This question-answer format also illustrates that Baptists combine freely what comes from the Bible. Their language ideology takes words as meaningful units that can be easily removed from their context without fear of misrepresenting God's intentions. Linguistic anthropologists call this process of the free shifting of chunks of discourse "entextualization," which means that "texts" can be taken from a particular context and inserted into new contexts (Bauman and Briggs 1990). The first question Pavel presented was a modified quotation from Acts (8:37) in which the baptism of an Ethiopian eunuch was described. Though most contemporary

Figure 6.2. Pavel baptizing Lida, August 2002.

versions of the Bible have omitted this passage, as it has been proved to be a "later" insertion, the Russian Synodal translation, which is the text the Baptists in Russia use, contains it. The Baptists, who rely on the Russian Orthodox exegetical work (but give no credit to this fact), avoid all questions of philological scholarship and take their version of the Bible as inerrant. Biblical criticism has therefore no importance whatsoever (Prokhorov 2013, 221; 294–302; see also Bennett 2011; Bielo 2009; Crapanzano 2000; Malley 2004; Sibgatullina 2020).[10]

If we look more closely at an extensive use of quotations in sermons as chunks of discourse, we see that the fixed words are not alien to the concept of spontaneity among the Baptists. The quotation practice of the Baptists is overwhelming in all spoken and written forms of language. Freely taking passages out of contexts is what gives the Baptists' speech not only its sense of authenticity and authority but also its flexibility. Pavel encouraged herders to memorize passages "which they liked most" and to use them at every convenient moment. And Yegor and some other Nenets Baptists did that often. For example, Andrei's favorite was "A righteous man regardeth the life of his beast" from Proverbs (12:10).

If we look at the semantic (constative, locutionary) side of this baptismal speech event, we see an inherent tension in the concept of belief. Anthropologists have repeatedly stressed that there is a difference between "to believe in" and "to believe that." The first means trust, certainty, and commitment toward the one that is believed in; the second is giving assent to a fact or proposition (Asad 1993; Pouillon 1982; Robbins 2007a, 2020; Ruel 1997; Smith 1998). It is worth noticing here that Pavel's question ("Do you believe *that* Jesus Christ is the Son of God?") is propositional ("believe that"). With his reply, Yegor aligned himself with something that was entirely experience distant. His answer "I believe" is best to be taken as pledging himself to God, claiming publicly the existence of God and trust in him, thus tying up both constative and performative dimensions. Belief is first and above all about alignment with propositional statements—in everyday life also with one's outer appearances, such as clothing and hairstyle, or disciplinary practices, such as kneeling before lunch—and taking responsibility for these claims. But as we shall see further below, in the evangelicals' morality and ethics, responsibility must be aligned with "right" feelings as well.

Not all manage the ritual as well as Yegor did. On a different occasion, I witnessed the baptism of Pukhutsya in the Pentecostal church in Vorkuta. The Pentecostals' first question is the same as the Baptists'. Unlike the latter, they also ask a second question, which is "Do you promise to serve God with a pure and good conscience?" Pukhutsya had been taught to reply to the first "I believe" and to the second "I promise." Despite earlier lengthy instructions by the presbyter, Pukhutsya, who knew almost no Russian, mixed up the order of two answers, which she gave in Nenets. Her daughter Tikynye, who was near the baptismal pool, translated her mother's incorrect replies to Russian not verbatim but as the script required. Russian participants did not notice, and the validity of ritual was never questioned.

What is significant here is that the relationship of Yegor's, Lida's, and Pukhutsya's words to their inner intentions becomes uncertain, as the event was ritualized. Let us take another look at sincerity in ritual. Humphrey and Laidlaw have argued that ritualization starts where intentions do not change the course of prescribed actions. "Ritualization involves the

modification—an attenuation but not elimination—of the normal intentionality of human action," they argue (2007, 256; see also 1994). Certainly,
we can see this happening in the cases of baptism above. One could say that
this goes against a general endeavor of the Baptists, whose language ideology is built on the idea of sincerity—imagined as a total correspondence of
interiority and exteriority that is expressed through language, as "a congru-
ence between avowal and actual feeling" (Trilling 1972, 2; see also Keane
2007; Pickett 2017; Rabinow 2008, 76–78). Furthermore, this departs from
the logic according to which intentions could be fully given in advance,
which are there to be expressed—that is, externalized. One could say that a
public act of alignment of words and inner thoughts is what is expected in
the Baptists' practices. Ideally, a person going through baptism must direct
all attention and intentionality ("right thoughts") toward the act. However,
the act of ritual in its fixity cannot guarantee the full alignment. As we saw
in the case of Yegor, he had no other choice than to align his statements
with authoritative discourse.

As only God has access to others' minds, humans must consider the
"opacity of other minds" (Robbins and Rumsey 2008; see chap. 5) and must
admit the impossibility of complete transparency of one's thoughts and sentiments. Being aware of the problem of insincere language, Protestants have
fought against the potential mismatch of intention and semiotic form since
the early days of the Reformation. For the Baptists, there have always been
two simultaneous forces at work. First, all fixed rituals, verbal or nonverbal
(breaking of bread, laying on of hands, etc.), required lots of explanation
beforehand. Bearing this in mind, lengthy readings, quotations, preaching, and question-answer sessions were performed to prevent the collapse
of meaning (Tomlinson and Engelke 2006). Second, to avoid a threatening
gap between one's words and their meaning, believers were told to invoke
the presence of the Holy Spirit through prayer (see chap. 4). As believers say,
without the presence of the Holy Spirit, one cannot understand God's Word,
even if one understands the meanings of words in the Bible.

Let us return to the scene of baptism to discuss how sincere Baptist
speech and emotion is learned. After Lida, Yegor, and Pavel came out of
the water, they were hidden behind large blankets, where they put on dry
clothes, then the congregants said prayers of thanks and sang joyful hymns
from the "Baptism" section of the hymnal. Then everybody moved to the
tent of Yegor's unbaptized mother, Granny Marina, where a postbaptismal
service was about to start. Before the beginning, Yegor came to me, rubbed

his chest with his right hand, a wide smile on his face, and said, "I can feel that my heart is filled with joy."[11] For the born-again person, this feeling is an embodied sign that the Holy Spirit is actively at work in a person (cf. Robbins et al. 2014). Yegor, who was learning how to read signs not only *around* himself but also *in* himself and how to express these to others, had reached the next level, where the Holy Spirit was dwelling in him more firmly than ever. He could call himself "born-again" in the sense that is described by Jesus to Nicodemus in one of the most often-quoted passages (John 3:3) among the Baptists. And most importantly, he made sure that others would know that his inner state conformed to the outward ritual.

Being born again is imagined to be an event that usually precedes the rite of baptism, having clearly recognizable features. Andrei's daughter Vera said that she felt that she was born again one day when she was fourteen. When I asked her what this experience was like, she described how she suddenly realized that the eternal life was what mattered most from then on. It was both an emotional and intellectual transformation. Suddenly, her heart was at peace and full of joy. It was the sense of being certain of the divine presence that took her over: "When I pray or read the Bible, I feel that God is near to me. When I read, inside me there is 'Forgive others.'" Vera explained that keeping this closeness becomes the main goal of a *punryoda*. This state could be sustained only through speech practices, reading, and following the rules for renewing one's commitment. Occasionally it required orchestrated bodily movements such as kneeling, closing eyes, and kissing as well.

The main element in the postbaptismal service is the laying on of hands on the freshly baptized, followed by the Lord's Supper (see fig. 6.4). In his sermon, Pavel read a passage from Acts (8:14–17) and explained how the apostles Peter and John laid hands on the Samaritans to mediate the Holy Spirit into them. Pavel said, "God wanted to show that he wanted to save all the people. Both Jews and Samaritans. Also Russians, Nenets, Estonians. All the people. . . . Laying on of hands unites us with the Holy Spirit; this mediates God's blessing." He named all the names of the unsaved present, including me. As we saw in the previous chapter, for Nenets, naming itself had potentially a cunning power to injure and bind.

In the following sermon, Pavel instructed Yegor and Lida in what to ask God for. Pavel said, "Yesterday, we heard from Yegor that his heart was afraid that it [living as a believer] may turn out to be too difficult. Ask the Lord to be faithful to him, ask courage and strength to remain certain."

Figure 6.3. Baptist missionaries and Nenets converts singing hymns, August 2002.

Yegor then started his prayer in Russian, which was slow and full of pauses, as if he was struggling to find the *right* words:

> Lord, today, I ask you that the Holy Spirit will come into my heart. That he will live in my heart so I shall reach God. And [that I shall] live on earth in this way. I also ask for your blessing. Lead me away from all evil. You are great . . . . And in the name of Jesus Christ, you know how to lead. You yourself hear every word. When I am in trouble, you hear me. Always strengthen . . . and you can strengthen. You can take care . . . . You can take care of the children. So that children will be dutiful, and that I shall be dutiful to my children. Since I cannot read, give me more wisdom. I praise your name. You see all that I have. Everything will be at your will. You can give all that I want. Therefore, I praise your name. In the name of the Father, the Son and the Holy Spirit. Amen.

After Yegor's and Lida's prayers, Pavel laid his hands above their heads and started his prayer in a loud and clear voice. His intonation moved like

Figure 6.4. Pavel performing the laying on of hands for Lida and Yegor, August 2002.

rolling waves: "You Lord saw how difficult they came to you. You saw how the enemy did not want to release them. Today you gave victory to their heart. Today is a joyful day for us as for them. They came to your, God's family. They gave the promise to you to serve you from a pure heart. And you saw it today. We here were witnesses of that. Be praised that you continue building the church. You love the Nenets people by saving them."

Then he went on *re*presenting more specifically Yegor's prayer in his prayer, doing that more smoothly and elegantly while correcting some of Yegor's dysfluencies: "Bless dear brother Yegor, give him strength. Let his heart be filled with the Holy Spirit. You have always responded to his prayers, listen to them now also and listen to our prayers. Turn him into a forceful Christian so that he can win against evil. You know that he struggles leading his heart. Give him the strength. With your strength he can defeat everything that he meets on his path."

As we see, praying is more than representation of one's inner thoughts, worries, and wishes, as it has embodied results. This is a spiritual embodiment that Yegor characterized to me in this way: "When a person prays, the Holy Spirit grows inside. The other, the bad side of the person then shrinks. . . . And this person who does not pray, his thoughts are sly." He needed external help to reform his own desires, thoughts, and speech, especially knowing that he committed minor sins with his tongue every day. For this reason alone, he had to purify himself through prayers as often as possible. This, again, required the right perspective and proper words (see chap. 7).

Authority and Disciplined Spontaneity

As we know from Austin's account, recognizing authority is a necessary constituent of performativity. Nenets converts saw in Pavel a person who was full of the Spirit, certainly more than any of them (maybe the closest to him among the Nenets was Andrei, the Nenets' ordained pastor). With his God-given authority, he commented on what was right and what was not. He spoke in the name of God using extensively reported speech and quotations. He explained that a prayer had to be relevant to the context (a theme of a sermon, a ritual at a hand, a concern shared). He insisted that one needed to learn to pray in the way it was pleasing to God.

In church performance, authority is bracketed in a specific context that privileges the pastor (Besnier 1995, 154–60). To have full control, all the prayers in Nenets had to be translated into Russian when missionaries were present. It was not enough that God heard them. For instance, Pavel explained once to a Nenets man who had finished his prayer that he should not have asked in his petition forgiveness for the sins committed in the past life, as he had been born again and forgiven his earlier sins already. Feeling themselves a bit lost in this new exercise, converts tried hard to imitate the way the missionary prayed. Pavel had assumed the position of an external commentator whose authority was perceived as almost indisputable because he knew God's ways better than others. Pavel took some of his—to use Niko Besnier's (1995, 158) phrase—"sermonic authority" into spheres other than strictly church issues, making comments on social relations or on raising children. I almost never saw any dodging of Pavel's authoritative claims by the Nenets congregants, except a few times. Once when he called for regular brushing of one's teeth, Andrei reacted, "Where does it say in the Bible that one ought to brush teeth?" Although the converted Nenets had accepted Christianity, they had to submit to an alien ritual form as the only right one; in some minor matters, they still negotiated the extent of the authority. Pavel had not assumed the position of a moral exemplar (Humphrey 1997) whose personal ways—commented on sometimes critically as *lutsa* ways—would have been admired uncritically.

Pavel insisted that it would be a mistake to see him or other missionaries as acting *from* themselves. Through his heteroglottic voice he presented himself as a mediator of the distant and truthful knowledge ("the power of words is nothing other than the *delegated power* of the spokesperson," Bourdieu 1991, 107, his italics).[12] Pavel explained to me that he saw evangelical work like Jesus's and the apostles'—that is, to sow the field with good seeds (i.e., words) and wait for what would happen. "It is not we who put pressure on a person. We wait for what God does inside the person's heart. Our job is to sow the field with seeds. But how they grow, we do not know. We only know that they grow as potatoes or wheat grow," he said. When somebody decided to repent, they argued that God had grown his Word in this person. Vata's initial mimetic speech and later silence as a refusal to engage in the new relationship is an instance where the good soil for an unknown reason turns into barren ground.

In contrast to the Russian Orthodox, evangelical converts must become fluent in words that circulate. Bakhtin's (1981, 293) concept of authoritative discourse and internally persuasive discourse in the novel are good concepts to think with here. He describes the process of making another's word one's own like this: "The word in language is half someone else's. It becomes 'one's own' only when the speaker populates it with his own intention, his own accent, when he appropriates the word, adapting it to his own semantic and expressive intention" (see also Harding 2000, 59, 289). He further writes, "When verbal disciplines are taught in school, two basic modes are recognized for the appropriation and transmission—simultaneously—of another's words (a text, a rule, a model): 'reciting by heart' and 'retelling in one's own words'" (Bakhtin 1981, 341). The first corresponds to authoritative discourse, while the latter is internally persuasive discourse. Bakhtin explains that "the authoritative word demands that we acknowledge it, that we make it our own; it binds us, quite independent of any power it might have to persuade us internally; we encounter it with its authority already fused to it. The authoritative word is located in a distanced zone, organically connected with a past that is felt to be hierarchically higher. It is, so to speak, the word of the fathers. Its authority was already *acknowledged* in the past. It is a *prior* discourse" (342, his italics).

The Word of God Nenets converts are immersed into serves as an authoritative word that cannot be changed and can only be learned and used; it is monologic. However, all spoken language is dialogic, as Bakhtin (1984, 183) stresses: "Language lives only in the dialogic interaction of those who make use of it" (cf. Mauss 2003, 32–37). By internalizing the language of the others, also that of God from the Bible, converts are called to actively construe the significance and relevance of the text through a dialogic process. As any God-talk is witnessing, it is in a dialogue with various voices, real or imagined. Harding (2000, 34–35) phrased a matching description in her analysis of evangelical conversion, "Witnessing is rhetorical in two senses, namely, as an argument about the transformation of self that lost souls must undergo, and as a method of bringing about that change in those who listen to it. Fundamental Baptist witnessing is not just a monologue that constitutes its speaker as a culturally specific person; it is also a dialogue that reconstitutes its listeners."

Baptists' language is thus a language of ethical transformation of high personal relevance. Bruno Latour (2005, 28) has argued that religious speech is a specific "regime of enunciation." Religious talk is not there to transport information but to transport persons. As when a lover says "I love you," it is not about giving new information but asserting and renewing commitment. Thus, love-talk produces lovers as God-talk produces believers—that is, lovers of God. Baptists are concerned with the efficacy of the language, the correct tonality, the capacity to renew the relationship or to represent (make present anew) the closeness of God. As Latour (2005) says (borrowing from speech act theorists without acknowledging it), for love-talk to have effect, it must meet felicity conditions that surround the speech with all its extralinguistic aspects. As lovers test each others' statements of love by "smiles, sighs, silences, hugs, gestures, gaze, postures" (30), so do the believers who need the right tone. However, in the interaction with God—at least in an ordinary sense of interaction—there is a deep asymmetry or nonmutuality, as one gets no reaction, at least not immediately, to the expressed intimate sentiments that would otherwise shape the dialogue in a face-to-face situation. Love-talk offers thus only an incomplete comparison with God-talk, as the latter usually fails to produce such intimacy as love-talk can produce between two people who mirror each other. And yet, both love-talk and God-talk have a capacity to change the speaker's sense of self when one hears oneself saying affectionate statements. Furthermore, they both demonstrate to the other people around one's deep involvement with and commitment to the addressee (cf. Holbraad and Pedersen 2017, 266–68).[13]

As discussed in the previous chapter, Nenets converts do not show the same degree of verbal eagerness and emotionality as Russian believers in the city. Therefore, the extent and intensity of Christian verbalization is a real challenge to earlier or "traditional" use of language among Nenets and their usual self-reserve and taciturnity. In numerous situations, I observed how—when praying or speaking on biblical matters—Nenets *punryodaq* struggled to cope with this emphasis on verbalism and emotion in Baptism (as in Pentecostalism, with its particular focus on speaking in tongues, see chap. 4). Rather, appearing not to enjoy public speaking or perhaps afraid of saying the wrong thing, some men and almost all women kept their prayers short and formulaic. In the following example, on his tundra trip, Pavel addressed the Nenets about the way believers should act and speak.

> PAVEL: We have to communicate [*obshchat'sya*] openly. We should not feel embarrassed.
>
> YEVGENI: It is still difficult.
>
> PAVEL: Don't worry. Time will do it. We need to be . . . feel free. We are the family of God. The teachings of the apostles, God's Word has to be in our families every day. We also have to gather more often and communicate with each other more often. The communication is a sacrifice to God. What else can we give to God? Fish? Meat? Vera, what else can we give to God? [Silence.] Firstly, to follow the teachings; secondly, to hold communion with each other; thirdly, to pray.

Pavel tried hard to urge converts to become more articulate and vocal.[14] He was convinced that there was lots of educational work to do before the Nenets would become the *same* as others (i.e., Russian *veruyushchie*). Pavel did not call for actions to be freely chosen, but he called for people to totally submit and let the Holy Spirit work inside. In other words, one must not hinder what wants—as the discourse defines—to come out from one's interior. Pavel's is a paradoxical call for a controlled spontaneity: Nenets converts must repudiate old ways and subsume themselves under the control of God, missionaries, and fellow believers and—most importantly—work on the self. In this way, the divine other, human other, and "I" are all bound in an entangled network of control, each on different premises.

But is disciplined spontaneity a logical or practical impossibility? In her discussion of the women of the Islamic piety movement, Saba Mahmood (2005) has argued that learned ritual behavior becomes spontaneous. She writes that "the enactment of conventional gestures and behaviors devolves upon the *spontaneous* expression of *well-rehearsed* emotions and individual intentions, thereby directing attention to how one learns to express 'spontaneously' the 'right attitudes'" (129, her italics; see also Hirschkind 2006; Simon 2009). She argues that the opposition between spontaneity and convention in anthropological discussion is drawn on a Cartesian distinction of "the inner life of individuals and their outward expressions" (129n18). However, as Laidlaw (2014) reminds us, this kind of pious practice should not be seen as a form of unthinking but rather a conscious work on oneself that creates new skills and dispositions. Ethical transformation starts from trying to speak a new language that contains description of oneself as a particular kind of person (not a "pagan" but a person loyal to God's will) who has certain emotions (e.g., joy, peace), thinks and speaks in a right manner, and does certain things (e.g., prays, behaves, and dresses like a believer). This practice creates the potential to acquire intellectual, embodied, and emotional skills to act and speak as a committed believer, which matches the expectations of others to whom one is supposed to give an account of oneself. As Tim Jenkins (2013, 70–71) aptly notes about evangelical Christians, "A disciplined tongue is the means of making the self."

Evangelical Magic

In evangelicals' language ideology, as we have seen, the main emphasis is on representing what one has inside. But despite the widespread ideology of representationalism and intentionalism, there is also a place for what we could call a magic use of signs. Stanley Tambiah (1990, 7) argues in his genealogical account of magic that "the Bible accepts the reality and efficacy of pagan magic." Take the belief, widespread among Christians, that mentioning the name of Jesus has power to drive away Satan (Cameron 1991, 47). What gives these words efficacy? What makes this magic different from Nenets magic?

Unlike the Calvinists on Sumba who deny the automatic efficacy of words (Keane 2007, 70), Baptists in Russia implicitly accept the idea of automatism in certain situations. Accounts of believing prisoners from the Soviet period abound with descriptions of how attempts to silence God's words failed. These accounts present as their favorite incidents in the cases in which atheists unwittingly quoted God's words—for example, when writing on a confiscation order the title of a religious painting, such as *God is our refuge and strength. . . . Therefore we shall not fear . . . though the waters roar* (Vins 1989, 9–13; the quote is from Psalms 46:1–3). Taken out of their initial context, God's words gain a quality of magical efficacy, as quoting the scriptures in an official document, as any form of witnessing, would invoke his presence and create real effects in the world.

However, in other contexts, missionaries still warn that having God's name in the mouth in the wrong context (e.g., nonserious language) can have unwanted consequences. Probably the best example of automatic language—separated from intentions—is when a born-again person blasphemes against the Holy Spirit. There the human words take on a force mechanically. This is said to be the only sin that God does not forgive (with the reference to Mark 3:28–29). Boyko, one of the leading Baptists of the Soviet period, describes how, when he was in the Gulag camp of Khalmer-Yu (the village north of Vorkuta where Independents came to trade, see chap. 1), he thought for a moment that he had blasphemed the Holy Spirit (*pokhulil Dukha Svyatogo*) with an unwilling utterance ("In Christ Satan"). He only later realized that he never said that—this sensation was Satan's trick who made him feel he had blasphemed God (Boyko 2006, 31).[15]

Converts in the tundra have also come to stress the dangers of uncontrolled self-expression. Consider this example. Nenets presbyter Andrei described how, in an Orthodox church, his grandfather's third wife had made a promise that changed her life for worse:

> She had *ikota* [hiccup possession, which old Vata had, see chap. 5]. She had it from an Orthodox church! She was betrothed at church and given a blessing

there. Then she was given an Orthodox Law [*pravoslavnyy zakon*] but she could not understand what the betrothal meant [that it was a promise to God, as Andrei later explained]. She did not follow the rules and, instead of a blessing, an impure spirit entered her. She herself rejoiced at it. You know the place in the Bible where it is told that if you clean only partly or incompletely from the impure, it returns with seven other miseries? Things are much worse than they were before. I usually talk to my sisters in faith that if you give a promise to God, you have to have a good conscience [*sovest'*], you have to be careful [not to break the promise].

For Andrei, the words of promise were powerful in themselves, as they tie a person to outside agents (as has often been noted about Nenets).[16] Therefore, a promise that is given as if unintentionally or not fully understood still counts as a promise that results in responsibility regardless of one's thoughts or motives. As we see, the automatic efficacy of words can take various forms in believers' thinking. In the end, one's intentions, speech, and moral character remain in a volatile and unpredictable relationship with each other.

To sum up, there are both continuous and discontinuous elements present in old and new understandings of speech and silence. Remember that Yegor's daily worry was to get his tongue (and heart and soul) right. He used the Bible and praying to master his tongue. And yet, as in his preconversion life, he still had to beware the power of words. The main shift was that he, like other believers, had become preoccupied with his inner self and the signs it exteriorized.

In the next chapter, I shall look more closely at the intricate link between evangelical language and personhood and how Nenets Baptist converts are involved in ethical self-transformation. The chapter deals with the challenge Lambek (2015a, xi) has described like this: "What it means to live in a world with ideals, rules, or criteria that cannot be met completely or consistently."

7

PURE SUBJECTS

Striving for Christian Individualism

In this last chapter, I ask how Nenets Baptist converts try to make themselves into new kinds of person, and more specifically, how they adopt the Christian concept of self in which the notions of purity and holiness are central. The ethnographic focus here is on committed converts who attempt to create new lives for themselves as they are instructed by God via missionaries, the scriptures, and divine signs around them. As we have seen in the case of Yegor and others, there are struggles related to the ideals of piety and everyday life, with its moments of vulnerability, contradiction, and failure.

I suggest that these tensions are part and parcel of the conversion experience, especially when these inconsistencies are made explicit and become a part of the ethical project of self-cultivation. Defining failures and mistakes as sins (*grekhi* in Russian, *khebyakhaq* in Nenets) and correcting oneself are integral parts of gradually becoming a different person—a born-again Christian—which in the long run should transform one's character with more lasting effects. According to Baptist logic, growing into a true believer involves sustained striving and investment: taking a new perspective on the world and oneself, learning Christian rules and developing new virtues, becoming alert to failures, talking about one's faith, and exposing oneself to criticism from others. Conversion thus entails continuous reworking of one's self, both in public and private

As Andrei said in the previous chapter, one's life as a believer is keeping one's promise to God. Swearing oaths and keeping promises, of course, are not Christian inventions. As Lambek (2010a, 27) has put it, "keeping one's word," or rather trying to, lies at the center of any ethical becoming.

He writes, "It is striking how often a central, primary, or salient feature of ethics is identified as keeping one's word, following through on what one has committed to, finishing what one has begun, or at least acknowledging that one has changed direction. This may be as ordinary and implicit as adhering to the conversational implicatures of speaking (as set forth by Grice or equivalent ones in a given speech community), as everyday as carrying through the obligations of kinship, or as grand and explicit as adhering to the Abrahamic covenant or redeeming the Christian sacrifice" (27–28; see also Grice 1975).

One's pledges and promises are constantly evaluated by other people (De Vries 2008, 82–84; Lambek 2015a, 34–35). Among Independents, these are not only fellow Christians but also non-Christians who comment on converts' behavior. Every *punryoda* knows that, at some level, minor failings to keep one's promise are unavoidable. But cases of breaking the promise to God, which in the evangelical language is "backsliding" (*otstuplenie*), are perceived as tragic among devout believers, even as the hope that "the lost son" (*bludnyy syn*) will return is still entertained. When I visited Yegor's camp in 2012, one of his adult sons, Vanya, had stopped praying. Yegor turned to the Bible for his daily reading and chose to read the parable of the prodigal son (Luke 15:11–32). While slowly reading out the words, he looked from time to time at Vanya, who sat silently nearby. Yegor's facial expressions reflected pain and reproach. Throughout my stay, he was not openly critical toward his son and fulfilled his duty to express Christian love for his child. In this case, personal attachments and affects were competing with explicit commitments to various human and nonhuman others creating hurtful moments for those involved.

Baptists insist that a believer who has made a promise and has sincere faith relies on God's promise to save his children who endeavor to be pure and holy. In this ascetic logic, it is not so much the achieved degree of piety but rather an ongoing striving for an ethically consistent life, especially in its public dimension. Believers can show their conviction and promise-keeping by bringing their words and acts into the realm of the explicit through their conduct—the verbal in particular, as this is the primary way to probe oneself and be visible and audible to others. Public commitment to one's words and deeds has far reaching consequences: it evokes evaluative measures of discipline, obedience, surveillance, and denunciation in the community; also it tests relations with oneself and others around that are inherited from the preconversion past and that continuously reemerge.

I suggest that we consider two aspects regarding the radically new experience of converts in the tundra camps. First, the converts become much more self-focused: they try to consciously cultivate themselves as born-again Christians by changing their embodied behavior and ways of speaking. The introduced cultivation of the self—a systematic virtue ethics—is a deeply novel experience for Independents, especially considering that they were not exposed to the transformative policies of state institutions (schools, the army, collective farms, etc.) that exerted a significant influence on most tundra dwellers' lives in the Soviet period. Second, the evangelical model teaches that one's self is a source of sinfulness and therefore one's human self must be, in theological language, renounced. This entails a promise of a kind of theosis in this life and salvation in the afterlife.[1] This somewhat paradoxical claim of a need to work on one's self and to renounce it will be in focus next.

Foucault's model of "technologies of the self" has been particularly productive for thinking about ethical self-fashioning in Christianity (Faubion 2011; Robbins 2004; Strhan 2015; Zigon 2010, 2011a, 2011b; see also Laidlaw 2014). In his later texts, he developed a genealogy of Christian practices of cultivation of the self by commenting, among others, on monk and theologian John Cassian's (c. 360–c. 435) writings on monasticism. Foucault (1997, 177) describes these ascetic technologies as "techniques that permit individuals to effect, by their own means, a certain number of operations on their own bodies, their own souls, their own thoughts, their own conduct, and this in a manner so as to transform themselves, modify themselves, and to attain a certain state of perfection, happiness, purity, supernatural power."[2] The fifth century monks had to engage in a constant practice of self-scrutiny, as Foucault (242) notes: "Each person has the duty to know who he is, that is, to try to know what is happening inside him, to acknowledge faults, to recognize temptations, to locate desires; and everyone is obliged to disclose these things either to God or to others in the community and, hence, to bear public or private witness against oneself. The truth obligations of faith and the self are linked together. This link permits a purification of the soul impossible without self-knowledge" (see also 2015, 54). Foucault (2015, 72) argues that, in the Christian practices of the self, verbalization plays a special role. Confessions articulated in the presence of others at once reveal one's sinful thoughts and help to distance oneself from the sinful ways, turning words into a form of self-renunciation or self-sacrifice.[3]

Christian practices of verbalization as self-transformative procedures have a profound impact on the world of those Nenets who have converted. Unlike in early Christianity, where purity of heart is gained through specifically monastic ways ("contempt of all possessions," "the mortification of desires" as phrased by Cassian, quoted in Paden 1988, 73), Baptist converts in the tundra are as much concerned with recognizing their sinful human nature as they are busy recognizing their own saintliness and purity.

In the following, my ethnographic focus stays with Yegor, his son Ngarka, and the young woman called Syado, who all, in one way or another, go through the struggle of becoming and being good Christian individuals. In their everyday lives, they all try to adapt to fundamental evangelical ideas such as human sinfulness, purity of soul, and certainty of salvation. Doubt and anxiety are an essential part of this process, as are the judgments of how to balance ideas, values, and commitments that are incommensurable with one another.

One night before falling asleep, Ngarka, lying next to me in the tent, said, "You know what keeps me awake in the night . . . why on earth Eve had to sin? If she had not sinned, we would all live happily in Eden now. But instead, we have to suffer here on earth." Ngarka's burst of anxiety showed me how much some Nenets converts were contemplating cosmic matters that had come to have relevance for their individual lives ages later, or by their account, "six thousand years later" than the initial event. The twenty-five-year-old Ngarka had just returned from his first missionary trip to the Yamal Nenets and Khanty across the Urals. He was one of those core young members whom missionary Pavel occasionally asked to give a sermon from the pulpit in the Vorkuta prayer house. Ngarka was determined to leave the tundra and enjoy all the benefits of city life, especially, as he said, close communion with church members elsewhere. For him, like many other younger devotees, leaving the tundra was also an issue of finding a partner, preferably a white Russian girl, and starting a proper family life, as God required every man to do. He knew that he could shape his life in a very different way from the lives of his ancestors, a conviction echoed by Protestants elsewhere who feel themselves "enticed to write new scripts for their lives" (Meyer 2004, 461). For Ngarka, as for Ivan and many others who enjoyed the new kind of communality associated with conversion, there was a pull to create a modern, individual self, filtered through specifically Christian concerns.

Ngarka's moment of anxiety over the character of fallen human nature and the consequent separation from the transcendent God was not exceptional among fresh converts. Like many others, he had become acutely aware of the new logic of loss and gain. The anxiety worked in a tension between the events at the two ends of history—falling into sin and the Second Coming. In her discussion on the problem of transcendence, Fenella Cannell (2006, 15) has described the significance of this idea to Christianity:

> The separation of man from the divine—the origin of the "unhappy consciousness" that recognizes this loss—sets up problems to which anthropologists and historians have recurred again and again in accounts of Christian thinking, including the need for mediation with this distant God, the centrality of a salvationist emphasis in which death (the only place in which man and God can be reunited) becomes the crucial defining moment of life, the setting up of a hierarchy between life and afterlife, with crucial implications for ideas about economy and exchange, and the creation of a new notion of interiority that has its origins in the need of the Christian to consider the fate of his or her own soul.

Ngarka's deeply personal anxiety—his "unhappy consciousness"—mirrors these cosmic tensions. I suggest this anxiety is not an impasse, however, but rather an inadequacy that is necessary for one's self-constitution as a good Christian here on earth. This is not only "a mournful awareness of the inevitability of moral failure" (Robbins 2004, 208) or morally right attitude of humility (Laidlaw 2014, 127–28) but also a necessary precondition to cultivating one's certainty of salvation. This is because transcendence is not understood as absolute: this "distant God," with the three-in-one composition (Father, Son, and Holy Spirit), is now and again spoken about as being nearby, dwelling inside oneself, and yet located in an elsewhere of the future. As Jon Bialecki (2017, 7) put it in his study on Vineyard Christians of California, "There is a perception of religious time as 'already/not-yet,' where God's grace is present in the world but has yet to complete its inevitable triumph over the Devil and his damaged earth." This is a "problem of presence," as Engelke (2007) has aptly characterized a perception of the divine being simultaneously present and absent.

Russian Baptists stress that between these two crucial events—falling into sin and the Second Coming—lies the resurrection of Christ, which gives Christians the possibility to lead a holy life through endeavors of purification (*ochishchenie*) and sanctification (*osvyashchenie*). Through these teachings, which are of particular importance for Unregistered Baptists (see *Ob osvyashchenii* 2006), Nenets converts have come to realize that they cannot entirely escape the sinful human condition, but they can still surmount the distance and have a taste of the heavenly future by having chosen salvation, being born again, and being filled with the Holy Spirit. Holiness—as a near reunion of man and God—is thus something that must be attempted in this life, even if becoming holy will never be completed here on earth. Therefore, one's objective can be only a partial restoration of the initial, prelapsarian communion with God, accompanied by a promise of full communion with God in heaven.

Even if a convert's sense of change may be sudden (especially in a self-narrative such as presented by Ivan, see chap. 2), sanctification—the process of becoming close to God—is seen as a gradual ethical self-transformation. Turning one's ideas, motives, habits, and desires into sustained practices of thought and talk require time (cf. Crapanzano 2000; Stromberg 1993, 2015). As Ngarka put it, the main objective in his life was to save his soul, and all other objectives were subordinated to that. Having gone through a rupture, having given God his promise to live a saintly life, and having been forgiven for all the sins from his past life through an act of repentance and the rite of baptism, Ngarka was now facing lifelong maintenance work with himself. Surrendering to God was possible only through rejection of his sinful nature in order to warrant the presence of the divine inside—an imagined site of new significance—and the constant exercise of vigilance in regard to Satan's evil acts.

The evangelicals' theology of self-perfection contains thus an inherent tension, as a believing individual has both fallen and saved components. The aim for believers is to recognize one's sinful desires and thoughts, to ask forgiveness for these and to try to live up to the exemplary role of a holy person, to be Christlike. Although the ideal is that a person stays saintly throughout one's life—and largely this is what Unregistered Baptists imagine to be the case—unconscious (*nesoznatel'noe*) sinning is still assumed to happen even in the lives of the born-again. This divided person is therefore always in flux, trying to live up to what one knows God would expect from oneself.

In practical terms, striving for sanctification required that Ngarka and other committed *punryodaq* dedicate themselves to various everyday activities such as praying, reading the Bible, avoiding sinful deeds (both visible and invisible), and responding to others'—especially missionaries'—evaluative comments. Ngarka's moment of anxiety, described above, would have been impossible before his exposure to Christian language. Speaking about his own inherited sinfulness and desire for salvation was part of the production of his Christian self. But to become a good believer, he needed to hold communion with others and engage in forms of collective prayers and Bible reading events that, as evangelists say, are more efficacious than solitary prayers or attempts to understand the Bible alone (recall what Pavel said on the benefits of communal reading in chap. 6; cf. Prokhorov 2013, 159, 273). Nevertheless, this form of collective work primarily serves the purpose of his individual salvation. On the one hand, Ngarka shared his religious aspiration and commitment with others in the family and nearby camps. On the other hand, he was also aware that only he was responsible for his failures and successes and that only as an individual—and not just by being a member of a believing family—could he conquer the sin he had inherited from Eve.

In the anthropological literature, it has become a common assumption that conversion to Christianity, and especially to evangelical Protestantism, makes people more individualist or has the power to individualize a person in a specific way.[4] This is not to say that Christianity necessarily would introduce individualism "into a world that formerly had lacked" it (Keane 2007, 52; see also Laidlaw 2014, 32–39) but that Protestant individualism, as a value and practice, promotes a new pattern of ethical self-formation by paying heightened attention to oneself as an object of scrutiny and taking public responsibility for one's words and acts.

A few remarks about earlier Nenets individualism and related ethical practices that existed before conversion may clarify what has changed since Nenets have converted to evangelical Christianity. As mentioned in the introduction, Nenets reindeer herders entertain a particular ideal of living on the land and being relatively independent from others (Golovnev 2004, 47). The preconversion Nenets model of autonomy, however, entails various kinds of dependencies and relationalities through exchanges—such as gifts, known as *myadonzey, myadinzey*, and *padarak*; or bride-price payment (*nye mirq*); or dowry—that form bonds temporarily or over one's life course.[5] As we have seen (see chap. 5), this model also contains distributed and detachable aspects of personhood that emerge through various constellations related to personal qualities (e.g., the excessive power of an adult compared to the vulnerability of a small child), things and animals (e.g., reindeer and puppies as extensions of their human owners), spirits and forces (e.g., hiccup worms moving in one's body; dangerous power coming from menstruating women), or words (e.g., being exposed to one's personal name or song; being asked about one's intentions and future plans). Nenets individualism is not so much an expression of indivisibility but an ideal of relative autonomy of action while dealing with aspects of vulnerability to certain forms of relationality. As we saw with the case of Tikynye's inherited shamanic kinship with wolves, various forms of relationality with nonhumans are common. Such instances of humans' porousness demonstrate that a person would need to be careful not to become exposed to others' intrusive and damaging forces (this is where shamans were believed to be different from ordinary people, as they were empowered with extraordinary capacities by being reconstituted by spirits during initiation). Furthermore, as we have discussed earlier, one needs to avoid emotionally charged relations and attachments with other humans, as they may have fatal consequences (as in verbal quarrels that can kill, see chap. 5).

In more mundane circumstances, the value of relative autonomy—taken as a form of nondependency—is evident in both collective and individual terms. A family that leads an independent life in the tundra marks its independence with the word *ngara*. This can be translated as "to lead an independent way of life," as when a young family starts to live on its own after securing enough reindeer, skins, and sledges; when somebody who has worked for another person or inside a collective farm is able to start an independent (*ngaryoi*) life; or when those who once settled in villages return to a tundra lifestyle in search of freedom. This form of autonomy for a family is primarily related to reindeer or, to be more precise, to many reindeer. Those who have too few reindeer are dependent on others as they get transport reindeer bulls on loan from wealthier herders or engage in other forms of exchange as insurance against misfortunes such as losing reindeer in an epidemic (see Yevladov 1992, 168–73).[6] This also has a cosmological dimension, as Yevladov notes, "Nenets believe that you should not regret the loss [of reindeer] because 'gods take these to themselves'" (171). However, the loss of reindeer to other humans, including state representatives (or just any *lutsa*), is looked upon differently and is considered an act of intrusion and theft. Wealthy and poor, Christian and non-Christian alike try to keep their independence from state institutions that, as they fear, would limit their options for increasing the number of their reindeer.

There is yet another layer of independence that is more personal (not necessarily solitary, rather cooperative) and has to do with individual ethical practices. As a young person, one can achieve autonomy by learning skills through listening, observation, example, and repeated trials. This is how one becomes good at herding, hunting, wayfinding, sewing, cooking, repairing snowmobiles—in short, managing things on one's own and not depending too much on others' help (Golovnev 2017, 50; see also Ingold

Figure 7.1. Mastering lasso is one of the most important skills for men, November 2006.

2000). This kind of autonomy ideally helps to raise a herd of several hundred animals, which gives a young family a wide-ranging economic independence. This (above all male) vision of becoming an independent herder, finding a partner, and starting a family is positively discussed among the (male) youth who still live with their parents.

After conversion new values of sociality have been introduced. On the one hand, the church as Christ's body aims at a "religious ethic of brotherhood" (Weber 2009, 348), which is supposed to create new forms of care and support at the expense of preconversion relationalities. And yet, people in the tundra share histories and reindeer pastures, and they must still cooperate with one another, regardless of their religious belonging and views. As Keane (2016, 214) notes, even the most pious depend on kin and community who might not share the same religious values and aspirations. Some

Nenets believers even continue their gift partnerships with nonbelievers (who are often their kin), or otherwise show respect, hospitality, or generosity based on established relationships. In Christian terms, this is discussed as the dictate to "love thy neighbor," which demonstrates how "habitual ethics" (207) is linked to the new ethics of explicit rules.

As missionaries discourage becoming too intimate with nonbelievers, so do they not recognize a positive version of intimacy with animals and things (while this kind of intimacy is imagined to exist; see chap. 4): this would constitute an illicit form of relationships for a believer. While converts sort relationships with humans versus nonhuman others on the basis of a binary principle of absolute good versus evil, the older Nenets concept of personhood allows for far more varied forms of partibility with spirits, animals, and things. But as Andrei once said in a sermon, "the old life," (*nyevkhy yil*), must be discarded fully. However, converts struggle with this new Christian logic, as the earlier logic of engagement with nonhuman others is difficult to abandon and forget. As Piers Vitebsky notes (2017a), sometimes it is not converting "*to* a new way of being" but converting "*from* an old one" (165, his italics), which is the key issue in a religious conversion.

Purity and Certainty

Nenets converts stressed repeatedly that one must live a pure life that would please God.[7] Becoming holy is related to the concept of purity (*chistota*, also "cleanliness," see chap. 2), as the missionaries taught. But purity is a notion that matters to both Christians and non-Christians, even if there is no straight translatability between the Christian and Nenets concepts. For Christians, purity is related to a life without sinful conduct such as drinking, smoking, or cursing, and, more broadly, to God's saving grace. One can attain God's grace by living with the right kind of intentions in mind, ensuring blessings in this life as well as eternal life thereafter. For non-Christian Nenets, purity is not related to inner intentions, desires, feelings, or introspection but to one's distributed personhood, bodily fluids, and relations with invisible spirits. Because of these conceptual discrepancies and translational difficulties, fresh converts struggle with the notion of purity and holiness, as we shall see in the following ethnographic example.

I witnessed a scene in 2002 when missionary Pavel—using the Pauline language from the New Testament—asked a recently married and baptized

Nenets woman, Syado, whether she saw herself as holy (*svyataya* in Russian). A male Nenets convert, who was interpreting Pavel to Syado, translated *svyataya* as *nyaro*, which means "unpolluted" or "pure," contrasting with *syaqmei*, which means "polluted" or "dangerously powerful." Among Nenets, *nyaro* and *syaqmei* are the key concepts regulating relations not only between men and women but also between the living and the dead or between Nenets and Russians.

Syaqmei is conceptualized as a certain kind of power that attracts various visible and invisible agents, be these diseases, wolves, Russians, or other predators into the sphere of the "real people." To ward off dangerous agents, a ritual of cleansing with the smoke of *torabtq*[8] and metal items are needed. This purification rite (*nibtyeva*) takes place after a woman has given birth, finished menstruating, or overstepped or touched certain objects belonging to men or related to reindeer; when somebody has died or visited a settlement; when a shaman starts a seance; or when men prepare to go to a sacred site. *Syaqmei* is partly gendered, as women are seen as a main source of dangerous pollution (Liarskaya 2005; Serpivo 2016). Until a girl's first menstruation, she is *nyaro* like any boy: after reaching the fertile age, she should not step over men's belongings, reindeer poles, or strings, and she should place her boots in a special bag (*syaqmei pad*, also used for catching evil words, as described in chap. 5) that she can carry on the special *syabu* sledge in order not to contract pollution to others. When women reach the end of childbearing age, they are *nyaro* again (Kharyuchi 2004, 156). Christianity has brought a change in these concepts and practices: after conversion, routine cleansing rituals where women repeat "*kyv, kyv, kyv*" in a low voice disappear; instead, purifying prayers are enacted with the words "Please cleanse me, O Lord."

Pavel's question about holiness and purity made Syado hesitate, look down, and say that she did not know whether she was *nyaro*. She had been raised with the knowledge that all fertile women had female power that was both procreative and destructive. But now she could not be sure what she was expected to say and feel. She knew that this had to be pleasing to God and missionaries. Pavel insisted that she ought to know that she was *svyataya*, saying that her confident words about her own holiness would mirror her inner condition as a saved person. Syado was probably confused not only by the mismatch between the old and new concept of purity but also by the complexity—and inherent contradictions—of the evangelical concepts of purity and impurity *and* certainty and uncertainty.

Pavel's claim that Syado ought to see herself as pure was based on the conviction that after having become a Christian, a person enshrines the Holy Spirit that helps to keep one's sins under control. Nevertheless, Syado could hear in sermons that even believers had to ask forgiveness for their sins. There was thus always an inherent tension between representing oneself as sinful and being truly confident in one's salvation. On the one hand, one is supposed to scrutinize oneself; on the other hand, this constant vigilance must coexist with the assurance of salvation. Furthermore, as we saw in the case of Nyeteta and her episode of mental breakdown (see chap. 4), one's sense of certainty could be undermined by extraordinary events that others could judge as signs of an impure spiritual condition. Even if one's thoughts and acts have not changed, being subject to evaluation—and potentially condemnation—by others is a force that one cannot fully control.

Among Unregistered Baptists, purity and certainty are entangled notions. Aleksandr, a senior Russian presbyter, once told me, "Every person carries inside a testimony [*svidetel'stvo*], a confident conviction of being saved or not. You have to inspect yourself. You need to open your heart to God." This rather Calvinistic statement partly echoes what Foucault has written about Christian efforts of purification of interiority as an ethical process, as we have seen above. Aleksandr's statement demonstrates that Russian Unregistered Baptists in the early twenty-first century demand an assertion of conviction (as celebrated in the lyrics of a popular hymn: "Yes, I am saved! That is not a word of pride"). Declaring certainty had to be supported by petitionary prayers to God to make it real and effective. And yet, in other places and moments, Baptists show doubt and anxiety over their status in God's eyes (Prokhorov 2013, 101–2). This performative talk of certainty and praying to God was thus accompanied by claims of doubt, a necessary balancing act so as not to sound too arrogant and to avoid losing one's salvation (Crapanzano 2000; see also Engelke 2007, 81–85).[9]

At least in the very first phase of conversion, we see that self-examination is guided by rules and ideals offered by missionaries rather than being a self-motivated act of self-scrutiny. Syado was expected to publicly declare herself to be pure and confident, even if she continued to keep her *syaqmei pad* in the entrance area of her tent and put it on the *syabu* sledge, as in the old days. As an explanation for this practice, Ivan said to me that using such old-style arrangements based on gender rules was now a matter of keeping order in the tenthold and no longer a spiritual problem.[10]

Never in Anger

For Nenets converts, following teachings and managing one's natural inclinations proves challenging. Baptist missionaries taught that the heart (*serdtse* in Russian, *syei* in Nenets) as an interior self was the battlefield between
sinful and divine inclinations, a cosmic fight taking place on a very intimate level.[11] I witnessed such a struggle over the years in Yegor, who made
continuous efforts at avoiding relapse into his previous life of sin and molding himself as a saved person (see chaps. 5 and 6). As we have seen, Yegor's
postconversion biography contained slippages to the past sinful self and
guilt over participating in the old kind of singing as well as feeling his heart
being filled with the Holy Spirit. We also saw that Yegor prayed to God to
strengthen his self-control—including getting his tongue right—and to improve his knowledge of the teachings.

Many in the tundra considered Yegor a tempestuous authoritarian.
Yegor used to say he had two big sins that were hard to get rid of. (I never
heard non-Christians engage in this kind of self-analytic statement.) One
was his inclination to make jokes, and another was his outbursts of anger.
Both were related to what he characterized as his inability to control himself. Almost every day, Yegor found a reason to laugh at children, me, or
other guests. Although this kind of joking is widespread among Nenets, it is
categorically condemned in the new Christian context. When others went
along with the laughter, often he stopped laughing and then others stopped
as well. Then Yegor said, in a serious tone, that laughing was not pleasing to
God. Thus he reestablished his "right" kind of self as a "serious" person in
the eyes of those present, either human or divine. He also became enraged
easily and occasionally shouted at children when they had not done what
was expected or when they just got something wrong. In these moments of
anger, he typically called the children *lutsaq*.[12]

Once in 2006, when on the road to the next campsite through deep snow,
I saw Yegor accidentally injure a stubborn harness reindeer (*pyelyei*) with his
driving pole (*tyur*). It started to bleed from its anus. Not only was there danger of losing a beautiful white reindeer cow but also this was a deeply em-
barrassing accident for him. He had behaved clumsily, like a *lutsa*. Watching
the bleeding animal, Yegor shouted at us when we came close to the heavily
breathing animal: "Does it look funny to you?" All silently retreated to our
sledges. Later in the evening, after we had set up our camp, Yegor seemed
unusually subdued. He took up the event again: "Anger is a big sin. But God

knows that we were only having fun. He knows that I am impatient and that I am always in haste to reach the next campsite before darkness. I have a habit to joke and to yell at others. I use to tell my sons that if I say things quietly, people think I am not serious." He went on with reading a passage in the Bible picked up from his reading plan and asked God in a prayer to forgive and assist him to get rid of his "bad habits." Yegor was troubled, but he expressed certainty that he could rely on God's help to restore his pure inner self, placate his excessive emotions, and undo all his failings. He lived with God's promise to help him keep his own promise to God.

Note that Yegor spoke from both the first-person singular and plural (compare this to the singing that took him back into his "pagan" self, as described in chap. 5). As a unitary individual, he ought to see himself as solely responsible for his actions. But Yegor asked forgiveness in the name of "us" by saying that "*we* were only having fun," even though no others were involved in his moments of rage or laughter that day (or at least did not initiate them). Yegor seeing "us" as the cause of his own rage reflects an older Nenets understanding, in which the source for one's actions may lie with other actors. The presupposed individual responsibility seemed to have made only a partial inroad into Yegor's ethical sensibilities. This kind of ambivalence, or the displacement of responsibility, is present in new converts' lives and, as a result, lots of self-rectifying claims were made among *punryodaq*. Yegor's nephew, young Andrei, who was perhaps the least serious Baptist youngster I knew among the Yamb-To converts, claimed that his jokes were just acts of his tongue: "Actually, my heart is not like that."

In the long run, this practice of striving for coherence in one's life should bring about the transformation of ethical character. As we have seen (see chap. 6), Baptist logic posits that one's self-transformation takes place only with God's help—that is, through divine grace. God could open human hearts, and this was frequently requested in prayers, once again illustrating how efficacious language was imagined to be. Recall what Pavel said about Poru in chapter 2: "But Poru loves to drink. Yet our Jesus is able to make his heart receptive." The inherent theo-logic here is that growing as a believer is letting Christ (or the Holy Spirit) take over one's self: when he lives in one's heart, he will lead the person's actions and desires, "for it is God who works in you to will and to act according to his good purpose" (*Ob osvyashchenii* 2006, 16). The Baptists' manual of teachings makes it clear that there is no self left, as "yet not I, but Christ liveth in me" (ibid.) or, as the same text puts it, "By fulfilling God's commands, the more we fulfill with the Holy Spirit

(Ephesians 5:18), the more we acquire knowledge and strength for the holy life, the more Christ expresses in us, and the less there is place for our 'I,' the manifestation of our character" (17). We see in the Baptist tenets that self-constitution works paradoxically by diminishing the share of one's self and giving more space to God inside a person through the Holy Spirit (or Christ). This is not only an intellectual but also an embodied experience, as we saw with Yegor, who rubbed his chest after his baptism and expressed his overwhelming joy (see chap. 6).

I suggest that, somewhat paradoxically, the verbal denial of the self is the actual production site of the individualist self and Christian character (cf. Bialecki 2018, 217). Missionaries who have accumulated lots of blessings and wisdom (*premudrost'*) have little of the human—meaning sinful—self left in them; therefore, what they say and command is seen as action of the Holy Spirit.[13] Circularly, the same spirit helps them in their prayers to the very same divine agent. While Pentecostals performed this circularity through speaking in tongues, the Baptists demonstrated it through a sober, measured language (see chaps. 4 and 6).

What every convert is supposed to know is that one becomes holy only when one's desire and choice are perfectly aligned with the right kind of external determinacy—expressing the will of God.[14] This requires assuming a God's-eye view on oneself, others, and the entire environment in which one lives. One morning, after reading a passage on God's rage, Yegor said, "If we do not remember God, the rage of God would come close to us." The same day, the two of us drove our sledges over the autumn ice of a lake. Water emerged from the trails of our sleds, showing how risky it was to make a shortcut over a layer of thin ice. Yegor said with a tone full of meaning, "You see, this water is like God's rage. We should keep to the edge of the lake." It was his daily practice to recall the Bible passage he had read that day. The questions "What is God trying to tell me?" or "What is God's intention?" are parts of converts' everyday work of reading the self in context (Harding 2000, 33; see also Crapanzano 2000, 89–90; 2017). Yegor was reading the landscape, as he always had done, only his moral interpretation had changed. Instead of identifying signs of local spirits in the landscape, Yegor was interpreting what God wanted to tell him through the freshly read or heard Word (see Vallikivi 2022 for more detail).[15] He was replacing preconversion ideas with the propositional knowledge acquired through everyday reading of scriptures. His duty was to hold present the divine gaze on himself and the world, listen to God, be open to unexpected moments of divine intervention (e.g., the sound of the cracking ice, dreams, etc.), and share them with others. Yegor's reflection of the world through scripture demonstrates how the formation of Christian character is constituted through shifting between perspectival positions: by self-reflection through a God's-eye view, which is a kind of reminder to oneself of God's presence, and by standing back and looking at one's deeds, words, and thoughts from a distance (cf. Nichols 2011, 221).

Embracing a God's-Eye View

It is often repeated in insiders' and outsiders' texts that religious conversion opens a new perspective (Schott 2016, 200). This expression is not only a metaphor for a change of faith; it can also be seen as the development of a new type of imaginative, affective, and embodied type of perspective-taking (Hage 2014, 150). To be a believer is to question how one appears to oneself in the eyes of God, which is inseparable from being evaluated by fellow humans, or by the generalized other—that is, our sensation of how society sees us (Mead 1962, 154; see also Strhan 2015, 16). For converts, assuming this gaze takes the form of the crucial question—What does God want from me (or us)? This is an imagined vantage point that has profound ethical consequences. The ideal is that the new perspective from God would always be held present to help the convert construct a coherent Christian life. In practice, however, assuming a divine point of view requires self-discipline, forming necessary habits, remembering God's teachings, and learning new words and rituals, all of which entail arduous work. It is a constant process of developing and maintaining obedience and loyalty to *a* point of view.

Keane (2016, 201) has also argued that piety regimes rely on "the inculcation of a God's-eye view," which "posits a single organizing vision" (213). It is seeing oneself from another's point view and imagining God's (or, in secular contexts, the state's, party's, leader's, etc.) perspective on oneself. He has noted about Christian and Muslim piety movements, "The participants in these movements actively and self-consciously strive to live ethically consistent lives. In both piety movements, that demand for consistency is partly explained by the inculcation of a God's-eye view, a version of the third-person perspective from which the faithful is expected to see the totality of his or her life and impose order on it" (200–201). Keane shows that the ability to take an external perspective on oneself is essential to ethics, from everyday acts of communication to complex religious systems such as Christianity or Islam—these ethical regimes can be highly organizing as well as rationalizing and universalizing. He stresses the significance of perspective-taking in reform movements like this: "The point of view of a transcendent deity offers a position on which to stand, from which one may survey the whole range of known ethical values available in any given cultural world, such that their inconsistencies become visible. It is the pressure exerted by this asymptotically transcendental point of view that provides at least the conceptual and ethical motivation for the kinds of purification or reform movements that are so characteristic of monotheistic religious history" (210). God's gaze is mediated not only by other people but also by things and signs all around, which are, in Keane's term, "ethical affordances" (e.g., new names for experiences, things, or ideas that emerge in social interactions), which offer, but do not determine, whether any of these are picked up and used. Although there is no God in Communist regimes, they can offer "a similar totalizing role" with the help of "the Marxist-Leninist theory of history and the social categories it presupposed" (240; see also 2014), or more specifically with such documents as the "Moral Code of the Builders of Communism" (Kharkhordin 1999, 250–51; Zigon 2010, 206), or various institutions such as the Communist Party (Groys 2009, 106; Kotkin 1995, 229; Laidlaw 2018, 186).

I would suggest that any conversion is a combined shift in a linguistic and moral vantage point (see also Jenkins 2013, 74). Expressing loyalty as a Christian requires the acquisition of the new language and speaking it to significant others, divine and human, in public. This language contains its own vocabulary, style, prosody, narratives, and texts that reflect a particular connection to the Christian morality system. To look at the interconnection of perspective and language, it is worth returning to Humphrey's reading of Badiou and her concept of decision-event (see chap. 2).[16] Let me recall that in Humphrey's (2008, 357) interpretation, a decision-event is part of subject formation in particular circumstances, such as "the advent of new regimes, convulsions wrought by war, schisms of former social wholes and, in general, the overturning of accustomed patterns of intelligibility and the advent of a radically new idea" (see also Laidlaw et al. 2018). A decision-event cannot happen without "universal ideas" or without "the deployment of a new language" and its specific vocabulary (such as "organization-creation of the mass," "common people," "Party," "us," and "together," as in Humphrey's [2008, 363] example of revolutionary figures of Inner Mongolia in the 1920s).

The Nenets who have decided to become believers know that they must change their perspective and speak the new language, which is the only way to constitute themselves as new subjects (compare with early Nenets Communists, such as Yevsyugin, introduced in chap. 1). It is not only new words and categories (sin, salvation, pagans, witnessing, and so on) that converts must learn, however, but also a whole set of new pragmatics. As discussed in chapter 6, one is expected to become fluent in this faith language, which becomes objective proof that one has stopped speaking the language of the past self or unsaved others. However, the new language—despite its claims of universal reach—has its inner limits, and in wider social contexts, it may need adaptation or translation. This is a revolutionary language that must become one's own, while it might not be fully comprehensible to those who are not fellow revolutionaries (cf. Prokhorov 2013, 260, 309–15). It can make sense only from within.

Badiou (2001, 82) calls this kind of language a "subject-language" that acclaims a truth (see also 2003). Žižek (1999) describes the concept of subject-language (which has some similarity with Latour's love-talk, discussed in chap. 6) as being engaged in a "subjective perspective" that is based on fidelity to the truth-event (e.g., resurrection of Christ, falling in love, etc.) and assessing everything from this standpoint. Žižek writes: "Let us imagine a person in love describing the features of his beloved to his friend: the friend, who is not in love with the same person, will simply find this enthusiastic description meaningless; he will not get 'the point' of it. . . . In short, subject-language involves the logic of the shibboleth, of a difference which is visible only from within, not from without" (136, original ellipsis; see also Badiou 2006, 398; Hallward 2003, 128). However, not all speech acts can be consistently attached to the truth-event in the same manner in different social circumstances, even by a subject-in-becoming. Real-life situations require a person to carefully choose where and when to use such enthusiastic subject-language; otherwise, communication would be hampered or outright impossible. As believers live among rather different kinds of people, both Christian and non-Christian, there is a need to shift between different registers, vocabularies, and natural languages, and thus, in some sense, between different vantage points.

It is once again helpful to turn to Bakhtin (1981) to discuss the linkage between language and perspective, with a focus on the shifting between different kinds of language when addressees change. He argued that people use varied languages (or registers) throughout their lives: "All languages of heteroglossia, whatever the principle underlying them and making each unique, are specific *points of view on the world*, forms for conceptualizing the world in words, specific world views, each characterized by its own objects, meanings and values" (291–92, my italics). Bakhtin illustrated this with an example of an illiterate peasant in eighteenth-century Russia, who "prayed to God in one language (Church Slavonic), sang songs in another, spoke to his family in a third and, when he began to dictate petitions to the local authorities through a scribe, he tried speaking yet a fourth language . . . he passed from one to the other without thinking, automatically: each was indisputably in its own place, and the place of each was indisputable" (295–96).

As in the example of Bakhtin's peasant, Yegor frequently shifted between different perspectival languages or registers. For instance, when speaking to non-Christian reindeer herders, he chose a different, more quotidian register, and when speaking to Russian acquaintances or officials, he used his limited Russian, opting for words that had entered the Nenets language relatively recently (e.g., *pasport, administratsiya*, etc.). In both settings, his aim was to get things done, yet he occasionally inserted references to God's commands and his own identity as a believer; at other times, he avoided evangelical language, his subject-language, entirely (cf. Engelke 2013, 66).

In a departure from Bakhtin, I would suggest that shifting between different registers does not need to be an entirely automatic or entirely self-reflective act either. When Yegor was making jokes, he was speaking Nenets in a "pagan" way; when he was condemning his jokes, he was speaking Baptist. My strong impression was that it shifted him between varied dispositions he was not able to fully control, even if he was able to reflect upon these later.[17] Unlike Bakhtin's peasant, Yegor knew that the ultimate ideal was to stay only in the Christian-language world and not to speak the language of his past self, as this entailed the danger of losing the perspective of "God's-gaze-on-me," which was the only moral way to anchor himself into the right perspective or subject position. This inability to fully control himself at all times, and thus his struggle for a Christian subjectivity, was also a reason why he avoided speaking of and to spirits or singing old songs, as these could have swayed his perspective and drowned him in the old "pagan" world (see chap. 5).[18]

Earlier Yamb-To Nenets used to say "Num [God] Mikola is watching" (*Num Mikola manie*) when someone committed a mistake or transgressed a taboo (e.g., women stepping over reindeer harnesses). These moments had the potential to shift one's perspective to that of a transcendental judge, an idea that probably came from Orthodox Christianity. However, this did not lead to a sustained practice of self-objectification, as the Orthodox God did not have the piercing gaze of the Baptists' God. Nenets *punryodaq* say that God's view penetrates everything, including one's soul. So, the evangelicals' God's gaze works rather as Foucault's internalized gaze in Bentham's panopticon, which is there to guard oneself in the absence of a visible other (Foucault 1977, 195–228).

In this context, we can ask, "*When* does a person occupy an ethical subject position?" (see also Faubion 2013; Humphrey 2008). Baptists, like many other Christians, often use kin terms when speaking of their relations with God. God is "our father" and we are his "children." If self-reflectively engaged, these are moments of the perceived presence of God as father who offers the perspective of "what pleases him."[19] I suggest that sensing the presence of God's gaze as a father's gaze could be characterized as having a different ontological perspective than when looking at the world from the perspective of human willfulness. We could argue that Baptist personhood is a site where various connections take place, analogous to perspectival stances in Melanesian persons as "dividuals," that is microcosms of relations that emerge through exchanges with others over time (Strathern 1996). Marilyn Strathern (1999, 253) suggests in the Papua New Guinean context that ontological consequences come from the position where people find themselves in kin relations at a particular moment, "being a son to these people and a sister's son to those, or to being a consanguine by contrast with an affine." Once again, this positionality is contextually set not only in "space" but also in time.

Taking another's perspective is a capacity that is essential to all human beings. However, it is never a total self-detachment. It is rather a "double perspective," as my gaze from elsewhere is at the same time a gaze from myself that witnesses me being looked upon. This simultaneity is only partial because at a particular point of time, a person is either *more* here or there. George Herbert Mead (1962, 174–76) expressed a similar idea by arguing that the "I" that observes cannot directly grasp itself. In Christian history, this has produced paradoxical situations when an observer "I" and observed "I" get hopelessly entangled with each other (see Paden 1988, 77, for such instances in the diaries of seventeenth-century Puritans of New England). Therefore, the third-person perspective is inseparable from the first-person perspective.

Converts in the tundra are taught to adhere to God's perspective through interiorized disciplinary practices and through talking about it to oneself and others. To live a good life as a believer thus requires striving to occupy the right subject position and stay in it. The crucial node is the shifting of viewpoints between the human and the divine, an oscillation that is probably necessary to live a complete life, with its moments of doubt and moments of certainty about one's salvation. This struggle does not end with either success or failure. Rather, verbal praise for success or admitting failure both serve as highly productive ways to craft a new Christian self and community (see Beekers and Kloos 2018). What matters, as they say, is a sincere intention to strive and hope that divine grace does the rest. There is the possibility of movement toward a more stable subject position, where one becomes an experienced and practiced believer. Such a person is said to be filled with the Holy Spirit (see chap. 6).

Believers in the tundra try to manage the paradox that is inherent in the demand for a coherent life and their lived lives, which are filled with irresolvable tensions. The ideal of achieving coherence guides one's life and puts one's thoughts and words in a specific mode. This occurs forcefully in moments when one can achieve a God's-eye view, especially when the challenges and contingencies of life would—as Laidlaw (2014, 128) phrases it—"provoke particularly intense ethical questioning." And yet we should not forget that there are always parallel, conflicting, and fragmented projects in one's life, even among the most committed and pious monotheists. Coherence is an ideal that has a fragile relationship with the lived life and its many connections and contingencies. As Robert Hefner (2019, 145) puts it, commenting on Muslim subjectivities: "Even the most fervent pietists . . . may aspire to other interests and ethical concerns."[20] Therefore, some maneuverability between "ethical traditions" is what makes life livable, as Laidlaw has argued. Giving an example of lay Jains in North India, Laidlaw (2014, 168) says that despite them knowing what it takes to act morally and be "a self-consistent virtuous self," they can yet do it "only at intervals and only in counterpoint to the pursuit of contrasting goods and ends." Even if people are torn apart by various conflicting projects in their everyday lives, we should not discount the power of aspiring to coherence and to the theo-logic of certainty in salvation.

We could argue that Nenets converts switched between different ethical regimes (like they moved between different registers and languages). In daily matters, Yegor continued to use his practical judgment to sustain the well-being of his family, reindeer herd, pastures, and pragmatic relations with various *lutsaq*. However, during the moments where he took God's gaze on him, he expressed these concerns under one total scheme, which was living for God through his prayers and his reading and witnessing practices. And yet, it was not easy to manage this ideal of living with God's gaze for longer periods. Once when I asked why he did not keep Sunday, he replied that God knows that he needs to pasture his reindeer every day and added, "We think that all the work we do, we do for God." He seemed to have forgotten what he had told me a few weeks earlier, when he complained that his back and legs were aching after he went on a Sunday to check fishing nets and fell from his snowmobile into a hole and injured himself. He explained that this was a punishment for him working on Sunday.[21]

As we see, everyday practical issues must be continuously renegotiated, rejustified, and re-accounted for because of the demand to look at one's life from a God's-eye view. In the end, Yegor and other converts can rely on God's power to forgive and resolve tensions once the right words are uttered, feelings expressed, and rituals performed. Furthermore, prayers always contain a reference to "the sins one has committed without knowing." Even if everyday misfortunes cannot always be avoided, there is hope for a delayed reward in the hereafter for all the pious words, sincere intentions, and correctly embodied behavior. This is a radically new world Yegor and other converts have entered, one they could not have imagined until recently. Their new life (*yedei yil*) is full of competing and sometimes incommensurable visions of a good life—achieving of which requires a new way of dealing with words and silences.

CONCLUSION

THROUGHOUT THIS WORK, I HAVE FOLLOWED HOW NENETS have looked for empowerment from outside, while trying not to be submerged by it. The nomads' understandings, sensibilities, and values have been in flux as a result of their encounters with outsiders, who are various kinds of Russians. Nenets have both avoided and engaged with *lutsaq* and the Soviet state, pursuing innumerable other messy forms of contact, including conflict, collusion, and cooperation. This is a story about social connections in formation, full of speech acts and silence acts, with the power to cut existing relations and form new ones. When evangelical missionaries reached the tundra, they offered a new model of relationality with (the more powerful) God and his Russians that promised protection from demanding, unpredictable, and sometimes outright dangerous engagement with spirits, witchcraft, predators, and "unfriendly" Russians. For many Nenets, there has been hope that the new faith would work as life insurance in this world as well as in the hereafter. However, for others, it has been a source of hesitation and an unwanted demand for relation-building and submission, which has been perceived as intrusive and perilous, making them vulnerable to unknown consequences.

Evangelists, who found their pre-apocalyptic "ends of the earth" in the Arctic tundra, arrive with words that are meant to radically change people. However, depending on the listener's viewpoint, these words have been seen as gibberish, invasive, or harmful weapons, or, on the contrary, as revelations of truth by those who are interested, even if the full message often remains obscure. We have seen how missionary Pavel's calls for repentance led Yegor to make self-analytic statements and Vata to obstinately keep silence; likewise, the Pentecostal pastor Vladislav's abundant explanations triggered Iriko's collusive repetitions. Those who have stopped dodging missionaries' words and responded to interpellation and have begun speaking the new evangelical language—by making thus an explicit promise—find themselves taking a course of action they could not have known beforehand: Christian logic often arrives later and the futures that were initially imagined must be reimagined.

After meeting evangelical missionaries, many Nenets have thus come under an obligation to speak for the first time, explaining themselves to others; aligning their thoughts, feelings, and deeds with the truth claims of a universalist ideology; and demonstrating motivation and obedience to its overseers, all of which require some solemnity and seriousness in its performativity. One is required to talk abundantly to God and about God, remembering that everything is judged by him and asking forgiveness and expressing praise to him (Bog in Russian; when speaking in Nenets, he is still called Num). This demands mastery of the correct words in situations such as initial repentance and subsequent praying, reading, witnessing, preaching, and admonishing. Protestant missionaries have introduced a logic in which the most powerful act that changes the world and oneself is a speech act, as it is speaking above all that conveys one's inner thoughts and feelings. Furthermore, one's words are said to be always (over)heard by a divine superaddressee, in whose name discipline is to be enforced. However, the force of the humans' words comes from their representation of what is inside: in a sincere prayer of repentance, words are believed to have the capacity to override nonverbal actions (including Christian good deeds, kneeling, or any other visible act) through their power to give an explicit demonstration of one's faith. For a newly sprouting individualist Christian, striving to make interiority and exteriority match each other is a challenging endeavor requiring a specific perspectival language.

In this process, this previously taciturn culture is unraveled and transformed by the verbose rhetoric of the evangelists, as a discreet, nonexplicit Nenets personhood is reshaped by the need to demonstrate and broadcast a new personhood that has a particular kind of moral interiority. Conversion has thus been a movement from a relatively silent animist world, in which most principles cannot be easily expressed in words and it is one's actual deeds that count, to a verbally explicit religion in which each act can and should be reflected and commented on, often through reference to some passage in the Bible. In this new ideology, silence, when it is taken to be an absence of a meaningful relationship with God, is no longer a legitimate state: such sinful silences must be mended by the right kind of words.

In Nenets ontology, local assumptions of the power of silence are directly linked to an understanding that words are forceful. Words can create effects outside the notion of representation or signification, to the extent that semantic and pragmatic meanings are in some sense irrelevant. This is because in various social contexts, words are seen as parts of specific persons and flows of exchange, not limited by the intentionality of an individual speaker but, once said out loud, having an autonomous force of their own. Therefore, one cannot be sure what kind of efficacy words take on once they are expressed, as this depends on the power or vulnerability of a particular person as well as on the tone and the intensity of relations involved. Thus, Nenets relate the problem of words to an inherent uncertainty about whether and in what way they take on magical effects. The old logic of distributed personhood and intentionality, in which words—including personal names and personal songs—create relations to one's past and to non-Christian kin may pose a threat to the converts' attempts to sustain conversion (as in case of Baptist Yegor whose old-style singing threatened his Christian self).

There is, therefore, noticeable tension that emerges when missionaries arrive and try to push Nenets into acting against their own previous rituals and deeply internalized cosmologies. While some fall silent and refuse to engage with the evangelists, others attempt to learn the new language and behavior. This becomes an everyday struggle against the Nenets' own earlier personhood, which was formed through a deep-seated engagement with their own memories and kinship relations, as well as with the spirits of the land on which they continue to live (as in case of Pentecostal Tikynye, who regarded herself to be kin to wolves). As in so many other places where Protestant missionaries have been active, this conversion has led to the destruction of sacred objects, to the demonization of places recently considered sacred, and to the condemnation of the Nenets' own ancestors, epic songs, and shamanic sensibilities. Furthermore, the entire Independent community is getting more divided, making it more difficult to exchange gifts, partners, and knowledge between Christians and non-Christians.

Even if one's words, ideals, and aspirations are Christian, this does not mean that a radical break with the past can emerge easily. This is why we can see elements of "continuity thinking" (Robbins 2007a) and perhaps also of continuity feeling popping up here and there. Robbins has called for taking Christianity seriously as cultural logic, and critically notes that "anthropologists assume that people's beliefs are difficult to change and therefore endure through time" (13), arguing in a series of influential publications that anthropologists studying religious conversion tend to overemphasize the role of local *bricolage*-like activities and cultural continuity with the past as if people were unable "to view the world except through their received categories" (2003, 221; see also 2007a, 10, 2009, 2014, 2020; Bialecki et al.

2008; Højer and Pedersen 2019). However, as this ethnography has demonstrated, there is often considerable tension between the exclusionary logic of "either/or" and the pluralist logic of "both/and" (Lambek 2015b). Furthermore, as Iriko's and Vladislav's (mis)communications show concerning the burning of Iriko's sacred objects, these crucial moments often take place in gaps where the two sides have rather different views on materiality and mediation; on the agency of humans, spirits, and words; and on the forms of responsibility for one's acts and their consequences. In these moments of what missionaries describe as people "beginning to understand," there is a lot of confusion and uncertainty, as with Syado, who struggled with the image of herself as both pure and impure.

While agreeing with the view that Christianity is a cultural logic that makes a particular kind of impact, I have argued that the capacity and willingness to take the new logic on board varies greatly. The mission encounter is a highly dynamic situation, with the inherent logic of Christianity making an impact, as do aspects of various power struggles, pragmatic interests, ethical choices, and moments of entertainment and aesthetics, which are not necessarily connected to Christian teachings as such. Even the most pious do not Christianize every moment of their lives, despite this being required by teachings. Perhaps it is not so much beliefs but character and habits that are difficult to change, although not entirely impossible. Old-time sensibilities tend to linger, as we have seen throughout the ethnography. At least this is so with many first-generation converts: they are not blank slates; they have earlier backgrounds, ideas, sentiments, and habits, even if some of these have been objectified and worked hard upon to be discarded. Taking on the novel is easier for the young than for the old. What we see when we compare Yegor and his son Ngarka is that the father, who is a well-formed person, is haunted by his past much more forcefully than his son.

Any molding of the self is not a straightforward process but is full of struggle and paradox. Not everybody who has become a member of the evangelical church would have begun to scrutinize him or herself with a same intensity to Ngarka, Yegor, or Andrei. Even if a convert like Yegor believed himself to be a new person, he struggled with his past ways, which he tried actively to overcome and forget. In the end, a radical break needs to be upheld through a continuous striving for self-perfection and repeated analysis of one's failures, often via public speaking. In this encounter, an explicit set of moral norms, institutionalized and hierarchically orchestrated, meets more tacit and fluid assumptions that sometimes remain hidden, at other times are made conscious and then reformed. Indeed, many Nenets have become tuned into the ethos of rupture, speaking as devout believers and keeping silence on ungodly matters, including their previous ways of relating to spirits, dead ancestors, and sacred sites when they were still "pagans." Nevertheless, even if conversion to evangelical Christianity has led to an obligatory articulacy, forgetting the old and remembering the new is harder than it looks. But as missionaries and more dedicated converts sometimes complain, there are many baptized Nenets in the tundra who "still don't understand." Some of these people were like Iriko and Pukhutsya, who were neither coerced nor persuaded to become Pentecostal converts but rather went along with events they did not fully control, hoping for protection from more dangerous *lutsaq*.

There are considerable generational differences in how the mission encounter is seen. In the background, there has been a fear of losing one's humanity (*nyeney nyenets'*) and of becoming "the other" (*lutsarakha*, "Russian-like"). This has been a worry, especially for older converts who do not want to see their children becoming alienated from a life on the land with reindeer. Paradoxically, the first converts, who were young men in the 1990s, are now middle aged and struggle with their own children's wishes to leave the tundra, just as their own parents—by now most of them dead already—once did not want them to accept the strange *lutsa* ways. There is a parallel with the sentiment among middle-aged Russian Baptists who criticize their children for being too eager to explore modern global culture or to leave the conservative church outright.

Nenets parents often warn their children against becoming too attracted to city life, fearing the metamorphosis of their children could become irreversible. Those who have lived longer are less attracted by the promise of modernity (including money, goods, and technology) and less worried about the sense of being marginal or isolated or about feeling embarrassed of not being sufficiently familiar with *lutsa* habits And even young people like Vera, who have dreamed of embracing urban ways (with Christianity included) have not moved away from the tundra but instead continue with the nomadic way of life. She has come to realize, like many others have—especially once they have created their own families—that the rough *lutsa* environment is not a better place. However, what all converts seem to appreciate is the possibility of improving their lives in one way or another—materially, socially, and spiritually—and of strengthening their sense of dignity in the larger world. The crucial point appears to be finding the right balance between the earlier ways of living with reindeer and families and the new demands of breaking with "paganism"—purity rules, *myenaruiq*, Nenets songs, raw blood, alcohol, and so forth. Giving up vodka has been particularly appealing for many, as they see fewer violent deaths around them and argue that their reindeer herds and families are more likely to prosper. Furthermore, missionaries who act as matchmakers help reindeer herders find future husbands and wives from distant camps that people cannot easily visit themselves.

Throughout the book I have pointed to several parallels between the Soviet and Christian reformisms, such as their passion to conquer unknown margins, including the people who live there, and to transform "souls" considered difficult to transform. Both kinds of reformers have attempted to master time within their linear logic, as they imagine making history by hurtling toward a better future. Tackling the final edge, in an Arctic that is full of dangers, is a definite sign of their success. These shifts have often occurred through a single Indigenous gatekeeper such as Ivan, who had long dreamed of becoming a mediator. But instead of becoming a shaman, he became a businessman and later an ordained evangelizer, as the new teachings and relations with missionaries precluded earlier patterns of transformation.

Evangelists know well that the younger generation in the tundra can more easily develop their Christian selves, as they have not actively been part of relation-making with local spirits in the landscape. These younger converts are school educated and literate, and they do not need to deal with "their demons from the past" since they did not have time to make local spirits their own. Just as early Communists in the 1920s paid attention to youth, so do evangelical missionaries who have told me that some problems will solve themselves once the older generation is gone. This demonstrates how both evangelical and Communist historical changes have their parallel yet specific logics: in both cases, youth is the main target and catalyst for change (Suslov 1931, 150; cf. Grenoble 2003, 167–68).

I have discussed how Christianity, in its specific expressions, has the potential to create and mold selves in certain ways and give impetus to the birth of ethical subjects of a particular kind, making completely new demands on thinking and acting, and leading to a shift in the "entire universe of causality and mutuality" (Vitebsky 2017a, 325). This new kind of ethics, which requires systematic objectification of oneself, was not part of these animists' world, as required in the large historical formations such as Christianity or Soviet Marxism.[1] For Nenets Independents, evangelical conversion has been the first close encounter with such organized ethical

Figure 8.1. A boy and a *myenarui*, reindeer bull dedicated to spirits, July 2002. *The young generation of Christians grows up without experiencing earlier intricate relations between humans, animals, and spirits.*

practices and self-technologies requiring introspection. The Russian Orthodox priests and Soviet state administrators were unable to impose efficient practices of self-objectification and did not have much influence on the reindeer nomads' ethical lives, at least as designed by these regimes.

What has been at stake is how much one or another regime—the Soviet and the Christian—has managed to make their transcendent projects relevant to people and turn them into self-motivated agents. The Independent Nenets stayed outside the *direct* impact of Soviet policies of subject formation, with their specific concerns such as claims of universal truths, aspiration for self-perfection, mutual surveillance, public penance, or condemnation of "outsiders." The Independents did not live in the world in which working for the Communist cause meant working heroically and tirelessly for the good of society, in which individuals had to be changed not for the sake of themselves but for the sake of the collective, which was shortly to be transformed into a paradise on earth (Zigon 2010, 205). This was a collectivist faith in progress, which had to be achieved by molding each person as a Soviet new man.[2] While the Soviets aimed to eradicate the tundra way of life—as their ideology prescribed—to civilize and rationalize Nenets, Khanty and others, Christian missionaries have worked along a somewhat—although not entirely—different trajectory, stressing a need to become fixed in communion with God, to look inward, and to make one's interior conform to God's will, which, as a collateral effect, introduces "a civilized way of life" into the tundra. Unregistered Baptists know well what it means to be a target of ideological indoctrination by the state. Their stories of persecution by the Soviet regime or other *lutsaq* have shown them to be more trustworthy in the eyes of many unregistered Independents. Both sides have had a long history of tension with the Soviets which, as we have seen, has played out in radically different ways.

Where Communists failed and Baptists succeeded among Independents— or at least among the most committed ones—was in the introduction of the transcendental gaze and its perspectival language in a way that led to profound ethical self-transformation. They both tried to impose total morality systems on the Nenets' tundra life while trying to eradicate the old ways. As Keane (2016, 211) puts it, "In monotheistic traditions . . . the transcendentalizing move always contains the latent possibility—the invitation—of further purification, such as iconoclasm, antiritualism, and other attacks on the material things and practices that prior religions had made use of." This observation can be extended to other highly organized religions as well as to secular ideologies such as Soviet Marxism. Inherently, this kind of shift involves various dimensions such as time, morality, and authority. Or as Vitebsky (2012, 192) describes in his comparison of transformations among Eveny collective farm reindeer herders in Siberia and Sora Baptist converts in India, "Where the local community's frame of reference is local it must be made universal, where their time is cyclical or non-destinational it must be made future-oriented, where their sense of morality comes from within it must be structured and validated by an outside source." It seems that in mission encounters of religious and secular kinds, a new social order requires a new cosmology, and vice versa.

Das (2007) has argued that any highly organized and centralized morality system that requires self-formation has the potential to create violence. As a result, caring for other humans is no longer primary; instead, the system motivates people to be brutal in the name of an ultimate and universal good. Soviet society, especially in its Stalinist version, serves as an example of this kind of highly repressive environment. While agreeing with Das in general, Laidlaw (2018, 185) points out that some morality systems can "also obviously lead people to heightened sensitivity or enlarged sympathy or motivate them much more strenuously to try to do good." Or these systems can be used as tools to break some patterns that are not considered desirable, offering efficient means for self-cultivation. Take alcohol in the Nenets tundra, which has caused much damage to individual lives while supporting certain cultural life forms. While some, after accepting evangelical Christianity, could celebrate the eradication of alcohol consumption in Nenets campsites, others would lament the loss of earlier patterns of sociality in which drinking had a key role (cf. Safonova and Sántha 2013). What is important to note here is that these instances are possibilities for strong ethical evaluations for all sides involved.

It must be stressed that none of these grand totalizing morality systems, with their particular secular or religious ideologies, produces change or stasis automatically. Values, agendas, and power relations that do not quite fit or that outright conflict keep shaping the local cultural world in various manners. On a broader scale, although there are considerable similarities in these ideologies of transcendence, like the logic of obedience and commitment, conversion to Christianity should not just be seen as yet another wave of modernization or globalization with predictable consequences (Cannell 2006, 45; cf. Jenkins 2012, 471). Most Nenets converts are still intimately linked to reindeer and the landscape, pursuing the value of having large herds and large families. Reindeer and the land, as well as the nomads' remote location, their ideal of independence, and their desire for innovation, thus continue to be affordances that link people with human and nonhuman others and thus have the creative potential to shape futures in unexpected ways. Despite promises of theological certainty, sociological unpredictability remains high.

MAIN CHARACTERS

Most personal names are pseudonyms that are chosen from an existing pool of Nenets personal names. Reindeer nomads have usually both Nenets and Russian names.

Yamb-To Baptists

Ivan, the first Nenets to convert to Baptism, a trader, and the unofficial leader of the Yamb-To community in the 1990s. Ivan moved to Vorkuta city and became an ordained preacher in 2012.

Andrei, Ivan's elder brother, the second convert and presbyter of "the Nenets church."

Lyuba, Andrei's wife, born into a family of Ural Independents whose reindeer were collectivized in 1976.

Vera, eldest daughter of Andrei and Lyuba. Vera dreamed of leaving the tundra but ended up having her own family there.

Yegor, elder brother of Ivan and Andrei, demands obedience from himself and others.

Lida, Yegor's wife, is from a Komi-speaking Nenets (*kholva yaran*) collective-farm hunting family. She is school educated.

Ngarka, Yegor and Lida's oldest son, was the first to be baptized in his family but convinced others to follow.

Ksenya, younger sister of Yegor, is cheerful and skillful with a lasso.

Yevgeni, Ksenya's husband and Lida's brother, is also a Komi-speaking Nenets (*kholva yaran*) and boarding school boy. Once in the tundra he quickly learned Nenets and reindeer herding.

Tyepas, daughter of Vata and Tado, their only married child and the only Baptist in the family. In 1983, she and her brother were taken to school without their parents' knowledge or permission.

Nyeteta, suffered a mental breakdown after conversion and marriage. Missionaries suspected she was possessed.

Syado, Lyuba's younger sister, lives with her Baptist husband. They live in a separate tent next to the husband's non-Christian family.

Yamb-To Nonconverts

Granny Marina, mother of Ivan, Andrei, Yegor, and Ksenya, immune to the "good news," lived with her daughter Ksenya, died a "pagan" in 2018.

Tyepan, Granny Marina's youngest son, first to leave for the state farm, now lives in Vorkuta, sometimes visits an Orthodox church, fights for the land rights of the Ural Nenets.

Vata, Ivan's uncle, remained silent in the presence of missionaries and died a recalcitrant non-Christian in 2018.

Tado, Vata's wife, the only woman in the camp, died in 2015.

Poru, one of the very few Independent men fluent in the Russian world, was already so during the Soviet period and a self-proclaimed "atheist."

Ancestors

Yarki Veli, a half-mythic ancestor whose soul-image, *ngytarma*, was burned by his great-great-great-grandson Yegor when he converted to Baptism.

Taras, grandson of Yarki, died in the early twentieth century in an epidemic after most of his reindeer had died.

Mikul, Taras's son, father of Vata and Sem, was also called *pop vesako* ("old priest"). Inspired by Russian Orthodoxy, he baptized children and died in 1976.

Mikhail, Mikul's brother, was chairman of a collective farm during the Stalinist era.

Ngel, Mikul's brother, was sent to the front in Second World War in 1942 and never returned.

Vas, Mikul's brother, joined the *mandalada*, a Nenets uprising in 1943. He was arrested and perished in the Gulag.

Sem, Mikul's son, father of Ivan, Andrei, Yegor, Ksenya, and Tyepan, died a recalcitrant non-Christian in 1999.

Ural Nenets Pentecostals or "Almost" Pentecostals

Iriko, a wealthy reindeer herder, became Pentecostal against his will.

Pukhutsya, Iriko's wife, always in good humor, was baptized with his husband.

Their Children, All Illiterate

Tikynye, a lively young woman with some shamanic skills, being attracted by the Russian world and church network. She became the first Pentecostal in the family.

Netyu, daughter, despite being illiterate, tried hard to read the Bible. Netyu would later marry a non-Christian Khanty collective farmer and stop being an active believer.

Maranga, youngest daughter, is a Pentecostal who dreams about joining the Baptist church, in which there are many more young Nenets.

Pubta, son, takes care of the family herd. He is recently married.

Tyakalyu, son, is a good traveling companion.

Ngelya, son, is the last to be baptized among the children.

Kolye, youngest son, is a tempestuous person.

Missionaries

Pavel, Baptist presbyter of the Vorkuta Unregistered Baptist church, is the initiator of the conversion campaign among the Nenets. He is a former coal miner, originally from Ukraine.

Vladislav, a Pentecostal missionary from Vorkuta, works as a railway inspector and is originally from Ukraine.

GLOSSARY OF SELECTED NENETS AND RUSSIAN WORDS

Nenets Words

ikota (from Russian *ikota*)—hiccup spirit that causes pain inside one's body and demands alcohol, also known as *ikota khalyq*, "hiccup worms"; the word comes from Russian *ikat'*, "hiccup"; known as *sheva* among the neighboring Komi

khabyenye—Russian (or any other non-Indigenous white) woman, see *lutsa*

khebyidya—sacred, holy; *khebyidya yindq*, "holy spirit"

khekhe—spirit, god, deity from the upper or middle world; spirit related (e.g., *khekhe ya* "spirit land," sacred site); sacred object, figure, or image imbued with a (guardian) spirit; "idol" or "fetish" in the missionary language

lutsa—Russian (or any other non-Indigenous white) man; person who has no reindeer; in the early Soviet period Communists were called *nyaryanaq lutsaq*, "red Russians"

lutsa khekhe—"Russian spirit"; Russian Orthodox icon

mandalada—"the gathered"; war gathering, uprising

mya—large tepee-shaped conical tent; Russian *chum*; in English also known as "chum" or "choom"

myad pukhutsya—"old woman of the tent," female spirit in the form of a doll-like figure that protects the tenthold and women in childbirth

myenarui—leading reindeer in a herd, usually not harnessed, owned by spirits

ngylyeka—spirit from the underworld; evil predatory spirit; wolf; devil for Christians

ngytarma—wooden and clothed image of a dead ancestor, kept in the tent and occasionally fed

num—sky; sky god, Christian deity in the language of Nenets converts

nyaro—pure, the opposite of *syaqmei*

nyeney—real; human; Nenets(-like)

nyeney nyenets' (plural, *nyeneyq nyenetsyaq*, "real people")—human; person; Nenets

nyeney yil—"real life," nomadic way of life with reindeer

porti—(from Russian *portit'*, "to spoil") witchcraft, harming

punryoda—Christian believer

sanggovo vada—"heavy word," unintended harmful word

si (*singgana, sinyakuy* as a Russianized version)—ritually pure "male" area of the tent, opposite side of the door area called *nyo*

sidyangg (*sidryangg*)—shadow; shadow soul; sacred image

255

syadei—wooden or stone image of spirit, usually placed at open sacred sites in the landscape

syaqmei—charged with dangerous power, related to female fertility and menstruation as well as to the dead

syaqmei pad—bag of female boots

symzy—central vertical pole in the tent along which spirits move in and out of the tent; it connects the middle world with the lower and upper worlds

tadyebya—shaman

tarq pad—piece of fur found inside a reindeer's throat, which is a sign of luck, *yab*

vada—word, speech, language

vesako—old man, husband; male name, including for gods (e.g., Num Vesako, "Old Man Num")

vevako vada—"evil word," curse

yabye syo—"drunken song," genre of personal song

yarabts—genre of epic song

yerv—master, leader; spirit

yindq—breath; breath-soul

Russian Words

lichniki—see *yedinolichniki*

svyatoy—holy; saint, holy one; in the language of evangelicals, it denotes all living Christians who have rejected the ways of the world

veruyushchie—believers, Russian Baptists' and Pentecostals' primary self-label; in Nenets, *punryodaq*

yazychniki—"pagans," Russian evangelicals mark all Nenets nonconverts with this word; some Nenets who practice ancestral religion ("Nenets religion") proudly use the term about themselves

yedinolichniki (also *lichniki*)—Independents, reindeer herders outside the collective or state farm (especially in the Soviet period), sometimes used interchangeably with *chastniki* ("private owners"); as Nenets do not distinguish between phonemes like "sh" and "ch," Independents thought they were called *lishnie*, which means "superfluous" or "out of place" in Russian; in Nenets, people mark those outside of farms as *khariq yilyenaq*, "the ones who live on their own," or *kharta yilyenaq nyenetsyaq*, "independently living Nenets"

NOTES

Introduction

1. I use the word *sides* for the sake of clearer exposition. I do not mean that the two sides—Indigenous Nenets nomads and evangelical white missionaries of Russian and Ukrainian ethnic backgrounds—are internally coherent or even oppositional in everything they do. However, one of the results of the mission encounter is that the boundaries of the sides are being redrawn and the idea of belonging to bounded groups has become more emphasized along the way.

2. Yamb-To (*yamb to*, "long lake") is a relatively new name that comes from the early 1990s when the process of the official clan-community formation began and a name was chosen for it. Among the Ural Nenets, the Yamb-To Nenets are known as the *yedei yakha tyerq*, "the people of the New River," which refers to the Korotaikha River where the group has winter pastures. The Ural Nenets call themselves *pe tyerq* ("the people of the mountains") or *pe mal tyerq* ("the people of the mountains' end"). The name *pe tyerq* also refers to those Nenets who live on the eastern (Asian or Siberian) side of the Polar Urals and who are not the focus of this book (cf. Adaev 2017; Vagramenko 2014).

3. According to various estimates, the number of Protestants in Russia is over two million, constituting between 1 to 2 percent of the entire population (Filatov 2016; Lunkin 2014).

4. Lambek has perceptively described the coexistence of spirit possession and Islam in Mayotte. He writes about a situation in which different religious regimes meet with one another in Mayotte: "The 'conversation' between spirit possession and Islam can be characterized as one in which Islam (i.e. certain arguments made by Muslims and *as* Muslims from within an Islamic tradition) asks people to select 'either/or' with respect to certain practices, whereas spirit possession offers a world of 'both/and'—one in which you can practice both, in which not only can a Muslim be a spirit medium, but some of the spirits too are Muslim" (Berliner et al. 2016, 8, Lambek's italics; see also Lambek 2015b, 60–61). This is similar to how Nenets animists entertain the both/and view of spirits by calling certain spirits "Russian spirits" (see chap. 4; cf. Stammler 2005, 328–31, on the wider logic of selective adaptation and creative innovation among the collectivized Yamal Nenets).

5. Bernard Williams (2011) writes about "the morality system" (pluralized as "morality systems" by Keane, see 2016) as a set of social norms that constrain individuals. In a roughly similar way, Foucault (1997) uses the term *moral code*, talking of this as rules and norms (see also Keane 2016, 18–20; Laidlaw 2014, 112–13). Both Williams and Foucault reserve the word *ethics* for a different aspect that primarily deals with the question of how one should live.

6. In anthropology, various aspects of self-cultivation in religious settings have been producitvely explored by many (see, e.g., Beatty 2012; Bialecki 2015, 2017; S. Coleman 2006; Csordas 1994, 1997; Daswani 2015; and Meyer 2010, 2015 for Pentecostal and charismatic strands; Mahmood 2005 for Islam).

7. So far, the Gospels of Luke (*Luka* 2004), Mark (*Mark* 2010), John (*Ioann* 2014), Matthew (*Matfey* 2018), and the Book of Jonah (*Num' Vadi* 2021) have been translated into

Nenets. In addition to local Nenets linguists, the translations are made by Eunsub Song, a South Korean exegetical adviser who lives in Salekhard and works for the Institute for Bible Translation based in Moscow (see Song 2015). The Baptist and Pentecostal missions under focus here have not been involved in the translation work. However, they distribute these translations, as this suits well their effort to spread the gospel.

8. The word *pagan* (also *heathen*, *idolater*) is part of Christian discourse about those who are not Christian and in particular about those who do not adhere to any world religion and are considered primitive (Masuzawa 2005). Furthermore, the word *religion* (also *faith*, *belief*, etc.) is similarly awkward, as Nenets animists have not usually considered their cosmology or ritual engagement with sentient environment to be a "religion" that could be replaced with another.

9. The 2021 Russian census counted 49,787 Nenets (this number also includes a couple thousand Forest Nenets, *nyeshchang*, in Western Siberia; the overall number had more than doubled since 1959 when there were 22,845 Nenets): 35,979 were registered in the Yamalo-Nenets Region (this area has the largest nomadic community of pastoralists in the entire Arctic), 6,722 in the Nenets Region, 3,853 in the Krasnoyarsk Territory, 1,383 in the Khanty-Mansi Region, and 222 in the Komi Republic.

10. Along with the Enets, Selkup, and Nganasan languages, the language of the Tundra Nenets (*nyenetsya vada*) belongs to the Samoyedic group of the Uralic or Finno-Ugric language family (Burkova 2022; Salminen 1998). There are some variations across dialects in Tundra Nenets, yet all dialects are mutually intelligible (Koshkareva 2010, 2017). The first written standard of Tundra Nenets, which is based on the Great Land tundra dialect (also spoken by Independents), was created in the early 1930s. However, written Nenets has had limited use as there are relatively few publications in Nenets (Ogryzko 2003; Toulouze 2004) and most literate Nenets would prefer reading in Russian anyway. Furthermore, there are also Komi-speaking Nenets. Due to long-term relations with Izhma Komi (*iz'vatas* in Komi), a few hundred self-identified Nenets (including some Yamb-To women) speak the Izhma Komi dialect as their native language. When speaking in Nenets, the latter are known as *kholva yaran* (*kholva* comes from the place name "Kolva," *yaran* means "Nenets" in Komi, see also Habeck 2005, 68; Istomin 1999, 2019, 88–105; Vallikivi 2014a).

11. Tundra Nenets is spoken by more than twenty thousand speakers and is one of the few Indigenous languages in the Russian Arctic that is also widely used by the youngest generation. However, the knowledge of Nenets is very uneven across Nenets regions. Many of these regional differences come from different Soviet-period sedentarization and education policies as well as from the variation of ethnic composition (see Vakhtin 2001). In the European North, the loss of ancestral language has been much more severe than among the Siberian Nenets, who have more children able to speak their ancestral language compared to any other Indigenous minority in the Russian Arctic: while in the Yamalo-Nenets Region 55 percent of all self-identified Nenets claimed to be able to speak Nenets in the 2010 census, the same indicator in the Nenets Region was only 10 percent—that is, 750 people (see Toulouze and Vallikivi 2016, 30–33). As Nenets journalist Irina Khanzerova (2022) notes, virtually the only Nenets children who know their ancestral language in the Nenets Region are from the Yamb-To, while others are monolingual Russian speakers (even if a few of them may understand some of their heritage tongue).

12. Today, officially the collective farms and state farms have been renamed joint-stock enterprises or such (Vladimirova 2017). However, locally people still refer to these enterprises as *kolkhozy* and *sovkhozy*.

13. Shamans were sometimes labeled as "kulaks-shamans," despite many of them being poor. They were typically accused of practicing illegal medicine, fraud, and extortion. When found, their ritual objects were confiscated or destroyed. Some were imprisoned, and if they survived and were released, they hid or discontinued their practice. In the Great Land tundra, the best-known shaman at the time was Ivan Ledkov (Ngebt Yamb Vanyu), who spent three years in a Gulag and returned to become a tailor and informant for Russian folklorists and linguists (Menshakova and Taleyeva 2011; Skachkov 1934, 28; Tereshchenko 1990, 55, 334; Tolkachev 2000b, 267–72).

14. There is extensive literature on the nature of collectivization in the North, its randomness, and the discrepancy between the declared objectives and actual repressive practices (see Balzer 1999; Bulgakova 2013; Bulgakova and Sundström 2017; Donahoe 2012, 107; Fondahl 1998; Slezkine 1994; Ziker 2002).

15. In Russian history, Pustozersk was a notorious settlement, as it was the place of exile and execution of Archpriest Avvakum (1620 or 1621–82) (Avvakum 2021; Okladnikov 1999; Yasinski and Ovsyannikov 2003). This uncompromising religious thinker and writer became the spiritual leader of those dissenters who later became known as Old Believers. The lower Pechora area (especially Ust-Tsilma) was one of the strongholds for the fugitive dissenters who refused to accept Patriarch Nikon's reforms (1652–66), including the three-fingered sign of the cross, the four-ended cross, and new liturgical texts. Nenets were not involved in these confessional fights, even if there are a few vague reports in which reindeer herders were accused of being followers of Old Belief (Okladnikov and Matafanov 2008, 72–73, 78; see also Lukin 2011, 217–22). Pustozersk was abandoned by the early 1960s; today there are various monuments, including one wooden figure representing "a Nenets spirit," which has caused controversies with the Russian Orthodox Church. The site of Pustozersk is twenty-five kilometers from the administrative center of the Nenets Region, called Naryan-Mar ("Red Town"), which was founded in 1930 to serve as a port for the Vorkuta coal region (see map 1).

16. Until the 1930s, Russians called Nenets *samoyedy* ("Samoyeds") and, in the eastern areas, *yuraki* ("Yuraks"). In Russian *samoyedy* sounds derogatory because, in part, its folk etymology links the word to "cannibal" (*samo* "self," *yed* "eater"; compare with the regular word for "cannibal"—*lyudoyed*, from *lyudi* "people," *yed* "eater").

17. Veniamin (1855, 114) reports that between 1825 and 1830 he and his entourage managed to baptize 3,303 souls, which is roughly three-quarters of all European Nenets. Around a thousand Nenets living west of the Urals remained unbaptized, mainly in the Great Land tundra (Okladnikov and Matafanov 2008, 83). The large majority of the "pagans" (*yazychniki*) were herd owners from the Great Land tundra whose knowledge of Russian was poor and whose contact with "rebellious" Yamal and Ural Nenets (*kamennye samoyedy*) was intense. To avoid the Orthodox mission altogether, many moved temporarily across the Urals (Shemanovskiy 2011, tome I, 187).

18. I have discussed pre-Soviet Russian Orthodox missionization elsewhere in more detail (Vallikivi 2003, 2023; Leete and Vallikivi 2011, 89–95; see also Ablazhey 2005; Khomich 1979; Lar and Vanuyto 2011; Mavlyutova 2001; Okladnikov and Matafanov 2008; Perevalova 2019; Shemanovskiy 2011; Templing 2003, 2004, 2007; Toulouze 2006, 2011a, 2011b).

19. Reindeer herding is the most thoroughly studied aspect of the Tundra Nenets cultural world: Nenets nomads keep around one million domesticated reindeer out of more than two million in the world (see Arzyutov and Lyublinskaya 2018; Golovnev and Osherenko 1999; Golovnev et al. 2018; Istomin and Dwyer 2021; Krupnik 1993; Kvashnin 2009a; Lehtisalo 1932; Niglas 1997a, 2000; Stammler 2005; Yoshida 1997).

20. There is a growing body of literature about the Russian Arctic landscape as a living environment in which animals, spirits, stories, memories, and dreams become entangled in a complex manner (see D. Anderson 2000, 2014; Haakanson and Jordan 2010; Istomin and Dwyer 2010; Kharyuchi 2004; Lukin 2011, 2022; Safonova and Sántha 2013; Vitebsky 2005; Vitebsky and Alekseyev 2015a, 2015b; Willerslev 2007; Willerslev et al. 2015).

21. Already in the nineteenth century, losing reindeer was frequently mentioned in travelers' reports (see, e.g., Nosilov 1895, 44; see also Krupnik 1993, 153–54). The latest cases of losing reindeer on a large scale, threatening to turn herders into reindeerless villagers or fishermen, are linked to several factors. On the one hand, the competition for lands has increased because of the rapidly expanding hydrocarbon industry and because of various legal restrictions, such as private owners not being officially allocated enough grazing areas (see Murashko 2013, 2016 on Ural Independent families being evicted from their pastures). On the other hand, the particularly fast global warming in the Arctic region creates unpredictable weather patterns. In recent years, frequent rain on snow and the formation of impenetrable ice crust in large areas has led to high reindeer mortality, as the animals cannot reach food (Golovnev 2017; Terekhina and Volkovitskiy 2023). Among the Independents, in the winter of 2013 and 2014 many families lost parts of their herds. Elsewhere, there have been other tragedies, also possibly linked to climate change. In 2016 an anthrax outbreak occurred in Yamal that was probably caused by the exposure of old grave sites of reindeer killed by anthrax when permafrost began melting (Laptander 2020a). Remarkably, a local cosmological explanation for this and other mass die-offs links it to evil spirits, such as *vevako khabtsya* and *posa khabtsya*, who live underground and kill animals and people. Some Yamal Nenets argue that these disastrous mass deaths are "caused by the disrespect to the sacred places and the dead" (Golovnev 2017, 41, see also 46); others talk about conspiracies such as the poisoning of their pastures with some liquid "by order from above" (Stammler and Ivanova 2020, 12). Tellingly, people complain that there are no shamans left to consult with to manage such disasters (9–10). As a rule, those who have been forced to quit the habitual mobile way of life try to acquire enough reindeer (for fish, sledges, clothes, etc.) to become full-time nomads again, which is still the key cultural value (Golovnev 1995, 52; Kharyuchi 2001, 12–13; Laptander 2020a, 22).

22. This idea is also visible in the semantics: in the Taimyr Nenets vocabulary, *lutsimz* means both "to become Russianized" and "to become sedentary" (Tereshchenko 2003, 195).

23. As Zoia Vylka Ravna (2021) shows, in addition to verbal directives such as prohibitions and warnings in a family setting, also stories, songs, and riddles have significant pedagogical value. Giving example and working together when crafting a sledge, marking reindeer calves, or moving in the landscape are typical forms of nonverbal education.

24. As one of my Nenets interlocutors in the tundra explained, not standing up straight is called *lusarta*, which in his view was related to the word *lutsa*, "Russian."

25. However, some Independent families have recently joined nearby collective farms because of the lack of free pastures in the context where their herds have grown several times and the farms have the legal right to use the vast majority of the pastures (cf. Vladimirova 2017, 2018).

26. It must be noted that the term *shamanism* (like *animism*) is highly problematic as the ending "-ism" implies it being a systematized and codified religion like Christianity or some other literate and doctrine-based religion. Even if there are numerous studies about "Nenets shamanism," there are very few detailed accounts of Nenets shamanic seances and related cosmology (see, e.g., Johnson 1903; see also Dobzhanskaya 2008, 2014; Khomich 1978,

1981; Lapsui et al. 2023; Lar 1998, 2001, 2005, 2006; Lar and Vanuyto 2011; Lehtisalo 1924, 1937; Lukin 2011, 2012, 2022; Pushkareva 1999, 2003, 2007, 2019; Pushkareva and Burykin 2011, 298–306; Pushkareva and Khomich 2001; Yadne 2006, 59, 167–69). This is so mainly because Nenets have hidden sacred matters from outsiders. Today, Nenets live in a "post-shamanistic" society (Vitebsky 1992, 244). However, among Nenets occasionally a few are still called shamans (*tadyebya* in Nenets, *shaman* in Russian) as they claim to have shamanic sensibilities and perform rituals, or as Nenets author Nina Yadne (2006, 169) writes, "Now there are few real shamans and those who are go further to the tundra" (see also Golovnev 2000b, 220; Kharyuchi 2004, 156–57; Pyrirko 2019; Vagramenko 2014, 29–31). Global neoshamanism with its "individualistic psychologization" and "environmentalist activism" (Vitebsky 1995, 189) has also reached the Nenets areas. For instance, Nikolai Taleyev, alias Shaman Kolya, a Nenets from Nelmin-Nos village, is known throughout Russia thanks to his public rituals of divination.

27. Following Keane (2013), I regard ontology to be local assumptions, representations, or theories that guide people's actions ("weak ontology"), which is different from Eduardo Viveiros de Castro's (1998) claims of ontology determining the way people inhabit their own world ("strong ontology"). I find the notion of ontology useful when talking of people's intuitions or views about what things are in the world (e.g., the wine of the Eucharist as Christ's blood for Christians, see Keane 2013, 190), which can be radically different from one another. These intuitions and views can, however, change in divergent contexts depending on, among other things, ethical criteria (Lambek 2021, 120). These are "practices in an 'ontology' . . . in which relations are drawn on different principles," as Caroline Humphrey (2018, 13) puts it with a reference to Philippe Descola's (2013) work.

28. There is some research done on evangelical communities among Siberian Nenets east of the Urals by Skvirskaja (2014) and Tatiana Vagramenko (2014, 2017a, 2017b, 2018). Vagramenko's work offers a valuable ethnographic insight into relations between various Christian denominations in Yamal, both in sedentary and nomadic settings, also shedding light on the widespread negative discourse on "sectarians" (*sektanty*) among Nenets and Khanty intelligentsia and beyond.

29. The biggest source of mission force today are Ukrainians, many of whom moved to Russia in the Soviet period, often attracted to the North by the possibility of earning the "long rouble"—that is, high pay. So are the central characters in my account, Baptist pastor Pavel and Pentecostal pastor Vladislav, both ethnic Ukrainians. Already in the Soviet period the largest Baptist community in Europe was in Ukraine, which was also called "the Bible Belt of the Soviet Union" (Wanner 2007, 1). As a result, Ukrainians have proselytized across the former Soviet Union, from Central Asia to the Far North (Pelkmans 2009b; Wanner 2009; White 2020). Among the northern Indigenous minorities, the Ukrainians, alongside Russians, are active not only among Nenets but also among the Khanty, Koryak, Chukchi, and others (King 2011, 96; Lunkin 2000, 130; Plattet 2013; Vagramenko 2014, 83; Vakhtin 2005; Vaté 2009; Wiget and Balalaeva 2007, 15; 2011, 168). With the full-scale invasion of Russia into Ukraine in February 2022, many Ukrainians ceased to have access to the mission fields in Russia. One-third of all brotherhood members live in Ukraine; many of them have been forced to become refugees and some have been killed (V zone 2022, 22–25). The brotherhood has declared the war to be the sure sign of the end times (https://iucecb.com /news/20220923-1851).

30. The word *veruyushchiy* ("believer") or *khristianin* ("Christian") is the primary marker of self-identification for Russian Baptists and Pentecostals. They rarely use names derived

from the denominational labels such as *baptist* ("Baptist") or *pyatidesyatnik* ("Pentecostal") (cf. Wanner 2009, 168, 180n10).

31. In the nineteenth century, Orthodox missionaries also complained that the locals who were baptized did not know the name of Christ (Khomich 1979, 21; see also Borisova 2022 on such "ignorance" today).

1. Dynamics of Avoidance and Engagement

1. I stress the word *sense* here, as reindeer herders' situations vary considerably. Unlike some other marginalized groups (such as Pentecostal Dalit women in a South Indian slum see Roberts 2016), Nenets families usually do not convert to Christianity to alleviate their poverty (many converts are well-off, while some nonconverts are struggling to get meat on the table). However, Ural Nenets who have been threatened with removal are motivated to seek protection from farm bosses through their alliance with Christian Russians (more below).

2. This distinction has its roots in an earlier debate on Robin Horton's (1975a, 1975b) "intellectualist theory" of conversion in Africa (see also Hefner 1993b).

3. It must be noted that firsthand knowledge of the cultural worlds both *before* and *after* conversion is rare among anthropologists, as this would require a rather long duration of ethnographic observation (but see Tuzin 1997; Vilaça 2016; Vitebsky 2017a; 2017b, 24).

4. The Veli is one of the oldest clans (*yerkar*) among the European Nenets. We know that some with the clan name Veli participated in assaults against Russians in Pustozersk in 1661. In the tax documents, the clan name first appears in 1683. They are then categorized as the dwellers of the forests (*pedara khasavaq*, "forest people") possibly living in the lower reaches of the Usa River. This earlier area largely matches Mikul's son Vata's version, which is that his ancestors began to move from the forest to the open tundra in summer only in the mid-nineteenth century; some other Veli families already nomadized in the open tundra by that time, especially in the Kanin peninsula (see Dolgikh 1970, 46, 61; Islavin 1847, 135; Kvashnin 2019, 83–84; Kolycheva 1956, 84; Lashuk 1958, 162; Okladnikov and Matafanov 2008, 251).

5. There were as many as 363 baptized Veli (or Valeyskiy, which is a Russianized form) by the end of the nineteenth century (Okladnikov and Matafanov 2008, 251).

6. I have chosen to use "Independents" rather than "private farmers," "noncollectivized peasant," or "small-holders" when translating the word *yedinolichniki*. This is a term that came into a wider usage in the early 1930s, designating the people who were not (yet) collectivized in the rural areas (see, e.g., Maslov 1934). In Stalin's constitution from 1936, as Karen Petrone (2000, 190) writes, "article 9 explicitly permitted the 'small-scale private economy of individual peasants and artisans based on their personal labor'" (see also Lévesque 2006). Nevertheless, most *yedinolichniki* could not survive, as they were not given (good) land, and most of what they grew or raised was taken through exorbitant taxation. Officially registered *yedinolichniki* became rare in the documents of the Nenets areas after 1940, as they were forced to pay exorbitantly high taxes to the state (Khomich 1966, 252; 1971a, 237; Stammler 2005, 141). Nenets Independents with their thousands of reindeer were officially not registered as *yedinolichniki*, although they were locally called this by other reindeer herders of the region.

7. Yevsyugin (1910–95) belonged to the cohort of the early northern graduates from the Herzen Pedagogical Institute in Leningrad (1930–33). In his memoirs Yevsyugin (1993)

describes approvingly how in 1920, as a schoolboy in Nizhnyaya Pyosha, the priest-teacher was confronted by school children who had been changed "under the influence of Red commanders, political instructors, and revolutionary songs." Further, he writes, "I am deeply grateful to the first Red Army men who came to us. Under their influence, I became an atheist and thereafter a Komsomol [member of the Communist Youth League] and a Communist" (7). Only a few Nenets went through this kind of conversion experience to cast themselves as revolutionary subjects, as the majority of them were out in the tundra and had little contact with political activists. In Yevsyugin's, as in many other early Soviet narratives of conversion to Communism, one can discern a pattern like that of Christianity in which the motifs of rebirth, confession, and repudiation of one's past self dominate (Hellbeck 2006, 311–12; see also Kharkhordin 1999).

8. Compare with what Nenets writer Vasiliy Ledkov writes in his novel on collectivization: "But they [*yedinolichniki*] also need the word of the Party. We leave them out of sight and they will be the prey of kulaks and shamans. And also the children of *yedinolichniki* need to be engaged. They must study . . . By all means . . ." (1977, 114, original ellipsis).

9. During the Great Purge in 1937, Prourzin was accused of, among other things, not carrying out "a decisive fight against the machinations [*vylazok*] of the kulaks, shamans, and clergy," and he spent fifteen years in prison camps (Tolkachev 2000a, 44; see also 525–26).

10. "Yadey Segery" is a Russianized version of *yedei syekhery*, which translates as "new ways" in Nenets. It was one of the two small collective farms that were based in the village of Karataika. Mikhail worked as its chairman until 1952, when the farm was merged with two others into a "consolidated collective farm" (*ukrupnennyy kolkhoz*) (Mamoylova 1997, 66). During this period of "rationalization," many Nenets lost their leading positions in rural collective structures.

11. Possibly he was caught as a participant in the *mandalada* uprising, even if he did not take part in it (more below).

12. Ngel was conscripted in 1942 and was declared "missing" (*propal bez vesti*) in 1943, which usually means death without the body being found but can also mean capture by the enemy or desertion (https://www.obd-memorial.ru/html/info.htm?id=68260918, checked 27/2/2019).

13. The archival documents provided by Tolkachev (2000b, 305) tell us that "Valey Vasiliy Tarasovich (Taras Vas')" was arrested among those putative "bandits" who were caught only after the event at a distance of up to thirty kilometers. It is known that there were random retributive arrests made among those who did not participate in the *mandalada*.

14. Among rather brief and vague reports of *yedinolichniki*, a more concrete example is given by Alexandra Lavrillier (2005, 123) who writes that "we still find today in the village [area] of Ust-Nyukzha some nomadic kin groups that never joined the state institutions and whose herds have never been requisitioned. This is the shaman Fyodor Vasil'ev's lineage and another family whose name I will not reveal. The latter are currently looked for by the police, who, despite many years of searching in the taiga, have not been able to locate them." I heard of a similar case of a nomadic family in the Ural Mountains whom the authorities have never "found" (as in 2007, more below).

15. Khalmer-Yu, a village with a Gulag history, was at the time the center of the Bolshezemelskaya District of the Nenets Region before it was transferred to the Komi ASSR in 1959 (Vorkuta was transferred in 1940). The changes in administrative borders must have made Independents less visible to the authorities. Furthermore, the copresence of Gulag

and civil administrations in the area made the issue of responsibility for dealing with such "illegals" less clear.

16. Also, many Baptist pastors who were not working were sentenced by the same law (see Bourdeaux and Filatov 2003, 171, 195).

17. Moving around in settlements was always dangerous, as the identity documents were occasionally checked, especially in the heavily guarded areas like the Vorkuta Gulag area (see Solzhenitsyn 1991, 82–83n42). However, the reindeer herders were not asked for documents on streets that often, as they wore reindeer coats and moved around with reindeer, which put them in a particular "savage slot."

18. Like in the tsarist era, so trading did not necessarily involve cash transactions. The Independents often engaged in the exchange of pelts for rifles, ammunition, tarpaulin, rubber boots, or similar illegal or difficult-to-get things with Russians.

19. Living without a *propiska* was a criminal offense in the Soviet Union, as it was a prerequisite for all citizens to have one; it secured housing, schooling, medical service, and employment. De facto it was a vicious circle as one could not get a *propiska* without being employed in an enterprise, which was a "primary unit of society" (Humphrey 2002, 25).

20. Many Izhma Komi are of Nenets origin, or as Otto Habeck (2005, 203) notes about the people with whom he did fieldwork, "The Khatanzeiskii families see themselves as 'somewhere in between' Komi and Nenets."

21. These are internal passports (*pasporta*) that were used as national identity cards and were issued to the rural population only in the 1970s (Baiburin 2021). The data in the Independents' passports are often rather approximate: for many, the date of birth is the first of July and the place of birth is "Bolshezemelskaya tundra," "Kara River," or similar.

22. There is a similar case of a Yamb-To child finding himself in the orphanage in 1976 as a result of his mother dying during childbirth. The family was visiting the village of Karataika to buy supplies when her labor unexpectedly started. The child was saved and taken to Arkhangelsk. Although the family name and patronymic of the newborn were known, his father and brothers were found only at the beginning of the 1990s when contacts emerged between *yedinolichniki* and Nenets in Naryan-Mar. The orphan joined his family in 1993 without knowing the Nenets language or reindeer herding. Although at the beginning he tried to escape several times, he has stayed and is living in the tundra (Khanzerova 2018).

23. This is a paraphrase of Stephen Kotkin's (1995, 220) expression "speak Bolshevik"—"the obligatory language for self-identification and as such, the barometer of one's political allegiance to the cause" (see also Petrov and Ryazanova-Clarke 2014). There is a certain parallel with the "Baptist dialect," with its "numerous archaisms, biblical allusions and euphemisms" (Prokhorov 2013, 309), which also works as an identity marker. As Konstantin Prokhorov notes, "Those familiar with this 'pious' dialect quickly distinguished the 'ins' from the 'outs'" (312).

24. As we shall see later, the issue of sincerity is much more contested than it would appear from these statements (see also Rappaport 1999).

25. The formal and informal property regimes have been rather complex in the tundra area over the last hundred years (see Konstantinov 2015; Ventsel 2005; Vladimirova 2006). Atsushi Yoshida, who has done research among Gyda Nenets (2001, 69), reports, "Most of the reindeer herders had officially been organized in *sovkhozy* (state farms) or *kolkhozy* (collective farms). But quite a large number remained as independent herder-smallholders called *yedinolichniki* in Russian. In documents, they are sometimes called hunters (*okhotniki*) or fishermen (*rybaki*), depending on their secondary specialized mode of subsistence.

Some also do double-duty working as herders for collective farms or working seasonally as fishermen in fish factories. However, if one looks beyond the statistics, most are at the same time also herders" (cf. Bogordayeva and Oshchepkov 2003, 170; Stammler 2005, 144). Unlike the Yamb-To and Ural Nenets, these *yedinolichniki* in Gyda still had links with the state farms, as their other citizen duties, such as schooling, army service, and identity papers were all managed through their offices. They are those who I would call "grey-zone herders" (cf. Lévesque 2006, 109). Furthermore, during the Soviet era, despite official restrictions, many managed to run big personal herds inside the collective farm system, hidden from the gaze of outsiders or enjoying silent agreement from farm administrations (especially in Yamal and Gyda, see D. Anderson 2000, 144; Golovnev and Osherenko 1999, 98; Golovnev 2004, 92–93; Stammler 2005, 135).

26. Initially the name was *Obshchina olenevodov-yedinolichnikov 'Yamb To'* (*Proyektnye* 1993; cf. Tuisku 2002). Only in January 2011, the Yamb-To clan-community (with the full Russian name: *semeyno-rodovaya obshchina korennykh malochislennykh narodov Severa Nenetskogo avtonomnogo okruga 'Yamb To' [Dlinnoe ozero]*), with fifteen families, was finally registered by the local authorities. A few Independents have also become "associate members" of the nearby collective farms based in Karataika, Ust-Kara, and Vorkuta or remained unaffiliated herders (*chastniki*) (Bobrova 2010). The existence of the official clan-community has been rather unstable. In 2015, it was liquidated by the federal authorities, as the necessary tax reports were not filed in time. Before paying a visit to the community the same year, I had accidentally discovered the official statement of "the liquidation" of the community on the official website of court acts (Reshenie 2015). No one among the Yamb-To reindeer herders I talked to had heard of the closing of the clan-community, including the illiterate head of the community. The following year the community was officially restored with the help of Nenets officials in Naryan-Mar. Since 2011 they have been allocated some pastures; however, these cannot accommodate their twenty thousand or so reindeer (cf. Korepanova 2019, 487).

27. The confrontation of the state and Indigenous understanding has often caused bureaucratic problems. A Nenets woman told me how her family had buried her grandmother, and as one of the items she asked to be buried with her was her passport; this was done. Afterward it caused significant problems for the registration of her death. These examples demonstrate, in different semiotic ideologies or ontologies (Henare et al. 2007, 19; Keane 2007), how material items can gain agency of their own and can pose a real threat to existing cultural forms.

28. The number of the Yamb-To Nenets (not considering their relationship to the Yamb-To *obshchina*) is around two hundred (in 2007 it was 205; most of them were registered in Amderma, the Nenets Region). The number of the Ural Nenets, who have always been more numerous, is almost double that. By 2001, Vorkuta City Council had issued documents for 253 Nenets who had previously no documents (Komandirovka 2001, 63; see also Bogoyavlenskiy 2001). In 2019, the Vorkuta municipal area had registered 237 Indigenous people (the majority of them are Nenets), 192 of them listed as nomads and others as part-time nomads (Status 2019). My rough estimate of the Ural Independents, based on my fieldwork material, is between 300 and 400. Many of them are registered in the Yamalo-Nenets Region, where more generous allowances are paid.

29. As Sovetskiy village was closed, in 2016 the four-year school was moved to Vorgashor, the coal-mining village on the other side of the Vorkuta industrial region, which is also planned to be shut down. In 2019, seventy Nenets children went to this school. However, the

number is decreasing, as many families have moved their children to schools in the Yamalo-Nenets Region (Romanova 2022; see also Kuwajima 2015).

30. Since the early 2010s, the Ural Independents have been under increasing pressure from the local joint-stock farms "Reindeer Herder" and "Red October" (an ex-sovkhoz and an ex-kolkhoz), whose bosses (father and son) have sued several Nenets heads of family for using the pastures of farms that have an official lease agreement with Vorkuta city (for the years 2005–2028). As there is no land to rent for the Independents, this can be seen an opportunity to "collectivize" the Ural Independents (Murashko 2016). There have been several court cases (I attended one session in 2012) and Nenets have been fined for using the pastures their parents and grandparents had used for decades. There is another dimension to this as well: various accusations have been made that the Independents not only are uncivilized and unable to manage their herds but also, being Baptists, are supported and manipulated by foreign churches, which implicitly means a moral danger to everyone, including the Nenets themselves (*Ezhegodnyy* 2015, 19; Murashko 2013, 58; see also Andreyev 2017; Opasnost' 2019 for examples of accusations against Protestants). Indeed, the Nenets who were sued have agreed that the Vorkuta Baptist church petitioned against their attempted eviction from their lands (http://iucecb.com/news/20140406-0254). In the early 2010s, a few Ural families formed an *obshchina* called "Tybertya" (from Nenets *ty pertya*, "reindeer herder") and acquired the rental rights for some pastures on the border of Komi Republic and Yamalo-Nenets Region in 2014. Some others have been forced to join a joint-stock farm so as not to be evicted from their pastures.

2. Trajectories of Conversion

1. The paradox of being simultaneously modern and antimodern is managed through the concept of interiority and exteriority, the dichotomy that defines most aspects of a believer's life. The part that will be saved is one's soul, while the body is above all an externality that is said to be mirroring what is "inside" (the role of body is not stressed in the doctrine of resurrection; see Cannell 2005). Yet, as we shall see below, the idea of mirroring interiority may become a source of significant anxiety for converts.

2. Also other gadgets such as smartphones became popular in the late 2000s. These were used primarily for entertainment, as most of the time there was no mobile coverage (cf. Stammler 2009).

3. The story has a few parallels that are known from shamanic initiation stories, such as suffering and losing consciousness (Lehtisalo 1924, 147; 1937, 3). However, Ivan's demonizing discourse based on the Christian value system did not reveal whether he thought in these categories himself. So, the parallel is rather "typological" here and based on Ivan's claim that he had earlier desired to become a shaman.

4. "Doth not even nature itself teach you, that, if a man have long hair, it is a shame unto him?" (1 Corinthians 11:14).

5. Reluctance and tormenting visions have been common in shamanic initiation among the Nenets, as reported by several commentators (Schrenk 1848, 403; Siikala 1978, 190; see also Vitebsky 1995, 74–77). Although Nenets shamanhood is hereditary, sometimes marked by a birthmark or a pellicle on the crown of the head (like in the case of Tikynye; see introduction), it is believed that spirits chose the future shaman and pressured the person into the apprenticeship of shamanhood (Khomich 1981; Lar 2005). Spirits were said to be

choosing the person and would punish an unwilling person with a disease or death (Popov 1944, 90). The motifs that keep repeating in shamanic initiatory accounts are spirits cutting up, boiling, and putting back together the initiate. Often some bones or organs are added to the person before being brought back to life. This is thus a kind of corporeal rebirth that gives the person shamanic powers.

6. When Andrei was being ordained, his wife, Lyuba, knelt next to him, indicating that the role of a fully functioning pastorship needs a believing and supporting wife as a household church.

7. Here is a strong parallel with the nineteenth-century Lutheran pietist movement known as Laestadianism that spread widely among Sámi reindeer herders in northern Scandinavia. This was started in the 1840s by Lars Levi Laestadius (1800–61), a Swedish Sámi pastor and botanist, who integrated a successful temperance program into his evangelization campaign.

8. There are many passing notes on this topic across Siberia (see Broz 2009, 31; Golovnev et al. 2014, 87; Khakhovskaya 2018, 219–20; Kharitonova 2004, 30; Pelkmans 2009b, 154; Sillanpää 2008, 87; Toulouze and Niglas 2019, 276; Vagramenko 2014; Vaté 2009, 50; Wanner 2007, 220–25; Wiget and Balalaeva 2011).

9. Also nonconverts were talking of conversion as becoming sober. For instance, when I refused to have a drink with nonconverts, they asked whether I had become a Baptist.

10. The female converts' relative invisibility among the Independents contrasts with what Vagramenko (2014, 2017a) describes about school-educated female converts in Beloyarsk, Yamal, where two middle-aged Nenets sisters helped Russian Baptist male missionaries to arrange most conversions via their kin networks.

11. Like the Nenets Independents, the Unregistered Baptists have reservations toward too much education. While the Nenets do not want their children to stay at school more than four years, the Baptists do not encourage their children to go to university, as this is not necessary for living the life of "a service to God." In the pages of *Herald of Truth*, senior Russian Baptist Vladimir Chukhontsev (2007, 11) condemns those believers who have pursued higher education: "They have invested resources and wasted their efforts and time. They lived five years under strain. . . . for what good? In order to boast when an opportunity presents itself: 'I have higher education!' This is open vanity."

12. Obviously, Ivan did not consider himself a Russian. When living in the city, this is virtually impossible, even if one wished. He said that Russians on the street call Nenets pejoratively *chukchi* (a stereotype of uncivilized reindeer herders, from an ethnonym of the Chukchi living in the Far East) or *churki* (people from the Caucasus or Central Asia) because of their Asiatic appearance and small stature.

3. Baptist Missionaries on the Edge

1. Until 2001, their name was "The Union of Churches of Evangelical-Christian Baptists," then they added "International" in front of their name. On the one hand, this reflects the fact that Russia and other ex-Soviet states where churches were located belonged to different political entities now. On the other hand, a claim for "internationality" helps them to strengthen their image as *the* Christ's church on earth (more below).

2. Those churches that survived the Stalinist purges or emerged after either remained independent, and thus illegal, or joined the state-sanctioned All-Union Council, which

united both Baptists and Pentecostals. The Vorkuta Baptist church existed as an independent congregation until the 1990s, when it joined the unregistered union. The Vorkuta Pentecostal Church has grown out of the official Pentecostal branch, which until 1989 was a part of the All-Union Council (Bourdeaux and Filatov 2003, 266–83; 2005, 195–200). The Registered Pentecostals were forced to adopt Baptist theological and ritual preferences, which were more acceptable to the secular authorities. While retaining believer's baptism, the Pentecostals had to give up their central rituals, which distinguished them from the Baptists: they were not allowed to speak in tongues or prophesy, or perform spiritual healing during joint church services (Sawatsky 1981, 93–95).

3. He was referring to Vladimir Yevladov's (1893–1974) book *Po tundram Yamala k Belomu ostrovu* ("Across the Tundra of Yamal toward the Belyi Island"). Yevladov worked for the Ural Regional Land Service and traveled on the Yamal Peninsula in 1928–29 and 1935–36, studying the land resources and Indigenous peoples (Yevladov 1992; see also 2010; Pika 1998).

4. There is a perennial problem for Christian missionaries who strive to find what is "cultural" (and can therefore be left alone or even positively used for Christianization purposes) and what is "pagan" (see also Pelkmans 2007). A discrepancy between missionaries' and Nenets converts' perceptions is apparent: the latter are sometimes even more radical in their attempts at eradication, as they can see "paganism" in things and habits that are invisible to the missionaries, who know very little of the local cosmologies and ritual practices (see also Vagramenko 2017b).

5. I sensed a symmetric suspicion by both state agents and missionaries. Pavel implied that my academic work could be used by the state. An official in Naryan-Mar whom I contacted to ask for permission to work in the closed border area where the Yamb-To summer pastures are located inquired whether I was working for the missionaries or was, in fact, a missionary myself (cf. Broz 2009, 34n8; Vagramenko 2014, 60–63).

6. This was the All-Russia agricultural census that took place in summer 2006. Note also a quote from an Unregistered Baptist: "When Christ comes to take his church, if she has registered her marriage with the State . . . of course, He will repudiate such a church! Would you be pleased if your bride registered her marriage with another man?" (quoted in Prokhorov 2013, 345, original ellipsis).

7. Other strands of Baptists and other evangelical Christians in Russia are involved in various social programs (Caldwell 2017, 25; Mikeshin 2016).

8. The author of the lyrics is Viktor Belykh, a Christian who was in a Gulag camp in Vorkuta. The song was already circulating in the 1960s. Interestingly, one can recognize the similar language of harshness in the Vorkuta punk subculture (Pilkington 2014, 162).

9. Born in Ukraine in a Baptist family, Pavel found his way to Vorkuta by being conscripted into the army in Vorkuta in 1979. After being released from the army, Pavel took his wife and son to Vorkuta and started working in a coal mine, attracted by a high salary and other "northern privileges." In the late 1990s, he retired from work; since then, he has dedicated most of his time to traveling and evangelizing in the tundra.

10. However, both the Registered and Unregistered Baptists shared the basic seven dogmatic principles shared widely among Baptists elsewhere: the Bible as the only rule and guidance, freedom of conscience, the church of only regenerated people, baptism of adult believers by immersion, independence of local churches, the priesthood of all believers, and the separation of the church from the state (Vins 1979, 103; cf. Sawatsky 1981, 338). Despite sharing the same set

of dogmas, the actual practices and church ideology in both groups were considerably different, mainly due to their different attitudes toward the state and secular modernity.

11. "For what have I to do to judge them also that are without? do not ye judge them that are within? But them that are without God judgeth. Therefore put away from among yourselves that wicked person."

12. In the Soviet period, some young believers wore photos of prisoners on themselves, as Prokhorov writes, "These small photos were being revered and were functioning almost like icons" (2013, 218–19). He has demonstrated that in this and many other cases Russian Orthodoxy has had a major impact upon the religiosity of Russian Baptists.

13. In recent years, Protestants have experienced hardships that they have not seen since the late Soviet period. In 2016, the new law (known as the Yarovaya Law after lawmaker Irina Yarovaya) was enacted (Zagrebina 2017), forbidding missionizing outside recognized church buildings without special registration, thus making the Unregistered Baptists' evangelization illegal in the eyes of the state.

14. The number 666 is a widespread worry among Christians in Russia, including Russian Orthodox (Benovska 2021, 1).

15. The language barrier poses serious challenges to the missionaries, who must read other signs to assess converts' Christianness. Pavel writes in a mission report on the importance of visible deeds: "In summer 2004, G. and D. experienced the joy of being born from above and were baptized. The language barrier often hinders understanding the inner world of our Nenets brothers and sisters. But deeds express their interior world and thoughts better than any words. So once again when visiting the Ural Nenets church, I saw how brothers from other tents came on their reindeer harnesses to visit one of the poor families. One of them brought the carcass of a reindeer calf, another took with him dried bread [*sukhari*] and the third brought sugar. When seeing the loving work of God in the life of those people, my heart fills with trembling and gratitude to God for His work among these people."

16. In this respect, Unregistered Baptists differ from many other Christians elsewhere in the world who often launch their mission through translation work (see, e.g., Handman 2015; Hanks 2010; Meyer 1999). In Russia, this stance is related to the dominant language ideology that represents the Russian language as an inevitable part of every citizen's life.

4. Destructive Persuasion

1. "But now I have written unto you not to keep company, if any man that is called a brother be a fornicator, or covetous, or an idolator, or a railer, or a drunkard, or an extortioner; with such an one no not to eat."

2. William Pietz (1985, 14) notes, "The discourse of the fetish has always been a critical discourse about the false objective values of a culture from which the speaker is personally distanced." But as we shall see below, this is an issue not only of values but also of ontological concepts of things and their agency.

3. "So then faith cometh by hearing, and hearing by the word of God."

4. Or take the fleshiness of a leather-bound Bible, which is good for waving when making a point, as we shall see further below (cf. Rutherford 2006). There are many reports from the Soviet period that Bibles were valued as sacred objects because physical copies were hard to come by (Prokhorov 2013, 224–33).

5. Orthodox Nenets avoided damaging *syadeyq*. The priest Nevskiy gives a telling account of this when he travels with Nenets in the Great Land tundra in 1905. He learned that a larch tree he had stopped by during the day was "an idol" with a carved face on it. Later in the day at a nomadic campsite, it was explained that Nenets smeared the face with vodka, as this helped to avoid getting lost in the tundra. When learning of these details, Nevskiy began explaining about the "falsity" of this belief. He then noted that "finally, they understood and laughed at the idol." But when he asked for an axe, they refused, saying, "What's it to you? You are a priest, so [the idol] will not touch you, but we shall suffer evil" (Nevskiy 1906, 271; see also Baryshev 2011; Mikhaylov 1898; Okladnikov and Matafanov 2008; Ovsyannikov and Terebikhin 1994, 68–69; Shashkov 1896; Yur'ev 1919, 64–65).

6. Like Orthodox icons, Indigenous sacred objects, such as shamanic drums, cloaks, and carved images, were publicly burned by Soviets (Balzer 2011, 43–45; Bulgakova 2013, 196, 213–15; Bulgakova and Sundström 2017, 246).

7. Many scholars have written about similar issues elsewhere in Siberia (see, e.g., Bloch and Kendall 2004, 94; Højer 2009, 579; Lukin 2010; Rethmann 2001, 39; Slezkine 1994; Ssorin-Chaikov 2001, 14–15; Vitebsky 2005, 323).

8. As Baptist missionary Pavel put it after his trip to Vaigach (using the language of the prophet Daniel, especially 9:27; 11:31): "The island in Nenets is called Khebyidya-Ya, which means 'sacred island' [he mistranslates *ya*, "land," as "island"]. Scholars call it 'a historical monument of the Nenets national culture,' but the Word of God calls these places 'the abomination of desolation' [*merzost'yu zapusteniya*] where everything is polluted with idols and idolaters. The world and God value phenomena and facts in a diametrically opposed manner." Note that the missionary speaks not from a human but from the divine point of view (see chaps. 3 and 7).

9. Khomich writes that *myad pukhutsya* ("old woman of the tent") does not always have a typical wooden or stone core but just a piece of cloth is taken around that the *khekhe* grows (1971b, 242; see also Ivanov 1970, 85; Menshakova and Taleyeva 2011, 21). Each time a child is born, mother adds a new overcoat or a scarf to the *myad pukhutsya* who has eased childbirth. Lehtisalo (1924, 123) describes how Forest Nenets shamans used to give clothes taken from a *khekhe* to ease the pain of an ailing person. Lapsui writes that *myad pukhutsya* is "an earthly, tent-dwelling part of goddess Ja-Minja [Yaminya]" (Lapsui et al. 2023, 19).

10. There is no guarantee that local spirits would always be protective for their owners. Some Nenets non-Christians said to me that *khekheq* could be rather moody and unpredictable (see also Golovnev 2000b, 213; Lehtisalo 1924, 118).

11. Finding a partner has always been a challenge in the areas where most around are close kin, which is sometimes further complicated by religious choices (Vallikivi 2009, 72–73). The missionaries who traveled widely acted as matchmakers, ensuring that young Nenets would form Baptist families (cf. Vagramenko 2014, 177–94; 2017a; 162–64; Wiget and Balalaeva 2011, 171).

12. These reindeer bulls with big antlers are considered leading animals in a herd. A young non-Christian Yamb-To man told me that the first *myenarui* appeared when a Nenets in the old times fell ill. He then promised a reindeer to a god and, as a result, he recovered quickly. Since then, every person has one. So, in his account, *myenarui* was necessary not only for the well-being of the herd but also for the owner's health.

13. Pe Mal Khada is known among most Nenets alongside some other gods (e.g., Yamal Khekhe, Ser Ngo Iri) whose dwelling places are visited from afar. Some Nenets identify her as the goddess of earth (also according to Tikynye) and the daughter of the sky god, Num,

whose caravan was transformed into stone (mountain) after the master of the underworld Nga attacked her (Khomich 1966, 199–200n20). One of many legends of origin tells that Pe Mal Khada traveled from south to north through the valleys: she stopped seven times, and each place became a sacred site (see Golovnev 2004, 319–20 for more details). She is a protector of calves and newborn babies (Lar 2003, 107–8; Lar and Vanuyto 2011, 101). Golovnev (1995, 491–92), who observed a sacrificial ritual there in 1993, has reported the following sacrificial words: "Grandmother, we brought you a reindeer calf, so others could live unharmed" (see also 1994). And in a shamanic song, Pe Mal Khada responds to the invocation call of a shaman, "Pe Mal Khadako, where have you gone?" by answering, "I stop at the nose [front end] of the sacred sledge" (Golovnev 1995, 381–82). The nose of the *khekhengan*, where the "material" *khekheq* are kept, is smeared with the blood of a sacrificially slaughtered reindeer (cf. Prokof'eva 1953, 227). This implies that the deity moves around and yet she (or part of her) may dwell in the doll-like figure.

14. One could argue that in this way reindeer herders solve the problem of being constantly on the move unable to visit distant sacred sites. It has to be noted that not all *khekheq* are collected from sacred sites (*khekhe ya*). Some are given by shamans or encountered in the landscape. People may choose something for a *khekhe* because of its unusual finding circumstances or shape (e.g., anthropomorphic). This is usually interpreted as spirits' volitional act of self-revelation (see also Golovnev 2000b; G. Kharyuchi 2001, 82, 107; 2012, 19; Lehtisalo 1924, 104, 133–34; Skvirskaja 2012, 156; Zhitkov 1913, 51).

15. A *khekhengan* is a sledge where only "pure" things can be kept. Iriko stored on it sacred items but also food and men's tools. It is on the other side of the tent entrance, farther away from the *syabu* sledge, which has things with dangerous female powers (see chap. 7).

16. The Pentecostal mission "Voice of Hope" (affiliated to the All-Ukrainian Union Churches of Evangelical Pentecostal Faith) was founded in Lutsk, Ukraine. From this mission, Fyodor Velichko first visited Vorkuta in 1990. He became a bishop of the church union in the Komi Republic, being integrated into the Russian Church of Christians of Evangelical Faith. All the churches of the union are registered with the state authorities. Unlike the Vorkuta Baptists, the Pentecostals are also involved in social programs like outreach to prisoners with HIV/AIDS and alcoholics (Bourdeaux and Filatov 2003, 266–83; 2005, 195–200; see also Wanner 2007).

17. Among Russian Baptists, joking and laughing, especially in religious settings, are signs of disrespect to God, if not a sacrilege (with a reference to Ephesians 5:4, cf. Prokhorov 2013, 180, 314, 321).

18. Note that demons or devils (*cherty* in Russian) and idols are discursively the same and not-the-same, just as the devil is one and many. It is commonly argued by Christian theologians that the devil (Satan) is a fallen angel who governs the world with all the other rebellious angels who are, strictly speaking, "demons." These spirits can manifest themselves in a myriad of visual guises (see, e.g., Valk 2001). Furthermore, it needs to be stressed that Nenets old-timers, young converts, and missionaries most likely understood "devils" to be rather different nonhumans "in their aspects both as persons and as concepts" (Lambek 2021, 33) with their particular histories, capacities, and motivations.

19. Tikynye also called a spirit effigy like Pe Mal Khada a *sidyangg*, which means "shadow" and "photo" (cf. Lar 2003, 82). The same word had a wide spectrum of use: from the recently deceased who wandered around to somebody's representation on a photo, as mentioned. This refers to the perception that the effigies were not classified along the line of material and immaterial or even visible and invisible, but rather in a hybrid way. Pretty

much like another part of a person, the breath (*yindq*) is both material and immaterial. Rane Willerslev (2007, 57), while discussing the Yukaghir concept of soul, makes a similar observation by quoting Valerio Valeri (2000, 24), who writes that breath is "most invisible in the visible, most immaterial in the material."

20. The idea that some people go to live in the sky where everything is pure has been around for some time among the Nenets. Yet only exceptional people could do this, such as a mythic shaman called Urier [Nguryer], who, being tired of the worsening conditions on the earth, drove with one of his wives on a reindeer sledge to the sky (Castrén 1853, 234; Schrenk 1848, 527; cf. Lehtisalo 1924, 115). This motif is likely influenced by the biblical ideas of the moral degradation of the earth and the rewards of paradise as well as by the story of St. Elijah (cf. Leete 2014, 99).

21. In her recent report on this sacred site, Ol'ga Poshekhonova (2016, 13 photo 4) has published a photo of "home spirits," *myad khekheq*, at this site that have possibly been returned by Nenets converts.

22. According to the Russian ethnographer Yekaterina Prokof'eva (1953, 225, who relies on the data gathered by Grigoriy Verbov and Georgiy Prokof'ev), a piece of wood, stones, or textile taken from a sacred site is called *khekhe-pyelya* (see also Kharyuchi 2013, 51, 65). This word can be translated as "spirit-part" (*pyelya*, meaning "half," or "part," or "patrilineal kin"; *ngamzani pyelya*, literally "part of my flesh," meaning "brother" from the same exogamous group, which refers to shared substantiality and close relationship, see also Verbov 1939, 49).

23. On his visit to the same site (also known as Yamal Khekhe Salya) in 1996, Golovnev (2000b, 223) notes that one is supposed to leave and take things at the site to return in three years' time. A related idea is to have sacred items detached from a person who cannot (e.g., those who live in settlements or are female widows, see Kharyuchi 2013, 92; Murashko 2004, 60) or need not keep them anymore (e.g., a person has no reindeer left, see Kharyuchi 2001, 99; 2004, 158–59; Khomich 1981, 22, 37).

24. Note that Vladislav's wish to return Iriko's icons to their place of origin ("an Orthodox church") bears a typological similarity with the idea discussed here. However, as we see, his cosmological and moral assumptions are radically different from those of Nenets animists.

25. Not only *khekheq* were burned but occasionally also card sets that they played for reindeer—as a result of gambling, some families had lost most of their herd.

5. Silence and Binding Words

1. The conspicuousness of silence among Nenets has been touched upon by several scholars (Khristoforova 1998, 2006; Laptander 2020a; Leete 2014, 2019; Novikova 2016; Ravna 2021; Simoncsics 2005; Toulouze and Niglas 2019, 206–22; Yadne 2006, 182). A well-known short novel called *Molchashchiy* ("The Silent") by Nenets writer Anna Nerkagi echoes uses of silence in a riveting way (1996, 231–305; see also Samson-Normand de Chambourg 1998). The inclination to few words among Nenets is also noted by cross-cultural psychologists who compared Nenets with Russians from Central Russia, who were found to be far more verbose (Draguns et al. 2000).

2. There are plenty of examples of similar speech avoidance practices throughout the Russian Arctic and Siberia (see Brandišauskas 2017, 64–65, 153–55; Kwon 1993; Ssorin-Chaikov 2003, 150–54; Vitebsky 2005, 67, 113; Vladimirova 2006, 311–14; Willerslev 2007, 159–80). Most commentators seem to agree that elliptic and abbreviated forms of

speech among herders and hunters stress the value of personal experience and relative unimportance of others' explicit instructions. In some Indigenous communities, there are also social situations when staying silent is discouraged (see, e.g., Vorob'ev 2013, 50 on a prohibition to keep silence in a hunting hut among Chirinda Evenki).

3. Falling silent may be simultaneously concealment and revelation. Consider, for instance, what Yelena Pushkareva (1999, 61) writes about a ritual event from 1997 in which Gennadi Lapsui "demonstrated the art of Nenets shamanism": "Then the shaman begins to predict the future to other spectators. Losses and misfortune can await some of them, in which case he will not mention the names, he will just give a hint. If the man guesses, he will ask the shaman a question: 'Tell me about my future, I didn't quite get what the deities said.' The shaman will heat the drum again and ask the deities again. The shaman stops, falls silent, he can't find words, he will only say: 'They didn't say a word.' The man will lapse into silence, while the shaman will predict the future to all those present. He predicted happiness to all with the exception of one man" (see also 2019, 190–217).

4. When in a tent, Nenets parents often use the word *munzyuq* ("keep silence") or *khursyn* ("you are noisy") to silence noisy children.

5. Among Nenets, conversion to evangelical Christianity has led to an obligatory articulacy, unlike in some places, where it has led to inarticulacy. Vitebsky gives an excellent description of how Sora Baptist converts in eastern India are left "literally lost for words" (2017a, 326), after they cannot articulate their feelings in the old mode of ritual dialogues with the dead.

6. On a similar campaign among Indigenous peoples in the Far North during the early Soviet era, see Slezkine (1994, 231–33).

7. Repetition as a "metamessage of involvement" (Tannen 2007, 61) is an everyday linguistic phenomenon across the world. However, it can be also highly ritualized, as in Nenets shamanic practices. Pushkareva (1999, 59) writes that "a good assistant must join the shaman when the latter finishes a sentence, and the shaman will in turn continue singing as soon as *teltanggoda* finishes his part" (see also 2003, 113–15; Dobzhanskaya 2008; Lukin 2017, 200–204; 2022). This practice was known among the Yamb-To Nenets as well. Vata said that his father Mikul, when he was young, had acted as a shaman helper *teltanggoda*. He had to repeat the shaman's text (and sometimes also the gestures) of the shaman during a seance. Among other things, this technique served for memorizing the text and allowed a repeater to be part of the story told.

8. Another Russian ethnographer, Andrey Popov (1984), describes a similar situation among the Dolgan, eastern neighbors of the Nenets on the Taimyr Peninsula: "Sometimes the bride's father remains silent and forces the matchmaker to 'open his mouth' by giving him a fox-skin. Sometimes even this does not help. Then it is up to the matchmaker somehow to provoke *at least one word* from the bride's father, to draw him into conversation" (207, my italics; see also Czaplicka 1916, 109). Among Nenets in the western tundra, once negotiation over the details has begun, as Vladimir Islavin (1847, 126–27) describes it, a matchmaker and a girl's father communicate with each other "almost without speaking": the visitor presents a fox skin as a gift and, if the gift is accepted, negotiating continues by cutting notches on a wooden staff, which alternately mark the offered and requested number of reindeer for the bride-price (see also Yadne 2006, 162).

9. Tim Jenkins (2013) depicts a parallel "modernist" language ideology among social scientists. In his critical and perceptive rereading of Leon Festinger's theory of cognitive dissonance in *When Prophecy Fails* (1956), based on the secret observation of a small group

that anticipated the end of the world, Jenkins shows how the scientists operated with similar assumptions of individuals being bounded and entailing a moral interiority (79–81).

10. According to Althusser (1971), hailing works as a "physical conversion," or as he writes, "Assuming that the theoretical scene I have imagined takes place in the street, the hailed individual will turn round. By this mere one-hundred-and-eighty-degree physical conversion, he becomes a *subject*. Why? Because he has recognized that the hail was 'really' addressed to him, and that 'it was *really him* who was hailed' (and not someone else)" (174, his italics).

11. Unlike in Foucault's (1997, 248) account on early Christians (see also chap. 7), Nenets are described as "confessing" silently. In the literature, a rare example of "confession" among Nenets is related to a difficult birth when a man, "without saying a word," ties as many knots in a piece of string as times he has committed adultery, which is then shown to the woman giving birth, after which she gets some relief (Kostikov 1930b, 42–43; see also Khomich 1995, 189; Kushelevskiy 1868, 120–21).

12. *Syo* is semantically related to "throat," "voice," and perhaps also "breathing" (Niemi and Lapsui 2004, 25; see also Lukin 2022, 15–16).

13. Niemi writes about the significance of silence in the context of singing: "Thus, in a sense, every song type is needed for different occasions for talking about the unsaid. Song is a special vehicle for communicating things that cannot be communicated with speech. . . . Individual songs are a way to place an individual in a larger network of family ties and continuum of generations. The 'unsaids' of the Nenets include deceased relatives. The individual song is considered as a suitable means of talking about the deceased and even then, the closest and dearest relatives are deeply revered [in] an inviolate silence" (Niemi and Lapsui 2004, 30; cf. Abramovich-Gomon 1999). Note that among Nganasan, as Oksana Dobzhanskaya (2008, 89) writes, singing another's song is not allowed, because this would steal the song owner's soul and mind.

14. Occasionally, Yegor asked me in the morning what I had dreamed. When discussing our dreams, he always insisted that it was dangerous to believe "too much" in dreams. Even if interpreting dreams is also a local practice (Liarskaya 2011), this ambivalence of dreams being truthful and deceptive is something that seems to have become more black and white after missionaries arrived (cf. Prokhorov 2013, 335–43).

15. Niemi (1998, 62–63) gives a vivid example recorded from a Yamal Nenets man called Gennadi Puiko, who describes how interrupting an epic song (*syudbabts*) by a performer can dangerously stop the flow of actions in the song and, as a result, the stuck character can come to the presenter's—or, as Nenets say, "the one who holds the song"—dream and kill him (cf. Pushkareva 2004).

16. During a shamanic seance, as explained by Pushkareva (1999), the song embodies a shaman's journey, which is described using the vocabulary of reindeer sledge riding: a shaman is the lead reindeer in the harness, his assistant is also in the harness; furthermore, the whole shamanic journey is acted out as traveling in the landscape and is measured by a leg, which equals the length of time the shaman sings in one go (see also Dobzhanskaya 2008; Lehtisalo 1947, 497–503; Lukin 2015, 2022; Siikala 1978, 197–211).

17. Natal'ya Tereshchenko (2003, 31) translates the expression of *vada yan khaqma(s')* as "to say something that others do not pay attention to (literally: 'the word falls down on the land')." The stress in the sacrificial incantation is thus on making the curse of the Russians fall down. Other related expressions are *man' vadin yan khaqmydq*, "my words were not paid attention to," and *vadam yan tankhalts'*, "do not fulfill somebody's request (literally: 'to trample the word into the land')" (see also Nenyang 1997, 198).

18. As I will discuss later, Baptists have a similar concept of unmentionability related to the blasphemy of the Holy Spirit (see chap. 6).

19. The Nenets word *porti* comes from Russian *portit'* ("to spoil"). A similar phenomenon of harming through words is spread all over Slavic Russia under the name of *porcha* (Ivanits 1989; Lindquist 2006) as well as among Komi (Il'ina 2008; Sidorov 1997) and other Indigenous groups (Brandišauskas 2017, 224; Zorbas 2021). Among the Nenets, the concept of *porcha* seems to have been better known among western groups who have been in closer contact with Russians and Komi (consider the expression in Komi *vezh kyv us'ködöm*, literally "dropping an envious word"; see also Napolskikh et al. 2003, 104). For instance, in the KGB report on shaman Ivan Ledkov from the Great Land tundra, he is said to have chosen to heal only those who were not seriously ill, claiming that they suffered from *porcha*. He would find the bewitcher and heal the patient. However, others who are ill from God should address a doctor (Tolkachev 2000b, 270; see also Khomich 2003, 67; Vagramenko 2014, 27 on cursing accusations).

20. *Khebyakha* is described as a misdeed or taboo by the Nenets interlocutors. A cognate word or root of it is *khebya* or *khebts(n)*, which means "exit." This possibly refers to the idea of the openness to the realm of spirits (cf. Anttonen 2005). Tikynye used the word *khebyakha* often also in a sense of "harm" or "accident." Another way to say something is forbidden is *khevy* (Kharyuchi 2012, 103) from *khebyos'*, "to be forbidden." Russian linguists (see, e.g., Tereshchenko 1990, 332; 2003, 796) usually translate *khebyakha* as *grekh* ("sin"), and it is used in the scriptural translations to mark "sin" (see, e.g., *Luka* 2004, 5).

21. Salt has power to repel invisible forces, both benevolent and malevolent. For example, salt cannot be added to a sacrificial cauldron that contains reindeer meat, as spirits would not eat from there. Likewise, using salt in protective magic is widespread among Komi (Napolskikh et al. 2003, 288–89) but also elsewhere in Europe, including in Catholic countries (e.g., consecrated salt, *sal sacerdotale*, with a reference to 2 Kings 2:19–22; cf. Siikala 2002, 77).

22. The Komi also use a pike's head to protect the family against witchcraft (Leete and Lipin 2015; Napolskikh et al. 2003, 357; see also Tolkachev 2000b, 268 for the above-mentioned shaman Ledkov's relationship with the pike; Vallikivi 2022 for the role of *yid yerv*).

23. This seems to indicate that the danger might come from the dead, as in the shamanic song of a Nenets who visits the underworld and whose speech is heard in the realm of the living through fire (Lehtisalo 1924, 135–37; see also Laptander 2020b, 2023; Laptander and Vitebsky 2021; Lar 2001, 85–89, 220–24; Pushkareva 2019, 210).

24. *Sanggovo vada* functionally parallels the Russians' concept of the evil eye (*sglaz*). In her Nenets dictionary, as a counterpart to *sglazit'* ("to put the evil eye"), Tereshchenko (2003, 66) gives an idiom from the Great Land tundra *vevako sevm khaqvra*, literally "send an evil eye." Intentionality is here central: *sglaz* is usually unintentional, while *porcha* is intentional. *Sglaz* is also an explanation for babies who cry a lot. In the context of Russian village life, Margaret Paxson (2005) writes that "excessive praise (*ogovor*), like the evil eye (*sglaz*) can wittingly or unwittingly cause *porcha* to attach itself to a victim by attracting the forces lying in wait" (171, my italics). A similar set of ideas can be found in Komi (Sidorov 1997) and Mongolia (Højer 2019).

25. As E. E. Evans-Pritchard noted, witchcraft accusations not only explain unfortunate events but also produce lots of uncertainty (1937; see also Favret-Saada 1980; Lambek 2015a, 20). Likewise, as Florian Stammler and Aytalina Ivanova (2020, 12) report, Nenets entertain conspiracy theories when explaining recent events of mass deaths of reindeer in the tundra, which has caused lots of "spiritual uncertainty."

26. Vitebsky describes a similar case among Eveny, who can tell by the taste of a reindeer intestine the character of the person to whom the animal belonged to (2005, 110–11).

27. Compared to Baptists, in charismatic strands of Christianity, words have a far stronger link to automatism, embodiment, and materiality. Consider what Simon Coleman (2006, 165) writes about Swedish Pentecostals: "When sacred words are regarded as thinglike in their autonomous force and their production of tangible results, the identity of the born-again person appears to be pervaded and even constituted by such language. To read and listen to inspired language is seen as a means of filling the self with objectified language, even in a physical sense."

28. As discussed in the introduction, I have taken speech act theory onto a slightly different path and followed what words do in the framework of Nenets language ideology. As Keane (2004) has argued, the implementation of speech act theory would not always help us to understand how our interlocutors in the field themselves see the characteristics and agency of words: "In many cases, the practitioners themselves do *not* see their rituals as achieving their effects simply by convention. They may, for instance, be concerned with influencing the spirit world through emotional effects or magical causality" (433, his italics).

29. As Nigel Thrift (2008, 131) puts it, Butler "cannot bear to part entirely with a textual model of performance based upon sign and referent."

30. This topic has been presented as the question of "opacity of other minds." Especially in Melanesia but also elsewhere, people avoid talking about others' intentions, as they claim that others' minds cannot be known (Robbins and Rumsey 2008). As Keane (2008a) and Rupert Stasch (2008) have stressed, this is not to say that people do not take others' thoughts and intentions as unknowable but that this is rather a moral stance that these should not be discussed.

6. Speaking Saves, Silence Damns

1. This story originates from *The Life of Aesop*. Yegor thought it came from the Bible. There is also certain cultural parallel here, as Nenets have various kinds of saying that warn against the misuse of words (e.g., "Fear your own tongue"). Consider also a riddle about the tongue: "Without blood, without wounds can it kill" (Nenyang 1997, 200, 223).

2. As briefly mentioned in chapter 1, Yurchak (2006) argues that, although all speech acts have a constative and performative dimension according to Austin, in one or other settings, one dominates over the other. For instance, in the late Soviet period, the importance of the constative dimension of authoritative discourse diminished, while the performative dimension as overwhelmingly ritualized use of authoritative language grew in importance. Nevertheless, as Yurchak suggests, this did not mean that ordinary Soviet citizens were mainly pretending when participating in speech acts of authoritative discourse: they used the language (and rituals) without necessarily being committed or opposing the meanings of what was said (or acted). In this and many other ritual contexts, sincerity understood as a match of inner thoughts and visible acts may become irrelevant, as, for example, in the case of irony known as *styob* (249–54; see also Prozorov 2009 for a different reading of Austin's theory through Agamben in the late Soviet context; Lambek 2015a, 22, 150–70 on irony).

3. As I have shown in chapter 3, Pavel believed that objective descriptions ("ethnography") can be produced about things that do not concern "spiritual life"—for instance, about reindeer herding or sledge making. Nevertheless, he doubted that there was any use to these descriptions.

4. This is why sermons entail frequent quotations like "For with the heart man believeth unto righteousness; and with the mouth confession is made unto salvation" (Romans 10:10), or "Let no corrupt communication proceed out of your mouth, but that which is good to the use of edifying, that it may minister grace unto the hearers" (Ephesians 4:29), or "Let your speech be always with grace, seasoned with salt, that ye may know how ye ought to answer every man" (Colossians 4:6).

5. Among the Baptists, it is perfectly normal to claim that the same act is done by human and God (see chap. 7).

6. There is an inevitable tension between the literalists' language ideology and the literalists' practices (Keane 2007, 101). Harding (2000, 28) has demonstrated this discrepancy in the case of the American fundamentalist evangelicals who were led by Jerry Falwell: "The interpretive tradition is literalist in the sense that it presumes the Bible to be true and literally God's Word, but the interpretive practices themselves are not simply literalist. The biblical text is considered fixed and inerrant, and it means what God intended it to mean, but discerning that meaning is not simple or sure or constant. The Bible is read within a complex, multidimensional, shifting field of fundamental Baptist (becoming evangelical) folk-narrative practices, and so are the lives of preachers and their peoples."

7. Unregistered Baptists are openly hostile to ritualism. For instance, they never use the Russian word *obryad* or *ritual* for their own religious acts, emphasizing thus their antiritualism.

8. Consider what Marcel Mauss (2003, 21) has written about the dynamics of prayer: "Almost empty at first, one sort suddenly becomes full of meaning, while another, almost sublime to start with, gradually deteriorates into mechanical psalmody."

9. The phrases in Russian are *"Verish' li, chto Iisus Khristos est' Syn Bozhiy?"* (during the explanatory service, Pavel said that this question comes from Acts 8:37: "And Philip said, If thou believest with all thine heart, thou mayest. And he answered and said, I believe that Jesus Christ is the Son of God") and *"Po poveleniyu Gospoda i po vere tvoey kreshchu tebya vo imya Ottsa, i Syna, i Svyatogo Dukha. Amin'"* (the reference is Matthew 28:19).

10. The Russian Baptists I know read the Bible every day: they use it as a manual and source of "self-authorization" (Crapanzano 2017), alongside other texts published and circulated by their own church, believing that these texts are highly pertinent to their lives. They interpret their everyday experiences in the scriptural mode, being "driven by a search for relevance" (Malley 2004, 117). This careful process of recasting one's thoughts and self-expression is not idiosyncratic but is in dialogue with the patterns of interpretations, which are shaped by authoritative members such as local pastors and visiting church leaders. Furthermore, the use of Bible quotations that one knows by heart and considers one's favorite depends on the dominant currents in the church at the time.

11. This reminds us of Cavell's discussion of his passionate utterances and particularly the idea that "expressions of emotion excite emotion" (2005, 191). Or as Alison Jaggar (quoted in Keane 2016, 193) writes, "We absorb the standards and values of our society in the very process of learning the language of emotion, and those standards and values are built into the foundation of our emotional constitution." Unlike the situation of "finding" the moral emotions in the existing repertoire, Nenets converts must learn these largely from scratch.

12. Missionaries thus present themselves as divine instruments, who talk of things as though they are for God and who spread his message of love (cf. Prokhorov 2013, 256–57). Consider parallels with the Soviet context, in which instrumentality took various forms. Slavoj Žižek (2008) describes in the somber political context of Stalinist totalitarianism

when people were killed for the sake of the Progress of Humanity: "What we encounter here is the properly *perverse* attitude of adopting the position of the pure instrument of the big Other's Will: it's not my responsibility, it's not me who is effectively doing it, I am merely an instrument of the higher Historical Necessity" (286–87, his italics). For the Russian Baptists who suffered directly from the Soviet authorities' perverted "sense of duty," these "Satanic acts" all made perfect sense. Militant atheists or KGB investigators were seen as instruments of Satan, as they now perceived themselves to be instruments of God. Despite fundamental differences between Stalinist and Baptist ideologies, the logics of instrumentality converged, as shifting one's sense of personal responsibility for one's own acts was part of both regimes.

13. As discussed above, even if people can speak religiously without commitment, like a schoolboy in a classroom performing a creed (Keane 2007, 71; see also 2016, 58; Lambek 2010b, 45), such compelled act of speaking potentially has the power to transform the self, partly because the speaker is evaluated by others.

14. I realized the particular significance of talking to God audibly when Pavel told a story about being on a mission trip to Yamal during which he fell ill and temporarily lost his voice. As he said, his biggest fear at that moment was that he could not ask forgiveness from God, should he die. In this case, even his sincerest intentions and thoughts were as if not enough. This account shows the importance of having voice as material medium, which is a necessary precondition for successful communication with God despite him being otherwise known as an all-knowing agent with the capacity to see into one's mind and hear one's thoughts.

15. A blasphemy, like any taboo, functions as a performative that almost always bears effects independent of one's intentions or other contextual parameters. Fleming (2011, 153) has called this "rigid performativity" (see Prokhorov 2013, 347–48 for other examples of word avoidances among Russian Baptists—e.g., *bes* meaning both "without" or "un-" *and* "demon").

16. Promising in the form of taking an oath or making a vow (*valytava, vatorava*) used to have a significant role in the Nenets tundra (see, e.g., Litke 1828, 239). Vows were made to the Russian God or Saint Nicholas, known as Mikola (Kostikov 1930a, 122–23; Lar and Vanuyto 2011, 138; Latkin 1853, 94; Lehtisalo 1924, 5; Schrenk 1848, 409; Shemanovskiy 2011; Templing 2003, 2004, 2007; Veniamin 1855, 115). Furthermore, Tikynye told me that there were women who were promised to Num and who thereafter were not allowed to marry (*numd vatormy nye, khayupa ni khanq*): this vow was made when the girl had been seriously ill and her parents had pledged her to the deity (cf. Lehtisalo 1924, 139; 1956, LII; Lukin 2022, 14; Vagramenko 2014, 29–31; 2017b; Yadne 2006, 184). These instances of promising do not necessarily refer to inner intentions but to contractual relations between humans and beyond, which, if they are broken, can result in a curse (*proklyatie*, a loanword from Russian) or punishment (*vangy*).

7. Pure Subjects

1. This problem is described in several ethnographies of new convert cultures in which people struggle with the impossibility of living a fully Christian life here on earth and are thus torn between Christian ideals and everyday "sinful" realities. In Robbins's (2016, 11) account, Urapmin "cultivate an 'easy' or 'quiet' heart filled with 'good thinking' that will lead them to live a lawful 'Christian life.'" And yet, as he explains, they "still need to rely on

traditional patterns of moral action in key stretches of everyday life, their lives are marked by a conflict between the values of wilfulness and lawfulness" which "leads them to define themselves as deeply sinful people" (see also 2004; Bialecki 2018, 217). Although Nenets converts talk about being sinners, their tools for dealing with this condition are somewhat different from the Urapmin, as I shall demonstrate below.

2. Foucault (1985, 26–28; 1997, 263–65) delineates four separate questions to consider when analyzing projects of self-formation, which could be outlined in a simplified way, like this: the part of oneself chosen (e.g., soul, body, desires, feelings, intentions), the rules and ideals applied (e.g., divine law, state law, cosmological order), the practical activities taken (e.g., self-examination, confession, prayer), and the goal set (e.g., purity, self-mastery) (see also Faubion 2011, 3–4; Laidlaw 2014, 103–4; Mahmood 2005, 30; Robbins 2004, 217).

3. This is an aspect, as Foucault (1997, 249) writes, "what was called in the spiritual literature *exagoreusis.* This is an analytical and continual verbalization of thoughts carried on in the relation of complete obedience to someone else; this relation is modeled on the renunciation of one's own will and of one's own self."

4. Bialecki (2017, 220n3) argues that "discussions of subjectivity tend to come in three different varieties: one relating to the phenomenological, psychological, and experiential; one concerning Foucaultian and Aristotelian ethics and techniques of self-formation; and one focusing on the architectonic structure of the subject"; much of the debate in anthropology has been around the "architectonic" (Bialecki 2017; Bialecki and Daswani 2015; Eriksen et al. 2019; Holbraad and Pedersen 2017; Mosko 2010, 2015; Robbins 2015, 2019; Robbins et al. 2014; Strathern 2018; Werbner 2011). I would suggest that becoming Christian is not so much antisocial as it is pro-individual.

5. Both dowry and bride-price are still practiced after conversion, even if to a lesser extent. Also, rich non-Christian Nenets give their animals to poorer Christian Nenets who use these reindeer for two or three years and then return them as castrated and trained harness animals (see also Stammler 2005, 195). Only a few converts have argued that these exchange practices were unnecessary (cf. Vagramenko 2014, 181). Ivan declared that he did not engage in exchanging reindeer as gifts any more, as this was morally suspicious or, as he said, futile (*pustoy* in Nenets, borrowed from Russian).

6. In Siberian Indigenous communities, various kinds of reciprocity rule involving humans as well as nonhumans are explained to outsiders as *zakon tundry,* "law of the tundra" in Russian (D. Anderson 2000; Stammler 2005; Ventsel 2005; Ziker 2002).

7. We saw in chapter 3 how the notion of purity had in the Soviet times occupied a strong collective dimension for Unregistered Baptists. They guarded the purity of the church by denouncing and excommunicating. Yet collective purification cannot replace individual maintenance work: it can only boost it.

8. *Torabtq* usually contains a piece of beaver fur (*lidyangg*)—obtained from the southern neighbors living in the forest (cf. Kharyuchi 2001, 159)—wrapped in the dried intestines (*palako*) of a reindeer that is killed ritually. It is used to fumigate, for instance, reindeer harnesses or human genital areas.

9. Engelke (2007, 84) describes the conundrum of certainty and uncertainty among evangelical Christians, with reference to the work of Harding and Crapanzano, when he writes that "work on sanctification raises two points. First, even when a subject comes to inhabit a religious language there is always a disconnect between that language and the subject. Second, and importantly for the discussion here, the religious subject can act with

certainty and still not understand what that certainty entails." Throughout this chapter, we see a similar struggle between the language of certainty and the sense of certainty.

10. The tent replicates the larger cosmological divisions with its horizontal and vertical lines. One of the invisible lines is behind the fireplace, which stretches the cosmological axis into the surrounding landscape and can also attract dangerous spirits and misfortune when overstepped throughout the time when the tent is up (see also Golovnev and Osherenko 1999, 32–39; Haakanson and Jordan 2010; Skvirskaja 2012, 151; Stammler 2005, 85). I noticed that baptized women generally avoided stepping across it, although in a few cases, I saw some of them cross it demonstratively.

11. Even if heart (*syei*) has been an important notion in preconversion Nenets society, one can see a certain shift taking place in the rhetoric of Nenets converts. The *syei* in the Nenets' non-Christian understanding is the locus of life-force, emotionality (e.g., courage, passion), and volition. Someone's evil words can hurt one's heart, as in the expression *tartsyaq vadakhavaq syeikhanan khartanarakhaq*, "these words pierced into my heart like a sharp knife" (Tereshchenko 2003, 752); there are many other sayings with *syei* to express losing courage, initiative, or will. Another close word is *syonzya*, which is "inner part," "character," as in the idiom *syonzyada lak*, "(s)he has an explosive temper." These words offer certain, although limited, continuity with the Russian biblical understanding of *serdtse*, which denotes one's emotional, volitional, and moral interiority but also "the locus of divine indwelling," as described (often in contradictory ways) in around one thousand mentions in the Bible (Comfort and Elwell 2001, 579; cf. Robbins et al. 2014; Vitebsky 2017a).

12. Being angry or otherwise losing one's temper is generally frowned upon among Nenets (as among many other Arctic communities where emotional control is highly valued; see, e.g., Briggs 1970). There are plenty of either individuals (Yadne 2006, 529) or entire clans (Golovnev 2004, 61) that are characterized as having such "dangerous" qualities as rage (cf. Basso 1970, 221–22).

13. The Baptist church leader Boyko (2006) has written how he had spent most of his life "in an uninterrupted prayer to God," which made his acts, strictly speaking, not his but divine: "The Lord taught me not to rely on my own intellect but to be constantly in fellowship with Him through prayers" (55). When the KGB-hired atheist lecturers tried to persuade him of the truth of the scientific worldview, he saw this as an action not against him but against God: "Lord, make them understand that they are not dealing with me, with an insignificant human but with You" (56). Such claims are frequent in the statements of senior Baptists who take on the role of divine tool and demonstrate their holiness, as discussed in chapter 6.

14. At least since Augustine, aligning one's will with that of God's has been a key issue and has been discussed a lot. Augustine (1997, 240) writes, "The good derive from you [God] and are your gift; the evil are my sins and your punishments." The Russian Baptists I know would argue that all good deeds are from God and all bad deeds are from Satan, who is the source of one's sinfulness ("For it is God which worketh in you both to will and to do of his good pleasure," Phil. 2:13; see *Ob osvyashchenii* 2006, 17). However, in everyday situations, the individual is still made responsible for the wish to be in the alliance with one of them, and it is rather a matter of situated interpretations and exercises of authority. The theological question "Who finally is responsible for an act? God or man?" (Crapanzano 2000, 94; see also Robbins 2020, 56–70) does not have one answer; instead, asking this question creates various performative effects in one's life as a believer.

15. When someone fell through the ice into the water, in the old days this would have been interpreted as the water spirit *yid yerv* taking a sacrifice (see also Golovnev 1995, 470–71; 2000b, 212; 2004, 305; Kharyuchi 2012, 94–95; Lar 2003, 108; Lar et al. 2003, 79–80; Pushkareva and Burykin 2011, 163).

16. In his account of Paul as a revolutionary, Badiou (2003, 63) argues that becoming a subject of truth (an evangelical convert, committed Communist, etc.) is an endless process that "has to be understood as a becoming rather than a state" (see also Robbins 2010, 647; 2020; Faubion 2013, 299). He unites in his revolutionary figure both rupture and evolution roughly in the same way, as Baptists would see the formation of one's self-transformation.

17. One possible way to look at this kind of shifting is through the notion of "moral moods" (Throop 2014, 68). Jason Throop argues that "moments of transgression, worry, and/or concern into both past and possible future horizons of experience . . . stretch well beyond the confines of the present." Moods are only partly controlled by the person alone, as ethical life is not fully reflected by oneself; moods are triggered by other agents.

18. Obviously, anthropologists also shift the perspective of their interlocutors, which I have experienced in the field again and again (see chap. 6). For instance, Tikynye once told me that my questions made her think differently about her past and see it as a valuable source of information, despite her occasional Christianity-inspired claims of the need to forget "the old." Consider what Vitebsky (2017a) writes about his presence as something that triggered strong emotions from the past in a newly Baptist Sora community.

19. There are considerable typological similarities with Soviet ideology once again and with the cult of Stalin, who was characterized as "our father" (Fürst 2010, 114). Even if Stalin's gaze was not commonly imagined to penetrate one's mind by Soviet citizens, there was anxiety that one would accidentally betray one's hidden feelings or splash out unsuitable words that could be read as the vestiges of one's past self still being present. Many early Soviets strove to conform to the model of the "new man," which required extraordinary adaptative measures. These techniques of the self are seen as a continuation of the pre-Bolshevik practices of ethical self-constitution and self-perfection (see Fitzpatrick 2005; Halfin 2002, 2009; Hellbeck 2006; Kharkhordin 1999). However, what is radically different between a majority state power and a minority religious group, is the use of violence and readmittance: while Communist revolutionaries rarely readmitted people after they had "sinned," the evangelicals let people repent and will readmit "the lost son" into the fold (cf. Humphrey 2014).

20. In her book about African American evangelical Christians' struggle when taking care of their severely ill children, Cheryl Mattingly (2010, 24) shows how they are not entirely determined by the evangelical logic of faith and hope in their attempts to lead a good life (see also 2014, 166; 2018). Which is to say that people lead several and fragmented projects, and despite the totalizing rhetoric of evangelical Christianity, other aspects of their cultural resources provide them with commitments and plans next to specifically Christian teachings.

21. A month later, this topic came up again when Yegor said that his grandfather had observed Sundays and considered working on a day of rest a transgression, *khevy*, and as a punishment a fire would be made on top of the person in the afterworld (see also Leete and Vallikivi 2011, 94). Paying visits to one another on Sundays had become common by the late nineteenth century under the influence of Orthodox priests who told to keep the Sabbath (Mikhaylov 1898, 164–65; Shashkov 1896, 183–84).

Conclusion

1. Or, following Bialecki (2017, 8–9), one should say that it was "actually existing Communism," with its particular relationship to the ideal, as it is with "actually existing Christianities" that take various local forms in specific ethical regimes.

2. There are significant differences in how much collectivized Nenets were indoctrinated by Soviet ideology, depending on many aspects such as age, gender, school education, Russian language proficiency, the intensity of contact with the *lutsaq*, reading habits, personal inclinations, and so on. This is well exemplified by Yaungad's dialogue with his father in chapter 1.

REFERENCES

Ablazhey, Anatoliy M. 2005. "The Religious Worldview of the Indigenous Population of the Northern Ob' as Understood by Christian Missionaries." *International Bulletin of Missionary Research* 29 (3): 134–39.

Abramovich-Gomon, Alla. 1999. *The Nenets' Song: A Microcosm of a Vanishing Culture.* Aldershot: Ashgate.

Abul'khanov, Anvar I., and Nikolay M. Kovyazin. 1977. *Nenetskiy avtonomnyy okrug.* Arkhangelsk: Severo-Zapadnoe knizhnoe izdatel'stvo.

Adayev, Vladimir N. 2017. "Gornye nentsy Polyarnogo Urala: osobennosti traditsionnoy kul'tury i landshaftnogo osvoyeniya." *Ural'skiy istoricheskiy vestnik* 55 (2): 25–34.

Agadjanian, Alexander. 2014. *Turns of Faith, Search for Meaning: Orthodox Christianity and Post-Soviet Experience.* Frankfurt am Main: Peter Lang.

Alekseyenko, Yevgenia A. 1981. "Shamanstvo u ketov." In *Problemy istorii obshchestvennogo soznaniya aborigenov Sibiri (po materialam vtoroy poloviny XIX–nachala XX v.),* edited by I. S. Vdovin, 90–128. Leningrad: Nauka.

Alekseyenko, Yevgenia A., and Rudol'f F. Its. 2005a. "Polozhenie korennogo naseleniya Turukhanskogo rayona Krasnoyarskogo kraya. 1960 g." In *Etnologicheskaya ekspertiza: narody Severa Rossii. 1959–1962 gody,* edited by Z. P. Sokolova and Ye. A. Pivneva, 114–25. Moscow: Institut etnologii i antropologii RAN.

———. 2005b. "O perspektivakh khozyaystvennogo i kul'turnogo razvitiya korennogo naseleniya Turukhanskogo rayona Krasnoyarskogo kraya. 1961 g." In *Etnologicheskaya ekspertiza: narody Severa Rossii. 1959–1962 gody,* edited by Z. P. Sokolova and Ye. A. Pivneva, 237–44. Moscow: Institut etnologii i antropologii RAN.

Alexopoulos, Golfo. 2003. *Stalin's Outcasts: Aliens, Citizens, and the Soviet State, 1926–1936.* Ithaca, NY: Cornell University Press.

Althusser, Louis. 1971 [1970]. "Ideology and Ideological State Apparatuses (Notes towards an Investigation)." In *Lenin and Philosophy and Other Essays,* translated by B. Brewster, 127–86. New York: Monthly Review.

Anderson, David G. 2000. *Identity and Ecology in Arctic Siberia: The Number One Brigade.* Oxford: Oxford University Press.

———. 2014. "Cultures of Reciprocity and Cultures of Control in the Circumpolar North." *Journal of Northern Studies* 8 (2): 11–27.

Anderson, David G., Jan Peter Laurens Loovers, Sara Asu Schroer, and Robert P. Wishart. 2017. "Architectures of Domestication: On Emplacing Human-Animal Relations in the North." *Journal of the Royal Anthropological Institute* 23 (2): 398–416.

Anderson, John. 1994. *Religion, State, and Politics in the Soviet Union and the Successor States, 1953–1993.* Cambridge: Cambridge University Press.

Andreyev, Igor'. 2017. "V NAO oruduyut missionery zapadnykh khristianskikh konfessiy." *MK v Arkhangel'ske,* March 22. https://arh.mk.ru/articles/2017/03/22/v-nao-oruduyut-missionery-zapadnykh-khristianskikh-konfessiy.html.

Anttonen, Veikko 2005. "Space, Body, and the Notion of Boundary: A Category-Theoretical Approach to Religion." *Temenos* 41 (2): 185–201.

Aromshtam, Marina. 2002. "Chemu nam uchit'sya u nenetskikh detey, ili Etnopedagogika dlya vzroslykh." *Doshkol'noe obrazovanie* 20 (October 23): 2–5. https://dob.1sept.ru /article.php?ID=200202002.

Arzyutov, Dmitriy V. 2016. "Samoyedic Diary: Early Years of Visual Anthropology in the Soviet Arctic." *Visual Anthropology* 29 (4–5): 331–59.

———. 2019. "Zhizn' vne seti: kochevniki i elektrichestvo na Yamale." In *Arkheologiya Arktiki*, vol. 6, edited by N. V. Federova, 76–95. Salekhard.

Arzyutov, Dmitriy V., and Marina D. Lyublinskaya, eds. 2018. *Nenetskoe olenevodstvo: geografiya, etnografiya, lingvistika.* St. Petersburg: MAE RAN.

Asad, Talal. 1993. *Genealogies of Religion: Discipline and Reasons of Power in Christianity and Islam.* Baltimore, MD: Johns Hopkins University Press.

———. 1996. "Comments on Conversion." In *Conversion to Modernities: The Globalization of Christianity*, edited by P. van der Veer, 263–73. New York: Routledge.

———. 2003. *Formations of the Secular: Christianity, Islam, Modernity.* Stanford, CA: Stanford University Press.

Augustine. 1997. *The Confessions.* Translated by M. Boulding and edited by J. E. Rotelle. Hyde Park: New City.

Austin, J. L. 1961. "A Plea for Excuses." In *Philosophical Papers*, edited by J. O. Urmson and G. J. Warnock, 123–52. Oxford: Oxford University Press.

———. 1962. *How to Do Things with Words.* Edited by J. O. Urmson. Oxford: Clarendon.

Avvakum, Petrovich (Archpriest). 2021. *The Life Written by Himself.* Translated by K. N. Brostrom. New York: Columbia University Press.

Babushkin, Aleksandr I. 1930. *Bol'shezemel'skaya tundra.* Syktyvkar: Komi obstatotdel.

Badiou, Alain. 2001 [1998]. *Ethics: An Essay on the Understanding of Evil.* Translated by P. Hallward. London: Verso.

———. 2003 [1997]. *Saint Paul: The Foundation of the Universalism.* Translated by R. Brassier. Stanford, CA: Stanford University Press.

———. 2006 [1988]. *Being and Event.* Translated by O. Feltham. London: Continuum.

Baiburin, Albert. 2021. *The Soviet Passport: The History, Nature and Uses of the Internal Passport in the USSR.* Translated by S. Dalziel. Cambridge: Polity.

Bakhtin, Mikhail M. 1981. "Discourse in the Novel." In *The Dialogic Imagination*, translated by C. Emerson and M. Holquist, edited by M. Holquist, 259–422. Austin: University of Texas Press.

———. 1984. *Problems of Dostoevsky's Poetics.* Translated and edited by C. Emerson. Minneapolis: University of Minnesota Press.

———. 1986. *Speech Genres and Other Late Essays.* Translated by V. W. McGee, edited by C. Emerson and M. Holquist. Austin: University of Texas Press.

Baklund, Oleg O. 1911. "Obshchiy obzor deyatel'nosti ekspeditsii br. Kuznetsovykh na Polyarnyy Ural letom 1909 goda." *Zapiski Imperatorskoy Akademii Nauk po fiziko-matematicheskomu otdeleniyu* 28 (1): 1–124.

Balzer, Marjorie Mandelstam. 1999. *The Tenacity of Ethnicity: A Siberian Saga in Global Perspective.* Princeton, NJ: Princeton University Press.

———. 2011. *Shamans, Spirituality, and Cultural Revitalization: Explorations in Siberia and Beyond.* New York: Palgrave.

Barayev, Oleg (director). 1997. *Missioner.* G. Grigor'ev (photography), Y. Berlin (producer). Arhangelsk: Dialog, Pomor'e. (TV documentary).

Barenberg, Alan. 2014. *Gulag Town, Company Town: Forced Labor and Its Legacy in Vorkuta.* New Haven, CT: Yale University Press.

Baryshev, Il'ya B. 2011. *Yazycheskie svyatilishcha ostrova Vaygach.* Moscow: Institut Naslediya.

Basso, Keith H. 1970. "'To Give Up on Words': Silence in Western Apache Culture." *Southwestern Journal of Anthropology* 26 (3): 213–23.

———. 1979. *Portraits of "The Whiteman": Linguistic Play and Cultural Symbols among the Western Apache.* Cambridge: Cambridge University Press.

Bauman, Richard. 1983. *Let Your Words Be Few: Symbolism of Speaking and Silence among Seventeenth-Century Quakers.* Cambridge: Cambridge University Press.

Bauman, Richard, and Charles L. Briggs. 1990. "Poetics and Performance as Critical Perspectives on Language and Social Life." *Annual Review of Anthropology* 19:59–88.

Beach, Hugh, and Florian Stammler. 2006. "Human–Animal Relations in Pastoralism." *Nomadic Peoples* 10 (2): 6–30.

Beatty, Andrew. 2012. "The Tell-Tale Heart: Conversion and Emotion in Nias." *Ethnos* 77 (3): 295–320.

Beekers, Daan, and David Kloos, eds. 2018. *Straying from the Straight Path: How Senses of Failure Invigorate Lived Religion.* New York: Berghahn.

Belyakova, Nadezhda, and Miriam Dobson. 2015. *Zhenshchiny v yevangel'skikh obshchinakh poslevoyennogo SSSR. 1940–1980-e gg.* Moscow: Indrik.

Bennett, Brian P. 2011. *Religion and Language in Post-Soviet Russia.* New York: Routledge.

Benovska, Milena. 2021. *Orthodox Revivalism in Russia: Driving Forces and Moral Quests.* London: Routledge.

Berliner, David, Michael Lambek, Richard Shweder, Richard Irvine, and Albert Piette. 2016. "Anthropology and the Study of Contradictions." *HAU: Journal of Ethnographic Theory* 6 (1): 1–27.

Besnier, Niko. 1995. *Literacy, Emotion, and Authority: Reading and Writing on a Polynesian Atoll.* Cambridge: Cambridge University Press.

Bialecki, Jon. 2009. "Disjuncture, Continental Philosophy's New 'Political Paul,' and the Question of Progressive Christianity in a Southern California Third Wave Church." *American Ethnologist* 36 (1): 110–23.

———. 2011. "No Caller ID for the Soul: Demonization, Charisms, and the Unstable Subject of Protestant Language Ideology." *Anthropological Quarterly* 84 (3): 679–704.

———. 2015. "Affect: intensities and Energies in the Charismatic Language, Embodiment, and Genre of a North American Movement." In *The Anthropology of Global Pentecostalism and Evangelicalism*, edited by S. Coleman and R. I. J. Hackett, 95–108. New York: New York University Press.

———. 2017. *A Diagram for Fire: Miracles and Variation in an American Charismatic Movement.* Berkeley: University of California Press.

———. 2018. "Character as Gift and Erasure." *Social Anthropology/Anthropologie Sociale* 26 (2): 211–21.

Bialecki, Jon, and Girish Daswani. 2015. "What Is an Individual? The View from Christianity." *HAU: Journal of Ethnographic Theory* 5 (1): 271–94.

Bialecki, Jon, Naomi Haynes, and Joel Robbins. 2008. "The Anthropology of Christianity." *Religion Compass* 2 (6): 1139–58.

Bielo, James S. 2009. *Words upon the Word: An Ethnography of Evangelical Group Bible Study.* New York: New York University Press.

Billig, Michael. 1999. *Freudian Repression: Conversation Creating the Unconscious.* Cambridge: Cambridge University Press.

Bjørklund, Ivar. 1995. "A Journey to the Bolshezemelskaja Tundra." In *The Barents Region,* edited by I. Bjørklund, J. J. Møller, and P. K. Reymert, 71–80. Tromsø: University of Tromsø, Tromsø Museum.

——— [B'erklund]. 2000. "Kochevaya shkola v tundra." In *Nenetskiy kray: skvoz' v'yugi let. Ocherki. Stat'i. Dokumenty,* edited by V. F. Tolkachev, 485–91. Arkhangelsk: Pomorskiy gosudarstvennyy universitet imeni M. V. Lomonosova.

Bloch, Alexia. 2004. *Red Ties and Residential Schools: Indigenous Siberians in a Post-Soviet State.* Philadelphia: University of Pennsylvania Press.

Bloch, Alexia, and Laurel Kendall. 2004. *The Museum at the End of the World: Encounters in the Russian Far East.* Philadelphia: University of Pennsylvania Press.

Bobrova, Yelena. 2010. "Slozhnaya struktura i sud'ba 'Krasnogo Oktyabrya.'" *Nar"yana Vynder* (Naryan-Mar), November 3.

Bodenhorn, Barbara, and Gabriele vom Bruck. 2006. "'Entangled in Histories': An Introduction to the Anthropology of Names and Naming." In *The Anthropology of Names and Naming,* edited by G. vom Bruck and B. Bodenhorn, 1–30. Cambridge: Cambridge University Press.

Bogordayeva, Aksana A., and Konstantin A. Oshchepkov. 2003. "Sovremennye etnokul'turnye protsessy." In *Etnografiya i antropologiya Yamala,* edited by A. N. Bagashev, 157–72. Novosibirsk: Nauka.

Bogoyavlenskiy, Dmitriy D. 2001. "Istoriko-demograficheskaya spravka po nentsam Respubliki Komi." *Mir korennykh narodov* 5:64–65.

Borisova, Natal'ya. 2022. "'Odna spasennaya dusha—eto malo ili mnogo?': Beseda s iereem Petrom Bogdanom o missionerskom sluzhenii v Salekhardskoy eparkhii." https://pravoslavie.ru/146011.html.

Bourdeaux, Michael. 1968. *Religious Ferment in Russia: Protestant Opposition to Soviet Religious Policy.* London: Macmillan.

Bourdeaux [Burdo], Michael, and Sergey B. Filatov, eds. 2003. *Sovremennaya religioznaya zhizn' Rossii. Opyt sistematicheskogo opisaniya. Tom 2.* Moscow: Logos.

———. 2005. *Atlas sovremennoy religioznoy zhizni Rossii. Tom 1.* Moscow: Letniy sad.

Bourdieu, Pierre. 1977 [1972]. *Outline of a Theory of a Practice.* Translated by R. Nice. Cambridge: Cambridge University Press.

———. 1991. *Language and Symbolic Power.* Translated by G. Raymond and M. Adamson. Cambridge: Polity.

Boyko, Nikolay Ye. 2006. *Veryu v bessmertie. Avtobiografiya.* Portland: Voice of Peace Christian Mission.

Braithwaite, Charles A. 1990. "Communicative Silence: A Cross-Cultural Study of Basso's Hypothesis." In *Cultural Communication and Intercultural Contact,* edited by D. Carbaugh, 321–27. Hillsdale, NJ: Lawrence Erlbaum.

Brandišauskas, Donatas. 2017. *Leaving Footprints in the Taiga: Luck, Spirits and Ambivalence among the Siberian Orochen Reindeer Herders and Hunters.* New York: Berghahn.

Bratskiy listok. 2001. *Bratskiy listok. Sbornik 1965–2000.* Moscow: Sovet tserkvey YeKhB.

Briggs, Jean L. 1970. *Never in Anger: Portrait of an Eskimo Family.* Cambridge, MA: Harvard University Press.

Brown, Kate. 2007. "Out of Solitary Confinement: The History of the Gulag." *Kritika: Explorations in Russian and Eurasian History* 8 (1): 67–103.

Broz, Ludek. 2009. "Conversion to Religion? Negotiating Continuity and Discontinuity in Contemporary Altai." In *Conversion after Socialism: Disruptions, Modernisms and Technologies of Faith in the Former Soviet Union*, edited by M. Pelkmans, 17–37. Oxford: Berghahn.

Bruce, Scott G. 2007. *Silence and Sign Language in Medieval Monasticism: The Cluniac Tradition c. 900–1200*. Cambridge: Cambridge University Press.

Brusco, Elizabeth E. 1995. *The Reformation of Machismo: Evangelical Conversion and Gender in Colombia*. Austin: University of Texas Press.

Buchli, Victor. 2010. "Presencing the Im-material." In *An Anthropology of Absence: Materializations of Transcendence and Loss*, edited by M. Bille, F. Hastrup, and T. F. Sørensen, 185–203. New York: Springer.

Bulgakova, Tatiana. 2013. *Nanai Shamanic Culture in Indigenous Discourse*. Fürstenberg: Kulturstiftung Sibirien.

Bulgakova, Tatiana, and Olle Sundström. 2017. "Repression of Shamans and Shamanism in Khabarovsk Krai: 1920s to the Early 1950s." In *Ethnic and Religious Minorities in Stalin's Soviet Union: New Dimensions of Research*, edited by A. Kotljarchuk and O. Sundström, 225–62. Huddinge: Södertörn University.

Burkova, Svetlana. 2022. "Nenets." *The Oxford Guide to the Uralic Languages,* edited by M. Bakró-Nagy, J. Laakso, and E. Skribnik, 674–708. Oxford: Oxford University Press.

Bur'yanov, Sergey A. 2007. *Ksenofobiya, neterpimost' i diskriminatsiya po motivam religii ili ubezhdeniy v sub"ektakh Rossiyskoy Federatsii*. Moscow: Moskovskaya Khel'sinkskaya gruppa.

Butler, Judith. 1993. *Bodies That Matter: On the Discursive Limits of "Sex."* New York: Routledge.

———. 1997a. *Excitable Speech: A Politics of the Performative*. New York: Routledge.

———. 1997b. *The Psychic Life of Power: Theories in Subjection*. Stanford, CA: Stanford University Press.

CAFF. 2004. *The Conservation Value of Sacred Sites of Indigenous Peoples of the Arctic: A Case Study in Northern Russia. Report on the State of Sacred Sites and Sanctuaries*. Akureyri: CAFF International Secretariat.

Caldwell, Melissa L. 2017. *Living Faithfully in an Unjust World: Compassionate Care in Russia*. Berkeley: University of California Press.

Cameron, Averil. 1991. *Christianity and the Rhetoric of Empire: The Development of Christian Discourse*. Berkeley: University of California Press.

Cannell, Fenella. 2005. "The Christianity of Anthropology." *Journal of the Royal Anthropological Institute* 11 (2): 335–56.

———. 2006. "Introduction: The Anthropology of Christianity." In *The Anthropology of Christianity*, edited by F. Cannell, 1–50. Durham, NC: Duke University Press.

Carrette, Jeremy R. 2000. *Foucault and Religion: Spiritual Corporeality and Political Spirituality*. London: Routledge.

Castrén, Matthias Alexander. 1853. *Reiseerinnerungen aus den Jahren 1838–1844*, hrsg. von A. Schiefner (*Nordische Reisen und Forschungen* 1). St. Petersburg: Kaiserliche Akademie der Wissenschaften.

Cavell, Stanley. 2005. "Passionate and Performative Utterance." In *Contending with Stanley Cavell*, edited by R. Goodman, 177–98. Oxford: Oxford University Press.

———. 2010. *Little Did I Know: Excerpts from Memory*. Stanford, CA: Stanford University Press.

Chernetsov, Valeriy N. 1987. *Istochniki po etnografii Zapadnoy Sibiri*. Edited by N. V. Lukina and O. M. Ryndina. Tomsk: Izdatel'stvo Tomskogo universiteta.

Chua, Liana. 2012. *The Christianity of Culture: Conversion, Ethnic Citizenship, and the Matter of Religion in Malaysian Borneo.* New York: Palgrave.

Chukhontsev, Vladimir N. 2000. "Uspekh i plod." *Vestnik istiny* 150 (2): 11–14.

———. 2007. "Samariyskiy grekh." *Vestnik istiny* 190 (6): 10–13.

Coleman, Heather J. 2005. *Russian Baptists and Spiritual Revolution, 1905–1929.* Bloomington: Indiana University Press.

Coleman, Simon. 2000. *The Globalisation of Charismatic Christianity: Spreading the Gospel of Prosperity.* Cambridge: Cambridge University Press.

———. 2006. "Materializing the Self: Words and Gifts in the Construction of Charismatic Protestant Identity." In *The Anthropology of Christianity*, edited by F. Cannell, 163–84. Durham, NC: Duke University Press.

———. 2007. "When Silence Isn't Golden: Charismatic Speech and the Limits of Literalism." In *The Limits of Meaning: Case Studies in the Anthropology of Christianity*, edited by M. Engelke and M. Tomlinson, 39–61. Oxford: Berghahn.

———. 2015. "Borderlands: Ethics, Ethnography, and 'Repugnant' Christianity." *HAU: Journal of Ethnographic Theory* 5 (2): 275–300.

Comaroff, Jean, and John Comaroff. 1991. *Of Revelation and Revolution. Vol. 1: Christianity, Colonialism and Consciousness in South Africa.* Chicago: University of Chicago Press.

Comfort, Philip W., and Walter A. Elwell, eds. 2001. *Tyndale Bible Dictionary.* Carol Stream: Tyndale House.

Corbey, Raymond. 2003. "Destroying the Graven Image: Religious Iconoclasm on the Christian Frontier." *Anthropology Today* 19 (4): 10–14.

Crane, Hillary K., and Deana L. Weibel, eds. 2012. *Missionary Impositions: Conversion, Resistance, and Other Challenges to Objectivity in Religious Ethnography.* Lanham, MD: Lexington.

Crapanzano, Vincent. 2000. *Serving the Word: Literalism in America from the Pulpit to the Bench.* New York: New Press.

———. 2017. "Textual Self-Authorization." *Journal of the Royal Anthropological Institute* 23 (1): 1–14.

Csordas, Thomas J. 1994. *The Sacred Self: A Cultural Phenomenology of Charismatic Healing.* Berkeley: University of California Press.

———. 1997. *Language, Charisma, and Creativity: The Ritual Life of a Religious Movement.* Berkeley: University of California Press.

Czaplicka, Maria A. 1916. *My Siberian Year.* London: Mills and Boon.

Dallmann, Winfried K., Vladislav V. Peskov, and Olga A. Murashko, eds. 2010. *Monitoring of Development of Traditional Indigenous Land Use Areas in the Nenets Autonomous Okrug, NW Russia: Project Report.* Tromsø: Norwegian Polar Institute.

Danziger, Eve, and Alan Rumsey. 2013. "Introduction: From Opacity to Intersubjectivity across Languages and Cultures." *Language and Communication* 33 (3): 247–50.

Das, Veena. 2007. *Life and Words: Violence and the Descent into the Ordinary.* Berkeley: University of California Press.

———. 2012. "Ordinary Ethics." In *A Companion to Moral Anthropology*, edited by D. Fassin, 133–49. Boston: Wiley-Blackwell.

———. 2015. *Affliction: Health, Disease, Poverty.* New York: Fordham University Press.

Daswani, Girish. 2015. *Looking Back, Moving Forward: Transformation and Ethical Practice in the Ghanaian Church of Pentecost.* Toronto: University of Toronto Press.

Derrida, Jacques. 1982 [1972]. "Signature Event Context." In *Margins of Philosophy*, translated by A. Bass, 307–30. Chicago: University of Chicago Press.

Descola, Philippe. 2013 [2005]. *Beyond Nature and Culture*. Chicago: University of Chicago Press.

de Vries, Hent. 2008. "Introduction: Why Still 'Religion'?" In *Religion: Beyond a Concept*, edited by H. De Vries, 1–98. New York: Fordham University Press.

Dobzhanskaya, Oksana E. 2008. *Shamanskaya muzyka samodiyskikh narodov Krasnoyarskogo kraya*. Norilsk: APEKS.

———. 2014. "Muzyka nenetskogo shamanskogo obryada: iz istoricheskikh istochnikov i novykh ekspeditsionnykh materialov." In *Issledovaniya po kul'ture nentsev*, edited by Ye. T. Pushkareva and N. V. Lukina, 168–89. St. Petersburg: Istoricheskaya illyustratsiya.

Dolgikh, Boris O. 1970. *Ocherki po etnicheskoy istorii nentsev i entsev*. Moscow: Nauka.

Dolzhno mne. 1995. "Dolzhno mne vozveshchat'." *Vestnik istiny* 131–32 (3–4): 26–53.

Donahoe, Brian. 2003. "A Line in the Sayans: History and Divergent Perceptions of Property among the Tozhu and Tofa of South Siberia." Unpublished doctoral dissertation, Department of Anthropology, Indiana University, Bloomington.

———. 2012. "'Trust' or 'Domination'? Divergent Perceptions of Property in Animals among the Tozhu and the Tofa of South Siberia." In *Who Owns the Stock? Collective and Multiple Property Rights in Animals*, edited by A. M. Khazanov and G. Schlee, 99–119. New York: Berghahn.

Donahoe, Brian, Joachim Otto Habeck, Agnieszka Halemba, and István Sántha. 2008. "Size and Place in the Construction of Indigeneity in the Russian Federation." *Current Anthropology* 48 (6): 993–1020.

Draguns, Juris G., Anna V. Krylova, Valery E. Oryol, Alexey A. Rukavishnikov, and Thomas A. Martin. 2000. "Personality Characteristics of the Nentsy in the Russian Arctic." *American Behavioral Scientist* 44 (1): 126–40.

Drama. 2000. "Drama vorkutinskikh nentsev." *Mir korennykh narodov* 3:74–80.

Du Bois, John W. 1993. "Meaning without Intention: Lessons from Divination." In *Responsibility and Evidence in Oral Discourse*, edited by J. H. Hill and J. T. Irvine, 48–71. Cambridge: Cambridge University Press.

Dudeck, Stephan. 2018. "Reindeer Returning from Combat: War Stories among the Nenets of European Russia." *Arctic Anthropology* 55 (1): 73–90.

Dudeck, Stephan, Aleksei A. Rud', Rudolf Havelka, Nikolai M. Terebikhin, and Marina N. Melyutina. 2017. "Safeguarding Sacred Sites in the Subarctic Zone—Three Case Studies from Northern Russia." In *Experiencing and Protecting Sacred Natural Sites of Sámi and Other Indigenous Peoples: The Sacred Arctic*, edited by L. Heinämäki, and T. M. Herrmann, 159–80. Cham: Springer.

Dumont, Louis. 1986. *Essays on Individualism: Modern Ideology in Anthropological Perspective*. Chicago: University of Chicago Press.

Duranti, Alessandro. 1993. "Intentionality and Truth: An Ethnographic Critique." *Cultural Anthropology* 8:214–45.

———. 2015. *The Anthropology of Intentions: Language in a World of Others*. Cambridge: Cambridge University Press.

Eire, Carlos M. N. 1986. *War against the Idols: The Reformation of Worship from Erasmus to Calvin*. Cambridge: Cambridge University Press.

Enfield, N. J., and Jack Sidnell. 2022. *Consequences of Language: From Primary to Enhanced Intersubjectivity*. Cambridge, MA: MIT Press.

Engelke, Matthew. 2007. *A Problem of Presence: Beyond Scripture in an African Church.* Berkeley: University of California Press.

———. 2010. "Number and the Imagination of Global Christianity: Or, Mediation and Immediacy in the Work of Alain Badiou." *South Atlantic Quarterly* 109 (4): 811–29.

———. 2013. *God's Agents: Biblical Publicity in Contemporary England.* Berkeley: University of California Press.

Englund, Harri. 2003. "Christian Independency and Global Membership: Pentecostal Extraversions in Malawi." *Journal of Religion in Africa* 33 (1): 83–111.

Englund, Harri, and James Leach. 2000. "Ethnography and the Meta-Narratives of Modernity." *Current Anthropology* 41 (2): 225–48.

Eriksen, Annelin, Ruy Llera Blanes, and Michelle MacCarthy. 2019. *Going to Pentecost: An Experimental Approach to Studies in Pentecostalism.* New York: Berghahn.

Etkind, Alexander. 2005. "Soviet Subjectivity: Torture for the Sake of Salvation?" *Kritika: Explorations in Russian and Eurasian History* 6 (1): 171–86.

Ezhegodnyy. 2015. *Ezhegodnyy doklad o deyatel'nosti upolnomochennogo po pravam cheloveka v Nenetskom avtonomnom okruge za 2014 god.* Naryan-Mar. https://map .ombudsmanrf.org/Karta_Yadro/prav_z_karta/sub_fed/sev-zapad_fed/nenezk_avt _okr/dokument_nenezk_av/dokument_2/dokument_2web.pdf.

Evans-Pritchard, E. E. 1937. *Witchcraft, Oracles and Magic among the Azande.* Oxford: Oxford University Press.

Fagan, Geraldine. 2013. *Believing in Russia—Religious Policy after Communism.* New York: Routledge.

Faubion, James D. 2011. *An Anthropology of Ethics.* Cambridge: Cambridge University Press.

———. 2013. "The Subject That Is Not One: On the Ethics of Mysticism." *Anthropological Theory* 13 (4): 287–307.

Favret-Saada, Jeanne. 1980 [1977]. *Deadly Words: Witchcraft in the Bocage.* Translated by C. Cullen. Cambridge: Cambridge University Press.

Fedorova, Natalia V. 2004. "Cultural Heritage in Yamal, Siberia: Policies and Challenges in Landscape Preservation." In *Northern Ethnographic Landscapes: Perspectives from Circumpolar Nations,* edited by I. Krupnik, R. Mason, and T. W. Norton, 343–57. Washington, DC: Arctic Studies Center, Smithsonian Institution.

Felman, Shoshana. 1983 [1980]. *The Literary Speech Act: Don Juan with J. L. Austin, or Seduction in Two Languages.* Translated by C. Porter. Ithaca, NY: Cornell University Press.

Fienup-Riordan, Ann. 1991. *The Real People and the Children of Thunder: The Yup'ik Eskimo Encounter with Moravian Missionaries John and Edith Kilbuck.* Norman: University of Oklahoma Press.

Figes, Orlando. 2008. *The Whisperers: Private Life in Stalin's Russia.* London: Penguin.

Filatov, Sergey B. 2016. "Parallel'nyy mir protestantskoy Rossii." In *Religioznye missii na obshchestvennoy arene: Rossiyskiy i zarubezhnyy opyt,* edited by A. A. Krasikov and R. N. Lunkin, 261–63. Moscow: Institut Evropy RAN.

Fitzpatrick, Sheila. 1994. *Stalin's Peasants: Resistance and Survival in the Russian Village after Collectivization.* New York: Oxford University Press.

———. 2005. *Tear off the Masks! Identity and Imposture in Twentieth-Century Russia.* Princeton, NJ: Princeton University Press.

Fleming, Luke. 2011. "Name Taboos and Rigid Performativity." *Anthropological Quarterly* 84 (1): 141–64.

Fleming, Luke, and Michael Lempert. 2011. "Introduction: Beyond Bad Words." *Anthropological Quarterly* 84 (1): 5–13.

———. 2014. "Poetics and Performativity." In *The Cambridge Handbook of Linguistic Anthropology*, edited by N. J. Enfield, P. Kockelman, and J. Sidnell, 485–515. Cambridge: Cambridge University Press.

Fleming, Luke, and James Slotta. 2018. "The Pragmatics of Kin Address: A Sociolinguistic Universal and Its Semantic Affordance." *Journal of Sociolinguistic* 22 (4): 375–405.

Fondahl, Gail A. 1998. *Gaining Ground?: Evenkis, Land, and Reform in Southeastern Siberia.* Boston: Allyn & Bacon.

Forsyth, James. 1992. *A History of the Peoples of Siberia: Russia's North Asian Colony, 1581–1990.* Cambridge: Cambridge University Press.

Foucault, Michel. 1977 [1975]. *Discipline and Punish: The Birth of the Prison.* Translated by A. Sheridan. New York: Vintage.

———. 1978 [1976]. *The History of Sexuality. Vol. 1: An Introduction.* New York: Pantheon.

———. 1985 [1984]. *The Use of Pleasure: The History of Sexuality. Vol. 2.* Translated by R. Hurley. New York: Vintage.

———. 1997. *Essential Works of Foucault 1954–1980. Vol. 1: Ethics: Subjectivity and Truth.* Edited by P. Rabinow. New York: New Press.

———. 2015. *About the Beginning of the Hermeneutics of the Self: Lectures at Dartmouth College, 1980.* Translated by G. Burchell. Chicago: University of Chicago Press.

Frazer, James George. 1911. *The Golden Bough. A Study in Magic and Religion. Part II. Taboo and the Perils of the Soul.* 3rd ed. London: Macmillan.

Freeman, Dena. 2017. "Affordances of Rupture and Their Enactment: A Framework for Understanding Christian Change." *Suomen Antropologi: Journal of the Finnish Anthropological Society* 42 (4): 3–24.

French, April L. 2018. "The 'Lived Religion' of Evangelical Christian-Baptist Women in Soviet Siberia (1945–1991)." *Quaestio Rossica* 6 (2): 454–67.

Fürst, Juliane. 2010. *Stalin's Last Generation: Soviet Post-War Youth and the Emergence of Mature Socialism.* Oxford: Oxford University Press.

Gagarin, Yuriy V. 1978. *Istoriya religii i ateizma naroda komi.* Moscow: Nauka.

Gell, Alfred. 1998. *Art and Agency: An Anthropological Theory.* Oxford: Clarendon.

Gellner, Ernest. 1988. *State and Society in Soviet Thought.* Oxford: Blackwell.

Glanzer, Perry L. 2002. *The Quest for Russia's Soul: Evangelicals and Moral Education in Post-Communist Russia.* Waco: Baylor University Press.

Glavatskaya, Yelena M. 2006. "'On velel pered smert'yu . . . borot'sya s shamanami': antireligioznaya politika na Obdorskom Severe." In *Yamal v XVII–nachale XX vv.: sotsiokul'turnoe i khozyaystvennoe razvitie (dokumenty i issledovaniya)*, edited by I. Poberezhnikov, 260–79. Salekhard: Bank kul'turnoy informatsii.

Golovnev, Andrey V. (author and director). 1994. *Khadampe.* Yekaterinburg: Etnograficheskoe byuro studiya. (Documentary).

———. 1995. *Govoryashchie kul'tury: traditsii samodiytsev i ugrov.* Yekaterinburg: UrO RAN.

———. 2000a. "Letter from Varandei." *Polar Research* 19 (1): 135–42.

———. 2000b. "Put' k semi chumam." In *Drevnosti Yamala* 1, edited by A. V. Golovnev, 208–36. Yekaterinburg: UrO RAN.

———. 2004. *Kochevniki tundry: nentsy i ikh fol'klor.* Yekaterinburg: UrO RAN.

———. 2017. "Challenges to Arctic Nomadism: Yamal Nenets Facing Climate Change Era Calamities." *Arctic Anthropology* 54 (2): 40–51.

Golovnev, Andrei V., and Sergei Kan. 1997. "Indigenous Leadership in Northwest Siberia: Traditional Patterns and Their Contemporary Manifestations." *Arctic Anthropology* 34 (1): 149–66.

Golovnev, Andrei V., and Gail Osherenko. 1999. *Siberian Survival: The Nenets and Their Story*. Ithaca, NY: Cornell University Press.

Golovnev, Andrey V., Denis A. Kukanov, and Yelena V. Perevalova. 2018. *Arktika: atlas kochevykh tekhnologiy*. St. Petersburg: MAE RAN.

Golovnev, Andrey V., Svetlana V. Lezova, Il'ya V. Abramov, Svetlana Y. Belorussova, and Natal'ya A. Babenkova. 2014. *Etnoekskpertiza na Yamale: nenetskie kochev'ya i gazovye mestorozhdeniya*. Yekaterinburg: AMB.

Gorter-Gronvik, Waling T., and Mikhail N. Suprun. 2000. "Ethnic Minorities and Warfare at the Arctic Front 1939–45." *Journal of Slavic Military Studies* 13 (1): 127–42.

Grant, Bruce. 1995. *In the Soviet House of Culture: A Century of Perestroikas*. Princeton, NJ: Princeton University Press.

Gray, Patty A. 2005. *The Predicament of Chukotka's Indigenous Movement: Post-Soviet Activism in the Russian Far North*. Cambridge: Cambridge University Press.

Grenoble, Lenore A. 2003. *Language Policy in the Soviet Union*. New York: Kluwer.

Grice, H. P. 1975 [1968]. "Logic and Conversation." In *Syntax and Semantics. Vol. 3: Speech Acts*, edited by P. Cole and J. L. Morgan, 41–58. New York: Academic.

Groys, Boris. 2009 [2006]. *The Communist Postscript*. Translated by T. H. Ford. London: Verso.

Gumperz, John J. 1968. "The Speech Community." In *International Encyclopedia of the Social Sciences*, edited by D. L. Sills and R. K. Merton, 381–86. New York: Macmillan.

Gurskiy, Konstantin P. 1999. *Moy Vaygach: zapiski zaklyuchennogo*. Naryan-Mar: Nenetskiy okruzhnoy krayevedcheskiy muzey.

Gurvich, Il'ya S. 2005. "O polozhenii yukagirov, evenov, chukchey, russkikh starozhilov ryada rayonov Yakutskoy ASSR i Magadanskoy oblasti. 1959 g." In *Etnologicheskaya ekspertiza: narody Severa Rossii. 1959-1962 gody*, edited by Z. P. Sokolova and Ye. A. Pivneva, 45–113. Moscow: Institut etnologii i antropologii RAN.

Haakanson, Sven, Jr., and Peter Jordan. 2010. "'Marking' the Land: Sacrifices, Cemeteries and Sacred Places among the Iamal Nenetses." In *Landscape and Culture in Northern Eurasia*, edited by P. Jordan, 161–77. Walnut Creek, CA: Left Coast.

Habeck, Joachim Otto. 2005. *What It Means to be a Herdsman: The Practice and Image of Reindeer Husbandry among the Komi of Northern Russia*. Münster: LIT Verlag.

———. 2011. "Komi Reindeer Herders: Syncretic and Pragmatic Notions of Being in the Tundra." In *Landscape and Culture in Northern Eurasia*, edited by P. Jordan, 279–95. Walnut Creek, CA: Left Coast.

Hage, Ghassan. 2014. "Eavesdropping on Bourdieu's Philosophers." In *The Ground Between: Anthropologists Engage Philosophy*, edited by V. Das, M. D. Jackson, A. Kleinman, and B. Singh, 138–58. Durham, NC: Duke University Press.

Halfin, Igal, ed. 2002. *Language and Revolution: Making Modern Political Identities*. London: Frank Cass.

———. 2009. *Stalinist Confessions: Messianism and Terror at the Leningrad Communist University*. Pittsburgh, PA: University of Pittsburgh Press.

Hallward, Peter. 2003. *Badiou: A Subject to Truth*. Minneapolis: University of Minnesota Press.

Handman, Courtney. 2015. *Critical Christianity: Translation and Denominational Conflict in Papua New Guinea*. Berkeley: University of California Press.

———. 2018. "The Language of Evangelism: Christian Cultures of Circulation beyond the Missionary Prologue." *Annual Review of Anthropology* 47:149–65.

Hanganu, Gabriel. 2010. "Eastern Christians and Religious Objects: Personal and Material Biographies Entangled." In *Eastern Christians in Anthropological Perspective*, edited by C. Hann and H. Goltz, 33–55. Berkeley: University of California Press.

Hanks, William F. 2010. *Converting Words: Maya in the Age of the Cross*. Berkeley: University of California Press.

Hann, Chris. 2007. "The Anthropology of Christianity Per Se." *Archives Européennes de Sociologie* 48 (3): 383–410.

Hann, Chris, and Hermann Goltz, eds. 2010. *Eastern Christians in Anthropological Perspective*. Berkeley: University of California Press.

Harding, Susan Friend. 2000. *The Book of Jerry Falwell: Fundamentalist Language and Politics*. Princeton, NJ: Princeton University Press.

Hefner, Robert, ed. 1993a. *Conversion to Christianity: Historical and Anthropological Perspectives on a Great Transformation*. Berkeley: University of California Press.

———. 1993b. "World Building and the Rationality of Conversion." In *Conversion to Christianity: Historical and Anthropological Perspectives on a Great Transformation*, edited by R. Hefner, 3–44. Berkeley: University of California Press.

———. 2019. "Reading and Remembering Saba Mahmood: Islam, Ethics, and the Hermeneutics of Tradition." *Contemporary Islam* 13:139–53.

Hellbeck, Jochen. 2006. *Revolution on My Mind: Writing a Diary under Stalin*. Cambridge, MA: Harvard University Press.

Henare, Amiria, Martin Holbraad, and Sari Wastell. 2007. "Introduction: Thinking through Things." In *Thinking through Things: Theorising Artefacts Ethnographically*, edited by A. Henare, M. Holbraad, and S. Wastell, 1–31. London: Routledge.

Hirschkind, Charles. 2006. *The Ethical Soundscape: Cassette Sermons and Islamic Counterpublics*. New York: Columbia University Press.

Højer, Lars. 2009. "Absent Powers: Magic and Loss in Post-Socialist Mongolia." *Journal of the Royal Anthropological Institute* 15 (3): 575–91.

———. 2019. *The Anti-Social Contract: Injurious Talk and Dangerous Exchanges in Northern Mongolia*. New York: Berghahn.

Højer, Lars, and Morten A. Pedersen. 2019. *Urban Hunters: Dealing and Dreaming in Times of Transition*. New Haven, CT: Yale University Press.

Holbraad, Martin, Bruce Kapferer, and Julia F. Sauma, eds. 2019. *Ruptures: Anthropologies of Discontinuity in Times of Turmoil*. London: UCL Press.

Holbraad, Martin, and Morten A. Pedersen. 2017. *The Ontological Turn: An Anthropological Exposition*. Cambridge: Cambridge University Press.

Hollywood, Amy. 2002. "Performativity, Citationality, Ritualization." *History of Religions* 42 (2): 93–115.

Horton, Robin. 1975a. "On the Rationality of Conversion. Part I." *Africa* 45 (3): 219–35.

———. 1975b. "On the Rationality of Conversion. Part II." *Africa* 45 (4): 373–99.

Hovi, Tuija. 2016. "Self-Fulfilling Words and Topics Not to Be Touched Upon: Noncommunication in Neo-Charismatic Rhetoric." *Ethnologia Europaea* 46 (2): 44–57.

Humphrey, Caroline. 1994. "Remembering an 'Enemy': The Bogd Khaan in Twentieth-Century Mongolia." In *Memory, History, and Opposition under State Socialism*, edited by R. S. Watson, 21–44. Santa Fe: School of American Research Press.

———. 1997. "Exemplars and Rules: Aspects of the Discourse of Moralities in Mongolia." In *The Ethnography of Moralities*, edited by S. Howell, 25–47. London: Routledge.

———. 1998. *Marx Went Away, but Karl Stayed Behind*. Ann Arbor: University of Michigan Press.

———. 2001. "Inequality and Exclusion: A Russian Case Study of Emotion in Politics." *Anthropological Theory* 1 (3): 331–53.

———. 2002. *The Unmaking of Soviet Life: Everyday Economies after Socialism*. Ithaca, NY: Cornell University Press.

———. 2005. "Dangerous Words: Taboos, Evasions, and Silence in Soviet Russia." *Forum for Anthropology and Culture* 2:374–96.

———. 2006. "On Being Named and Not Named: Authority, Persons, and Their Names in Mongolia." In *The Anthropology of Names and Naming*, edited by G. vom Bruck and B. Bodenhorn, 158–76. Cambridge: Cambridge University Press.

———. 2008. "Reassembling Individual Subjects: Events and Decisions in Troubled Times." *Anthropological Theory* 8 (4): 357–80.

———. 2014. "Schism, Event, and Revolution: The Old Believers of Trans-Baikalia." *Current Anthropology* 55 (S10): S216–25.

———. 2018. "The Fateful Landing of the Hoopoe: Omens from the World." *Terrain: anthropologie et sciences humaines*. https://doi.org/10.4000/terrain.16579.

Humphrey, Caroline, and James Laidlaw. 1994. *The Archetypal Actions of Ritual: A Theory of Ritual Illustrated by the Jain Rite of Worship*. Oxford: Clarendon.

———. 2007. "Sacrifice and Ritualization." In *The Archaeology of Ritual*, edited by E. Kyriakidis, 255–76. Los Angeles: Cotsen Institute of Archaeology, University of California.

Hymes, Dell H. 1974. "Ways of Speaking." In *Explorations in the Ethnography of Speaking*, edited by R. Bauman and J. Sherzer, 433–51. Cambridge: Cambridge University Press.

Igumnov, German'. 1912. "S Yugorskago Shara." *Pravoslavnyy blagovestnik* 9:409–13.

Il'ina, Irina V. 2008. *Traditsionnaya meditsinskaya kul'tura narodov Yevropeyskogo Severo-Vostoka (konets XIX–XX vv.)*. Syktyvkar: Institut yazyka, literatury i istorii Komi nauchnogo tsentra UrO RAN.

Ingold, Tim. 2000. *The Perception of Environment: Essays in Livelihood, Dwelling and Skill*. London: Routledge.

———. 2013. "Anthropology beyond Humanity." *Suomen Antropologi: Journal of the Finnish Anthropological Society* 38 (3): 5–23.

Ioann. 2014. *Ioann' padvy Maymbabtso Yun*. Moscow: Num' Padarm' pertya Institut. [*Gospel of John* in Nenets.]

Islavin, Vladimir A. 1847. *Samoyedy v domashnem i obshchestvennom bytu*. St. Petersburg.

Istomin, Kirill V. 1999. "Kolva Volost and Kolva Ethnographic Group as an Example of Transition from Nomadic to Settled Way of Life." *Pro Ethnologia* 8 (*Arctic Studies* 3): 19–34.

———. 2019. "Yazykovaya situatsiya sredi olenevodov-kochevnikov i poluosedlogo naseleniya severa yevropeyskoy Rossii i Zapadnoy Sibiri: sfery bytovaniya, situatsii ispol'zovaniya, yazykovye kompetentsii." *Voprosy etnopolitiki* 3:75–112.

Istomin, Kirill V., and Mark J. Dwyer. 2010. "Dynamic Mutual Adaptation: Human-Animal Interaction in Reindeer Herding Pastoralism." *Human Ecology* 38 (5): 613–23.

———. 2021. *Reindeer Herders' Thinking: A Comparative Research of Relations between Economy, Cognition and Way of Life*. Fürstenberg: Kulturstiftung Sibirien.

Ivanits, Linda J. 1989. *Russian Folk Belief*. Armonk: Sharp.

Ivanov, Sergey V. 1970. *Skul'ptura narodov Severa Sibiri XIX–pervoy poloviny XX v.* Leningrad: Nauka.

Jackson, Frederick George. 1895. *The Great Frozen Land (Bolshaia Zemelskija Tundra): Narrative of a Winter Journey across the Tundras and a Sojourn among the Samoyads*. London: Macmillan.

Jaworski, Adam. 1993. *The Power of Silence: Social and Pragmatic Perspectives*. Newbury Park: Sage.

Jenkins, Timothy. 2012. "The Anthropology of Christianity: Situation and Critique." *Ethnos* 77 (4): 459–76.

———. 2013. *Of Flying Saucers and Social Scientists: A Re-Reading of* When Prophecy Fails *and of Cognitive Dissonance*. New York: Palgrave.

———. 2018. "Theology's Contribution to Anthropological Understanding in T. M. Luhrmann's *When God Talks Back*." In *Theologically Engaged Anthropology*, edited by J. D. Lemons, 102–22. Oxford: Oxford University Press.

Johnson, Richard. 1903 [1598–1600]. "Certaine Notes Unperfectly Written." In *The Principal Navigations, Voyages, Traffiques and Discoveries of the English Nation*, vol. II, edited by R. Hakluyt, 345–49. Glasgow: James MacLehose.

Jorgensen, Dan. 2005. "Third Wave Evangelism and the Politics of the Global in Papua New Guinea: Spiritual Warfare and the Recreation of Place in Telefolmin." *Oceania* 75 (4): 444–61.

Josephson, Paul R. 2014. *The Conquest of the Russian Arctic*. Cambridge, MA: Harvard University Press.

Kazmina, Olga. 2008. "Negotiating Proselytism in Twenty-First Century Russia." In *Proselytization Revisited: Rights Talk, Free Markets and Culture Wars*, edited by R. I. J. Hackett, 339–64. London: Equinox.

Keane, Webb. 1997. *Signs of Recognition: Powers and Hazards of Representation in an Indonesian Society*. Berkeley: University of California Press.

———. 1998. "Calvin in the Tropics: Objects and Subjects at the Religious Frontier." In *Border Fetishisms: Material Objects in Unstable Spaces*, edited by P. Spyer, 13–34. New York: Routledge.

———. 2004. "Language and Religion." In *A Companion to Linguistic Anthropology*, edited by A. Duranti, 431–48. Malden, MA: Blackwell.

———. 2006. "Epilogue: Anxious Transcendence." In *The Anthropology of Christianity*, edited by F. Cannell, 308–23. Durham, NC: Duke University Press.

———. 2007. *Christian Moderns: Freedom and Fetish in the Mission Encounter*. Berkeley: University of California Press.

———. 2008a. "Others, Other Minds, and Others' Theories of Other Minds: An Afterword on the Psychology and Politics of Opacity Claims." *Anthropological Quarterly* 81 (2): 473–82.

———. 2008b. "The Evidence of the Senses and the Materiality of Religion." *Journal of the Royal Anthropological Institute* 14 (S1): S110–27.

———. 2013. "Ontologies, Anthropologists, and Ethical Life." *HAU: Journal of Ethnographic Theory* 3 (1): 186–91.

———. 2014. "Rotting Bodies: The Clash of Stances toward Materiality and Its Ethical Affordances." *Current Anthropology* 55 (S10): S312–21.

———. 2016. *Ethical Life: Its Natural and Social Histories*. Princeton, NJ: Princeton University Press.

Kee, Howard Clark. 1980. *Christian Origins in Sociological Perspective*. London: SCM Press.

Kertselli, Sergey V. 1911. *Po Bol'shezemel'skoy tundre s kochevnikami*. Arkhangelsk.

Khakhovskaya, Lyudmila N. 2008. *Korennye narody Magadasnkoy oblasti v XX–nachale XXI vv*. Magadan: SVNTs DVO RAN.

———. 2018. *Kul'tura etnolokal'nogo soobshchestva: koryaki sela Verkhniy Paren'*. Moscow: Nestor-Istoriya.

Khanzerova, Irina. 2003. "Sud'by lyudskie." *Nar''yana Vynder* (Naryan-Mar) 40, March 18.

———. 2004. "Uchitelya priekhali." *Nar''yana Vynder* (Naryan-Mar) 108, June 30.

———. 2007. "Skazaniya i byli Khal'mer Yakhi." *Nar''yana Vynder* (Naryan-Mar) 105–6, July 19.

———. 2017. "'Yamb to'—eto chto?" *Nar''yana Vynder* (Naryan-Mar) 106, September 30.

———. 2018. "Skazhite otkuda ya rodom." *Nar''yana Vynder* (Naryan-Mar) 131, November 29.

———. 2022. "La survie de la langue nénetse." *Études finno-ougriennes* 51–53:315–22.

Kharitonova, Valentina I. 2004. *Religioznyy faktor sovremennoy zhizni narodov Severa i Sibiri*. Moscow: Institut etnologii i antropologii RAN.

Kharkhordin, Oleg. 1999. *The Collective and the Individual in Russia: A Study of Practices*. Berkeley: University of California Press.

Kharyuchi, Galina P. 2001. *Traditsii i innovatsii v kul'ture nenetskogo etnosa (vtoraya polovina XX veka)*. Tomsk: Izdatel'stvo Tomskogo universiteta.

———. 2004. "Nenets Sacred Sites as Ethnographic Landscape." In *Northern Ethnographic Landscapes: Perspectives from Circumpolar Nations*, edited by I. Krupnik, R. Mason, and T. W. Horton, 155–76. Washington, DC: Arctic Studies Center, Smithsonian Institution.

———. 2012. *Priroda v traditsionnom mirovozzrenii nentsev*. St. Petersburg: Istoricheskaya illyustratsiya.

———. 2013. *Svyashchennye mesta v traditsionnoy i sovremennoy kul'ture nentsev*. St. Petersburg: Istoricheskaya illyustratsiya.

———. 2018. "Sacred Places in the Nenets Traditional Culture." *Sibirica* 17 (3): 116–37.

Kharyuchi, Galina P., and Liudmilla Lipatova. 1999. "Traditional Beliefs, Sacred Sites and Rituals of Sacrifice of the Nenets of the Gydan Peninsula in the Modern Context." In *The Archaeology and Anthropology of Landscape: Shaping Your Landscape*, edited by P. J. Ucko and R. Layton, 284–97. London: Routledge.

Khlinovskaya Rockhill, Elena. 2010. *Lost to the State: Family Discontinuity, Social Orphanhood and Residential Care in the Russian Far East*. Oxford: Berghahn.

Khomich, Lyudmila V. 1966. *Nentsy: istoriko-etnograficheskie ocherki*. Moscow: Nauka.

———. 1971a. "Sotsialisticheskoe stroitel'stvo v Nenetskom natsional'nom okruge." In *Osushchestvlenie leninskoy natsional'noy politiki u narodov Kraynego Severa*, edited by I. S. Gurvich, 229–44. Moscow: Nauka.

———. 1971b. "O nekotorykh predmetakh kul'ta nadymskikh nentsev." In *Religioznye predstavleniya i obryady narodov Sibiri v XIX–nachale XX veka*, edited by L. P. Potapov and S. V. Ivanov, 239–47. Leningrad: Nauka.

———. 1976. "Predstavleniya nentsev o prirode i cheloveke." In *Priroda i chelovek v religioznykh predstavleniyakh narodov Sibiri i Severa*, edited by I. S. Vdovin, 16–30. Leningrad: Nauka.

———. 1977. "Religioznye kul'ty u nentsev." In *Pamyatniki kul'tury narodov Sibiri i Severa (vtoraya polovina XIX–nachalo XX v.)*, edited by I. S. Vdovin, 5–28. Leningrad: Nauka.

———— [Khomič]. 1978. "A Classification of Nenets Shamans." In *Shamanism in Siberia*, edited by V. Diószegi and M. Hoppál, 245–53. Budapest: Akadémiai Kiadó.

————. 1979. "Vliyanie khristianizatsii na religioznye predstavleniya i kult'y nentsev." In *Khristianstvo i lamaizm u korennogo naseleniya Sibiri (vtoraya polovina XIX–nachalo XX v.)*, edited by I. S. Vdovin, 12–28. Leningrad: Nauka.

————. 1981. "Shamany u nentsev." In *Problemy istorii obshchestvennogo soznaniya aborigenov Sibiri (po materialam vtoroy poloviny XIX–nachala XX v.)*, edited by I. S. Vdovin, 5–41. Leningrad: Nauka.

————. 1995. *Nentsy: ocherki traditsionnoy kul'tury*. St. Petersburg: Russkiy Dvor.

————. 2003. *Nentsy*. St. Petersburg: Drofa.

————. 2006. "O sovremennom polozhenii korennogo naseleniya v Yamalo-Nenetskom natsional'nom okruge Tyumenskoy oblasti. 1966 g." In *Etnologicheskaya ekspertiza: narody Severa Rossii. 1963–1980 gody*, edited by Z. P. Sokolova and Ye. A. Pivneva, 145–76. Moscow: Institut etnologii i antropologii RAN.

Khorev, Mikhail. 1988. *Letters from a Soviet Prison Camp*. Eastbourne: Monarch.

Khristoforova, Ol'ga B. 1998. *Logika tolkovaniy: fol'klor i modelirovanie povedeniya v arkhaicheskikh kul'turakh*. Moscow: Rossiyskiy gosudarstvennyy gumanitarnyy institut.

————. 2006. "Interpretatsii molchaniya: rechevoy etiket narodov Severa v zametkakh puteshestvennikov i po dannym fol'klora." *Arbor Mundi. Mirovoe drevo* 12:82–104.

————. 2016. *Oderzhimost' v russkoy derevne*. Moscow: Neolit.

Kibenko, Valeriy A., Sergey M. Zuyev, Yekaterina A. Sukhova. 2017. "Deyatel'nost' religioznykh organizatsiy v srede korennykh malochislennykh narodov Severa, vedushchikh traditsionnoy obraz zhizni." *Nauchnyy vestnik Yamalo-Nenetskogo avtonomnogo okruga* 97 (4): 89–93.

King, Alexander D. 2011. *Living with Koryak Traditions: Playing with Culture in Siberia*. Lincoln: University of Nebraska Press.

Kirsch, Stuart. 1997. "Lost Tribes: Indigenous People and the Social Imaginary." *Anthropological Quarterly* 70 (2): 58–67.

Klokov, Konstantin B., and Sergey A. Khrushchev. 2006. "Olenevodcheskoe khozyaystvo korennykh narodov Severa Rossii." In *Mezhetnicheskie vzaimodeystviya i sotsiokul'turnaya adaptatsiya narodov Severa Rossii*, compiled by Ye. A. Pivneva, edited by V. I. Molodin and V. A. Tishkov, 13–33. Moscow: Strategiya.

Klokov, Konstantin B., and Dzhon P. Zayker [Ziker], eds. 2010. *Pripolyarnaya perepis' 1926/27 gg. na Yevropeyskom Severe (Arkhangel'skaya guberniya i avtonomnaya oblast' Komi)*. St. Petersburg: EtnoEkspert.

Kolycheva, Yevgeniya I. 1956. "Nentsy yevropeyskoy Rossii v kontse XVII–nachale XVIII veka." *Sovetskaya Etnografiya* 2:76–88.

Komandirovka. 2001. "Komandirovka v Vorkutu." *Mir korennykh narodov* 5:60–64.

Konstantin. 2014. "Missioner v strane samoyedov." *Foma* 6 (134). http://foma.ru/missioner-v -strane-samoyedov.html.

Konstantinov, Yulian. 2015. *Conversations with Power. Soviet and Post-Soviet Developments in the Reindeer Husbandry Part of the Kola Peninsula*. Uppsala: Uppsala universitet.

Koosa, Piret. 2016. "Evangelical Silence in a Komi Village." *Ethnologia Europaea* 46 (2): 58–73.

————. 2017. "Negotiating Faith and Identity in a Komi Village: Protestant Christians in a Pro-Orthodox Sociocultural Environment." PhD diss., University of Tartu Press, Tartu.

Korepanova, Lyudmila Yu. 2019. "Yamb to." In *Nenetskiy avtonomnyy okrug. Entsiklopediya. Tom II*, edited by L. Yu. Korepanova, 486–87. Moscow: OST PAK NT.

Koroleva, Larisa A., Aleksey A. Korolev, and Svetlana F. Artemova. 2013. *Vlast' i yevangel'skie khristiane-baptisty v Rossii. 1945–2000 gg.: evolyutsiya vzaimootnosheniy*. Penza: PGUAS.

Koshkareva, Natalya B., ed. 2010. *Dialektologicheskiy slovar' nenetskogo yazyka*. Yekaterinburg: Basko.

———, ed. 2017. *Dialektologicheskiy atlas ural'skikh yazykov, rasprostranennykh na territorii Yamalo-Nenetskogo avtonomnogo okruga*. Kaliningrad: ROST-DOAFK.

Kostikov, Leonid V. 1930a. "Bogovy oleni v religioznykh verovaniyakh khasovo." *Etnografiya* 1–2:115–32.

———. 1930b. "Zakony tundry. K voprosu o polozhenii zhenshchiny u samoyedov." *Trudy Polyarnoy komissii Akademii Nauk* 3. Leningrad: Izdatel'stvo Akademii Nauk SSSR, 1–68.

Kotkin, Stephen. 1995. *Magnetic Mountain: Stalinism as a Civilization*. Berkeley: University of California Press.

Kovalenko, Leonid. 2006. *Oblako svideteley Khristovykh*. 4th ed. Kyiv: Tsentr Khristianskogo Sotrudnichestva.

Kozmin, N. 1903. "Sovremennoe religioznoe sostoyanie samoyedov, kochuyushchikh na o. Vaygache i Yugorskom share i usloviya missionerskoy sredi nikh deyatel'nosti." *Pravoslavnyy blagovestnik* 18:67–77.

Kroskrity, Paul V. 2004. "Language Ideologies." In *A Companion to Linguistic Anthropology*, edited by A. Duranti, 496–517. Malden, MA: Blackwell.

Krupnik, Igor I. 1976. "Pitanie i ekologiya khozyaystva nentsev Bol'shezemel'skoy tundry v 20-kh godakh XX v." In *Nekotorye problemy etnogeneza i etnicheskoy istorii narodov mira*, edited by P. I. Puchkov, 64–85. Moscow: Institut Etnografii AN SSSR.

———. 1993 [1989]. *Arctic Adaptations: Native Whalers and Reindeer Herders of Northern Eurasia*. Expanded English edition, translated and edited by M. Levenson. Hanover: University Press of New England.

Kryuchkov, Gennadiy K. 2000. "Svyataya otvetstvennost'." *Vestnik istiny* 149 (1): 2–4.

———. 2008. *Velikoe probuzhdenie XX veka. 1961–2006*. n.p.: Izdatel'stvo "Khristianin," Mezhdunarodnyy sovet tserkvey YeKhB.

Kulick, Don, and Bambi B. Schieffelin. 2004. "Language Socialization." In *A Companion to Linguistic Anthropology*, edited by A. Duranti, 349–68. Malden, MA: Blackwell.

Kupriyanova, Zinaida N. 1965. *Epicheskie pesni nentsev*. Moscow: Nauka.

Kushelevskiy, Yuriy I. 1868. *Severnyy polyus i zemlya Yalmal: Putevye zapiski*. St. Petersburg.

Kuwajima, Ikuru. 2015. *Tundra Kids*. Vienna: Schlebrügge.

Kvashnin, Yuriy N. 2009a. *Nenetskoe olenevodstvo v XX–nachale XXI veka*. Tyumen: Koleso.

———. 2009b. *Nentsy Yevropeyskogo Severa v materialiakh pokhozyaystvennykh perepisey 1924 i 1925 godov*. Tobolsk: Institut problem osvoyeniya Severa SO RAN.

———. 2018. *Zhizn' i byt samoyedov i loparey v kratkom opisanii odnogo volter'yantsa*. Tobolsk: Popligrafist.

———. 2019. "'This Family Has Been Found and Is Now Located in Obdorsk Region . . .' (Reflections on the List of Samoyeds of Berezovsky District in 1832)." *Arctic and North* 35:76–97.

Kwon, Heonik. 1993. "Maps and Actions: Nomadic and Sedentary Space in a Siberian Reindeer Farm." Unpublished doctoral dissertation, University of Cambridge, Cambridge.

Laidlaw, James. 2000. "A Free Gift Makes No Friends." *Journal of the Royal Anthropological Institute* 6 (4): 617–34.

———. 2014. *The Subject of Virtue: An Anthropology of Ethics and Freedom*. Cambridge: Cambridge University Press.

———. 2018. "Fault Lines in the Anthropology of Ethics." In *Moral Engines: Exploring the Ethical Drives in Human Life*, edited by C. Mattingly, R. Dyring, M. Louw, and T. S. Wentzer, 174–96. New York: Berghahn.

Laidlaw, James, Barbara Bodenhorn, and Martin Holbraad, eds. 2018. *Recovering the Human Subject: Freedom, Creativity and Decision*. Cambridge: Cambridge University Press.

Lambek, Michael. 2010a. "Introduction." In *Ordinary Ethics: Anthropology, Language and Action*, edited by M. Lambek, 1–36. New York: Fordham University Press.

———. 2010b. "Toward an Ethics of the Act." In *Ordinary Ethics: Anthropology, Language and Action*, edited by M. Lambek, 39–63. New York: Fordham University Press.

———. 2015a. *The Ethical Condition: Essays on Action, Person, and Value*. Chicago: University of Chicago Press.

———. 2015b. "Both/And." In *What Is Existential Anthropology?*, edited by M. Jackson and A. Piette, 58–83. Oxford: Berghahn.

———. 2017. "On the Immanence of Ethics." In *Moral Engines: Exploring the Ethical Drives in Human Life*, edited by C. Mattingly, R. Dyring, M. Louw, and T. S. Wentzer, 137–54. New York: Berghahn.

———. 2021. *Concepts and Persons*. Toronto: University of Toronto Press.

Lane, Christel. 1981. *The Rites of Rulers: Ritual in Industrial Society—The Soviet Case*. Cambridge: Cambridge University Press.

Lapsui, Anastasia, Markku Lehmuskallio, Pekka Lehmuskallio, and Kirsikka Moring. 2023. *Jäähyväiset tundralle—Siperian nenetsien matkassa*. Helsinki: SKS Kirjat.

Laptander, Roza. 2014. "Processes of Remembering and Forgetting Tundra Nenets' Reminiscences of the 1943 *Mandalada* Rebellions." *Sibirica* 13 (3): 22–44.

———. 2017. "Collective and Individual Memories: Narrations about the Transformations in the Nenets Society." *Arctic Anthropology* 54 (1): 22–31.

———. 2020a. *When We Got Reindeer, We Moved to Live to the Tundra: The Spoken and Silenced History of the Yamal Nenets*. Rovaniemi: Lapin yliopisto.

———. 2020b. "V poiskakh goryachego ochaga: ogon' v fol'klore i zhizni yamal'skikh nentsev." *Etnografiya* 1 (7): 166–87.

———. 2023. "The Tundra Nenets' Fire Rites, or What is Hidden Inside of the Nenets Female Needlework Bag *Tutsya*." In *The Siberian World*, edited by J. Ziker, J. Ferguson, and V. Davydov, 96–109. New York: Routledge.

Laptander, Roza, and Piers Vitebsky. 2021. "The Covid-19 App and the Fire Spirit: Receiving Messages in Britain and Siberia." *Anthropology Today* 37 (6): 17–20.

Lar, Leonid A. 1998. *Shamany i bogi*. Tyumen: Institut problem osvoyeniya Severa SO RAN.

———. 2001. *Mify i predaniya nentsev Yamala*. Tyumen: Institut problem osvoyeniya Severa SO RAN.

———. 2003. *Kul'tovye pamyatniki Yamala. Khebidya Ya*. Tyumen: Institut problem osvoyeniya Severa SO RAN.

———. 2005. *Shamans and Gods*. Translated by G. V. Korotayeva. Tyumen: Institut problem osvoyeniya Severa SO RAN.

———. 2006. "Religioznye traditsii nentsev i ikh evolyutsiya v XVIII–nachale XX v." Unpublished doctoral dissertation, Tobol'skaya gosudarstvennaya sotsial'no-pedagogicheskaya akademiya, Yekaterinburg.

Lar, Leonid A., Konstantin A. Oshchepkov, and Nina A. Povod. 2003. "Dukhovnaya kul'tura nentsev." In *Etnografiya i antropologiya Yamala*, edited by A. N. Bagashev, 50–112. Novosibirsk: Nauka.

Lar, Leonid A., and Valentina Yu. Vanuyto. 2011. *Religioznye traditsii nentsev v XVIII– nachale XX vv.* Tyumen: Ekspress.

Lashov, Boris V. 1964. "Voprosy osedaniya korennogo naseleniya Kraynego Severa (na primere Nenetskogo natsional'nogo okruga)." *Izvestiya vsesoyuznogo geograficheskogo obshchestva* 5:408–13.

Lashuk, Lev P. 1958. *Ocherk etnicheskoy istorii Pechorskogo kraya*. Syktyvkar: Komi knizhnoe izdatel'stvo.

Latkin, Vasiliy N. 1853. *Dnevnik Vasiliya Nikolayevicha Latkina, vo vremya puteshestviya na Pechoru, v 1840 i 1843 godakh. Chast' I. (Zapiski Imperatorskogo Russkogo geograficheskogo obshchestva 7).* St. Petersburg.

Latour, Bruno. 1993 [1991]. *We Have Never Been Modern*. Translated by C. Porter. Cambridge, MA: Harvard University Press.

———. 2005. "'Thou Shall Not Freeze-Frame,' or, How Not to Misunderstand the Science and Religion Debate." In *Science, Religion, and the Human Experience*, edited by J. D. Proctor, 27–48. Oxford: Oxford University Press.

———. 2010. *On the Modern Cult of the Factish Gods*. Durham, NC: Duke University Press.

Lavrillier, Alexandra. 2005. "Nomadisme et adaptations sédentaires chez les Évenks de Sibérie postsoviétique: 'jouer' pour vivre avec et sans chamanes." Unpublished doctoral dissertation, École Pratique des Hautes Études, Paris.

Ledkov, Vasiliy. 1977. *Lyudi "Bol'shoy medveditsy."* Translated from Nenets by N. Leontev. Moscow: Sovremennik.

Leete, Art. 2005a. "Anti-Soviet Movements and Uprisings among the Siberian Indigenous Peoples during the 1920–40s." In *The Northern Peoples and States: Changing Relationships (Studies in Folk Culture 5)*, edited by A. Leete and Ü. Valk, 55–89. Tartu: Tartu University Press.

———. 2005b. "Religious Revival as Reaction to the Hegemonization of Power in Siberia in the 1920s to 1940s." *Asian Folklore Studies* 64:233–45.

———. 2014. *Guileless Indigenes and Hidden Passion: Descriptions of Ob-Ugrians and Samoyeds through the Centuries*. Translated by K. Hakkinen. Helsinki: Suomalainen Tiedeakatemia.

———. 2019. "Silence in the Woods: Finno-Ugric Peoples of the Russian North and Western Siberia in the Ethnographic Literature from the Eighteenth to the Beginning of the Twentieth Century." *Sibirica* 18 (2): 1–26.

Leete, Art, and Vladimir Lipin. 2015. "The Concept of Truth in the Komi Hunting Stories." *Acta Borealia* 32 (1): 68–84.

Leete, Art, and Laur Vallikivi. 2011. "Imitating Enemies or Friends: Comparative Notes on Christianity in the Indigenous Russian Arctic during the Early Soviet Period." *Asian Ethnology* 70 (1): 81–104.

Lehtisalo, Toivo. 1924. *Entwurf einer Mythologie der Jurak-Samojeden*. Helsinki: Société Finno-Ougrienne.

———. 1932. *Beiträge zur Kenntnis der Renntierzucht bei den Juraksamojeden*. Oslo: Aschehoug.

———. 1937. "Der Tod und die Wiedergeburt des künftigen Schamanen." *Journal de la Société Finno-Ougrienne* 48 (3): 1–34.

———. 1947. *Juraksamojedische Volksdichtung*. Helsinki: Suomalais-Ugrilainen Seura.

———. 1956. *Juraksamojedisches Wörterbuch*. Helsinki: Suomalais-Ugrilainen Seura.

Lepekhin, Ivan I. 1805. *Puteshestviya akademika Ivana Lepekhina v 1772 godu. Chast' IV*. St. Petersburg: Imperatorskaya Akademiya Nauk.

Lévesque, Jean. 2006. "'Into the Grey Zone': Sham Peasants and the Limits of the Kolkhoz Order in the Post-War Russian Village, 1945–1953." In *Late Stalinist Russia: Society between Reconstruction and Reinvention*, edited by J. Fürst, 103–19. London: Routledge.

Lezova, Svetlana V. 2001. "Severnyy Yamal: velikoe pereselenie 1947 goda." In *Samodiytsy: Materialy IV Sibirskogo simpoziuma "Kul'turnoe nasledie narodov Zapadnoy Sibiri,"* edited by A. V. Golovnev, 132–35. Tobolsk: OmGPU.

Liarskaya [Lyarskaya], Yelena V. 2002. "Sovremennoe sostoyanie sistemy lichnykh imen u yamal'skikh nentsev." In *Antropologiya. Fol'kloristika. Lingvistika: sbornik statey 2*, edited by S. A. Shtyrkov and B. V. Kolosova, 90–130. St. Petersburg: Izdatel'stvo Yevropeyskogo universiteta v Sankt-Peterburge.

———. 2003. "Severnye internaty i transformatsiya traditsionnoy kul'tury." Unpublished doctoral dissertation, Yevropeyskiy universitet v Sankt-Peterburge, St. Petersburg.

———. 2005. "Female Taboos and the Nenets System of Concepts of the Unclean." *Forum for Anthropology and Culture* 2:266–75.

———. 2011. "A Working Model of a Sacred Place: Exhibits Appearing in Dreams and Other Miracles in a Small Museum at the Edge of the World." *Sibirica* 10 (2): 1–25.

———. 2013. "Boarding School on Yamal: History of Development and Current Situation." In *Sustaining Indigenous Knowledge: Learning Tools and Community Initiatives for Preserving Endangered Languages and Local Cultural Heritage*, edited by E. Kasten and T. de Graaf, 159–80. Fürstenberg: Kulturstiftung Sibirien.

Lienhardt, Godfrey. 1961. *Divinity and Experience: The Religion of the Dinka*. Oxford: Clarendon.

Lind, Tore Tvarnø. 2021. "The Quietude." In *The Bloomsbury Handbook of the Anthropology of Sound*, edited by H. Schulze, 311–20. New York: Bloomsbury.

Lindquist, Galina. 2006. *Conjuring Hope: Magic and Healing in Contemporary Russia*. New York: Berghahn.

Litke, Fedor P. 1828. *Chetyrekratnoe puteshestvie v Severnyy Ledovityy okean. Chast' II*. St. Petersburg.

Luehrmann, Sonja. 2010. "A Dual Quarrel of Images on the Middle Volga: Icon Veneration in the Face of Protestant and Pagan Critique." In *Eastern Christians in Anthropological Perspective*, edited by C. Hann and H. Goltz, 56–78. Berkeley: University of California Press.

———. 2012. *Secularism Soviet Style: Teaching Atheism and Religion in a Volga Republic*. Bloomington: Indiana University Press.

Luhrmann, Tanya M. 2004. "Metakinesis: How God Becomes Intimate in Contemporary U.S. Christianity." *American Anthropologist* 106 (3): 518–28.

———. 2012. *When God Talks Back: Understanding the American Evangelical Relationship with God*. New York: Knopf.

———. 2018. "The Faith Frame: Or, Belief Is Easy, Faith Is Hard." *Contemporary Pragmatism* 15:302–18.

———. 2020. *How God Becomes Real: Kindling the Presence of Invisible Others*. Princeton, NJ: Princeton University Press.

Luka. 2004. *Luka' padvy Maymbabtso Yun.* Moscow: Bibliyam' pertya Institut. [*Gospel of Luke* in Nenets.]

Lukin, Karina. 2010. "Animating the Unseen: Landscape Discourses as Mnemonics among Kolguyev Nenets." *Suomen Antropologi: Journal of the Finnish Anthropological Society* 35 (1): 23–42.

———. 2011. *Elämän ja entisyyden maisemat: Kolgujev nenetsien arjessa, muistelussa ja kerronnassa.* Helsinki: Suomalaisen Kirjallisuuden Seura.

———. 2012. "Narrating the Last Shaman." In *Mythic Discourses: Studies in Uralic Traditions,* edited by Frog, A.-L. Siikala and E. Stepanova, 355–79. Helsinki: Finnish Literature Society.

———. 2015. "Lonely Riders of Nenets Mythology and Shamanism." In *Between Text and Practice: Mythology, Religion and Research,* a special issue of *RMN Newsletter* 10, edited by Frog and K. Lukina, 118–27. Helsinki: University of Helsinki. https://www.helsinki.fi/assets/drupal/2022-12/rmn_10_2015.pdf.

———. 2017. "Matthias Alexander Castrén's Notes on Nenets Folklore." *Suomalais-Ugrilaisen Seuran Aikakauskirja—Journal de la Société Finno-Ougrienne* 96:169–211.

———. 2022. "Rendering Comfort and Control in Tundra Nenets *Sambadabc.*" *Études finno-ougriennes* 51–53:9–30.

Lunkin, Roman. 2000. "Russia's Native Peoples: Their Path to Christianity." *Religion, State and Society* 28 (1): 123–33.

———. 2014. "Rossiyskiy protestantizm: yevangel'skie khristiane kak novyy sotsial'nyy fenomen." *Sovremennaya Yevropa* 59 (3): 133–43.

MacCulloch, Diarmaid. 2013. *Silence: A Christian History.* London: Penguin.

Mahmood, Saba. 2005. *Politics of Piety: The Islamic Revival and the Feminist Subject.* Princeton, NJ: Princeton University Press.

Makariy [Mirolyubov, Nikolay K.]. 1878. *Khristianstvo v predelakh Arkhangel'skoy eparkhii.* Moscow: Obshchestvo istorii i drevnostey rossiyskikh pri Moskovskom universitete.

Malley, Brian. 2004. *How the Bible Works: An Anthropological Study of Evangelical Biblicism.* Walnut Creek, CA: Altamira.

Mamoylova, Tat'yana. 1997. "Iz istorii poselka Khorey-Ver." In *Istoki: zhurnal shkol'nogo nauchnogo obshchestva Nenetskoy shkoly-internata,* edited by N. A. Vostrikova, 65–70. Naryan-Mar.

Mark. 2010. *Mark' padvy Maymbabtso Yun.* Moscow: Bibliyam' pertya Institut. [*Gospel of Mark* in Nenets.]

Marsh, Christopher. 2011. *Religion and the State in Russia and China: Suppression, Survival, and Revival.* New York: Continuum.

Maslov, Pavel P. 1934. "Kochevye ob"edineniya yedinolichnykh khozyaystv v tundre Severnogo Kraya." *Sovetskiy Sever* 5:27–34.

Masuzawa, Tomoko. 2000. "Troubles with Materiality: The Ghost of Fetishism in the Nineteenth Century." *Comparative Studies in Society and History* 42 (2): 242–67.

———. 2005. *The Invention of World Religions: Or How European Universalism Was Preserved in the Language of Pluralism.* Chicago: University of Chicago Press.

Matfey. 2018. *Matfey' padvy Maymbabtso Yun.* Moscow: Num' Padarm' pertya Institut. [*Gospel of Matthew* in Nenets.]

Mattingly, Cheryl. 2010. *The Paradox of Hope: Journeys through a Clinical Borderland.* Berkeley: University of California Press.

———. 2014. *Moral Laboratories: Family Peril and the Struggle for a Good Life*. Berkeley: University of California Press.

———. 2018. "Ethics, Immanent Transcendence and the Experimental Narrative Self." In *Moral Engines: Exploring the Ethical Drives in Human Life*, edited by C. Mattingly, R. Dyring, M. Louw, and T. S. Wentzer, 39–60. New York: Berghahn.

Mattingly, Cheryl, and Jason Throop. 2018. "The Anthropology of Ethics and Morality." *Annual Review of Anthropology* 47:475–92.

Mauss, Marcel. 2003 [1909]. *On Prayer*. Translated by S. Leslie and edited by W. S. F. Pickering. New York: Berghahn.

Mavlyutova, Gul'nara Sh. 2001. *Missionerskaya deyatel'nost' russkoy pravoslavnoy tserkvi v Severo-Zapadnoy Sibiri (XIX–nachalo XX veka)*. Tyumen: Izdatel'stvo gosudarstvennogo universiteta.

Mead, George Herbert. 1962 [1932]. *Mind, Self, and Society: From the Standpoint of a Social Behaviorist*. Chicago: University of Chicago Press.

Menshakova, Yelena G., and Lyudmila P. Taleyeva. 2011. *Sakral'nye predmety nentsev arkhangel'skikh tundr: katalog*. Nar'yan-Mar: Nenetskiy krayevedcheskiy muzey.

Meyer, Birgit. 1999. *Translating the Devil: Religion and Modernity among the Ewe in Ghana*. Trenton, NJ: Africa World Press.

———. 2004. "Christianity in Africa: From African Independent to Pentecostal-Charismatic Churches." *Annual Review of Anthropology* 33:447–74.

———. 2010. "Aesthetics of Persuasion: Global Christianity and Pentecostalism's Sensational Forms." *South Atlantic Quarterly* 109 (4): 741–63.

———. 2015. *Sensational Movies: Video, Vision, and Christianity in Ghana*. Berkeley: University of California Press.

Michalski, Sergiusz. 1993. *The Reformation and the Visual Arts: The Protestant Image Question in Western and Eastern Europe*. London: Routledge.

Mikeshin, Igor. 2016. *How Jesus Changes Lives: Christian Rehabilitation in the Russian Baptist Ministry*. Helsinki: University of Helsinki.

Mikhaylov, Ioann. 1898. "Poyezdka na Yugorskiy Shar (iz dnevnika svyashchennika)." *Arkhangel'skie eparkhial'nye vedomosti* 4:106–12; 5:133–39; 6:163–70; 9:257–62.

Mitrokhin, Lev N. 1997. *Baptizm: istoriya i sovremennost'*. St. Petersburg: Izdatel'stvo Russkogo khristianskogo gumanitarnogo instituta.

Miyazaki, Hirokazu. 2000. "Faith and Its Fulfillment: Agency, Exchange, and the Fijian Aesthetics of Completion." *American Ethnologist* 27 (1): 31–51.

Mosko, Mark. 2010. "Partible Penitents: Dividual Personhood and Christian Practice in Melanesia and the West." *Journal of the Royal Anthropological Institute* 16 (2): 215–40.

———. 2015. "Unbecoming Individuals: The Partible Character of the Christian Person." *HAU: Journal of Ethnographic Theory* 5 (1): 361–93.

Murashko, Ol'ga, ed. 2004. *Znachenie okhrany svyashchennykh mest Arktiki: issledovanie korennykh narodov Severa Rossii*. Moscow: AKMNS i DV RF.

———. 2013. "'Oleni—nelegaly.'" *Mir korennykh narodov* 29:57–70.

———. 2016. "Vorkutinskikh nentsev vnov' pytayutsya podvergnut' kollektivizatsii." July 18. http://www.csipn.ru/glavnaya/novosti-regionov/2608-vorkutinskikh-nentsev-vnov -pytayutsya-podvergnut-kollektivizatsii#.XsaIg2j7SiM.

Napolskikh, Vladimir, Anna-Leena Siikala, and Mihály Hoppál, eds. 2003. *Komi Mythology*. Authored by N. D. Konakov, I. V. Il'ina, P. F. Limerov, O. I. Ulyashev, Yu. P. Shabayev,

V. E. Sharapov, and A. N. Vlasov. Budapest: Akadémiai Kiadó; Helsinki: Finnish Literature Society.

Nenyang, Lyubov'. 1997. *Khodyachiy um naroda*. Krasnoyarsk: Fond severnykh literatur "Khelgen."

Nerkagi, Anna. 1996. *Molchashchiy. Povesti*. Tyumen: SoftDizayn.

Neverov, Pavel. 1999. "Gospodnya volya i zemnoy proizvol." *Nezavisimaya gazeta—Religii* 19 (October 13).

Nevskiy, Vasiliy P. 1906. "Poyezdka v samoyedskie chumy." *Pravoslavnyy blagovestnik* 6:270–73.

Nichols, Gregory L. 2011. *The Development of Russian Evangelical Spirituality: A Study of Ivan V. Kargel (1849–1937)*. Eugene, OR: Pickwick.

Niemi, Jarkko. 1998. *The Nenets Songs. A Structural Analysis of Text and Melody*. Tampere: University of Tampere.

Niemi, Jarkko, and Anastasia Lapsui. 2004. *Network of Songs. Individual Songs of the Ob' Gulf Nenets: Music and Local History as Sung by Maria Maksimovna Lapsui*. Helsinki: Société finno-ougrienne.

Niglas, Liivo. 1997a. "Reindeer in the Nenets Worldview." *Pro Ethnologia* 5 (*Arctic Studies* 1): 7–33.

———. 1997b. "La femme chez les éleveurs de renne Nenets." *Études Finno-Ougriennes* 29:85–104.

———. 2000. "Reindeer as the Moulder of the Ethnic Identity of the Yamal Nenets." *Pro Ethnologia* 10 (*Arctic Studies* 4): 87–92.

Nikol'skaya, Tat'yana K. 2009. *Russkiy protestantizm i gosudarstvennaya vlast' v 1905–1991 godakh*. St. Petersburg: Izdatel'stvo Yevropeyskogo universiteta v Sankt-Peterburge.

Noble, John H. 1970 [1959]. *I Found God in Soviet Russia*. London: Lakeland.

Norget, Kristin, Valentina Napolitano, and Maya Mayblin, eds. 2017. *The Anthropology of Catholicism: A Reader*. Oakland: University of California Press.

Nosilov, Konstantin D. 1895. "Moi zapiski o zhizni, obychayakh i verovaniyakh samoyedov." *Pravoslavnyy blagovestnik* 1:38–46; 3:154–63.

Novikova, Natal'ya I. 2016. "Sur quoi les autochtones gardent-ils le silence, et pourquoi?" *Études finno-ougriennes* 47:45–60.

Num' Vadi. 2021. *Num' Vadi vadeta Iona' padvy padar". Kniga proroka Iony*. Moscow: Institut perevoda Biblii. [*Book of Jonah* in Nenets and Russian.]

Ob osvyashchenii. 2006. *Ob osvyashchenii. Verouchenie. Ustav MSTs YeKhB*. n.p.: Izdatel'stvo "Khristianin," Mezhdunarodnyy sovet tserkvey YeKhB.

Ogryzko, Vyacheslav, ed. 2003. *Nenetskaya literatura*. Moscow: Literaturnaya Rossiya.

Okladnikov, Nikolay A. 1999. *Pustozersk i nentsy (XVI–XIX vv.)*. Naryan-Mar: Nenetskiy okruzhnoy krayevedcheskiy muzey.

Okladnikov, Nikolay A., and Nikolay N. Matafanov. 2008. *Ternistyy put' k pravoslaviyu. Iz istorii obrashcheniya v khristianstvo nentsev arkhangel'skikh tundr*. Arkhangelsk: Pravda Severa.

Opasnost'. 2019. "Opasnost' vozbuzhdeniya religioznoy vrazhdy v Komi." https://baptistnorth.ru/bratstvo/news/komi/dangerous/.

Osherenko, Gail. 1995. "Property Rights and Transformation in Russia: Institutional Change in the Far North." *Europe-Asia Studies* 47 (7): 1077–108.

Ovsyannikov, Oleg V., and Nikolai M. Terebikhin. 1994. "Sacred Space in the Culture of the Arctic Regions." In *Sacred Sites, Sacred Places*, edited by D. L. Carmichael, J. Hubert, B. Reeves, and A. Schanche, 44–81. London: Routledge.

Paden, William E. 1988. "Theaters of Humility and Suspicion: Desert Saints and New England Puritans." In *Technologies of the Self: A Seminar with Michel Foucault*, edited by L. H. Martin, H. Gutman, and P. H. Hutton, 64–79. Amherst: University of Massachusetts Press.

Panych, Olena. 2012a. "Children and Childhood among Evangelical Christians-Baptists during the Late Soviet Period (1960s–1980s)." *Theological Reflections* 13:155–79.

———. 2012b. "A Time and Space of Suffering: Reflections of the Soviet Past in the Memoirs and Narratives of the Evangelical Christians-Baptists." In *State Secularism and Lived Religion in Soviet Russia and Ukraine*, edited by C. Wanner, 218–43. Washington, DC: Woodrow Wilson Center Press; New York: Oxford.

Parry, Jonathan. 1986. "The Gift, the Indian Gift and the 'Indian Gift.'" *Man* 21 (3): 453–73.

Paxson, Margaret. 2005. *Solovyovo: The Story of Memory in a Russian Village*. Washington, DC: Woodrow Wilson Center Press; Bloomington: Indiana University Press.

Pedersen, Morten Axel. 2011. *Not Quite Shamans: Spirit Worlds and Political Lives in Northern Mongolia*. Ithaca, NY: Cornell University Press.

Pelkmans, Mathijs. 2007. "'Culture' as a Tool and an Obstacle: Missionary Encounters in Post-Soviet Kyrgyzstan." *Journal of the Royal Anthropological Institute* 13 (4): 881–99.

———. 2009a. "Introduction: Post-Soviet Space and the Unexpected Turns of Religious Life." In *Conversion after Socialism: Disruptions, Modernisms and Technologies of Faith in the Former Soviet Union*, edited by M. Pelkmans, 1–16. Oxford: Berghahn.

———. 2009b. "Temporary Conversions: Encounters with Pentecostalism in Muslim Kyrgyzstan." In *Conversion after Socialism: Disruptions, Modernisms and Technologies of Faith in the Former Soviet Union*, edited by M. Pelkmans, 143–62. Oxford: Berghahn.

Perevalova, Yelena V. 2019. *Obskie ugry i nentsy Zapadnoy Sibiri: etnichnost' i vlast'*. St. Petersburg: MAE RAN.

Peris, Daniel. 1998. *Storming the Heavens: The Soviet League of the Militant Godless*. Ithaca, NY: Cornell University Press.

Pesn'. 2004. *Pesn' vozrozhdeniya. Sbornik dukhovnykh pesen yevangel'skikh khristian-baptistov*. 2nd ed. n.p.: Izdatel'stvo "Khristianin."

Petrone, Karen. 2000. *Life Has Become More Joyous, Comrades: Celebrations in the Time of Stalin*. Bloomington: Indiana University Press.

Petrov, Petre, and Lara Ryazanova-Clarke, eds. 2014. *The Vernaculars of Communism: Language, Ideology and Power in the Soviet Union and Eastern Europe*. London: Routledge.

Pickett, Howard. 2017. *Rethinking Sincerity and Authenticity: The Ethics of Theatricality in Kant, Kierkegaard, and Levinas*. Charlottesville: University of Virginia Press.

Pietz, William. 1985. "The Problem of the Fetish, I." *Res* 9:5–17.

Pika, Tat'yana I., comp. 1998. *Zemlya Yamal. Al'bom yamal'skikh ekspeditsiy V. P. Yevladova. The Land of Yamal. Album of Yamal Expeditions by V. Evladov*. Translated by V. Tsarev, K. Volkova, and T. Gindilis. Moscow: Sovetskiy sport.

Pilkington, Hilary. 2014. "Sounds of a 'Rotting City': Punk in Russia's Arctic Hinterland." In *Sounds and the City: Popular Music, Place, and Globalization*, edited by B. Lashua, K. Spracklen, and S. Wagg, 162–82. Vancouver: Palgrave.

Plattet, Patrick. 2013. "Sick of Shamanizing: In Search of Healing on the Kamchatkan Roads of World-Jesus." *Civilisations (Chamanismes en mouvement)* 61 (2): 69–88.

Podrazhayte. 2001. *Podrazhayte vere ikh. 40 let probuzhdennomu bratstvu*. n.p.: Izdatel'stvo "Khristianin," Sovet tserkvey YeKhB.

Popov, Andrey A. 1944. "Yeniseyskie nentsy (yuraki)." *Izvestiya Vsesoyuznogo geograficheskogo obshchestva* 76 (2–3): 76–95.

———. 1984. "The Family Life of the Dolgans." In *Kinship and Marriage in the Soviet Union*, edited by T. Dragadze, 192–219. London: Routledge.

Popova, Ul'yana G. 1981. "Perezhitki shamanizma u evenov." In *Problemy istorii obshchestvennogo soznaniya aborigenov Sibiri (po materialam vtoroy poloviny XIX–nachala XX v.)*, edited by I. S. Vdovin, 233–52. Leningrad: Nauka.

Poshekhonova, Ol'ga E. 2016. *Akt gosudarstvennyy istoriko-kul'turnoy ekspertizy o vklyuchenii v yedinyy gosudarstvennyy reyestr ob"ektov kul'turnogo naslediya "Svyashchennoe mesto Khada-Pe (Starushka-kamen')."* Tyumen.

Pouillon, Jean. 1982. "Remarks on the Verb 'to Believe.'" In *Between Belief and Transgression: Structuralist Essays in Religion, History, and Myth*, edited by M. Izard and P. Smith, 1–8. Chicago: University of Chicago Press.

Prokhorov, Constantine. 2013. *Russian Baptists and Orthodoxy, 1960–1990: A Comparative Study of Theology, Liturgy, and Traditions*. Carlisle: Langham Monographs.

Prokof'eva, Yekaterina D. 1953. "Materialy po religioznym predstavleniyam entsev." In *Sbornik Muzeya antropologii i etnografii* 14, edited by S. P. Tolstov, 194–230. Moscow: Izdatel'stvo Akademii Nauk SSSR.

———. 2018. "Sotsialisticheskaya rekonstruktsiya olennogo khozyaystva nentsev, 1949?" In *Nenetskoe olenevodstvo: geografiya, etnografiya, lingvistika*, edited by D. V. Arzyutov and M. D. Lyublinskaya, 133–54. St. Petersburg: MAE RAN.

Proyektnye. 1993. "Proyektnye predlozheniya po organizatsii territorii olen'ikh pastbishch krestyanskikh/fermerskikh khozyaystv olenevodcheskogo napravleniya na baze semey olenevodov-yedinolichnikov na territorii Nenetskogo okruga Arkhangel'skoy oblasti." Unpublished report by a land management organization. Murmansk.

Prozorov, Sergei. 2009. *The Ethics of Postcommunism: History and Social Praxis in Russia.* New York: Palgrave.

Pushkareva, Yelena T. 1999. "The Experience of Ethnological Reconstruction of Nenets Shamanistic Ritual on the Topic 'Prediction of the Future.'" In *Etnomusikologian Vuosikirja 1999*, edited by J. Niemi, 55–61. Helsinki: Suomen Etnomusikologinen Seura.

———. 2000. *Nenetskie pesni-khynabtsy: syuzhetika, semantika i poetika*. Moscow: Vostochnaya Literatura.

———. 2003. *Istoricheskaya tipologiya i etnicheskaya spetsifika nenetskikh mifov-skazok.* Moscow: Mysl'.

———. 2004. "Images of the Word in Nenets Folklore." *Anthropology & Archeology of Eurasia* 42 (4): 64–84.

———. 2007. *Kartina mira v fol'klore nentsev: sistemno-fenomenologicheskiy analiz.* Yekaterinburg: Basko.

———. 2019. *The Image of the Universe in the Folklore of the Nenets: Systematic and Phenomenological Analysis.* St Petersburg: Istoricheskaya Illustratsiya.

Pushkareva, Yelena T., and Aleksey A. Burykin. 2011. *Fol'klor narodov Severa*. St. Petersburg: Peterburgskoe Vostokovedenie.

Pushkareva, Yelena T., and Lyudmila V. Khomich, comp. 2001. *Fol'klor nentsev*. Novosibirsk: Nauka.

Pyrirko, Vasiliy. 2019. "V Yamal'skoy tundre zatikhaet zvuk shamanskogo bubna." *Krasnyy Sever* (Salekhard), June 22. https://ks-yanao.ru/news/obshchestvo/v-yamalskoy-tundre-ne-zatikhaet-zvuk-shamanskogo-bubna.

Rabinow, Paul. 2008. *Marking Time: On the Anthropology of the Contemporary*. Princeton, NJ: Princeton University Press.

Rappaport, Roy. 1999. *Ritual and Religion in the Making of Humanity*. Cambridge: Cambridge University Press.

Ravna, Zoia Vylka. 2019. *The Inter-Generational Transmission of Indigenous Knowledge by Nenets Women: Viewed in the Context of the State Educational System of Russia*. Tromsø: Arctic University of Norway.

———. 2021. "'Skills Come with Experience': A Pedagogical Study of Different Forms of Communication in Nenets Nomadic Communities in Northern Russia." *Learning and Instruction* 71:1–10.

Reshenie. 2015. "Reshenie 2–53/2015. Naryan-Marskiy gorodskoy sud." http://sudact.ru /regular/doc/8SwEHIvjROxl/.

Rethmann, Petra. 2001. *Tundra Passages: History and Gender in the Russian Far East*. University Park: Pennsylvania State University Press.

Richters, Katja. 2013. *The Post-Soviet Russian Orthodox Church*. London: Routledge.

Robbins, Joel. 2001a. "God Is Nothing but Talk: Modernity, Language, and Prayer in a Papua New Guinea Society." *American Anthropologist* 103 (4): 901–12.

———. 2001b. "Secrecy and the Sense of an Ending: Narrative, Time, and Everyday Millenarianism in Papua New Guinea and in Christian Fundamentalism." *Comparative Studies in Society and History* 43 (3): 525–51.

———. 2003. "On the Paradoxes of Global Pentecostalism and the Perils of Continuity Thinking." *Religion* 33 (3): 221–31.

———. 2004. *Becoming Sinners: Christianity and Moral Torment in a Papua New Guinea Society*. Berkeley: University of California Press.

———. 2007a. "Continuity Thinking and the Problem of Christian Culture." *Current Anthropology* 48 (1): 5–38.

———. 2007b. "You Can't Talk Behind the Holy Spirit's Back: Christianity and Changing Language Ideologies in a Papua New Guinea Society." In *Consequences of Contact: Language Ideologies and Sociocultural Transformations in Pacific Societies*, edited by M. Makihara and B. Schieffelin, 125–39. Oxford: Oxford University Press.

———. 2009. "Afterword." In *Native Christians: Modes and Effects of Christianity among Indigenous Peoples of the Americas*, edited by A. Vilaça and R. M. Wright, 229–38. Farnham: Ashgate.

———. 2010. "Anthropology, Pentecostalism, and the New Paul: Conversion, Event, and Social Transformation." In *Global Christianity, Global Critique*, special issue, *The South Atlantic Quarterly* 109 (4): 633–52.

———. 2011. "On Messianic Promise." In *Echoes of the Tambaran: Masculinity, History and the Subject in the Work of Donald F. Tuzin*, edited by D. Lipset and P. Roscoe, 183–94. Canberra: ANU E Press.

———. 2014. "The Anthropology of Christianity: Unity, Diversity, New Directions." *Current Anthropology* 55 (S10): S157–71.

———. 2015. "Dumont's Hierarchical Dynamism: Christianity and Individualism Revisited." *HAU: Journal of Ethnographic Theory* 5 (1): 173–95.

———. 2016. "What Is the Matter with Transcendence? On the Place of Religion in the New Anthropology of Ethics." *Journal of the Royal Anthropological Institute* 22 (4): 767–81.

———. 2019. "Pentecostalism and Forms of Individualism." In *Going to Pentecost: An Experimental Approach to Studies in Pentecostalism*, edited by A. Eriksen, R. L. Blanes, and M. MacCarthy, 187–92. New York: Berghahn.

———. 2020. *Theology and the Anthropology of Christian Life*. Oxford: Oxford University Press.

Robbins, Joel, and Alan Rumsey. 2008. "Introduction: Cultural and Linguistic Anthropology and the Opacity of Other Minds." *Anthropological Quarterly* 81 (2): 407–20.

Robbins, Joel, Bambi Schieffelin, and Aparecida Vilaça. 2014. "Evangelical Conversion and the Transformation of the Self in Amazonia and Melanesia: Christianity and New Forms of Anthropological Comparison." *Comparative Studies in Society and History* 56 (3): 1–32.

Roberts, Nathaniel. 2012. "Is Conversion a 'Colonization of Consciousness'?" *Anthropological Theory* 12 (3): 271–94.

———. 2016. *To Be Cared For: The Power of Conversion and Foreignness of Belonging in an Indian Slum*. Berkeley: University of California Press.

Rogers, Douglas. 2009. *The Old Faith and the Russian Land: A Historical Ethnography of Ethics in the Urals*. Ithaca, NY: Cornell University Press.

Romanova, Polina. 2022. "Ledkovy, Laptandery, Taybarey i Valey . . . ." *Region* 302 (8): 20–24.

Rosaldo, Michelle Z. 1980. *Knowledge and Passion: Ilongot Notions of Self and Social Life*. Cambridge: Cambridge University Press.

———. 1982. "The Things We Do with Words: Ilongot Speech Acts and Speech Act Theory in Philosophy." *Language in Society* 11 (2): 203–37.

Rouillard, Rémy. 2013. "Nomads in a Petro-Empire: Nenets Reindeer Herders and Russian Oil Workers in an Era of Flexible Capitalism." Unpublished doctoral dissertation, McGill University, Montréal.

Rozanova, Marya. 2019. "Indigenous Urbanization in Russia's Arctic: The Case of Nenets Autonomous Region." *Sibirica* 18 (3): 54–91.

Ruel, Malcolm. 1997. *Belief, Ritual and the Securing of Life: Reflexive Essays on a Bantu Religion*. Leiden: Brill.

Rutherford, Danilyn. 2006. "The Bible Meets the Idol: Writing and Conversion in Biak, Irian Jaya, Indonesia." In *The Anthropology of Christianity*, edited by F. Cannell, 240–72. Durham, NC: Duke University Press.

Safonova, Tatiana, and István Sántha. 2013. *Culture Contact in Evenki Land: A Cybernetic Anthropology of the Baikal Region*. Leiden: Brill.

Sahlins, Marshall. 1992. "The Economics of Develop-Man in the Pacific." *Res* 21:13–25.

———. 2013. *What Kinship Is—And Is Not*. Chicago: University of Chicago Press.

Salminen, Tapani. 1998. "Nenets." In *The Uralic Languages*, edited by D. Abondolo, 516–47. London: Routledge.

Samson-Normand de Chambourg, Dominique. 1998. *Ilir d'Anna Nerkagui: une page de vie autochtone dans le Grand Nord sibérien, 1917–1997*. Paris: Harmattan.

Sawatsky, Walter. 1981. *Soviet Evangelicals since World War II*. Scottdale, PA: Herald.

Schieffelin, Bambi B. 1990. *The Give and Take of Everyday Life: Language Socialization of Kaluli Children*. Cambridge: Cambridge University Press.

———. 2007. "Found in Translating: Reflexive Language across Time and Texts in Bosavi, Papua New Guinea." In *Consequences of Contact: Language Ideologies and Sociocultural Transformations in Pacific Societies*, edited by M. Makihara and B. Schieffelin, 140–65. Oxford: Oxford University Press.

Schott, Nils F. 2016. "Intuition, Interpellation, Insight: Elements of a Theory of Conversion." In *Words: Religious Language Matters*, edited by E. van den Hemel and A. Szafraniec, 199–210. New York: Fordham University Press.

Schrenk, Alexander G. 1848. *Reise nach dem Nordosten des europäischen Russlands, durch die Tundren der Samojeden, zum Arktischen Uralgebirge. Erster Theil*. Dorpat.

Scott, James C. 2009. *The Art of Not Being Governed: An Anarchist History of Upland Southeast Asia*. New Haven, CT: Yale University Press.

Serpivo, Stella Ye. 2016. *Zhenskoe prostranstvo v kul'ture nentsev*. St. Petersburg: Istoricheskaya illyustratsiya.

Severo-Zapadnoe. 2004. "Severo-Zapadnoe ob"edinenie MSTs YeKhB (iz zhizni bratstva)." *Vestnik istiny* 170 (4): 10–13.

Shashkov, Aleksandr. 1896. "Missiya na Yugorskom Share v poslednee desyatiletie." *Pravoslavnyy blagovestnik* 11:115–24; 12:178–85.

Shearer, David R. 2009. *Policing Stalin's Socialism: Repression and Social Order in the Soviet Union, 1924–1953*. New Haven, CT: Yale University Press.

Shemanovskiy, Ivan S. [Irinarkh]. 2011. *I. S. Shemanovskiy: izbrannye trudy. Tom 1–2*. Comp. L. F. Lipatova. Moscow: Sovetskiy sport.

Shestakova, Nadezhda. 2002. "Chelovek dvukh mirov." *Tyumenskie izvestiya* (Tyumen) 157, August 22.

Shevzov, Vera. 2004. *Russian Orthodoxy on the Eve of Revolution*. Oxford: Oxford University Press.

Sibgatullina, Gulnaz. 2020. *Languages of Islam and Christianity in Post-Soviet Russia*. Leiden: Brill.

Sidorov, Aleksey S. 1997 [1928]. *Znakharstvo, koldovstvo i porcha u naroda komi: materialy po psikhologii koldovstva*. St. Petersburg: Aleteyya.

Siikala, Anna-Leena. 1978. *The Rite Technique of the Siberian Shaman*. Helsinki: Suomalainen Tiedeakatemia.

———. 2002. *Mythic Images and Shamanism: A Perspective on Kalevala Poetry*. Helsinki: Suomalainen Tiedeakatemia.

Sillanpää, Lennard, ed. 2008. *Awakening Siberia: From Marginalization to Self-Determination: The Small Indigenous Nations of Northern Russia on the Eve of the Millennium*. Helsinki: University of Helsinki.

Simon, Gregory M. 2009. "The Soul Freed of Cares? Islamic Prayer, Subjectivity, and the Contradictions of Moral Selfhood in Minangkabau, Indonesia." *American Ethnologist* 36 (2): 258–75.

Simoncsics, Péter. 2005. "Pause and Silence in Nenets Poetic Diction." In *Shamanhood: An Endangered Language*, edited by J. Pentikäinen and P. Simoncsics, 77–83. Oslo: Novus.

Skachkov, I. F. 1934. *Antireligioznaya rabota na Kraynem Severe*. Moskva: OGIZ.

Skvirskaja, Vera. 2012. "Expressions and Experiences of Personhood: Spatiality and Objects in the Nenets Tundra Home." In *Animism in Rainforest and Tundra: Personhood, Animals, Plants and Things in Contemporary Amazonia and Siberia*, edited by M. Brightman, V. E. Grotti, and O. Ulturgasheva, 146–61. New York: Berghahn.

———. 2014. "Contested Souls: Christianisation, Millenarianism and Sentiments of Belonging on Indigenous Rural Yamal, Russia." *Études mongoles et sibériennes, centrasiatiques et tibétaines* 45:2–16.

Slezkine, Yuri. 1994. *Arctic Mirrors: Russia and the Small Peoples of the North*. Ithaca, NY: Cornell University Press.

Smith, Wilfred Cantwell. 1998 [1977]. *Believing: An Historical Perspective*. Oxford: One World.

Smolkin, Victoria. 2018. *A Sacred Space Is Never Empty: A History of Soviet Atheism*. Princeton, NJ: Princeton University Press.

Sneath, David. 2007. *The Headless State: Aristocratic Orders, Kinship Society, and Misrepresentations of Nomadic Inner Asia*. New York: Columbia University Press.

———. 2009. "Reading the Signs by Lenin's Light: Development, Divination and Metonymic Fields in Mongolia." *Ethnos* 74 (1): 72–90.

Solzhenitsyn, Aleksandr I. 1991 [1973]. *The Gulag Archipelago, 1918–1956: An Experiment in Literary Investigation. Vol. 1.* Translated by T. P. Whitney. New York: Harper and Row.

Song, Eun Sub. 2015. "The Effect of Bible Translation on Literacy among Nenets Christians." In *Language Vitality through Bible Translation*, edited by M. Beerle-Moor and V. Voinov, 217–23. New York: Peter Lang.

Ssorin-Chaikov, Nikolai. 2001. "Evenki Shamanistic Practices in Soviet Present and Ethnographic Present Perfect." *Anthropology of Consciousness* 12 (1): 1–18.

———. 2003. *The Social Life of the State in Subarctic Siberia*. Stanford, CA: Stanford University Press.

———. 2006. "On Heterochrony: Birthday Gifts to Stalin, 1949." *Journal of the Royal Anthropological Institute* 12 (2): 355–75.

Stammler, Florian. 2005. *Reindeer Nomads Meet the Market: Culture, Property and Globalisation at the "End of the Land."* Münster: LIT Verlag.

———. 2009. "Mobile Phone Revolution in the Tundra? Technological Change among Russian Reindeer Nomads." *Electronic Journal of Folklore* 41:47–78.

———. 2010. "Animal Diversity and Its Social Significance among Arctic Pastoralists." In *Good to Eat, Good to Live With: Nomads and Animals in Northern Eurasia and Africa*, edited by F. Stammler and H. Takakura, 215–43. Sendai: Center for Northeast Asia Studies, Tohoku University.

———. 2011. "Oil without Conflict? The Anthropology of Industrialisation in Northern Russia." In *Crude Domination: An Anthropology of Oil*, edited by A. Behrends, S. P. Reyna, and G. Schlee, 243–69. Oxford: Berghahn.

Stammler, Florian M., and Aytalina Ivanova. 2020. "From Spirits to Conspiracy? Nomadic Perceptions of Climate Change, Pandemics and Disease." *Anthropology Today* 36 (4): 8–12.

Stasch, Rupert. 2008. "Knowing Minds Is a Matter of Authority: Political Dimensions of Opacity Statements in Korowai Moral Psychology." *Anthropological Quarterly* 81 (2): 443–53.

———. 2009. *Society of Others: Kinship and Mourning in a West Papuan Place*. Berkeley: University of California Press.

———. 2011. "Word Avoidance as a Relation-Making Act: A Paradigm for Analysis of Name Utterance Taboos." *Anthropological Quarterly* 84 (1): 101–20.

Status. 2019. "Status gorozhan lishil olenevodov iz Vorkuty sotsial'noy pensii." https://www.bnkomi.ru/data/news/101694/.

Stépanoff, Charles, Charlotte Marchina, Camille Fossier, and Nicolas Bureau. 2017. "Animal Autonomy and Intermittent Coexistences: North Asian Modes of Herding." *Current Anthropology* 58 (1): 57–81.

Strathern, Marilyn. 1996. "Cutting the Network." *Journal of the Royal Anthropological Institute* 2 (3): 517–35.

———. 1999. *Property, Substance and Effect: Anthropological Essays on Persons and Things*. London: Athlone.

———. 2018. "Persons and Partible Persons." In *Schools and Styles of Anthropological Theory*, edited by M. Candea, 236–46. London: Routledge.

Strhan, Anna. 2015. *Aliens and Strangers? The Struggle for Coherence in the Everyday Lives of Evangelicals*. Oxford: Oxford University Press.

Stromberg, Peter G. 1993. *Language and Self-Transformation: A Study of the Christian Conversion Narrative*. Cambridge: Cambridge University Press.

———. 2015. "Wesleyan Sanctification and the Ethic of Self-Realization." *Ethos* 43 (4): 423–43.

Suslov, Innokentiy M. 1931. "Shamanstvo i bor'ba s nim." *Sovetskiy Sever* 3–4:89–152.

Szuchewycz, Bohdan. 1997. "Silence in Ritual Communication." In *Silence: Interdisciplinary Perspectives*, edited by A. Jaworski, 239–60. Berlin: De Gruyter.

Tambiah, Stanley J. 1990. *Magic, Science, Religion, and the Scope of Rationality*. Cambridge: Cambridge University Press.

Tannen, Deborah. 2007. *Talking Voices: Repetition, Dialogue, and Imagery in Conversational Discourse*. 2nd ed. Cambridge: Cambridge University Press.

Tannen, Deborah, and Muriel Saville-Troike, eds. 1985. *Perspectives on Silence*. Norwood, NJ: Ablex.

Tarasov, Oleg. 2002. *Icon and Devotion: Sacred Spaces in Imperial Russia*. London: Reaktion.

Tarkka, Lotte. 2013. *Songs of the Border People: Genre, Reflexivity, and Performance in Karelian Oral Poetry*. Translated by L. Virtanen. Helsinki: Suomalainen Tiedeakatemia.

Taylor, Charles. 1989. *Sources of the Self: The Making of Modern Identity*. Cambridge, MA: Harvard University Press.

Templing, Vladimir Ya., comp. 2003. *"I zdes' poyavlyaetsya zarya khristianstva . . .": Obdorskaya missiya 30-e–80-e gg. XIX v.* Tyumen: Mandr i ka.

———, comp. 2004. *Iz istorii Obdorskoy missii*. Tyumen: Mandr i ka.

———, comp. 2007. *Putevye zhurnaly missionerov Obdorskoy missii (60–70-e gg. XIX veka)*. 2nd ed. Tyumen: Mandr i ka.

Terekhina, Alexandra, and Alexander Volkovitskiy. 2023. "Climate Change through the Eyes of Yamal Reindeer Herders." In *The Siberian World*, edited by J. Ziker, J. Ferguson, and V. Davydov, 166–78. New York: Routledge.

Tereshchenko, Natal'ya M. 1990. *Nenetskiy epos. Materialy i issledovaniya po samodiyskim yazykam*. Leningrad: Nauka.

———. 2003 [1965]. *Nenetsko-russkiy slovar'*. St. Petersburg: Prosveshchenie.

Thibaudat, Jean-Pierre, and Franck Desplanques. 2005. *Nénètses de Sibérie: les Hommes debout*. Paris: Editions du Chêne.

Thompson, Niobe. 2008. *Settlers on the Edge: Identity and Modernization on Russia's Arctic Frontier*. Vancouver: UBC Press.

Thrift, Nigel. 2008. *Non-Representational Theory: Space, Politics, Affect*. London: Routledge.

Throop, C. Jason. 2014. "Moral Moods." *Ethos* 42 (1): 65–83.

Tishkov, Valeriy A., ed. 2016. *Rossiyskaya Arktika: korennye narody i promyshlennoe osvoyenie*. Moscow: Nestor-Istoriya.

Tolkachev, Viktor F. 1990. "Otshel'niki tundry, ili lyudi, kotorykh . . . net." *Pravda Severa* (Arkhangelsk), September 9.

———. 1999. *Svyashchennye narty*. Arkhangelsk: Severo-Zapadnoe knizhnoe izdatel'stvo.

———, ed. 2000a. *Nenetskiy kray: skvoz' v'yugi let. Ocherki. Stat'i. Dokumenty*. Arkhangelsk: Pomorskiy gosudarstvennyy universitet imeni M. V. Lomonosova.

———. 2000b. "Rossiya. Krayniy Sever. Vlast'." In *Nenetskiy kray: skvoz' v'yugi let. Ocherki. Stat'i. Dokumenty*, edited by V. F. Tolkachev, 260–316. Arkhangelsk: Pomorskiy gosudarstvennyy universitet imeni M. V. Lomonosova.

———. 2004. *Zakon kapkana*. Arkhangelsk: Elmor.

Tomlinson, Matt. 2009a. "Efficacy, Truth, and Silence: Language Ideologies in Fijian Christian Conversions." *Comparative Studies in Society and History* 51 (1): 64–90.

———. 2009b. *In God's Image: The Metaculture of Fijian Christianity*. Berkeley: University of California Press.

Tomlinson, Matt, and Matthew Engelke. 2006. "Meaning, Anthropology, Christianity." In *The Limits of Meaning: Case Studies in the Anthropology of Christianity*, edited by M. Engelke and M. Tomlinson, 1–37. Oxford: Berghahn.

Toulouze, Eva. 2004. "The Beginning of Literacy and Literature among the Tundra Nenets." *Suomalais-Ugrilaisen Seuran Aikakauskirja—Journal de la Société Finno-Ougrienne* 90:215–29.

———. 2006. "Irinarh Šemanovskij et la mission d'Obdorsk: une page de l'évangélisation des Khantys et des Nenets." *Études finno-ougriennes* 37:29–63.

———. 2011a. "Indigenous Agency in the Missionary Encounter: The Example of the Khanty and the Nenets." *Journal of Ethnology and Folkloristics* 5 (1): 63–74.

———. 2011b. "Movement and Enlightenment in the Russian North." *Folklore: Electronic Journal of Folklore* 49:97–112.

Toulouze, Eva, and Liivo Niglas. 2019. *Yuri Vella's Fight for Survival in Western Siberia: Oil, Reindeer and Gods*. Cambridge: Cambridge Scholars.

Toulouze, Eva, and Laur Vallikivi. 2016. "Les langues dans un miroir déformant: Que reflète le recensement russe de 2010 en matière de langues finno-ougriennes?" *Études finno-ougriennes* 47:7–43.

Toulouze, Eva, Laur Vallikivi, and Art Leete. 2017. "The Cultural Bases in the North: Sovietisation and Indigenous Resistance." In *Ethnic and Religious Minorities in Stalin's Soviet Union: New Dimensions of Research*, edited by A. Kotljarchuk and O. Sundström, 199–223. Huddinge: Södertörn University.

Trilling, Lionel. 1972. *Sincerity and Authenticity*. Cambridge, MA: Harvard University Press.

Troeltsch, Ernst. 1960 [1912]. *The Social Teaching of the Christian Churches. Vol. 2*. Translated by O. Wyon. New York: Harper Torchbooks.

Tserkov'. 2008. *Tserkov' dolzhna ostavat'sya Tserkov'yu: neobratimye desyatiletiya 1917–1937 gg. v istorii yevangel'skogo i baptistskogo dvizheniy*. n.p.: Mezhdunarodnyy sovet tserkvey YeKhB.

Tugolukov, Vladilen A. 2005. "O rezul'tatakh obsledovaniya evenkiyskikh kolkhozov Amurskoy oblasti. 1960 g." In *Etnologicheskaya ekspertiza: narody Severa Rossii. 1959–1962 gody*, edited by Z. P. Sokolova and Ye. A. Pivneva, 228–36. Moscow: Institut etnologii i antropologii RAN.

Tuisku, Tuula. 1999. *Nenetsien ankarat elämisen ehdot tundralla ja kylässä. Poronhoidon sopeutumisstrategiat ja delokalisoitumisprosessi Nenetsiassa*. Rovaniemi: Lapin yliopisto.

———. 2001. "The Displacement of Nenets Women from Reindeer Herding and the Tundra in the Nenets Autonomous Okrug, Northwestern Russia." *Acta Borealia* 18 (2): 41–60.

———. 2002. "Transition Period in the Nenets Autonomous Okrug: Changing and Unchanging Life of Nenets People." In *People and the Land: Pathways to Reform in Post-Soviet Siberia*, edited by E. Kasten, 189–205. Berlin: Dietrich Reimer Verlag.

Tumarkin, Nina. 1983. *Lenin Lives! The Lenin Cult in Soviet Russia*. Cambridge, MA: Harvard University Press.

Tuzin, Donald. 1997. *The Cassowary's Revenge: The Life and Death of Masculinity in a New Guinea Society*. Chicago: University of Chicago Press.

Ulturgasheva, Olga. 2012. *Narrating the Future in Siberia: Childhood, Adolescence and Autobiography among Young Eveny*. New York: Berghahn.

Ural'skoe. 1999. "Ural'skoe ob"edinenie (iz zhizni bratstva)." *Vestnik istiny* 146 (2): 33–35.

Vagramenko, Tatiana. 2014. "Religious Conversion and Nenets Bricolage: Making Modernity in the Polar Ural Tundra." Unpublished doctoral dissertation, National University of Ireland Maynooth, Maynooth.

——. 2017a. "'Blood' Kinship and Kinship in Christ's Blood: Nomadic Evangelism in the Nenets Tundra." *Journal of Ethnology and Folkloristics* 11 (1): 151–69.

——. 2017b. "Indigeneity and Religious Conversion in Siberia: Nenets 'Eluding' Culture and Indigenous Revitalization." In *Marginalised and Endangered Worldviews: Comparative Studies on Contemporary Eurasia, India and South America*, edited by L. Guzy and J. Kapaló, 207–30. Münster: LIT Verlag.

——. 2018. "Chronotopes of Conversion and the Production of Christian Fundamentalism in the Post-Soviet Arctic." *Sibirica* 17 (1): 63–91.

Vakhtin, Nikolay B. 2001. *Yazyki narodov Severa v XX veke. Ocherki yazykovogo sdviga*. St. Petersburg: Dmitriy Bulanin.

——. 2005. "The Russian Arctic between Missionaries and Soviets: The Return of Religion, Double Belief and Double Identity?" In *Rebuilding Identities: Pathways to Reform in Post-Soviet Siberia*, edited by E. Kasten, 27–38. Berlin: Dietrich Reimer Verlag.

——. 2006. "Transformations in Siberian Anthropology: An Insider's Perspective." In *World Anthropologies: Disciplinary Transformations within Systems of Power*, edited by G. L. Ribeiro and A. Escobar, 49–68. Oxford: Berg.

Valeri, Valerio. 2000. *The Forest of Taboos: Morality, Hunting, and Identity among the Huaulu of the Moluccas*. Madison: University of Wisconsin Press.

Valk, Ülo. 2001. *The Black Gentleman: Manifestations of the Devil in Estonian Folk Religion*. Helsinki: Suomalainen Tiedeakatemia.

Vallikivi, Laur. 2003. "Minority and Mission: Christianisation of the European Nenets." *Pro Ethnologia* 15:109–30.

——. 2005. "Two Wars in Conflict: Resistance among Nenets Reindeer Herders in the 1940s." In *The Northern Peoples and States: Changing Relationships (Studies in Folk Culture* 5), edited by A. Leete and Ü. Valk, 14–54. Tartu: Tartu University Press.

——. 2009. "Christianisation of Words and Selves: Nenets Reindeer Herders Joining the State through Conversion." In *Conversion after Socialism: Disruptions, Modernities and the Technologies of Faith*, edited by M. Pelkmans, 59–83. Oxford: Berghahn.

——. 2014a. "Les rennes maintiennent la langue nenets en vie." *Études finno-ougriennes* 45:169–194.

——. 2014b. "On the Edge of Space and Time: Evangelical Missionaries in the Tundra of Arctic Russia." *Journal of Ethnology and Folkloristics* 8 (2): 95–120.

——. 2017. "Taking Religion Seriously: Fieldwork among Animists and Evangelical Christians in Arctic Russia." *Forum for Anthropology and Culture* 13:112–21.

——. 2022. "On Thin Ice: Nenets Reindeer Herders' Changing Perception of Their Environment after Conversion to Evangelical Christianity." *Lagoonscapes* 2 (1): 55–74.

——. 2023. "Missionaries in the Russian Arctic: Religious and Ideological Changes among Nenets Reindeer Herders." In *The Siberian World*, edited by J. Ziker, J. Ferguson, and V. Davydov, 461–74. New York: Routledge.

van Asselt, Willem. 2007. "The Prohibition of Images and Protestant Identity." In *Iconoclasm and Iconoclash: Struggle for Religious Identity*, edited by W. van Asselt, P. van Geest, D. Müller, and T. Salemink, 299–311. Leiden: Brill.

van der Veer, Peter, ed. 1996. *Conversion to Modernities: The Globalization of Christianity*. New York: Routledge.

———. 2006. "Conversion and Coercion: The Politics of Sincerity and Authenticity." In *Cultures of Conversions*, edited by J. N. Bremmer, W. J. van Bekkum, and A. L. Molendijk, 2–14. Leuven: Peeters.

Vasil'ev, Vladimir I. 2006a. "O deyatel'nosti sovkhozov i predpriyatiy rybnoy promyshlennosti Yamalo-Nenetskogo natsional'nogo okruga Tyumenskoy oblasti v sfere pod"ema ekonomiki promyslovogo khozyaystva i uluchsheniya material'nogo blagosostoyaniya korennogo naseleniya Severa. 1974 g." In *Etnologicheskaya ekspertiza: narody Severa Rossii. 1963–1980 gody*, edited by Z. P. Sokolova and Ye. A. Pivneva, 218–28. Moscow: Institut etnologii i antropologii RAN.

———. 2006b. "Sovremennoe sostoyanie naseleniya yuzhnogo poberezh'ya Yamala (Panayevskiy sel'sovet Yamalo-Nenetskogo avtonomnogo okruga). 1982 g." In *Etnologicheskaya ekspertiza: narody Severa Rossii. 1981–1984 gody*, edited by Z. P. Sokolova and Ye. A. Pivneva, 187–98. Moscow: Institut etnologii i antropologii RAN.

Vasilevich, Glafira M. 2005. "Evenki Katangskogo rayona Evenkiyskogo natsional'nogo okruga." In *Etnologicheskaya ekspertiza: narody Severa Rossii. 1959–1962 gody*, edited by Z. P. Sokolova and Ye. A. Pivneva, 7–44. Moscow: Institut etnologii i antropologii RAN.

Vaté, Virginie. 2009. "Redefining Chukchi Practices in Contexts of Conversion to Pentecostalism." In *Conversion after Socialism: Disruptions, Modernisms and Technologies of Faith in the Former Soviet Union*, edited by M. Pelkmans, 39–57. Oxford: Berghahn.

Veniamin [Smirnov, Vasiliy N.]. 1851. *O obrashchenii v khristianstvo mezenskikh samoyedov v 1825–1830 godakh. Zapiski Arkhimandrita Veniamina*. St. Petersburg.

———. 1855. "Samoyedy mezenskie." *Vestnik Imperatorskogo Russkogo geograficheskogo obshchestva* 14:77–136.

Ventsel, Aimar. 2005. *Reindeer, Rodina and Reciprocity: Kinship and Property Relations in a Siberian Village*. Münster: LIT Verlag.

Verbov, Grigoriy D. 1939. "Perezhitki rodovogo stroya u nentsev." *Sovetskaya etnografiya* 2:43–66.

Vershinin, Yevgeniy V., and Georgiy P. Vizgalov, comp. 2004. *Obdorskiy kray i Mangazeya v XVII veke. Sbornik dokumentov*. Yekaterinburg: Tezis.

Vilaça, Aparecida. 2016. *Praying and Preying: Christianity in Indigenous Amazonia*. Berkeley: University of California Press.

Vins, Georgi. 1979 [1976]. *Three Generations of Suffering*. Translated by J. Ellis. London: Hodder and Stoughton.

———, comp. 1989. *Let the Waters Roar: Evangelists in the Gulag*. Grand Rapids, MI: Baker Book House.

Vitebsky, Piers. 1992. "Landscape and Self-Determination among the Eveny: The Political Environment of Siberian Reindeer Herders Today." In *Bush Base, Forest Farm: Culture, Environment and Development*, edited by E. Croll and D. Parkin, 223–46. London: Routledge.

———. 1993. *Dialogues with the Dead: The Discussion of Mortality among the Sora of Eastern India*. Cambridge: Cambridge University Press.

———. 1995. *The Shaman*. London: Duncan Baird.

———. 2005. *Reindeer People: Living with Animals and Spirits in Siberia*. London: HarperCollins.

———. 2008. "Loving and Forgetting: Moments of Inarticulacy in Tribal India." *Journal of the Royal Anthropological Institute* 14 (2): 243–61.

———. 2012. "Repeated Returns and Special Friends: From Mythic First Encounter to Shared Historical Change." In *Returns to the Field: Multitemporal Research and Contemporary Anthropology*, edited by S. Howell and A. Talle, 180–202. Bloomington: Indiana University Press.

———. 2017a. *Living without the Dead: Loss and Redemption in a Jungle Cosmos*. Chicago: Chicago University Press.

———. 2017b. *The Sora "Tribe"—Animist, Hindu, Christian*, online supplement to *Living without the Dead: Loss and Redemption in a Jungle Cosmos*. Chicago: Chicago University Press. http://www.press.uchicago.edu/sites/Vitebsky.

Vitebsky, Piers, and Anatoly Alekseyev. 2015a. "What Is a Reindeer? Indigenous Perspectives from Northeast Siberia." *Polar Record* 51 (4): 413–21.

———. 2015b. "Casting Timeshadows: Pleasure and Sadness of Moving among Nomadic Reindeer Herders in North-East Siberia." *Mobilities* 10 (4): 518–30.

Vittenburg, Yevgeniya P. 2003. *Pavel Vittenburg: geolog, polyarnik, uznik GULAGa (vospominaniya docheri)*. St. Petersburg: Nestor-Istoriya.

Viveiros de Castro, Eduardo. 1998. "Cosmological Deixis and Amerindian Perspectivism." *Journal of the Royal Anthropological Institute* 4 (3): 469–88.

Vladimirova, Vladislava. 2006. *Just Labor: Labor Ethic in a Post-Soviet Reindeer Herding Community*. Doctoral dissertation, Uppsala: Uppsala universitet.

———. 2017. "Producers' Cooperation within or against Cooperative Agricultural Institutions? The Case of Reindeer Husbandry in Post-Soviet Russia." *Journal of Rural Studies* 53:247–58.

———. 2018. "Security Strategies of Indigenous Women in Nenets Autonomous Region, Russia." In *Gender in the Arctic*, special issue, edited by J. O. Habeck and V. Vladimirova. *Polar Geography* 3:164–81.

Volzhanina, Yelena A. 2010. *Etnodemograficheskie protsessy v srede nentsev Yamala v XX– nachale XXI veka*. Novosibirsk: Nauka.

Vorob'ev, Denis V. 2013. "Contemporary Beliefs of Northern Wild Deer Hunters: (The Case of the Chirinda Evenki)." *Anthropology & Archeology of Eurasia* 52 (3): 34–58.

V zone. 2022. "V zone voyennogo konflikta." *Vestnik istiny* 262 (2): 23–25.

Walters, Philip. 1993. "A Survey of Soviet Religious Policy." In *Religious Policy in the Soviet Union*, edited by S. P. Ramet, 3–30. Cambridge: Cambridge University Press.

Wanner, Catherine. 2007. *Communities of the Converted: Ukrainians and Global Evangelism*. Ithaca, NY: Cornell University Press.

———. 2009. "Conversion and the Mobile Self: Evangelicalism as 'Travelling Culture.'" In *Conversion after Socialism: Disruptions, Modernisms and Technologies of Faith in the Former Soviet Union*, edited by M. Pelkmans, 163–82. Oxford: Berghahn.

———, ed. 2012. *State Secularism and Lived Religion in Soviet Russia and Ukraine*. Washington, DC: Woodrow Wilson Center Press.

Weber, Max. 2001 [1930]. *The Protestant Ethic and the Spirit of Capitalism*. Translated by T. Parsons. London: Routledge.

———. 2009. *From Max Weber: Essays in Sociology*. Translated and edited by H. H. Gerth and C. Wright Mills. London: Routledge.

Webster, Joseph. 2013. *The Anthropology of Protestantism: Faith and Crisis among Scottish Fishermen*. New York: Palgrave.

Werbner, Richard. 2011. "The Charismatic Dividual and the Sacred Self." *Journal of Religion in Africa* 41 (2): 180–205.

White, John Edward. 2020. *Factors Behind the Ukrainian Evangelical Missionary Surge from 1989 to 1999*. Eugene, OR: Pickwick.

Wiget, Andrew, and Olga Balalaeva. 2007. "Crisis, Conversion, and Conflict: Evangelical Christianity, Rapid Change, and the Eastern Khanty." *Sibirica* 6 (1): 1–29.

———. 2011. *Khanty, People of the Taiga: Surviving the Twentieth Century*. Fairbanks: University of Alaska Press.

Willerslev, Rane. 2007. *Soul Hunters: Hunting, Animism, and Personhood among the Siberian Yukaghirs*. Berkeley: University of California Press.

Willerslev, Rane, Piers Vitebsky, and Anatoly Alekseyev. 2015. "Sacrifice and the Ideal Hunt: A Cosmological Explanation for the Origin of Reindeer Domestication." *Journal of the Royal Anthropological Institute* 21 (1): 1–23.

Williams, Bernard. 2011 [1985]. *Ethics and the Limits of Philosophy*. London: Routledge.

Witte, John, Jr. 1999. "Introduction." In *Proselytism and Orthodoxy in Russia: The New War for Souls*, edited by J. Witte and M. Bourdeaux, 1–27. New York: Orbis.

Yadne, Nina N. 1995. *Ya rodom iz tundry*. Tyumen: SoftDizayn.

———. 2006. *Drevo zhizni*. Nadym: Zaural'e.

Yamalo-Nenetskiy. 1998. "Yamalo-Nenetskiy avtonomnyy okrug; do kraya zemli (iz zhizni bratstva)." *Vestnik istiny* 141 (1): 30–40.

Yasinski, Marek E., and Oleg V. Ovsyannikov. 2003. *Pustozersk. Russkiy gorod v Arktike*. St. Petersburg: Peterburgskoe vostokovedenie.

Yevladov, Vladimir P. 1992. *Po tundram Yamala k Belomu ostrovu. Ekspeditsiya na Krayniy Sever poluostrova Yamal v 1928–1929 gg*. Tyumen: Institut problem osvoyeniya Severa SO RAN.

———. 2010. *Polyarnaya yamal'skaya zimovka: Severo-Obskaya Ikhtiologicheskaya ekspeditsiya Vsesoyuznogo Arkticheskogo Instituta 1935–1936 godov*. Yekaterinburg: Ural'skiy rabochiy.

Yevsyugin, Arkadiy D. 1979. *Nentsy arkhangel'skikh tundr*. Arkhangelsk: Severo-Zapadnoe knizhnoe izdatel'stvo.

———. 1993. *Sud'ba kleymennaya GULAGom*. Naryan-Mar.

Yoshida [Esida], Atsushi. 1997. *Kul'tura pitaniya gydanskikh nentsev (interpretatsiya i sotsial'naya adaptatsiya)*. Moscow: Institut etnologii i antropologii RAN.

———. 2001. "Some Characteristics of the Tundra Nenets Reindeer Herders of Western Siberia and Their Social Adaptation." In *Parks, Property, and Power: Managing Hunting Practice and Identity within State Policy Regimes*, edited by D. G. Anderson and K. Ikeya, 67–80. Osaka: National Museum of Ethnology.

Yurchak, Alexei. 2006. *Everything Was Forever, Until It Was No More: The Last Soviet Generation*. Princeton, NJ: Princeton University Press.

Yur'ev, Gennadiy. 1919. "Zimniy mesyats v Bol'shezemel'skoy i vesna v Karskoy tundre." *Izvestiya Arkhangel'skogo obshchestva izucheniya Russkogo Severa* 3–4:62–66.

Zagrebina, Inna. 2017. "Pravovoe regulirovanie missionerskoy deyatel'nosti v Rossii: kak ne stat' zhertvoy 'zakona Yarovoy'?" In *Religiya i pravo v sovremennoy Rossii*, edited by R. Lunkin and I. Zagrebina, 174–90. Moscow: Yurisprudentsiya.

Zhilin, Nikolay T. 1963. *Nesushchie svet (rasskazy o rabote kluba ateistov Vorkuty)*. Syktyvkar: Komi knizhnoe izdatel'stvo.

Zhitkov, Boris M. 1913. *Poluostrov Yamal*. St. Petersburg.

Zhuravleva, Tat'yana Yu. 2000. "K voprosu ob organizatsii i funktsionirovanii kochevoy shkoly v obshchine nentsev-yedinolichnikov 'Yambto.'" In *Korennye etnosy Severa Yevropeyskoy chasti Rossii na poroge novogo tysyacheletiya: istoriya, sovremennost', perspektivy*, edited by E. A. Savel'eva, 524–27. Syktyvkar: Komi Nauchnyy Tsentr UrO RAN.

Zigon, Jarrett. 2010. *Making the New Post-Soviet Person: Moral Experience in Contemporary Moscow*. Leiden: Brill.

———. 2011a. *HIV Is God's Blessing: Rehabilitating Morality in Neoliberal Russia*. Berkeley: University of California Press.

———, ed. 2011b. *Multiple Moralities and Religions in Post-Soviet Russia*. Oxford: Berghahn.

Ziker, John P. 2002. *Peoples of the Tundra: Northern Siberians in the Post-Communist Transition*. Prospect Heights: Waveland.

Žižek, Slavoj. 1999. *The Ticklish Subject*. London: Verso.

———. 2008. *The Plague of Fantasies*. 2nd ed. London: Verso.

Znamenski, Andrei A. 1999. *Shamanism and Christianity: Native Encounters with Russian Orthodox Missions in Siberia and Alaska, 1820–1917*. Westport: Greenwood.

———. 2003. *Shamanism in Siberia. Russian Records of Indigenous Spirituality*. Dordrecht: Kluwer.

Zorbas, Konstantinos. 2021. *Shamanic Dialogues with the Invisible Dark in Tuva, Siberia: The Cursed Lives*. Cambridge: Cambridge Scholars.

Zuyeva, Tat'yana N. 2017. *Zapiski zapolyarnogo vracha*. Naryan-Mar.

INDEX

Adam, 132

aesthetics, 119, 143, 245; Baptist style, 175; in human-reindeer relationship, 26

Agamben, Giorgio, 276n2

agency, 14, 16–17, 37, 92, 131–132, 137, 139, 148, 150, 180, 201–202, 245, 265n27, 269n2, 276n28

Alekseyenko, Yevgenia, 9

Aksarka, 49

alcohol (vodka): being offered to Nenets, 22, 48, 65; in Christians' rhetoric, 89–90, 96, 123, 149, 150, 160; and coupons, 63; destructiveness of, 70, 95–96, 166, 175, 190, 250 (*see also* devil); and hospitality, 78, 95, 250; and imitating Russians, 43, 61; offered to spirits, 97, 141, 155, 161, 175, 176f, 186, 270n5 (*see also* sacrifice); rejection motivating conversion, 37, 85, 94–98, 247, 250; and singing, 182 (*see also* personal song); struggling to abandon, 96, 200, 204. See also *ikota*, Independents, non-Christians, spirits

allowances, 66–67, 69–70, 143, 265n28

all-terrain vehicle (*vezdekhod*), 3, 54, 119, 121, 122f, 125; "white vehicle", 3, 146

All-Union Council of Evangelical Christians-Baptists: Baptists dissatisfied with, 113; complying with the state regulations, 113, 115; formation of, 112; monitored by the authorities, 112, 116; and Vorkuta Pentecostal Church, 268n2. *See also* Council of Churches of Evangelical Christians-Baptists, Pentecostals, Registered Baptists, Unregistered Baptists

Althusser, Louis, 179, 274n10

Amderma, 24, 51, 55, 64f, 65f, 66–67, 96, 181, 265n28; and Gulag, 47, 49; Village Council of, 63

anger, 200, 232–233, 280n12. *See also* emotion, heart, sin

animists, 4, 10, 37, 243, 247, 257n4, 258n8, 260n26, 272n24; and ontology, 33–34;

and rituals, 23, 34. *See also* ethics, non-Christians, "pagan", promise, sacrifice

antireligious campaign: and Khrushchev, 112; and Soviet institutions, 112–113. *See also* atheism

Arctic Ocean, xiv, 3, 24, 25, 47, 56; and missionaries' ends of the earth, 121–122. *See also* ends of the earth

Aristotle, 13, 279n4

Arkhangelsk, 50, 119, 264n22; Province of, 56

army, 4, 49, 50, 53–54, 60, 67, 222; and Baptists, 112, 116; conscripted to, 49, 61, 67, 265n25, 268n9; Nenets trading with personnel from, 32, 55, 59f

articulacy: missionaries demanding, 14, 178, 217, 246, 273n5. *See also* Baptist language, language, speech

Asad, Talal, 81–83

atheism: atheist agitators in Vorkuta, 112–113; League of Militant Atheists, 112; in a life story of a Nenets, 62, 96; and the Soviet state, 9. *See also* antireligious campaign, heart

Augustine, 280n14

Austin, J. L., 12, 16–17, 191, 194, 199, 201, 213, 276n2

authoritative discourse, 205, 209, 214–215, 276n2

authority, 202; among Christians, 13, 78–80, 146, 148, 166, 207–208; and women, 97

autonomy (value), 32, 167, 173, 226–228. *See also* Independents

Avvakum, archpriest, 259n15

Badiou, Alain, 83–84, 102, 236–237, 281n16

Baidarata, 50, 58

Bakhtin, Mikhail, 201–202, 214–215, 237–238

baptism (ritual), 2f, 3, 5, 6, 92, 93, 118, 203–213, 225; compared among Baptists and Pentecostals, 93, 143; examination before,

16, 204; by immersion, 205, 268n10; and intentionality, 165, 209 (*see also* intention); Nenets version of, 36; and Nenets women, 93; among Pentecostals, 140, 143-144, 145f, 149, 208; and postbaptismal service, 209–213; as a promise, 11, 205; Spirit baptism, 148, 150. *See also* prayer, sermon

Baptist language, 13, 102, 197–219; and automatism, 218; and entextualization, 206; focused on representation and intention, 196; and language ideology, *see* language ideology; as love-talk, 215–216 (*see also* love speech); and public speaking, 145; and rigidity in rituals, 205–209, 278n15; as "speaking Baptist", 204, 238, 264n23; struggling with, 216–217; and witnessing, 215. *See also* articulacy, language, prayer, repentance, sermon, speech, witnessing, words

Baptist missionaries, 3–4, 77, 101, 104–130; author's relations with, 105–108; compared to Pentecostals, 143, 148, 151, 160; competing with Pentecostal missionaries, 5, 6, 139–148; complaining over converts' ignorance, 246; and evangelizing strategy, 132, 181, 267n10; and language barrier, 269n15; as matchmakers, 270n11; on Pentecostals, 147; perceived as "foreign" in Russia, 36; prohibit women to sermonize, 146; on secular entertainment, 127, 134; on translating, 126, 258n7, 269n16 (*see also* translation); and women, 146. *See also* conversion, pastor, Pentecostal missionaries, Unregistered Baptists

Baptists. *See* Baptist missionaries, Registered Baptists, Unregistered Baptists

Basso, Keith, 172

Baturin, Nikolay, 111

bears, 189

Belarus, 68

belief, 11, 32, 81, 244, 245, 258n8, 270n5; and language, 4; and loyalty, 150, 199, 208; system of, 8. *See also* certainty, devil, God, Jesus

Beloyarsk, 267n10

Belyi Island, 123, 268n3

Belykh, Viktor, 268n8

Benedictines, 197

Besnier, Niko, 214

Bialecki, Jon, 224, 279n4, 282n1

Bible (scriptures), 36, 68, 90, 92, 127, 134–136, 138, 153, 154, 156, 157, 162, 182, 198, 199, 201–202, 206–207, 209, 214, 215, 218, 219, 220, 268n10, 276n1, 280n11; Nenets translations from, 14, 126, 258n7 (*see also* translation); as physical copies, 88, 110, 135, 144–145, 151, 269n4; quoting from, 10, 79, 88, 135, 201, 218, 243, 277n10; reading of, 3, 6, 14, 15f, 78–79, 93, 98, 114, 118, 143, 146, 200, 210, 221, 225–226, 233, 234–235, 277n6, 277n10; Russian version of, 126. *See also* God's Word, literalism, sacred objects

Billig, Michael, 174

birth, 33, 162, 264n22; birth control denounced by Baptists, 128–129; certificates, 65, 264n21; and Nenets spirits, 142, 230, 270n9, 271n13; and silent "confession", 274n11

Bjørklund, Ivar, 68

body, 4, 13, 194, 222, 279n2; Christian view of, 90, 129, 266n1; *ikota* in, 175, 226 (*see also* ikota); of a *khekhe*, 164–165; and soul, 187. *See also* language, soul

Bolshezemelskaya District, 47–48, 54, 263n15

Bolshezemelskaya tundra. *See* Great Land tundra

born-again Christian, 107, 200, 202, 204, 205, 210, 214, 218, 220, 222, 224–225, 269n15, 276n27. *See also* conversion

Bourdieu, Pierre, 7, 172, 214

Boyko, Nikolay, 111, 218

Brezhnev, Leonid, 62, 96

bridewealth, bride-price (*nye mirq*), 23, 226, 273n8, 279n5. *See also* matchmaking

Brown, Kate, 46

Brusco, Elizabeth, 97

burial, 4, 23, 91, 190, 265n27. *See also* dead, death

Butler, Judith, 179–180, 192, 194, 199, 276n29

burning of sacred objects. *See* fire, sacred objects, shaman

California, 224

Calvinists, 132, 201, 218, 231

Cannell, Fenella, 102, 224

cards (playing), 78, 90, 177, 190, 204, 272n25
Cassian, John, 222–223
Castrén, Matthias, 92
Catholics, 12, 275n21
Cavell, Stanley, 12, 277n11
Central Asia, 153, 261n29, 267n12
certainty: and belief, 208, 210, 230–231, 233, 245, 279n9; and lack of it, 203–204, 275n25; of salvation, 223, 224, 231, 240, 251 (*see also* salvation)
Cervantes, Miguel de, 158
character (moral), 183, 191, 193, 219, 220, 233–234, 235, 245, 276n26, 280n11. *See also* ethics
Chernov, Georgi, 23–24
Christ's body (church), 102, 116, 228. *See also* Jesus
Chukchi, 261n29; as pejorative label, 267n12
Chukhontsev, Vladimir, 267n11
city (*marq*), 3, 24, 62, 63, 89, 105, 110, 113, 148, 216, 267n12; dangers related to, 103, 246; prayer house in, 77, 80, 86, 135; youth being attracted to, 29, 99–100, 173, 223 (*see also* youth). *See also* sedentarization, Vorkuta
clan-community (*obshchina*), 81, 88, 257n2, 265n26, 265n28, 266n30. *See also* Tybertya, Yamb-To
clan, 23, 188, 262n4, 280n12. *See also* kin, name
climate change, 260n21
coherence, 240; Christians striving for, 11–12, 38, 233, 235. *See also* ethics, self-transformation
Coleman, Simon, 13, 276n27
collective farm (kolkhoz), xiii, 8, 9, 19, 26, 48–49, 52–53, 61, 62, 227, 250, 264–265n25; "Friendship of Peoples" in Karataika, 58; Independents joining, 62–63, 260n25, 265n26; members compared to Independents, 25, 32, 37, 39, 40, 58, 60, 62, 91, 98, 222; pressuring Independents, 53; and privatization, 64, 258n12; "Red October" in Ust-Kara (Kara), 53, 56, 62, 67, 95, 266n30; as total social institution, 19; "Vyucheiskiy" in Nelmin-Nos, xiii, 42f; "Yadey Segery" in Karataika, 263n10. *See also* collectivization, state farm

collectivization, 19, 24, 44, 46, 47–49, 52, 54–55, 259n14, 262n6, 263n8; in the late Soviet period, 58; Nenets Independents avoiding, xiii, 4, 19, 44, 49–53; in post-Soviet period, 32, 266n30; Soviet ideology of, 19–21. *See also* collective farm, Independents, kulaks, reindeer, state farm
Colombia, 97
Comaroff, Jean, 7
Comaroff, John, 7
commitment, 6, 8, 11, 14, 16, 77, 89, 144, 177, 193, 203, 208, 210, 215, 216, 217, 220–223, 225–226, 240, 250, 276n2, 278n13, 281n20
Communists, 8, 23, 46, 51, 61, 62, 249; Christians on, 154; Communist Youth League (Komsomol), 60, 112–113, 263n7; compared with Christians, 124–125, 236, 237, 247, 249, 263n7, 281n16, 281n19, 282n1; and evangelicals, 112–113; Nenets Independents on, 161, 186; on the origin of humans, 43–44; as Party activists, 5, 34, 48, 61; repressing other *lutsaq*, 47; spirits punishing, 137; and their values, 8, 39. *See also* rupture, sincerity
consciousness: colonization of, 7, 10; and evil, 150–151; and God's Word, 134; located in idols, 132–133; politics of, 83; in Soviet ideology, 9, 53, 61; unhappy, 224. *See also* conversion
Constantine, 105
conversion, 33, 77–103; and alcohol, *see* alcohol; anthropological research on, 262n3; collective, 93; and consciousness, 7, 10, 11–12, 83 (*see also* consciousness); and cultural logic, 244–245; and cutting relations, 7, 228, 244; and ethical self-transformation, *see* ethics, self-transformation; and generations, 6, 10, 98–101, 245–246, 247 (*see also* youth); going along with, 246; and language, *see* language; as learning, 13, 17, 204, 209, 215; and modernity, *see* modernity; narratives, 88–93, 263n7; Pauline model of, 84, 92; and perspective-taking, 235–241 (*see also* perspective-taking); reasons for, 36, 40, 60, 62, 71–72, 85, 94–96, 99, 166, 246, 262n1; as rejection of the old, 32, 217, 229;

resistance to, *see* non-Christians; role of local actors in, 85–86; sustaining, 210, 244; utilitarian and intellectualist approaches to, 40, 85, 262n2. *See also* baptism, Baptist missionaries, devil, ethics, Independents, Pentecostals, personhood, promise, Protestantism, Russian Orthodoxy, shaman, women

Corbey, Raymond, 131–132

Council of Churches of Evangelical Christians-Baptists: ideology of separation from the state, 115; its leaders repressed, 114; split from All-Union Council, 114. *See also* All-Union Council of Evangelical Christians-Baptists, Unregistered Baptists

Crapanzano, Vincent, 279n9

curses, 16, 135, 173, 185–189, 195, 229, 274n17, 275n19, 278n16. *See also* evil word, gossip, witchcraft, words

Das, Veena, 12, 250

dead (the deceased), 4, 26, 164, 183, 190, 230, 260n21, 271n19, 273n5, 274n13, 275n23. *See also* burial, death, emotion, *ngylyeka*

death, 49, 95, 137, 160, 164, 179, 190, 265n27; Christians' rhetoric of, 118, 151, 152, 178, 181, 205, 224; leaving tundra life as, 102; in Nenets cosmology, 187, 267n5; violent, 166, 247. *See also* alcohol, burial, dead, devil, Nga

decision-event, 84, 89, 236. *See also* truth-event

Derrida, Jacques, 194, 199

Descola, Philippe, 261n27

devil (demon, Satan): acting through alcohol, 96–97, 182 (*see also* alcohol); acting through idols, 132–133, 138–139, 142, 149–151, 160, 161, 162, 189, 205 (*see also* idol); Baptists regarding Pentecostals to be possessed by, 147; being possessed by, 34, 98, 163; believing in, 162, 184, 247; challenging missionaries, 99, 121, 123–124; in conversion narrative, 89–90; entrapping Christians, 105, 107, 114; fearing, 135, 148; hindering conversion, 181, 213; and human words, 193; and

Internet, 120, 127; one and many, 271n18; Orthodoxy as worship of, 36; and power of name, 162, 187, 218, 278n15; and singing, 182; and Soviet Union, 126, 278n12; as underworld spirit, 78; vigilance in regard of, 225, 280n14; and the world, 83, 107, 109, 115, 120, 127, 129, 224. *See also* idol, God, *khekhe*, Nga, *ngylyeka*, spirits

dignity (sense of): and conversion, 40, 246; and private herders, 32, 173

Dinka, 26

disease (illness), 91, 142, 161, 184, 187, 191, 267n5, 270n12, 278n14; of reindeer, 28, 260n21; as spirit, 141, 172, 230. *See also* epidemic

Ditskaln, Aleksandr, 48

Dobzhanskaya, Oksana, 274n13

Dolgans, 273n8

Donbas, 53

dreams, dreaming, 108, 161, 184–185, 195, 235, 260n20, 274n14

Dumont, Louis, 117

Duranti, Alessandro, 195

Dutch, 22, 132

Eikhmans, Fyodor, 46, 48

emotion (feelings), 14–16, 53, 127, 132, 142, 173, 279n2, 281nn18–19; and the dead, 190, 227, 273n5; and language, 4, 13, 17, 151, 185, 203, 276n28, 277n11; learning of Christian, 7, 14, 79, 102, 146, 166, 208, 209–210, 216–217, 233, 241, 243; and Nenets children, 69; Nenets concept of, 192–193, 196, 229, 280nn11–12; in personal song, 182, 183. *See also* anger, dead, heart, laughter, quarrels

ends of the earth, 35, 37, 121–125, 242, 247. *See also* Arctic Ocean, eschatology

English (travelers), 22

Enets language, 258n10

Engelke, Matthew, 135, 224, 279n9

epic song (*yarabts, syudbabts*), 175, 184, 274n15. *See also* singing

epidemic, 45, 58, 98, 227, 260n21. *See also* disease, reindeer

eschatology (end times), 37, 105, 119–129, 151, 154, 261n29; as Second coming, 35, 119–122, 132, 224. *See also* ends of the earth, temporality

Estonians, 210

ethics, 153, 261n27, 281n17, 282n1; among animists, 33, 227; in conversion, 6–8, 10–15, 82, 95, 208, 219, 220–223, 225–226, 228–229, 231–241, 245, 247–250, 279n4; and language, 12–13, 15, 17, 84, 171, 174, 204, 215, 217; and morality, 10, 257n5; among Soviets, 281n19. *See also* character, conversion, language, morality system, self-transformation

Eucharist (Lord's Supper), 209, 210, 261n27

Evans-Pritchard, E. E., 275n25

Eve, 132, 223

Evenki, 52, 273n2

Eveny, 52, 250, 276n26

evil word (*vevako vada*), 186–189, 193, 230, 280n11. *See also* curses, gossip, heavy word, *syaqmei pad*, words

Ewe, 83

exchange, 26, 44, 95, 153, 178, 224, 227, 239, 244, 264n18, 279nn5–6; of gifts, 4, 26, 36, 177, 193, 196, 226, 229, 244, 273n8. *See also* non-Christians, personhood, reindeer

Falwell, Jerry, 277n6

fasting, 163, 205. *See also* baptism, prayer, words

Felman, Shoshana, 194

Festinger, Leon, 273n9

Figes, Orlando, 46

Finno-Ugric (Uralic) languages, 258n10

Finland, 49

fire, 78, 171, 177, 280n10; for burning idols, 138, 142, 151, 154–155, 157, 161; of hell, 151, 154, 281n21; speaking to warn, 189, 275n23; spirit (*tu yerv, tu khada*), 155, 189. *See also* idol, sacred objects, speech, spirits

fish, fishing, 32, 39, 44, 45, 49, 54, 55, 80, 88, 95, 123, 186, 216, 241, 260n21, 265n25. *See also* pike, *yid yerv*

Forest Nenets, 258n9, 270n9

forgiveness, 12, 62, 79, 90, 124, 138, 163, 181, 201, 203, 210, 214, 218, 225, 231, 233, 241, 243, 278n14. *See also* prayer, purification, repentance, sin

Forsyth, James, 23

Foucault, Michel, 10, 222, 231, 239, 257n5, 274n11, 279nn2–4

foxes, 32, 49, 55, 62, 273n8. *See also* furs

Friday Masowe Church, 135

furs, 22, 32, 44, 49, 55, 62, 140, 146, 177, 264n18, 279n8; fur tax (*yasak*), 22. *See also* foxes, taxation

future, 125, 247, 250, 251; Christians imagining, 7, 37, 81, 83, 89, 99, 102, 105, 119, 125, 185, 201, 224, 242; foretelling, 8, 50, 190, 273n3; Nenets not discussing, 196, 226; Soviets on, 48, 154. *See also* past, salvation, shaman, temporality

Gagarin, Yuriy (Soviet historian), 112

geologists, 23–24, 32, 46–47, 54, 55

Germans (of Volga), 112

Ghana, 83

gift. *See* exchange

glossolalia. *See* speaking in tongues

God (Christian deity): authority of, 86, 186, 213–214; believers' relationship with, 11, 13, 93, 99–102, 110, 145, 157, 160, 198–219, 220–225, 229–241, 242–243; believing, 3, 133, 161, 193, 203, 205, 208 (*see also* belief); children of, 82, 100, 105, 108–109, 114, 116, 117, 199, 239; conforming to the will of, 3, 80, 86, 91, 101, 121, 229, 230–249, 280n14; going against the will of, 34, 62, 78, 100, 162, 205, 232, 271n17, 280n13; and his performative speech, 179, 201; against idols and devils, 133, 137–138, 149–150, 156 (*see also* devil, idol); ignorance of, 202; incarnated, 134–135; instituting rulers, 114–115; intentions of, 206, 223, 234 (*see also* intention); as judge, 120; loving, 90, 153–154, 180; and making choices, 82, 96; miraculous intervening of, 124; missionaries as instruments of, 90, 124, 277–278n12; oneness of, 147, 149; perspective from, 102, 185 (*see also* God's-eye view); and promise, 219, 220–221, 225, 233 (*see also* promise); protection of, 34, 81, 96, 150, 163, 166, 174, 193; and providence, 68, 88, 90, 93, 99, 105–106, 121, 123, 126–127, 201; refusing to respond to, 178, 179; as savior, 93, 210, 213, 229; sees in a person, 108, 181, 209, 239;

separation from, 223–224; and singing, 182; speaking to, 12–17, 79, 89, 98, 145, 148–151, 163, 171, 172, 174, 176, 184, 200–205, 208–219, 231–232, 238, 243, 278n14 (*see also* prayer); submission to, 15, 202, 217, 225; and supremacy over Satan, 124. *See also* Jesus, God's-eye view, God's Word, Holy Spirit, name, Num, tolerance, words

God's-eye view, 11–220, 234–241. *See also* God, perspective-taking

God's Word (Word of God), 14, 68, 78, 93, 110, 121, 124, 134–135, 176, 178, 193, 200–202, 209, 214–215, 216, 218, 270n8. *See also* Bible, God

Golovnev, Andrei, 26, 271n13, 272n23

goods (consumer goods), 22, 47, 54, 59, 63, 86, 88, 128, 246. *See also* trade

Gorbachev, Mikhail, 127

gossip, 62, 183, 185, 188–189. *See also* curses, evil word, words

Great Land tundra (Bolshezemelskaya tundra), xiii, 3, 22, 23, 24, 37, 45, 52, 259n13, 259n17, 264n21, 270n5, 275n19; dialect of, 258n10, 275n24

Greek Orthodox, 197

grey-zone herders, 265n25. See also *yedinolichniki*

Groys, Boris, 124

Gulag (labor camps), xiii, xvi, 3, 24, 44, 46–47, 48–49, 50, 54, 110, 112, 141, 218, 259n13, 263n15, 264n17, 268n8. *See also* Amderma, Khabarovo, repressions, Stalinist period, Vaigach, Vorkuta

Gyda, 122, 177, 264–265n25

Habeck, Otto, 264n20

hair, 89, 90–92, 208, 266n4. *See also* shaman

Hamlet, 146

Harding, Susan, 13, 102, 200, 215, 277n6, 279n9

hate speech, 180. *See also* love speech, speech

heart: in atheists' rhetoric, 113; in Christians' rhetoric, 79, 82, 96, 108, 116, 117, 132, 133, 134, 149, 154, 161, 164, 181, 200, 201, 210–213, 214, 219, 223, 231, 232, 233, 269n15, 277n4, 277n9, 278n1; in Nenets vocabulary, 280n11; of reindeer, 193. *See also* Holy Spirit, interiority

heavy word (*sanggovo vada*), 191–193. *See also* curses, evil word, intention, words

Hefner, Robert, 240

Heidegger, Martin, 195

Holy Spirit, 16, 78, 80, 92, 93, 102, 108, 114, 121, 123, 127, 135, 143, 145, 146, 164, 176, 200, 201, 205, 209–210, 210–213, 217, 224–225, 232, 234; blasphemy of, 218, 231, 275n18; growing inside, 233–234, 240. *See also* baptism, Jesus, God, prayer

Horton, Robin, 262n2

human-animal relations, 24, 26, 33. *See also* aesthetics, bears, predators, reindeer, wolves

Humphrey, Caroline, 83–84, 178–179, 180, 208, 236, 239, 261n27

hunters, 55, 61, 62, 264n25, 273n2

hygiene, 23, 59

icon: Eastern Orthodox theology of, 134–135; in Nenets camps, 23, 36, 133, 135; Pentecostal missionary on, 155–160, 272n24. *See also* Jesus, *khekhe*, kissing, *lutsa*, Russian Orthodoxy, sacred objects, sacrifice

idol, idolatry: Baptists considering modern technologies as, 87, 123, 134; Christians on, 131–139, 142–143, 149–151, 154–165, 202–205, 270n8, 270n5, 272n25; and devils, 271n18; Martin Luther on, 133. *See also* devil, *khekhe*, sacred objects

ikota (hiccup spirit), 97–98, 175, 218. *See also* alcohol, devil, spirits

illiteracy, 61, 62, 68, 80, 87, 113, 135, 145, 146, 238, 265n26

Ilongots, 195

Independents, xiii–xiv, 5, 10, 21, 23, 24, 29, 117, 129, 164, 186, 218, 260n21, 264n18; and alcohol, 94–98 (*see also* alcohol); avoiding the authorities, 22, 36, 44–60, 263n15; compared to collectivized Nenets, 39–40, 60–63; compared to Unregistered Baptists, 129–130; conversion of, 81, 85–94, 104, 222, 247–249 (*see also* conversion); generational differences among, 98–101; getting divided, 244; names for, 4, 29, 262n6; in the post-Soviet period, 63–70, 260n25,

265n26, 266n30; seen as last true nomads, 32; and the value of independence, 29, 32, 226–228. *See also* autonomy, collective farm, collectivization, Communists, past, promise, Ural Nenets, Yamb-To, *yedinolichniki*

India, 240, 250, 262n1, 273n5

individualism: and Christians, 117, 164, 226, 234, 243; and Nenets, 226; and shamanism, 261n26. *See also* interiority, personhood, Protestantism

Indonesia, 132, 201

industrialization, 23–24, 46–47, 151

Ingold, Tim, 195

intention, intentionality, 14, 17, 215, 217, 275n24, 278n16, 279n2; attribution of, 191, 192, 195; and Christians, 12, 108, 192, 193, 196, 198, 201–202, 206, 217–218, 229, 234, 240, 241, 278nn14–15; mismatch of, 160, 166, 219; and Nenets personhood, 194, 195, 244; in ritual, 203, 208–209; Western and non-Western concepts of, 195, 276n30; and words, 185, 188, 195, 226. *See also* baptism, Baptist language, heavy word, interiority, responsibility, sincerity, speech, words

interiority (inner self): and Christian personhood, 14–15, 91, 102, 127, 145–146, 163, 178, 192, 199, 203, 208–210, 213, 217, 219, 224, 229, 230, 231, 232, 233, 243, 249, 266n1, 269n15, 280n11; church as collective, 78, 116; and idols, 138; in Western dichotomous thinking, 195, 217, 274n9. *See also* intention, sincerity

interpellation, 179, 242. *See also* name

Islam, 217, 235–236, 240, 257n4

Islavin, Vladimir, 273n8

Izhma Komi, 36, 41, 45, 56, 202, 258n10, 264n20. *See also* Komi

Ivanova, Aytalina, 275n25

Jaggar, Alison, 277n11

Jains, 240

Jenkins, Tim, 217, 273n9

Jerusalem, 121

Jesus (Christ), 3, 78, 80, 90, 110, 115, 117, 148, 149, 151, 157, 160, 165, 178, 179, 210, 211, 214, 218, 261n27, 267n1; believing in, 205,

208, 277n9; the film on, 134; ignorance of, 36–37, 125, 202; and mission command, 120–121, 125; narrow path after, 108, 202, 224, 237, 266n1; represented on icon, 156, 160 (*see also* icon); resurrection of, 83, 84, 92; saving from addiction, 96–98. *See also* God, Holy Spirit, name

Kanin Peninsula, 18, 262n4

Karataika, 58, 67, 123, 263n10, 264n22, 265n26

Kara: river, 264n21; sea, 44, 45, 77; tundra, 47

Karelia, 49, 119

Karskiy Village Council, 56

Keane, Webb, 10–11, 16, 81–82, 132, 201, 228, 235–236, 249, 261n27, 276n28, 276n30, 277n11

Kets, 9

Khabarovo: church building in, 45, 48; Gulag in, 24, 47

Khaen-Sale, 165

Khabtam Pe (mountain), 141

Khadam Pe (mountain), 123, 141, 164

Khalmer-Yu, 54–55, 58, 61, 62–63, 69, 218, 263n15

Khanty, 41, 139, 223, 249, 261n29, 261n28

Khanty-Mansi Autonomous Region, 258n9

Khanzerova, Irina, 66, 258n11

khekhe, 34, 132, 142; burning of, *see* sacred objects; missionaries demonizing, 158, 160; in Nenets rituals, 141, 161, 186, 270n10, 271n13; obtaining and making of, 138, 141, 157, 164, 270n9, 271n14, 272n22; as relational person, 142 (*see also* part-person); returning of, 164–165, 166; as Russian spirits (*lutsa khekheq*), 45, 133, 155 (*see also* icon); and sacred sites, 164–165, 272n21; translation of the term, 131. *See also* body, devil, idol, *myad pukhutsya*, sacred objects, sacred site, sacred sledge, shaman, soul, spirits, *syadei*

Khorev, Mikhail, 113

Khoseda-Khard, 23

Khrushchev, Nikita, 35, 112

kin, kinship, 23, 26, 33, 50, 171, 188, 190, 192, 221, 227, 228, 239, 244, 274n13; among Christians, 91, 97, 139, 178, 239, 244, 267n10. *See also* clan, non-Christians kissing, 50; among Baptists, 80, 210; of icon, 156, 160. *See also* icon

Kolva, 23, 140

Kolva Yaran, 60, 258n10

Komi (Republic, ASSR), 53, 56, 69, 258n9, 263n15, 266n30, 271n16, 275n24

Komi language, 60, 62, 79, 258n10

Komi people, 125, 164, 275n19, 275nn21–22. *See also* Izhma Komi

Korotaikha River, 25, 56, 257n2

Koryak, 34, 52, 261n29

Kostikov, Leonid, 177

Kotkin, Stephen, 264n23

Kovtun, Grigoriy, 111

Krasnoyarsk Territory, 19, 258n9

Kremlin, 115

Kryuchkov, Gennadiy, 105, 113, 115–116, 118, 119, 126–127

kulaks, 19, 29, 47, 110, 259n13, 263nn8–9. *See also* collectivization, shaman

labor camps. *See* Gulag

Laestadius, Lars Levi, 267n7

Laidlaw, James, 6, 10, 208, 217, 240, 250

Lambek, Michael, 6, 12, 13, 203–204, 219, 220, 257n4

language, 41; of Baptists and Pentecostals compared, 234, 276n27; biblical, 3, 124, 229; and body, 194; and quotation practice, 206–207; in conversion, 3–4, 10–17, 37–38, 62, 84, 90, 93, 102, 110, 126, 193, 197–199, 214–217, 219, 226, 235–238, 242–244, 269n15, 273n5 (*see also* articulacy); evangelical, 4, 17, 93, 110, 200, 216, 225; and gaps in understanding, 148; and internalization, 214–215, 279n9; and performativity, 16–17, 199; and personhood, *see* personhood; and perspective, 90, 236–238, 240, 243, 249 (*see also* perspective-taking); and representation, 13, 16, 132, 180, 184–185, 193–196, 198, 213, 217–218, 243. *See also* Baptist language, conversion, emotion, ethics, language ideology, materiality, name, personhood, prayer, Protestantism, silence, Soviet language, speech, subject-language, words

language ideology, 269n16, 273n9; Baptist, 178, 193, 198–200, 202, 206, 209, 217–218,

277n6; in mission encounter, 16–17, 172, 180, 197; Nenets, 177, 185, 193, 194–195, 276n28. *See also* language, literalism, words

Lapsui, Anastasia, 182–183, 270n9

Lapsui, Gennadi, 273n3

Latour, Bruno, 102, 215–216, 237

laughter, 62, 78, 87, 98, 173, 175, 183, 197, 200, 232, 233, 270n5, 271n17. *See also* emotion, sin

Lavrillier, Alexandra, 263n14

laying on of hands, 209, 210, 211, 212f

Ledkov, Ivan (Nenets shaman), 259n13, 275n19, 275n22

Ledkov, Vasiliy (Nenets writer), 263n8

Lehtisalo, Toivo, 270n9

Lenin, Vladimir, 46f, 48, 154, 186

Lienhardt, Godfrey, 26

literalism: among Baptists, 114, 121, 202, 207, 277n6; among Pentecostals, 133; in Soviet society, 60. *See also* Bible

love speech, 180, 190. *See also* hate speech, sermon, speech

Luhrmann, Tanya, 13

Luther, Martin, 133, 134

Lutherans, 147, 267n7

lutsa ("Russian"), 28, 241, 242, 282n2; being skillful with, 65, 86; dangers coming from, 4, 37, 39–44, 47, 49–50, 63, 67–68, 70, 72, 83, 161, 177, 227, 246, 249; folk etymology of, 260n24; Nenets becoming, 98, 100–101; regarding someone's behavior as, 43, 61, 172, 214, 232; and their spirits, 45, 133, 155 (*see also* icon, *khekhe*); and their way of life, 28, 41, 186; unskillful person as, 42–43. *See also* Bible, Communists, predators

Mahmood, Saba, 217

Malozemelskaya tundra, xiii

mandalada (uprising), 21, 49–51, 263n11, 263n13. *See also* collectivization, shaman, *yedinolichniki*

marginalization (sense of), 7, 40, 70, 72, 246, 262n1. *See also* conversion

marriage, 51, 61, 62, 141, 229–230, 278n16; arranged, 23, 99, 139; among Christians, 4, 99–100, 128, 139, 147, 152, 268n6; between cousins, 34; and negotiations, 177, 186–187. *See also* matchmaking, *porti*, witchcraft martyrdom: Soviet-era experience of, 36, 117–118. *See also* persecutions, Unregistered Baptists

Marxism (Soviet), 9, 23, 236, 247, 249–250. *See also* materiality

matchmaking, 177–178, 187, 247, 270n11, 273n8. *See also* Baptist missionaries, bridewealth, marriage, silence

materiality, 249, 265n27, 271n19; and Christians, 102, 124, 131, 132, 133–135, 139, 156, 160, 162, 245, 276n27; and language, 194, 278n14; as object of ethnography, 106–107; for Soviet Marxists, 9

Mattingly, Cheryl, 281n20

Mauss, Marcel, 277n8

Mayotte, 257n4

Mead, George Herbert, 239

medical care (by the state), 9, 23, 32–33, 58–59, 65, 82, 89–90, 162, 181, 264n19

Melanesia, 239, 276n30

men: becoming shift workers, 41, 42f; the Bible on, 91; and bodily gestures, 32; as Christians, 40, 65, 80, 216, 246; herding reindeer, 26, 32, 171; hiding from the authorities, 54; repressed by the Soviets, 21, 49–50; and ritual pollution, 187, 226 (*see also* pollution); starting independent life, 228; in the tent, 78; and urban clothing, 128; and women making decisions, 97. *See also* women

Mennonites, 112

Merleau-Ponty, Maurice, 195

Michalski, Sergiusz, 136–137

Mikola, 45, 238, 278n16. *See also* Nicholas

mining, 24, 47, 137; of coal, 24, 54, 99, 110, 113, 259n15, 265n29, 268n9. *See also* oil and gas

missionaries. *See* Baptist missionaries, Pentecostal missionaries

modernity, 7–8, 41, 63, 103, 132, 134, 246, 268n10; and conversion, 81–83, 85, 102, 250. *See also* idol, Protestantism

Mongolia, 8, 275n24; Inner Mongolia, 236

Mongols, 178

monkey (*ngayatar*), 43–44, 100. *See also* name

morality system, 7, 8, 10–11, 17, 236, 249–250, 257n5. *See also* ethics

Moscow, 26, 41, 58, 137, 258n7

museum, 107, 137, 138

myad pukhutsya (female spirit figure), 137, 142, 163, 270n9. *See also* birth, *khekhe*, spirits, women

myenarui (lead reindeer), 141, 247, 248f, 270n12. *See also* reindeer

Nadym, 122

name, naming: avoiding of, 172, 178–179, 183, 273n3; in Christians' addresses, 107, 178, 192; of clan or lineage, 188, 190, 262n4; given by Russian Orthodox Church, 23; God's, 218, 243; ignorance of Jesus', 36, 262n31; injurious, 192, 194, 210, 226; invoking spirits by, 98, 187; of neighboring groups, 41–42, 257n2, 258n10; nicknames, 100–101; in passport, 148, 210–211 (*see also* passportization); and personhood, 16, 65–66, 183, 244; registered by authorities, 58, 65–67; and subjectivation, 179–180, 194. *See also* devil, God, interpellation, Jesus, language, personhood, subjectivation

Naryan-Mar, xiii, xiv, 32, 47, 48, 53–54, 60, 63–65, 68, 88, 99, 119, 162, 259n15, 264n22, 265n26, 268n5

Ned-Yu (mountain), 50

Nelmin-Nos, 261n26

Nenets language, xiii, 19, 53, 79–80, 123, 161, 258nn10–11; as barrier, 269n15; Russians' ignorance of, 67; switching between Russian and, 3, 78, 93, 243. *See also* language ideology, Russian language

Nenets Autonomous Region, xiii, 19, 26, 32, 41, 48, 49, 52–54, 56, 121, 258n9, 258n11, 259n15, 263n15, 265n28

"Nenets church", 40, 93, 269n15

Nerkagi, Anna, 272n1

Nevskiy (Orthodox priest), 270n5

Nga (Nenets deity), 43–44, 187, 271n13. *See also* devil, *ngylyeka*, spirits

Nganasan, 274n13; language, 258n10

Nganorakha (mountains), 50

Ngutos Pe (mountain), 141

ngylyeka (underworld spirit), 43, 78–79, 92, 164. *See also* dead, devil, Nga, spirits

Nicholas (saint), 23, 45, 46f, 202, 278n16. *See also* icon, Mikola

Niemi, Jarkko, 182, 274n13, 274n15

Nikon, patriarch, 259n15

Nizhnyaya Pyosha, 263n7
nomads, nomadism, xiii, 5, 10, 19, 23,
    24–25, 28, 32, 39, 45, 52, 62, 68, 70, 88,
    100, 108, 242, 246, 249, 251, 257n1, 258n9,
    259n19, 260n21, 262n4, 263n14, 265n28;
    abandoning life of, 41, 98, 99; and seasonal
    migration, 25–26, 39, 45, 77, 86, 139, 262n4;
    and spirits, 271n13; the state attempting to
    control, 58–59; visiting settlements, 32, 61,
    69, 142, 230, 246. See also Independents,
    pastures, reindeer, sedentarization
non-Christians (nonconverts, nonbelievers),
    15, 34, 77, 91, 109, 123, 148, 166, 227, 238,
    262n1, 270n12, 280n11; and alcohol,
    95–97, 267n9 (see also alcohol); criticizing
    converts, 12, 80, 98; distanced from their
    Christian kin, 85, 97, 244 (see also kin);
    and exchange with Christians, 229, 279n5
    (see also exchange); joking, 131, 139, 200;
    and purity, 229; resisting conversion, 34,
    61, 99, 163, 172, 174, 176–179, 193; and sacred
    objects, 162, 189, 270n10; and words, 194,
    196, 221, 232, 237, 244 (see also words). See
    also animists, conversion, "pagan"
nonverbal communication (gestures), 4, 6,
    10, 14, 194, 197, 205, 208, 209, 210, 216,
    217, 243, 260n23, 273n7. See also men,
    silence
Norwegians, 22, 68
Novyi Port, 122
Num (sky deity), 270n13; in converts'
    rhetoric, 205, 243; shaped by Orthodoxy,
    43, 202, 238; women promised to, 278n16.
    See also God
nyaro (pure), 230. See also pollution,
    purification, syaqmei pad, women
nyeney (real, human), 28, 42, 100, 183, 246.
    See also nomads, ontology

Ob River, 22, 23, 49
Obdorsk, 22
oil and gas, 24, 154, 166
Old Believers, 9–10, 259n15
ontology, 6, 7, 16, 17, 28, 33–34, 131–132, 160,
    165, 185, 195, 200, 239, 243, 261n27, 265n27,
    269n2. See also animists, human-animal
    relations, nyeney, shamanism, words

oral, orality: and Nenets tradition, 43, 177;
    and written texts, 14, 78, 135, 186, 202–203,
    207. See also language, words
"pagan", xiv, 79, 91, 124, 132, 162, 218, 259n17;
    converts struggling with aspects defined
    as, 233, 238; evangelicals' view of, 15, 23,
    34–35, 37, 78, 93, 97, 138, 198; idols, 150 (see
    also idol); the past defined as, 43, 173, 175,
    180, 185, 217, 246, 268n4; rituals, 34, 173;
    term discussed, 258n8. See also animists,
    non-Christians, past

Papua New Guinea, 13, 71, 239
parasitism (social), 53–54
Parry, Jonathan, 153
part-persons, 16, 165, 180, 194. See also
    khekhe, personhood, words
passportization, 59, 65, 66f, 69, 81, 264n21.
    See also name,
past, 37, 125; Baptists glorifying, 118; breaking
    with, 81, 82, 90, 103, 133, 175, 180, 214, 225,
    237, 238, 244; ideas and habits from, 4, 6,
    7, 79, 184–185, 194–195, 221, 232, 244–245,
    247, 281n18; Independents as from, 32, 55;
    Soviets denouncing, 8, 263n7, 281n19. See
    also future, "pagan", rupture, temporality
pastor (minister, presbyter), 12, 213, 261n29,
    267n7; Baptist, xiii, 40, 77, 78, 79, 86,
    89–90, 93, 100, 108, 109–116, 118, 123, 125,
    127, 145, 205, 213, 218, 231, 264n16, 267n6,
    277n10; Pentecostal, 34, 139, 143, 148, 154,
    208, 242. See also Baptist missionaries,
    Pentecostal missionaries
pastures, 12, 23–25, 50, 53, 56, 64, 77, 153–154,
    161, 181, 197, 228, 241, 257n2, 260n21,
    260n25, 265n26, 266n30, 268n5. See also
    nomads, reindeer
Paul (apostle, saint), 84, 91, 92, 115, 117, 124,
    134, 146, 229, 281n16. See also conversion
Paxson, Margaret, 275n24
Pechora, 22, 259n15
Pe Mal Khada (Nenets deity), 141–142, 161,
    164, 186, 270–271n13, 271n19. See also birth,
    Khadam Pe, khekhe
Pelkmans, Mathijs, 85
Pentecostal missionaries, 4, 139–161;
    competing with Baptist missionaries, 5,

6, 139–148; and their organizations, 143, 271n16. *See also* Baptist missionaries, icon, Pentecostals

Pentecostals, xiv, 34, 104, 131–167, 261n29; in All-Union Council, 267n2; Baptists about, 147; charismatic neo-Pentecostals, 34; church (prayer house), 143; conversion to, 17, 139, 185, 246 (*see also* conversion); and finding partner, 139; identifying as Christian, 147, 261n30; perceived as "foreign", 36; and personhood, 33–34, 150, 187; and registration, 36, 104, 112; and speaking, 145, 242 (*see also* speaking in tongues); and style of worship, 145; thinking about joining Baptists, 139, 144, 147; and women, 146. *See also* All-Union Council of Evangelical Christians-Baptists, baptism, Baptist missionaries, devil, icon, language, literalism, pastor, Pentecostal missionaries, prayer, registration, singing, tolerance, Vorkuta, words

Perm Territory, 9

persecutions: of minority Christians in Russia, 5, 9, 105, 109, 110, 117–118, 249; of shamans, 51. *See also* martyrdom, repressions, Unregistered Baptists

personal song (*yabye syo*), 175, 182–184. *See also* alcohol, emotion, name, singing

personhood: in conversion, 226, 229, 243, 244; and evangelicals, 14–15, 116, 180, 239; and language, 13, 17, 172–173, 184, 185–186, 193, 194, 195–196, 244; and name, *see* name; and reindeer, *see* reindeer; and songs, 183–184, 198. *See also* conversion, exchange, individualism, words

perspective-taking, 11, 26, 81, 90, 185, 200, 213, 220, 235–241, 243, 249, 281n18. *See also* conversion, God, God's-eye view, language, "pagan", subject-language, subject position

Petrone, Karen, 262n6

Petrozavodsk, 125

Pietz, William, 269n2

pike (fish), 135, 188–189, 275n22

pollution (ritual impurity): avoiding among Christians, 116; Christians regarding idols as, 270n8; in mission encounter confusion over, 230–231; related female things and qualities, 187–188, 226, 230, 271n15 (*see also* women); and Russians, 130. *See also* men, *nyaro*, purification, reindeer

Pomors, 22

Popov, Andrey, 273n8

porti, 187–188, 275n19. *See also* curses, evil word, gossip, pollution, witchcraft, words

prayer, praying, 3, 14, 34, 77, 79–80, 94f, 123, 127, 174, 203, 210, 216, 225, 230, 231, 232, 233, 234; of baptismal service, 211–213 (*see also* baptism); centrality of, 200, 216; communal, 79, 98, 124; introductory, 78, 146, 209, 213; missionary's instructions on, 213–214; Nenets sacrificial, 185–186, 230; and Nenets women, 216; among Pentecostals, 143–144, 148, 150, 154; by plan, 117; of repentance, 11, 181, 184, 204, 241, 243 (*see also* repentance); for rulers, 117; spontaneous, 88; of thanks, 209. *See also* Baptist language, forgiveness, God, language, sincerity

predators, 26, 34, 44, 188, 230, 242. *See also* bears, *lutsa*, reindeer, wolves

Prokhorov, Konstantin, 264n23, 269n12

Prokof'ev, Aleksey, 113

Prokof'ev, Georgiy, 47, 272n22

Prokof'eva, Yekaterina, 272n22

promise (oath): in Christian rituals, 11, 205, 208, 213, 218–219; in conversion, 6–7, 11, 14, 98, 163, 185, 200, 220–222, 225, 242, 251; God's, 121, 125, 201, 221, 233; Independents giving to the authorities, 58; among Nenets animists, 270n12, 278n16. *See also* baptism, conversion, God, Num

Protestantism: conversion to, 10, 223; on idols, 132–133, 137, 164, 244; and individualism, 164, 226 (*see also* individualism); and language, 12, 243 (*see also* language); and missionaries, 36–37, 187; and modernity, 81, 83; perception among Baptists, 108; in Russia, 4–5, 104, 112, 134, 257n3, 269n13; on sincerity, 203, 209 (*see also* sincerity); and theology, 117, 201. *See also* conversion, Reformation, Russian Orthodoxy

Prourzin, Ivan, 48, 263n9

purification: Christians on, 79, 90, 213, 222, 224, 229–231, 279n7 (*see also* sanctification); as Nenets ritual, 189, 230 (see also *nyaro, torabtq*, women); of reform movements, 102, 236, 249. *See also* non-Christians, pollution, shaman

Puritans (of New England), 239

Pushkareva, Yelena, 273n3, 273n7, 274n16

Pustozersk, 22, 259n15, 262n4

Quakers, 197

quarrels, 88, 142, 189; creating an emotional bond, 180, 190, 227. *See also* emotion, dead

Rappaport, Roy, 203

Ravna, Zoia Vylka, 260n23

Reformation, 132, 134, 136, 209. *See also* Protestantism

Registered Baptists, 114–115, 127–128, 129, 268n10. *See also* All-Union Council of Evangelical Christians-Baptists, Unregistered Baptists

registration, 112–113; of Baptists, 4, 35, 109, 129, 268n6, 269n13; of Baptists and Independents compared, 129; of Pentecostals, 36, 104, 112. *See also* Pentecostals, Registered Baptists, Unregistered Baptists

reindeer, 24–32, 41, 106, 155, 171, 205, 259n19; alienated from, 28, 41, 246; and being Nenets, 19, 28, 33, 41–43, 70, 98, 100–101, 226, 246, 250, 260n21; and collectivization, 19, 24, 32, 44, 47, 48–49, 50, 56, 58–59, 109; dedicated to gods, 161 (see also *myenarui*); consuming raw blood of, 34, 35f, 78, 150, 177; enabling independence, 227; as gift, 193, 196, 269n15, 279n5; given on loan, 227, 279n5; human-reindeer relations, 26; losing of, 28, 45, 61, 95, 99, 163–164, 227, 260n21, 275n25; migration of, 25; in missionaries' rhetoric, 136, 153; personal or private ownership of, xiii, 19, 29, 39, 53, 64, 100; and personhood, 26, 101, 193, 194, 196, 226, 276n26; and practical knowledge, 17, 32, 49, 189, 232, 240–241, 260n23; and predation, 33–34, 142, 186, 189 (*see also* predators); reindeer

luck (*ty yab*), 29, 140–141; reindeer races, 65, 78, 89; and ritual pollution, 230, 238, 279n8 (*see also* pollution); sacrifice of, *see* sacrifice; shaman as, 274n16; and spirits or gods, 155–156, 161, 227, 271n13; stealing of, 89–90, 186; tensions over pastures of, 12, 23–24; toys of, 69; various uses of, 24, 26, 62, 63, 68, 86, 88, 100, 138, 146, 166, 197–198, 200, 264n17, 272n25, 273n8. *See also* collectivization, disease, epidemic, exchange, heart, men, nomads, pastures, Reindeer Day, *tarq pad*

Reindeer Day, xiii, 48, 65

repentance, 11, 14, 15, 84, 89, 114, 181, 200, 204, 214, 225, 243; calls for, 242; as readmittance, 281n19. *See also* forgiveness, prayer, conversion

repetition, 3, 154, 172, 175–176, 242, 273n7; Baptists' view of, 175, 181; Christian practices of, 80, 205; Nenets participatory, 151, 176–177; shamanic practice of, 273n7. *See also* language, words

repressions, 5, 21, 32–33, 39, 46, 47, 110, 114, 118, 250, 259n14, 263n9, 267n2. *See also* Communists, Council of Churches of Evangelical Christians-Baptists, Gulag, men, persecutions, shaman, Stalinist period, Unregistered Baptists

residence permit (*propiska*), 55, 63, 66, 264n19

responsibility, 131, 180, 191, 195, 245, 264n15; among Christians, 13, 16, 107, 162, 208, 219, 226, 233, 278n12, 280n14; shifting, 165, 166–167. *See also* intentions, interiority, sincerity, words

Robbins, Joel, 7, 13, 40, 71–72, 102, 119, 244, 278n1

Rogers, Douglas, 9

Rosaldo, Michelle, 195

rupture: in Christians' and Communists' ideologies, 125, 281n16; and evangelicals, 82, 88, 102, 225, 246; and modernity, 81. *See also* past, temporality

Russian. See *lutsa*

Russian language, 54, 60, 67, 143, 204, 258n10, 282n2; Christians' usage of, 3, 205, 211; enabling interethnic missionization, 126; poor knowledge of, 3, 19, 63, 87, 238;

and singing, 61, 80, 182 (*see also* singing).
 See also Nenets language
Russian Orthodoxy: and animosity toward
 Protestants, 36; Baptists' view on, 108; and
 condemnation of idols, 259n15; conversion
 to, 23 (*see also* conversion); and icons, 134,
 135, 155; and language, 12, 214; among Nenets
 reindeer herders, 36–37, 43, 45, 48, 95, 102,
 133, 135, 139, 164, 202, 218–219, 239, 262n31,
 270n5, 281n21; and Old Believers, 9; and
 proselytization in tsarist period, 5, 22–23, 45,
 92, 137, 249, 259nn17–18; and proselytization
 today among Nenets, 36; and Russian
 Synodal Bible, 207; and Soviet state, 46, 155.
 See also devil, icon, name, Num, sacrifice

sacred objects (figures, images), 78, 97, 135,
 138, 141–142, 157, 161, 164–165, 186, 188, 204,
 259n15, 270n9, 271n19, 271nn13–14, 272n22;
 Bible as, 269n4; burning of, 3, 34, 37, 45,
 131, 139, 142, 143, 154–161, 163, 165, 166, 244,
 245, 270n6, 272n25 (*see also* fire). *See also*
 icon, idol, *khekhe*, non-Christians, sacred
 site, sacred sledge, *syadei*, temporality
sacred site (*khekhe ya*), 45, 123, 137, 141–142,
 161, 165, 230, 244, 246, 260n21, 270n8,
 271nn13–14, 272nn21–22. *See also* idol,
 khekhe, sacred objects, spirits, *syadei*
sacred sledge (*khekhengan*), 142, 155, 163, 164,
 189, 271n13, 271n15. See also *khekhe*, sacred
 objects
sacrifice, 44, 45, 155, 164, 281n15; abandoning,
 94; Christian concept of, 3, 153, 216, 221,
 222; converts on animist, 93; for the
 newborn, 33; to Orthodox icons, 23 (*see
 also* icon); of reindeer, 8, 34, 141, 186,
 271n13, 275n21; Russian missionaries
 condemning, 34; words used during,
 185–186, 271n13, 274n17. *See also* alcohol,
 animists, prayer, reindeer, spirits
Sahlins, Marshall, 72
Saint Petersburg (Leningrad), 68, 99, 262n7
Salekhard, 22, 53, 58, 153, 258n7
salvation, 13–14, 45, 68, 81, 93, 96, 154, 174,
 178, 185, 199, 201, 222, 223, 224–226, 231,
 237, 240, 277n4. *See also* future
Sámi, 267n7

Samoyeds, in historical sources, 22–23,
 259n17; language group of, 258n10; as old
 name for Nenets, 259n16
sanctification, 114, 224–225, 279n9. *See also*
 purification
sanggovo vada. See heavy word
Scandinavia, 267n7
school (boarding school, *internat*): and
 Baptist missionaries, 68, 112, 126, 267n11;
 and effect on Nenets youth, 33, 60, 61–62,
 67, 86, 204; forcibly taken to, 59–60;
 Nenets avoiding, xiii, 4, 43, 53–54, 222;
 and post-Soviet period, 67, 69, 70f, 81, 91,
 99, 247, 265n29; and Soviet reformism,
 23, 59, 63, 91, 186, 263n7, 264n19, 265n25;
 Summer Nomadic School, xiii, 68. *See
 also* Independents, Vorkuta, youth
Second World War, 44–45, 49, 151–153
secret police (OGPU, NKVD, KGB), 46, 54,
 112, 113, 275n19, 278n12, 280n13
sedentarization, 9, 26, 28, 39, 41, 59, 99–100,
 227, 258n11, 260n22. *See also* city, nomads
self-transformation (self-cultivation, self-
 formation): among Christians, 4, 8, 10, 13,
 38, 81, 84–85, 101, 219, 220, 222–226, 233–234,
 249–250, 257n6, 279n2, 279n4, 281n16,
 281n19 (*see also* coherence); among Soviets,
 249, 281n19. *See also* conversion, ethics
Selkup language, 258n10
semiotic ideology, 16, 132, 265n27. *See also*
 language ideology
senses: and faith, 14, 134–135, 269n3
Ser Ngo Iri (Nenets deity), 270n13
sermon, 3, 78–79, 107, 125, 127, 135, 143, 202,
 223, 229, 231, 277n4; Baptist postbaptismal,
 210; on love, 151–154; women not allowed
 to deliver, 80, 207. *See also* baptism
Seventh-day Adventists, 112
shaman (*tadyebya*): acting in the
 mandalada, 50–51 (see also *mandalada*);
 avoiding the state, 263n14; and Christian
 conversion, 84, 88–93, 101–102, 247;
 "Christian shaman", 102; desire to
 become, 33, 92, 266n3; and drums burned,
 270n6; giving *khekheq*, 271n14 (see also
 khekhe); and hair, 91; and harmful magic,
 187, 191, 275n22; and healing, 270n9,

275n19; and helper during a seance, 273n7; and initiation, 92, 227, 266n3, 266n5; in missionary narratives, 138; predicting future, 50, 261n26, 273n3; and purification rite, 230; and related abilities, 33, 227; repressed as class enemies, 21, 47, 112, 137, 259n13, 263n9 (*see also* kulaks); and singing, 184–185, 271n13, 273n7, 274n16, 275n23; in Soviet narratives, 263n8; and spirit helpers (*tadyebtsoq*), 90, 92, 188–189 (*see also* spirits); travelling to the sky, 272n20. *See also* conversion, persecutions, shamanism, reindeer, repetition

shamanism, 9; Christians denouncing, 33, 51, 182, 244; different from organized religions, 8, 260n26; disappearing in the 20th century, 23, 92–93, 260n21; and neo-Pentecostals, 34; as neoshamanism, 261n26; persisting in ontological sensibilities, 33, 261n26 (*see also* ontology). *See also* shaman

Siberia, 32, 52, 137, 171, 183, 250, 257n2, 258n9, 258n11, 261n28, 267n8, 270n7, 272n2, 279n6

silence, 3, 6, 11, 37, 219, 241, 243, 272n1, 273nn2–4, 274n11, 274n13; biblical command to keep, 146; Christians on, 172–173, 178, 197, 243, 246; inherent in language, 12; and matchmaking, 177–178, 186, 273n8; misread as pensiveness, 181; Nenets being in, 54, 62, 69, 77, 86, 98, 171, 185; as a refusal and self-protection, 3, 174, 176, 178, 179, 214, 242, 244; silencing the other, 180–181, 214. *See also* birth, language, matchmaking, nonverbal communication, silence act, speech

silence act, 17, 171–182, 193, 242. *See also* silence, speech act theory

sin, 62, 110, 115–116, 157, 163, 178, 182, 184, 198, 218, 223–226, 232, 237, 279n1, 281n19. *See also* anger, forgiveness, laughter, taboo

sincerity: and Communists, 61, 264n24; and intention, 240, 241 (*see also* intention); and interiority, 14, 276n2; and ritual, 208–209; and words, 3, 15–16, 150, 174, 175, 196, 203–204, 221, 243, 278n14. *See also* interiority, language ideology, prayer, Protestantism

singing: among Christian converts, 14, 68, 80, 121, 146, 194–195, 211f; and Christian hymns, 3, 80, 110, 135, 143, 148, 161, 182, 209, 231; denounced by Christians, 182; Nenets way of (*khynots'*), 78, 94, 175, 177, 179, 182–185, 198, 204, 232, 233, 238, 244, 274n13; and Pentecostals, 143; and Reindeer Day, 65; Russian way of (*yanggerts'*), 80, 182 (*see also* Russian language); and shamans, *see* shaman. *See also* alcohol, devil, epic song, God, personal song

Skvirskaja, Vera, 165, 261n28

sky, 119, 165, 202, 270n13, 272n20. *See also* Num, shaman

Sneath, David, 8

snowmobiles, 86, 87f, 88, 121, 227, 241

Solzhenitsyn, Aleksandr, 174

Song, Eunsub, 258n7

Sora, 250, 273n5, 281n18

soul, 183, 247; breath-soul (*yindq*), 164–165, 187, 272n19; Christians' view of, 90, 107, 108, 117, 123, 129, 138, 178, 181, 184, 199, 200, 215, 219, 222–225, 239, 266n1; of *khekhe*, 164–165 (see also *khekhe*); among Nganasan, 274n13; shadow soul (*sidyangg*), 91, 157, 164–165, 271n19; soul-image (*ngytarma*), 204; among Yukaghir, 272n19. *See also* body, interiority

South Korea, 258n7

Sovetskiy (village), 69, 71f, 91, 190, 265n29; Village Council of, 69, 142

Soviet language, 60, 62, 264n23, 276n2. *See also* Communists, language, words

Sovietization, 21, 39, 44. *See also* youth

Soyuzpushnina, 55

speaking in tongues (glossolalia), 112, 143, 148, 152, 216, 234, 268n2. *See also* Pentecostals

speech: avoiding, 272n2; embodied and disembodied, 193–196; evangelicals', 16, 178, 180–181, 197, 202, 203, 205, 207, 209–210, 213, 219, 243; of the fire, 189, 275n23; and intentions, 195 (*see also* intention); making public, 58, 65, 88; and silence, 172, 174, 214, 242 (*see also* silence); speech community, 11, 221; speech event, 37, 148, 200, 208. *See also* articulacy, Baptist language, fire, God, hate speech,

language, love speech, speech act, speech act theory, spirits, tongue, words
speech act, 200, 237, 276n2. *See also* silence act, speech, speech act theory
speech act theory, 16–17, 18, 60, 194, 199, 216, 276n28. *See also* speech, speech act
spirits (gods, deities), 4, 26, 29, 34, 45, 50, 79, 92, 93, 123, 133, 137, 140–141, 150, 155, 161, 165, 185, 226–227, 229, 234, 245, 270n13, 271n14, 275nn20–21, 280n10; alcohol offered to, *see* alcohol; converts disengaging from, 157, 161, 162–165, 166, 238, 244, 246, 247; harm coming from, 91, 98, 155–156, 189, 260n21, 270n10, 281n15; and Russian saints, 45, 159, 257n4; Russians originating from, 43–44; and shamans, 188–189, 242, 266n5; and speech, 172, 185, 188, 196 (*see also* speech). *See also* birth, Communists, devil, disease, fire, *ikota*, *khekhe*, *lutsa*, *myad pukhutsya*, name, Nga, *ngylyeka*, nomads, reindeer, sacred sites, sacrifice, shaman, *syadei*, tent, *yid yerv*
spontaneity, 217; as conceptualized among Christians, 14, 206–207, 217. *See also* prayer
Ssorin-Chaikov, Nikolai, 124
St. Elijah's Day, 48; turned into Reindeer Day, 48. *See also* Reindeer Day
Stalin, Joseph, 23, 44, 51–52, 54, 112, 262n6, 273n6, 281n19
Stalinist period, 4, 19, 39, 44, 46, 124, 250, 267n2, 277–278n12. *See also* collectivization, Gulag, industrialization, repressions, Stalin
Stammler, Florian, 275n25
Stasch, Rupert, 276n30
state farm (sovkhoz), 8, 19, 47, 56, 62, 166, 258n12, 264–265n25, 264n25; of Baidarata, 58; in Komi, 56; of Usinsk, 56; of Vorkuta, *see* Vorkuta. *See also* collectivization, collective farm
Strathern, Marilyn, 239
Stundists (Shtundists), 136
subject-language, 237–238. *See also* language, perspective-taking
subject position, 200, 238–240. *See also* perspective-taking

subjectivation, 179–180, 196. *See also* interpellation, name
Sudan, 26
Sumba, 16, 132, 218
Sunday: among evangelicals, 11, 77–80, 205, 241; keeping in the past, 97, 281n21
Swedish, 13, 267n7, 276n27
syadei (spirit figure), 45, 137, 165, 270n5. *See also* devil, idol, *khekhe*, sacred objects, sacred site, spirits
syaqmei pad (bag of female boots), 187–188, 230, 231. *See also* evil word, pollution, *porti*, women
Syoyakha, 118, 122

taboo (*khebyakha*, *khevy*), 184, 187, 238, 275n20, 281n21. *See also* sin, women
tacit and explicit, 6, 7, 10, 245. *See also* silence
Taimyr Peninsula, 260n22, 273n8
Taleyev, Nikolai (Shaman Kolya), 261n26
Taleyeva, Lyudmila, xiii, xiv
Tambiah, Stanley, 218
tarq pad, 140, 142. *See also* reindeer
taxation, 22, 47, 49, 50, 109, 262n4, 262n6, 265n26. *See also* furs
Taylor, Charles, 146
teltanggoda (shaman helper), 273n7. *See also* shaman
temporality, 48, 247, 250; and Christians, 37, 83, 105, 119, 121–122, 124, 154, 175, 224; and Nenets sacred objects, 165; and Soviets, 124. *See also* eschatology, future, past, rupture
tent (*chum*, *mya*), 3, 24, 26, 41, 48, 58, 60, 61, 92, 100, 107, 138, 141, 146–148, 149, 163, 171, 175, 176, 177, 185, 188–189, 197, 209, 223; Baptists redecorating, 135, 175; covers of, 26, 32, 48, 65, 136; ritually pure and impure parts of, 36, 187, 231, 271n15, 280n10 (*see also* men, pollution, women); and spirits, 142, 155, 270n9 (*see also* spirits)
Tereshchenko, Natal'ya, 274n17, 275n24
Thrift, Nigel, 276n29
Throop, Jason, 281n17
tobacco, 22, 78, 97, 181
tolerance: Baptist missionary denouncing, 108; God's, 154; Pentecostals on, 147

Tolkachev, Viktor, 53
tongue: disciplining one's, 197–200, 213, 217, 219, 232, 233; Nenets sayings of, 276n1. *See also* Baptist language, language, speech, words
torabtq, 230, 279n8. *See also* purification
Tozhu, 52
trade, 22, 32, 45, 55, 69, 95, 97, 218, 264n18; as post-Soviet business, 40, 85, 86, 100, 102, 247. *See also* army, goods
translation, 86, 229–230, 237, 269n16, 270n8; of the Bible, 14, 126, 207, 257–258n7, 275n20 (*see also* Bible); of hymns, 182; during rituals and services, 3, 78, 208, 213. *See also* Baptist missionaries
Troeltsch, Ernst, 117
truth-event, 84, 237. *See also* decision-event
Turner, Frederick Jackson, 46
Tybertya (clan-community), 266n30

Ukraine, 53, 68, 146, 261n29, 268n9, 271n16
Ukrainians, xiii, 11, 126, 134, 146, 178, 257n1, 261n29
United States, 46, 88; evangelicals in, 13, 200, 277n6, 281n20
Unregistered Baptists, 5, 9, 14, 104–130; being repressed, 114, 118–119, 218; as descendants of early church, 105, 107, 124–125; evangelizing ethnic minorities, 125–126; and ideology on separation from the state, 104, 107, 109, 114–119, 127, 129; on marriage, 128; and myth of Holy Russia, 126; official and other names of, 104, 267n1; and registration, 4, 35, 109, 129, 268n6, 269n13; schismatic tendencies of, 109; seen as dissidents, 115; self-identifying as believers, 261n30; and their definition of outsiders, 107; and their journals, 110, 114, 118, 134, 267n11; on worldly rulers, 114. *See also* Baptist missionaries, Council of Churches of Evangelical Christians-Baptists, martyrdom, persecutions, Registered Baptists, registration, repressions, Vorkuta Baptist church
Ural Nenets (community of Independents), xiv, 4, 19, 24–25, 32, 37, 44, 51, 58, 61, 63, 69–70, 86, 91, 93–94, 100, 141, 164, 166,
186–187, 191, 257n2, 259n17, 260n21, 262n1, 263n14, 265n25, 265n28, 266n30, 269n15. *See also* Independents, nomads, Ural Mountains, Yamb-To, *yedinolichniki*
Ural Mountains (Ngarka Pe), 18, 26, 41, 45, 49–50, 51, 56, 123, 137, 139, 141–142, 163, 223, 259n17, 261n28; and its northernmost part (Polar Urals), 21–37, 50, 52, 56, 69, 166, 257n2
Urapmin, 71–72, 278n1
Urier (mythic shaman), 272n20
Usa River, 262n4
Usinsk, 56
Ust-Kara, 33, 58, 60, 62, 67; collective farm in, 51, 53, 56, 62, 67, 95, 265n26
Ust-Tsilma, 259n15

Vagramenko, Tatiana, 261n28, 267n10
Vaigach, 22, 122–123; Gulag on, 46, 48; as sacred island, 45, 123, 137, 141, 270n8
Valeri, Valerio, 272n19
Varnek, 123
Vasil'ev, Vladimir, 55–56
Velichko, Fyodor, 271n16
Veniamin (archimandrite), 23, 137, 259n17
Verbov, Grigoriy, 272n22
Vesako (Nenets deity), 137
vevako vada. See evil word
vigilance, 107, 109, 225, 231. *See also* devil
Vineyard Christians, 224
Vins, Georgiy, 113
Vitebsky, Piers, 229, 250, 273n5, 276n26, 281n18
Viveiros de Castro, Eduardo, 261n27
vodka. *See* alcohol
Vorgashor, xiv, 265n29
Vorkuta, xiii–xiv, 3, 24, 99, 122, 128, 162, 218, 259n15, 263n15, 265n28; and Gulag, 24, 110, 264n17, 268n8 (*see also* Gulag); history of Baptist church in, 109–114, 117–118, 119, 267–268n2; hymn on, 80, 110; missionaries from, 105, 139, 142, 268n9; Nenets settling in, 61–62, 63, 100; Nenets visiting, 69, 89, 95, 161; Pentecostals in, 143, 208, 268n2, 271n16; prayer house in, 77, 86, 93, 107, 142, 223; school in, 68; state farm of, 63, 141, 265n26, 266n30. *See also* atheism, city, Vorkuta Baptist church

Vorkuta Baptist church, 109–114, 267n2; as autonomous congregation, 114. *See also* Baptist missionaries, Unregistered Baptists, Vorkuta
Vorkuta River, 24

Wanner, Catherine, 11, 129
Western Apache, 43, 172
Willerslev, Rane, 272n19
Williams, Bernard, 257n5
witchcraft, 44, 186–187, 190, 192, 242, 275n22, 275n25. *See also* curses, evil word, marriage, *porti*
witnessing (Christian testimony), 16, 110, 121, 125, 132–133, 178, 199, 200, 213, 215, 218, 222, 237, 241, 243. *See also* Baptist language
Wittenberg, 133
Wittgenstein, Ludwig, 12
wolves, 33–34, 44, 56, 189, 227, 230, 244. *See also* predators, reindeer
women: and Baptists, 78, 79, 80, 93, 128, 146, 216, 267n6; and labor division, 32, 49; and motivation to convert, 96–97, 267n10; and purity rules, 142, 187, 226, 230, 231, 238, 271n15, 280n10 (see also *nyaro, syaqmei pad*); and Soviets, 23, 26, 41. *See also* authority, baptism, Baptist missionaries, men, *myad pukhutsya*, Num, Pentecostals, pollution, prayer, purification, sermon, taboo
Word of Life, 13
words: abounding among Christians, 3, 13, 148, 171, 197; being cautious with, 4, 276n1, 278n15, 281n19; being fixed in Christian rituals, 205, 207; being justified by, 200; being underdetermined, 160, 166; in conversion, *see* language; and deeds, 12, 17, 226, 243, 269n15; efficacious through God, 201–202, 218; and fasting, 205; and inner intentions, 14–15, 192, 194, 195, 208–209, 215, 241, 243 (*see also* intention); "living word", 135; and ontologies, 16–17, 98, 124, 131, 171, 182, 185, 193–194, 198, 218, 226, 243, 274n17 (*see also* ontology); among Pentecostals, 148, 276n27; and personhood, *see* personhood; and

representation, 16, 37; Russians' intrusive, 4, 16, 176–177, 186, 193, 242 (*see also* evil word); of Soviets, 48, 113, 263n8 (*see also* Soviet language); and tacit knowledge, 10, 172, 243; taking responsibility for, 13, 16 (*see also* responsibility); and their binding force, 38, 172, 180. *See also* Baptist, language, God's Word, language, language ideology, non-Christians, repetition, speech
wordscapes, 17, 38, 172. *See also* words

Yabtam Pe (mountain), 142
yabye syo. See personal song
Yamal Khekhe (Nenets deity), 123, 270n13
Yamal Peninsula, 52, 53, 55–56, 118, 123, 141, 165, 260n21, 268n3; etymology of, 122–123
Yamalo-Nenets Autonomous Region, 19, 41, 56, 58, 92, 149, 258n9, 258n11, 261n28, 265n25, 265n28, 266nn29–30; Nenets of, 165, 223, 257n4, 259n17, 267n10, 274n15, 278n14
Yamb-To (community of Nenets Independents), xiii–xiv, 4, 19, 24–25, 32–33, 36, 44, 51, 56–58, 61, 63–69, 77–80, 86, 93, 95, 96, 138, 162, 163, 166, 174, 178, 233, 238, 257n2, 258nn10–11, 264n22, 265nn25–26, 265n28, 268n5, 270n12, 273n7. *See also* Independents, Ural Nenets
Yaminya (Nenets deity), 270n9
Yarovaya Law, 269n13
Yaungad, Khabecha, 61, 282n2
Yavtysyi, Prokopi, xiii, xiv, 32
yedinolichniki (lichniki): elsewhere in Siberia, 263n14; in the *mandalada*, 50; Soviet activists trying to collectivize, 53, 59, 81, 263n8; Soviet category of, 4, 47, 52, 262n6, 264n25. *See also* collectivization, grey-zone herders, Independents, Ural Nenets, Yamb-To
Yenisei River, 18
Yevladov, Vladimir, 106, 165, 166, 227, 268n3
Yevsyugin, Arkadi, 48–49, 54–55, 237, 262n7
yid yerv (water spirit), 186, 189, 275n22, 281n15. *See also* pike
Yoshida, Atsushi, 264n25

youth, 228; alienated from tundra life, 28; and Baptists, 9, 99, 112, 113, 118, 126, 247; becoming independent, 227–228; being adaptive to change, 28–29, 39–40, 72, 83, 85, 87–88, 98–101, 173, 223, 245, 246, 247; and Soviet policies, 113, 247; and Sovietization, 60, 61. *See also* city, conversion, school

Yugor Peninsula, 56
Yugor Strait, 45
Yukaghir, 272n19
Yurchak, Alexei, 60, 276n2
Yusharskiy Village Council, 56

Zimbabwe, 135
Žižek, Slavoj, 237, 277n12

LAUR VALLIKIVI is Associate Professor at the Arctic Studies Centre and the Department of Ethnology at the University of Tartu.

For Indiana University Press

Tony Brewer, Artist and Book Designer
Brian Carroll, Rights Manager
Sophia Hebert, Assistant Acquisitions Editor
Brenna Hosman, Production Coordinator
Katie Huggins, Production Manager
Nancy Lightfoot, Project Editor and Manager
Bethany Mowry, Acquisitions Editor and Director
Dan Pyle, Online Publishing Manager
Stephen Williams, Marketing and Publicity Manager
Jennifer Witzke, Senior Artist and Book Designer